Historic Places of Worship

ALSO BY PAUL D. BUCHANAN

Famous Animals of the States:
True-to-Life Tales of the Most Unusual Beasts
of the 50 States, Puerto Rico, and the District of Columbia
(McFarland, 1996)

HISTORIC PLACES OF WORSHIP

*Stories of 51 Extraordinary
American Religious Sites Since 1300*

by
PAUL D. BUCHANAN

McFarland & Company, Inc., Publishers
Jefferson, North Carolina, and London

Acknowledgments: My thanks to Mary Ann Akao, State of Hawaii Archives; Lila Beasterfeld, The Beecher Bible and Rifle Church; Jeffrey D. Berg, Beaufort County Library; Ron D. Bryant, Kentucky Historical Society; Dee Collura, St. Louis Cathedral Gift Shop; Father Thomas Connelly, Society of Jesus; Olive Crowe, Thunder on the Tygart, Inc.; Leigh Darbee, Indiana Historical Society; Reverend Father James Dokos, Annunciation Greek Orthodox Church; Kathy English, Hawaiian National Historical Association; David Free, Kawaiaha'o Church Board of Trustees; Ellen Gamache, Albany Library; Neal Hatayama, Hawaii State Library; Jenni James, New Mexico State Library; Eric P. Johnson, Shrine of Our Lady of La Leche; Mildred Jones, the First Parish Church; Gordon B. Joyce, Pu'uhonua o Hōnaunau National Historical Park; Sandra Kinney, St. Anne's Shrine; Lachlan Mackay, Kirtland Temple Historical Center; Deborah Malone, Buddhist Churches of America Archives; Linda Martin, United States Department of Interior; Lorelei McClure, Baha'i National Center; Susan McNamee, International Peace Garden; Reverend Bob Myers, The Little Brown Church in the Vale; Ray Nichols, Holy Trinity (Old Swedes) Church Foundation, Inc.; Earl H. Sanderson, Center Church; Sr. Marilyn Schatz, El Santuario de Chimayo; Kristine Schmucker, Mennonite Heritage Museum; William P. Schoenberg, Society of Jesus; Debra Smith, the First Baptist Church of America; Mary Ellen Snyder, Women's Rights National Historical Park; Roger Trick, Whitman Mission National Historical Site; Barbara Wolf, Alcorn State University; Bette Yoder, St. John's at Lafeyette Square; and Penni Thorpe, photographic consultant and partner.

On the cover (*clockwise from top left*): Holy Trinity ("Old Swedes Church"), Wilmington, Delaware (photograph by Lisa Nichols, courtesy Holy Trinity Church); Friends' Great Meeting House, Newport, Rhode Island (photograph by Jay Walters); Annunciation Greek Orthodox Church, Wauwatosa, Wisconsin (courtesy Annunciation Greek Orthodox Church of the Milwaukee Hellenic Community); Hale o Keawe, Pu'uhonua o Hōnaunau National Park, Hawaii (courtesy Hawai'i Natural History Association).

British Library Cataloguing-in-Publication data are available

Library of Congress Cataloguing-in-Publication Data

Buchanan, Paul D., 1958–
    Historic places of worship : stories of 51 extraordinary American
religious sites since 1300 / by Paul D. Buchanan.
      p. cm.
    ISBN 0-7864-0588-0 (illustrated case binding : 50# alkaline paper) ∞
    1. Shrines — United States.   2. Christian shrines — United States.
3. Church buildings — United States. I. Title.
    BL2525.B83 1999
    291.3'5'0973 — dc21   99-18282
                                                CIP

Manufactured in the United States of America

McFarland & Company, Inc., Publishers
  Box 611, Jefferson, North Carolina 28640

To
Patricia and Duncan Buchanan

TABLE OF CONTENTS

INTRODUCTION

The stories presented here depict places of worship which have stood as centerpieces for larger cultural, political, or social movements. Although many places of worship have affected the history and development of the surrounding community, these stories involved influences reaching well beyond the immediate community, touching the nation, and even the world. This is not a comprehensive guide to old churches, but rather a narrative collection of historically significant stories.

The interesting thing about religion is how the profound so often accompanies and counterbalances the absurd. No matter how one might view the doctrines or practices followed in these places of worship, there is no doubt these structures embody the hopes, dreams, and visions of the people who built them.

This book is also filled with stories of attempts to explain the unexplainable. Sometimes, the explainers become so caught up in their own rationale, they forget the subject of discourse is, inherently, unexplainable. Although it may be easy to understand there is a profound difference between divine inspiration and delusion, it is not so easy to determine the boundaries between the two. Simply claiming revelation from God does not refute the possibility of delusion.

If God is truly God, then God can manifest its Godness in any way it chooses. It matters not the religion, the culture, the language, the society, the gender, or the nation through which the manifestation comes. It also matters not the finite perceptions or limitations which humans inevitably attempt to impose.

It is amazing how many of these stories' paths intersect. The history classes I recall were taught in a very linear, event-by-event manner. But the true theme of history is relationships: between people, between places, between nations, between events. How one event involving one people in one place affects another, no matter the distance or obscurity, is often the issue at hand.

Something very interesting happened to religions when they came to America. The churches, like the people, became immersed in the ambiguous yet evident concept known as "the American Way." Most of the faiths came from a history of absolute authority. Because of the democratization, plurality, and freedom of choice which characterizes America, the churches have had to adapt, and in some case, actually sell themselves to the people. The churches no longer choose the people; the people choose the churches.

1

Historic Places
of Worship

THE ANASAZI KIVAS

Affiliation: Anasazi (Native American)
Location: Southeastern Utah, Southwestern Colorado,
Northeastern Arizona, Northwestern New Mexico
Circa 1–1300

A taut leather drum pounds a hypnotic beat within the humid chamber. The smoke from a fire of mesquite and sage, crackling within the central fire pit, saturates the air with an intoxicating aroma. The sipapu — the portal to the underworld from which everything originally emerged — remains covered, preventing the spirits of the ancestors from entering the chamber until the precise time. Wooden figures depicting birds, animals, horns, discs, prayer sticks, lightning lattices and plume circles — painted in bright greens, browns, blacks, yellows, reds, and blues — stand at various points of the chamber. They draw attention to the six absolute directional points: northeast, northwest, southeast, southwest, straight up, and straight down.

More often the men, but sometimes the women, gather in the underground chamber for the ritual, which might celebrate birth, death, rites of passage, harvest, war, and other episodes of life. The rituals might feature bright costumes, dancing, chanting, and the invocation of spirits. These spirits flow from the water, the air, the animals, the stones, the people, the trees, the crops, the fire itself and, of course, the ever-present father of all, the sun. The rituals are as much a part of life as eating, sleeping, breathing, thinking. And, more often than not, they are performed in the underground ceremonial chamber known as the Kiva.

A kiva — which is Hopi for "old house" — is cavernous, circular in shape, and completely underground. It may be huge, more than sixty feet in diameter, serving an entire community; or small, perhaps twenty feet, serving one ex-

tended family. There is no door or window, but only a ladder leading to a portal at the roof of the chamber, made of earth and stone supported by lumber cut from local trees. There are twenty-three of these ceremonial chambers found among the two hundred or more rooms within the Cliff Palace at Mesa Verde National Park in Colorado. Hundreds of other examples can be found among the pit houses and apartment-style pueblos found throughout the four corners region of the United States: where the borders of Arizona, Utah, Colorado, and New Mexico meet. These structures, and thousands of artifacts found in them by archaeologists, are the legacy of a people called Anasazi, a Navajo term for "The Ancient Ones."

The Anasazi civilization is believed to have first appeared in the four corners area around the first century A.D. It is considered the most influential and enduring of all early southwestern cultures. Their pottery and basket weaving, architecture, and farming techniques would affect countless future generations of Navajo, Hopi, Hohokum, and other tribes of southwestern United States.

The Anasazi civilization manifested itself in two fairly distinct, yet overlapping, periods called the Basketmaker Period and the Pueblo Period.

The Basketmaker era spanned from 1 A.D. to about 700 A.D. During this time the Anasazi demonstrated considerable skill in weaving vegetable fibers: baskets, foot-coverings, clothes, utensils, transport equipment, storage containers. The weavers constructed baskets so fine and airtight that they could be used for cooking or carrying water. Toward the end of

An Anasazi kiva in Mesa Verde National Park, Colorado. (Courtesy National Park Service.)

the Basketmaker period the pottery took the shape of the baskets, but later appeared in more complex and intricate designs. Eventually, the Anasazi produced some of the finest pottery ever seen in the southwest.

The Basketmakers practiced food gathering, hunting, and farming to sustain themselves. They planted, harvested, and ate maize; they hunted elk, deer, buffalo, and bear. They gathered wild plant food such as seeds, acorns, mesquite beans, walnuts, yucca leaves, and roots. They also began developing social structures and religious ceremonies that have been passed down and used — in one form or another — for thousands of years.

During the Basketmaker period the Anasazi built shelters in caves and in the open. They constructed pit houses, whose roofs of mud and tree trunk remained level with the ground, and whose rooms were dug twenty feet or more deep down into the earth.

Between 700 A.D. and 1000 A.D., dwellings appeared above ground, made out of wood, stone, and adobe. The stones were laid horizontally into intricate masonry works, and they supported roofs of wooden beams. In addition to pottery, the Anasazi began developing jewelry from shells and beads, creating bracelets, pendants, and rings of exquisite craftsmanship

Finally, during the "Golden Age" of the Pueblo period from 1000 A.D. to 1300 A.D., the famous apartment-style pueblos, high atop mesas or deep within the recesses of sheer cliff walls, began to appear. These pueblos were sturdy and durable (some are more than 1000 years old), efficient and easily warmed, as most faced south, protected from rain and snow. Because hundreds of apartments comprised the pueblos, they provided intimate, easily defended communities. The Anasazi could pool the labor force, share the water supply, and develop more intricate and specialized tools.

Among the best examples of the pueblos are Chaco Canyon in western New Mexico, featuring 800 rooms and 36 kivas, and Cliff Palace at Mesa Verde National Park in Colorado, featuring more than 200 rooms and 23 separate kivas. Other notable sites are at Aztec, in the northwest corner of New Mexico, and Canyon De Chelly in Northwestern Arizona.

By the advent of the Golden Age, the Anasazi had developed into a remarkably sophisticated and astute culture. They had developed roads connecting the wide-spread pueblos, and had established trades routes as far south as Mexico, and west to the Pacific Coast. The Anasazi had also constructed irrigation canals to better control the little water which fell on their land. On at least one site — Fajada Butte in Chaco Canyon — they had created a complex sun calendar out of slabs of stone, which intricately marked the orbital cycles of both the sun and the moon. By these cycles the Anasazi apparently anticipated the richest agricultural seasons, and planned their schedule of seasonal rituals.

The kivas were not only the site for religious ceremonies, but they were also the social center for the community — sort of the tavern for the tribe. The men of the village would gather to socialize, weave, conduct community business and, of course, gossip. The kivas functioned as the social and spiritual center for life for the Anasazi culture.

After six hundred years of relatively prosperous living and development, the Old Ones had abruptly disappeared by the year 1300 A.D. One theory says a superior enemy invaded the old ones' domain, killing and driving them out of the four corners area. But the ruins left no signs of struggle, and the Anasazi so easily defended their cliff cities the possibility of conquest seems highly unlikely.

Others have postulated that famine drove the Anasazis away. Archaeological and geological excavations have determined that a severe drought struck the four corners area between 1276 and 1299 A.D. Facing crop failures, the absence of game, and an inadequate water supply, it is supposed the Anasazi left for a more prosperous environment.

Another theory says a form of "urban blight" drove the Anasazi out. Although cliff apartment dwelling appeared highly efficient and secure, it also brought a greater variety of people into a relatively small area. Often the cliff apartments drew several smaller towns with its own customs and mores together creating bigger cities. Internal dissent festered among the communities; essentially the cities became "overcrowded," and the Anasazi split up and left, looking for the "simpler life."

Odds are all of these factors — and perhaps more — merged together in one era, and the community dissipated. The Old Ones split up: Some assimilated with the Zuni Culture in New Mexico, others with the Hopi Villages in Arizona. Others, still, probably migrated south to Central and South America. The Anasazi Culture, which influenced southwestern culture for more than 700 years, was no more.

Sources
Frazier, Kendrick. *People of Chaco*. 1986, W.W. Norton & Company, New York.

Scully, Vincent. *Pueblo: Mountain, Village, Dance*. 1972, The Village Press, New York.

Silverberg, Robert. *The Old Ones*. 1965, New York Graphic Society Publishers, Ltd.

Terrell, John Upton. *American Indian Almanac*. 1971, Barnes and Noble Books, New York.

PUʻUHONUA O HŌNAUNAU

Affiliation: Hawaiian
Location: Kona Coast, Island of Hawaii, Hawaii
Circa 1550

Six well-armed islanders chase among the course sand and coconut trees along the southeast Kona Coast, on the big island of Hawaii. The islanders pursue, at a desperate pace, a lone runner witnessed violating one of the many *kapus* or sacred taboos. The pursuers know if the lawbreaker is not captured and punished, they risk bringing the horrible wrath of the gods upon the entire island population. The consequences — typhoon, flood, earthquake, volcano — could be devastating. The only chance of appeasing the Divine — as proclaimed by the ancestral king according to a tradition perhaps one thousand years old — is to bring the culprit to just punishment.

For the lone runner, the chase is even more critical. His crime was curiosity; he dared to raise his eyes from his prostrate position on the ground, as the King passed in royal procession. Several royal guards directly witnessed his indiscretion — a direct violation of the *kapu.* The guards sent in pursuit of the lawbreaker are several of his fellow islanders. All of them have been raised since birth to be watchful and merciless toward kapu-breakers, for the safety of the entire community. Justice will be swift and non-negotiable: he will be executed by spear, club, strangulation, or fire.

The kapu-breaker races for his life, southeast through the sun-baked ancient lava flows where the kiawe brush thrives, past hundreds of coconut trees. He spent the night in the shelter of huge lava rocks, but now the posse returns fresh to his trail. The kapu-breaker knows there is only one way out, one way to save his own life. There, up ahead, his salvation awaits.

The pursuers, wielding wooden spears and shark-tooth clubs, close in on the quarry. But now they see what the kapu-breaker sees. They sprint faster, as much to push the runner forward as to snare him.

Finally, his body racked with strained exhaustion, the lone runner stumbles forward, throwing himself on the ten-foot, lava stone fence, which separates an A-frame thatch temple from the outside. In a final act of desperation, the runner crawls over the lava wall, falling limply over the barrier. He presses his sweat-drenched face to the earth, gasping and weeping. His pursuers, meanwhile, stop their chase, for they know the race is over. They shake their heads, and mutter among themselves; but they also smile, knowing the kapu-breaker is where he needs to be.

He has reached the *Puʻuhonua*, a sacred spot of land respected by all. Here, all is forgiven. Within a few hours, the kapu-breakers will be blessed by the *kahuna pules*, or temple priests. He would be absolved of fault in the eyes of the gods, and within a few hours he will be welcomed back to his community, unthreatened and unashamed. By reaching the kahuna pules at the puʻuhonua, he has atoned for his kapu-breaking, and he is redeemed as a viable member of society.

The Puʻuhonuas — which means "Places of Refuge" — could at one time be found on all the Hawaiian Islands. Before the Hawaiians ever knew of the existence of *haoles* (Caucasians or outsiders), each island dwelt under its own sovereignty, which reigned over the people through the divinely sanctioned kapus. At the same time, all the islands remained at more or less constant war with each other.

The system of kapu — referring to the sacred, the forbidden, the taboo — regulated nearly every aspect of island life: food, politics, possessions, sex, marriage, and more. Of course, as with most socio-political systems, the prohibitions landed hardest on the backs of the poor and powerless. With so many rules to follow, ample opportunities existed to break the kapus, whose violation nearly always meant a swift and certain death. The island kings in their spiritual power, or *mana*, apparently created the Puʻuhonuas as a way for the common folk to beat the sanctions of the kapus.

The kapu system, which was practiced by untold generations of Hawaiians, came to a jolting demise under the influence of Kaʻahumanu, mother of King Liholiho, son of King Kamehameha the Great. When England's Captain James Cook visited the islands in 1778, and the natives observed no natural punishment for Cook's systematic violation of the kapus, many Hawaiians began questioning the veracity of the system. After the death of Kamehameha I, his favorite wife Kaʻahumanu — a defiantly strong woman who must have recognized the old system's particular encumbrance on her gender — convinced her son Liholiho (known also as Kamehameha II) to dismiss the old kapus. As a gesture toward the new ways, Liholiho would dine among gatherings of women, foreigners, and common

Hale o Keawe, Pu'uhonua o Hōnaunau National Historical Park. (Courtesy Hawai'i Natural History Association.)

people — all strict taboos under the old system. In his actions — influenced by the influx of foreign peoples, strange ideas, and organized religions on the islands — Liholiho all but declared the kapus to be false. Almost immediately, the Hawaiians began tearing down the ancient idols and temples. But Pu'uhonua o Hōnaunau, the most famous of the places of refuge, survived — a tribute to the engineering which created it.

As many as six separate pu'uhonuas are thought to have once occupied the big island of Hawaii. The six-acre Pu'uhonua o Hōnaunau, the largest and best preserved, consists of three main structures:

Palace Grounds

Ten thatch-roofed compartments comprise the palace, built for King Keawe-ku-i-ke-ka'ai some time in the sixteenth century. The palace provided a home for the King, his entourage, and his family — which often included several wives and all their children. The Hawaiians of the time believed in interbreeding, believing the fittest offspring descended from mates most closely related.

Hale o Keawe Heiau

This was the temple in which the priests, or the *kahuna pules*, performed the absolution rituals for the kapu-breakers. This is the third heiau or temple built on the Hōnaunau site, the original constructed around 1650. The heiau also functions as a kind of mausoleum, where the remains of past rulers were harbored. The Hawaiians believed the rulers were endowed with mana, or spiritual power infused in them by the gods. The kahuna pules believed if the remains of the rulers were kept in the heiau, the spiritual power of the temple would be greatly enhanced. At one point, the remains of 23 kings were kept in Hale o Keawe. Carved wooden totems of gods and idols surrounded Hale o Keawe.

Great Wall

Hawaiians built the wall – the most dominant structure at Puʻuhonua o Hōnaunau — in the 1500s, as a means of separating the palace grounds from the temple. Longer than three football fields, the Great Wall is L-shaped, ten feet high, and more than seventeen feet wide. It is constructed of gigantic lava stones, some weighing as much as 6000 pounds, which the builders apparently moved, miraculously, with simple wooden rollers and levers. The builders pieced these stones together so intricately, that they have managed to survive human attacks, tsunamis, and earthquakes without so much as a drop of mortar to cement them together. Nevertheless, the Great Wall has now stood for more than five hundred years.

In addition to absolution for kapu-breaking, the puʻuhonua also offered refuge in time of war. The very old, the very young, and the very frail could find shelter and solace within the puʻuhonua. Warriors, defeated in battle, would also seek asylum within the puʻuhonua wall. Here, they could sit out the battle and dress their wounds; at the end of the war, they would peacefully offer their allegiance to the victor.

After the end of the kapu system, Hawaiians began wholesale destruction of the ancient icons and temples, in an attempt to deny the old ways. A razing of the Puʻuhonua took place in 1829, but the impervious design structure of the wall and the temple withstood the attacks. The site stood dormant until the 1890s, when Charles R. Bishop purchased the site from the waning monarchy for $5000, preserving it for posterity. On July 1, 1961, through an act of Congress, Puʻuhonua o Hōnaunau was declared a National Historic Site.

Sources
Barlow, Bernice. *Sacred Sites of the West*. 1996, LLewellyn Publications, St. Paul, MN.
Doughty, Andrew and Friedman, Harriet. *Hawaii: The Big Island Revealed*. 1997, Wizard Publications, Honolulu.
Frierson, Pamela. *The Burning Island*. 1991, Sierra Club Books, San Francisco.
Uprichard, Brett. "Sanctuary for Kapu-Breakers," 1998.

MISSION NOMBRE DE DIOS

Affiliation: Roman Catholic
Location: St. Augustine, Florida
1620

On San Marcos Avenue in the northeast corner of the city of St. Augustine, Florida, stands the replicated Mission Nombre de Dios. Within the compound walls rests the tiny jewel of a chapel, the Shrine of Nuestra Señora de la Leche, honoring the Mother of Christ, whose devotion began in 16th century Madrid. Outside the mission grounds towers the 208 foot stainless steel cross, which marks the site of the first known Catholic mass celebrated in Florida, when the city of St. Augustine was named for the renowned 4th century Catholic bishop and scholar.

The tradition of veneration of the saints in the Roman Catholic Church stems from the belief in the Communion of Saints. The saints, human beings made immortal, residing with God in heaven, were believed to be able to intercede with God — in a sort of ecclesiastical debate with God — on the petitioner's behalf. Believers dedicated statues, shrines, cathedrals, even cities to saints, with the hope that the saint would convince the Almighty to shower good fortune upon the faithful. Although Church doctrine and tradition clearly delineates between the divinity of God and the humanity

Mission Nombre de Dios, Shrine of Nuestra Señora de la Leche, in St. Augustine, Florida. (Photograph by Chuck Profrock, courtesy Shrine of Nuestra Señora de la Leche.)

of the saints, the protracted and often elaborate worship of these saints would easily lead outsiders to believe the saints were worshipped as gods. Protestants therefore historically regarded and labeled the Catholics as idolaters.

The steel cross and mission at St. Augustine commemorate the 250 year reign of the Spanish Empire in Florida. Throughout this period of time, a bitter tug of war ensued between the Spanish colony, and alternately the French and the British governments, over possession of the northeast corner of the future state of Florida. It was a time of devastating pirate attacks; the construction of one of the most unusual and impregnable fortresses in the world; and the wild and woolly early days of the oldest permanent European settlement in the continental United States.

Father Francisco Lopez de Mendoza Grajales, a Spanish diocesan priest, celebrated Catholic mass for the first time in St. Augustine on Sept. 8, 1565. It was the first of 11 missions situated on the east coast of Florida; the priest had the initial stone chapel constructed in 1595. The first La Leche Shrine was created in 1620, destroyed and rebuilt several times during the next three hundred years, and reconstructed for the last time in 1915.

As typical for the Spanish Empire, the missions accompanied the military and the government, with the goal of making the fierce-fighting Timucua Indians — the largest tribe in Florida at that time — "Civilized, Christianized, and Hispanized." Founded by secular priests, and managed for a time by the Jesuits, the mission finally attained its height of success under the Franciscans. In all, thirty missions arose in the Florida territory by 1655, and claimed to convert and educate more than 26,000 Indians. Yet, by the time the Spaniards left St. Augustine for good in 1821, only 19 Christianized Indian families remained.

The original discovery of Florida is credited to the mercenary explorer Juan Ponce de Leon. Considering the fervent hostility with which the natives responded to Ponce de Leon's arrival, however, it is likely he was not the first Spanish visitor to the Florida Peninsula. Ponce de Leon landed at the mouth of the St. John's River while on his quest for the legendary island of Bimini, whose existence was foretold by the Arawak Indians of the Caribbean. Although history highlights Ponce de Leon's longing for the enchanted Fountain of Youth, he coveted wealth as his true objective; for, according to the Arawaks, the Bimini soil was comprised almost entirely of pure gold. Ponce de Leon sighted the east coast of Florida on March 27, 1513, and landed on April 2, 1513. He claimed the discovery for Spain, naming it Pascua Florida, for the Easter time "Feast of Flowers."

Juan Ponce de Leon came from San Servos, Province of Campos, in the Kingdom of Leon, in Spain. He had accompanied Columbus' second voyage, which in 1493 established the settlement of Hispanola (on modern day Haiti), and the discovery of the island of San Juan Bautista, which would become Puerto Rico. Hispanola became the first permanent Spanish settlement in North America. Ponce de Leon served as governor of nearby Puerto Rico from 1508 to 1512, finally leaving San Juan Bautista for Florida, one thousand miles to the northwest. After three years, finding the Timucuas particularly unfriendly, Ponce de Leon left Florida. He did not return until 1521, at Charlotte's Harbor in the southwest. There, the arrow of a Calusa Indian wounded him, and he died days later in Cuba.

For the next 50 years the land between the Atlantic Ocean and St. John's River, though claimed by Spain, remained unoccupied. Finally, a French expedition, sponsored by Huguenot Gaspard de Coligny, established a colony and fort at the Bay of Dolphins on St. John's River. Although Spain remained the dominant European power, France gradually lost its fear of the Catholic Iberian Empire. The French looked for inroads into Spanish possessions, establishing colonies for Protestant France. Lead by Jean Ribault, and later Rene Goulant de Laudonneir, the French established Fort Caroline five miles from the mouth of the St. John's River, on June 25, 1564.

Apparently demonstrating no desire to assimilate the natives into their culture — unlike the Spaniards — the French developed friendly relations with the Timucuas, even convincing them to help construct the building in their palm-thatched settlement. Still, due to poor climactic and agrarian conditions, plus a lack of adequate food resources, some of the French colonists mutinied, stealing two ships for transportation home. One of the ships fell into capture by the Spanish navy, which soon gained knowledge of the French fort illicitly perched on the edge of Spanish soil.

In response, King Philip II sent Captain-General Don Pedro Menendez de Aviles to rout the French from their fort, and establish a permanent Spanish settlement. One of the king's favorite citizens, Menendez had already compiled a considerable fortune colonizing and claiming land for the king, and eagerly anticipated opportunities for more wealth and power. An ardent Catholic, Menendez harbored a burning hatred for Protestants, all of whom he referred to as "Lutherans."

On August 15, 1565, armed with five ships, 500 soldiers, 200 sailors, and 100 passengers, Menendez sailed with banners flying and artillery firing, up St. John's River toward Fort Caroline. A timely hurricane struck the French ships gathering north of the fort, effectively disabling the French naval defense. Menendez established St. Augustine on September 8, 1565, the feast day of the saint, and mass was celebrated in St. Augustine's honor. It was 42 years before Jamestown, and 55 years before Plymouth Rock.

Menendez knew Fort Caroline stood isolated from its navy. He led an armed troop across the swampy overland, and destroyed the French settlement. He executed 300 French colonists at the Bay of Dolphins, which he justified as the extermination of heretic "Lutherans." The Bay of Dolphins was renamed Matanzas, the Spanish term for "slaughter." Fort Caroline fell on September 28, 1565, and Menendez renamed it Fort San Mateo.

The Spanish spent the next 20 years building the colony at St. Augustine. Farmers, crops, livestock, artisans and building materials, wives and children traveled from Spain or Cuba to settle in St. Augustine. The settlement eventually ballooned to more than 1,500 residents. But isolated and under-supplied by Spain, St. Augustine proved a vulnerable target.

As the century drew toward a close, the English became emboldened by their successes at sea, particularly through the adventures of privateer Sir Francis Drake. Between 1577 and 1580 Drake gained fame as the first Englishman to circumnavigate the globe. By 1586, Drake had gained a reputation as a rather ruthless corsair (or rich man's pirate). Private investors would sponsor his voyages, for a portion of the booty Drake accumulated by his infiltration, extortion, and destruction of Spanish Empire possessions. Over the years, Drake obtained an estimated total of 160,000 pounds in stolen Spanish booty for Queen and countrymen, for which he was knighted in 1580. As one of his favorite strategies, Drake would hold an entire town for ransom, threatening to destroy the village, building by building, if its treasures were not surrendered to him.

In 1586, on its way to pillage Spanish Santa Elena on Parris Island in South Carolina, Drake's expedition, 23 ships and 2000 men strong, happened to spot St. Augustine from offshore. By then, the timber at forsaken Fort San Mateo crumbled from rot. Drake approached the settlement with nearly one thousand invaders. When St. Augustine colonists meekly attempted to defend their city, Drake had it destroyed, and confiscated the colony's riches.

Two years later, Francis Drake became co-commander of the fleet which drove off the Spanish Armada, signaling the decline of Spain as a world power.

After the Drake raid, some doubted whether the settlement at St. Augustine would continue. The colonists persevered, however, and rebuilt the town. Clashes between British and Spanish Florida increased as Britain established colonies in Georgia and the Carolinas, infringing on Spanish territory. Then on May 9, 1668, a pirate captain named John Davis, made another daring raid upon the hapless res-

idents of St. Augustine. Stealing two Spanish ships, Davis and his crew anchored quietly at the harbor, and in the dark of night ransacked the sleeping town, plundering homes and leaving sixty colonists dead in the streets of St. Augustine.

The Davis invasion convinced the Spaniards a new fortification was needed to protect the city. On October 2, 1672, work commenced on the marvelous Castillo de San Marcos, which would be completed in 1696. The Spanish discovered an amazing building material called coquina on Anastasia Island, just east of the settlement. Coquina is a rock-like substance, made of a mixture of limestone and millions of sea shells. It could be cut from the quarry, and shaped with an ax while still pliable. But after exposure to the open air, coquina becomes harder than stone, extremely durable and impervious to fire (unlike St. Augustine's previous nine forts, all constructed of wood).

The Spanish situated Castillo de San Marcos on the coast east of St. Augustine, facing the ocean, where the Matanza and St. Mark's rivers join the channel alongside Anastasia Island. Any fleet daring to invade would run smack into the mighty Castillo. Its fabulous stellar design provided a central square parade ground which could hold 1500 (the entire population of St. Augustine). It featured a well of drinking water at one end and utilized the tide as a latrine on the other end. At each corner of the parade ground a four-sided bastion extended. The walls of the Castillo reached 33 feet in height, with a thickness of 19 feet at the base, and 11 feet at the top. The bastion bases lay 100 feet thick. A moat, 17 feet wide and five feet deep, surrounded the Castillo.

The Castillo de San Marcos literally saved the town of St. Augustine during two fearful 17th century British raids. Stocked with corn and livestock, plentiful enough to supply the 1500+ residents, the townspeople survived a two-month siege led by Gov. James Monroe of Carolina in 1702. Leading a 1000-man army, consisting of English soldiers and friendly Yemassee Indians, Moore still lacked the artillery sufficiently powerful to open up the Castillo de San Marcos. By the time he sent for larger cannons from Jamaica, four Spanish warships arrived at St. Augustine, driving off the invasion force.

In 1740, the Castillo survived a 30-day barrage led by the maniacal British General James Oglethorpe of Georgia. Oglethorpe led 1600 men and five ships against the fortress, but it again proved too strong for the British. A Spanish force stole out of the Castillo and attacked Oglethorpe outside the fort. Finally, weakened and racked with illness, Oglethorpe's British colony troops left St. Augustine, and limped back to Georgia.

During both invasions, the buildings, houses, and churches of St. Augustine fell to looting and burning. But the townspeople survived within the massive Castillo de San Marcos. For the next 20 years, St. Augustine lived in relative peace, secure in the shadow of the old coquina fort. But with Britain having overrun or destroyed most of the rest of the territory, St. Augustine became the last important Spanish settlement in Florida.

In 1763, in the Treaty of Paris following the French and Indian War, Spain exchanged eastern Florida with Great Britain for the newly conquered Havana. Britain ruled St. Augustine for the next 20 years, and the long Spanish reign in Florida was all but over.

In 1783, another Treaty of Paris, following the American Revolution, returned Florida Territory to Spain. However, this second Spanish occupation from 1784 to 1821 proved nominal at best. Its global power waning, experiencing growth unrest in Mexico and California, Spain now lacked the resources to adequately maintain its holdings in Florida. By the end of the War of 1812, residents of the upstart United States of America had settled in greater numbers in Spanish Florida Territory, soon demanding independence from Spain. Runaway slaves sought refuge in the Spanish lands, and the United States military, under General Andrew Jackson, pushed deeper down the Peninsula in its campaign against the Seminoles. The military had also moved in to quell the unrest among the locals in the western edge of Florida, where border disputes flared between Spanish officials and U.S. settlers.

In 1800, the Spanish gave the Louisiana Territory, which surrounded northwest Florida and spread west beyond the Mississippi, to strife-plagued France. The French sold the territory to the United States in 1803 to obtain funding for its continuing war effort with England and Russia. By then, U.S. territory had already infringed upon Spanish claims. Clearly, the end of Spain's presence in Florida was imminent. Florida had become "a refuge for runaway slaves, renegade whites and Indians, and foreign adventurers and pirates" (Tebeau, p. 115), which Spain could no longer police.

On February 22, 1821, congressional ratification of the Adams-Onis Treaty was completed, ceding Florida from Spain to the United States.

But even today, remnants of the Spanish Empire remain in America's oldest city: A 208-foot cross, marking the landing of Menendez in Florida; the great Coquina Fort, Castillo de San Marco, which successfully guarded the Spanish city of St. Augustine for more than a century; and the lovely Shrine of Nuesta Señora de la Leche, commemorating Mission Nombre de Dios, and the first mass in St. Augustine in 1565.

Sources

Davis, Kenneth C. *Don't Know Much About Geography*. 1992, Avon Books, New York.

Douglas, Marjory Stoneman. *Florida, The Long Frontier*. 1967. Harper and Row, Publishers, New York.

Gannon, Michael. *Florida, A Short History*. 1993, University Press of Florida.

Tebeau, Charlton W. *A History of Florida*. 1971, University of Miami Press, Coral Gables, Florida.

Terrell, John Upton. *American Indian Almanac*. 1994, Barnes & Noble Books.

CENTER CHURCH

(Hartford Meeting House)

Affiliation: Congregational (Puritan)
Location: Hartford, Connecticut
1636

"Take you wise men, and understanding, and known among your tribes, and I will make them rulers over you" (Proverbs 1:13).

A hush had fallen over the men who gathered in the meeting house at Hartford on this 31st day of May, 1638. The wooden benches laid end to end across the meeting house floor were filled, yet nary a sound could be detected, as the audience focused their ears and their attentions toward the preacher at the pulpit. As they listened, faces somber and pensive, each man could feel the words expressed touch his heart, as if the preacher described the emotions he had felt deeply for a very long time. For these men were residents of newly settled Connecticut, where they had come to escape a life of religious and political oppression in Massachusetts. But the ideas of this preacher offered hope that such subjugations would burden them no longer.

Reverend Thomas Hooker addressed this meeting of the Connecticut General Court at the Hartford Meeting House, the predecessor of Center Church, the First Church of Christ. The audience consisted of men from the newly established colonies of Hartford, Weathersford, and Windsor.

"The foundation of authority is laid in the free consent of the people," Hooker told them. Hooker wanted the men of Connecticut to understand they possessed the sacred right and duty to not only create but supervise the government which would manage their community. In his sermon, he emphasized three crucial points: (1) The people have the God-given right to appoint their own public officers; (2) The people should do this thoughtfully and in the fear of God; (3) The people who appoint the officers should also set the limits of the power and duties of those offices.

They had all felt the repression of Puritan authority in Massachusetts, and Hooker knew they had a chance to make certain such an administration never arose in Connecticut. "As God hath given us liberty," he implored, "take it!" The action they would take, inspired by Reverend Thomas Hooker's address, would profoundly influence political thought for the next three hundred years, and become a primary basis for representative democracy in America.

These revolutionary ideas — proposed by Hooker and accepted by the new citizens of Connecticut 137 years before the American Revolution — had formed within Hooker's consciousness after years of religious persecution in England as well as New England. Thomas Hooker was born in Marefield, England in 1586. With the intention of becoming a minister, Hooker attended Emmanuel College at Cambridge University, at the time a veritable cauldron of new and dissident thought.

Shortly after leaving Cambridge in 1620, Hooker delivered sermons at St. Mary's Church in Chelmsford, Essex. A powerful and eloquent preacher, he presented nonconformist and unorthodox topics, such as questioning the authority of the state to determine personal beliefs; discussing predestination and the authenticity of indulgences; and contemplating the nature of God's grace.

The Church of England considered preaching ideas contrary to its own doctrine — something Hooker practiced on a regular basis — tantamount to treason. Before long, the bishop of London brought Hooker before a royal commission to explain his actions. To escape the inevitable tortures to follow, Hooker fled England for Holland. Convinced by some of his former parishioners, he finally ventured on to the New World, to the newly established colony at Massachusetts.

The Massachusetts Bay Company formally emerged on March 23, 1629. Designed as a corporation for trade and commerce, it served as a refuge for Puritans wishing to escape the confines of the Church of England. Unlike the Pilgrims, the Puritans did not seek to abandon the national church. Instead, the Puritans planned to develop an ideal community in Massachusetts, which would in turn influence the reform of the entire church. The Puritan community included those who maintained a steadfast loyalty to the Mother Church, as well as the Congregationalists, who advocated the autonomy of one's individual congregation, and the piety of its members.

By 1633, Hooker became pastor of a Congregational church in Newtown (now, Cambridge, Massachusetts). He was amazed to find the Puritans of the Massachusetts Bay Colony, who had come to the New World to escape the persecution of the British Crown, practicing the same kinds of ecclesiastic tyranny against their own colonists. Hooker found himself opposed by many of the Puritan state and religious leaders, including Governor John Winthrop.

Winthrop believed those born into power or wealth were predestined by God to rule. He professed "the best part is always least, and of the best part, the wiser is always the lesser." He did not trust "the people," and dreaded the potential of mass tyranny. Under the original Massachusetts Bay charter, a general assembly of freemen — that is, approved members of the Puritan Church who swore an allegiance to the Commonwealth of Massachusetts — would elect the governor and develop the laws. But Winthrop and his associates arranged for the freemen to elect the assistants, who would in turn elect the governor. Together, the governor and his assistants would decree the laws of the community. Thus, Governor Winthrop obtained the power to change the company charter whenever he deemed it necessary.

The theocratic totalitarianism of Boston had already driven out Roger Williams, as well as Anne Hutchinson (who had the gall to offer her own Bible study in which participants could draw their own meaning of the scriptures). Williams and Hutchinson would find refuge in the new colony of Rhode Island, where political participation did not depend on religious affiliation. Hooker, as well, could not tolerate a government which was so deaf to the dissenting voice, and a church with such a vast gulf between ministers and people. He refused to sign the colony's required oath of allegiance. Like Williams and Hutchinson (both of whom he had known and often disagreed with in Boston), Hooker and his parishioners decided the best future would be elsewhere.

In June of 1636, Thomas Hooker and 110 of his followers — who had experienced similar kinds of oppression in Massachusetts — left Boston, and headed southwest towards lands charted by Edward Winslow four years earlier. Encumbered by 160 head of cattle, the great ensemble could manage to traverse only about ten miles a day. After eight days they settled on the west bank of the Connecticut River. They named the site Hartford, after Hertford, England, where Samuel Stone, a teacher in Hooker's company, was born. The communities of Windsor and Wethersfield arose near Hartford.

The original Hartford meeting house, where Hooker delivered his stirring sermon, was constructed in 1636. Square in shape, built of logs with a plain facade and pointed roof, the meeting house spanned probably no more than 260 square feet in girth. It stood at the present site of the Old State House in Hartford, and served as the meeting house for the congregation for four years. At that point Hooker, ever the pragmatic Puritan, turned the house into a livestock stable.

A second meeting house was built in 1640 near the site of the original church structure. Substantially larger, a single steeple extended from the center of the roof, housing what was at the time the second oldest bell used for church purposes in the American colonies. The third meeting house replaced it in 1739 where Center Church stands today, on the southeast corner of the Ancient Burying Ground. Larger still than the second meeting house, it featured a towering spire steeple. It served as the site where the United States

Opposite: *Center Church (Hartford Meeting House), Hartford, Connecticut. (Courtesy Center Church.)*

Constitution gained ratification by Connecticut General Assembly in January 1788.

The Fourth Meeting House, now called Center Church or the First Church of Christ, appears very nearly as when originally built in 1807. It stands at the same corner of the Burying Ground. Designed by amateur architect Daniel Wadsworth, Center Church is patterned after St. Martin's in the Field Church in London. Its steeple is 185 feet high, and features in its belfry a bell recast in England in 1727. The sanctuary features the Hooker Window, a stained glass memorial to the founder of the Hartford Community. Although his grave has never been marked, legend has Thomas Hooker's remains buried beneath the foundation of Center Church. Clearly, Hooker's influence has marked the meeting house since that May day in 1638.

By the time the Reverend Hooker finished his impassioned plea, the men of the General Court of Connecticut were reaffirmed to their purpose. Almost immediately, they assembled a committee to form a government for the colony. John Ludlow — a lawyer who studied at Balliol College at Oxford — set about the task of drafting the Fundamental Orders, which were presented to and accepted by a general assembly from Windsor, Wethersfield, and Hartford on January 14, 1639.

The Fundamental Orders of 1639, consisting of a preamble and eleven laws, dictated the following ideals of representative government: (1) All authority of government comes from the people. (2) There shall be no taxation without representation. (3) The number of men that the town shall choose to help make their laws shall be in proportion to the population of the town. (4) All freemen (excludes women, apprentices, servants, slaves, and convicts) who take an oath to be faithful to the state shall have a right to vote. (5) New towns may join the original towns and live under the same government

The "Fundamental Orders" is the first written constitution in history to permanently limit a state's power. It has served as a basis and model for all subsequent written constitutions in the United States. The original Fundamental Orders are on display at the Museum of Connecticut History in Hartford.

Sources
Johnston, Johanna. *The Connecticut Colony.* 1969, The MacMillan Company.
Pomfret, John E. *Founding the American Colonies, 1583–1660.* 1970, Harper & Row, Publishers, New York.
Soderlind, Arthur E. *Colonial Connecticut.* 1976, Thomas Nelson Inc., Publishers.

PAHA SAPA

Affiliation: Lakota, Western, or Teton Sioux Indian
Location: South Dakota
Circa 1640

Rising swiftly and majestically over the golden prairie, the Black Hills tower up to 7000 feet above the flat plains of southwest South Dakota. Once engulfed in a vast lake which covered much of the northern Great Plains, the Black Hills are the oldest mountain range in North America; older than the Rockies, older than the Appalachians, older than the Sierra Nevada. They spread 125 miles north to south, 65 miles east to west. Anglo settlers and prospectors gave the name "Black Hills," for the way the thick pine forests darkened the wild slopes. But to another people, they are known as *Paha Sapa:* "the hills that are black"; the Sacred Mountain.

These people once called themselves *Icke Wicasa* but they are known alternately as the Lakota, Teton, or Western Sioux. Historically, seven separate bands comprised this linguistically related people: the Oglala, the Brule (known as Sicangu), the Minnecojou, the Hunkpapa (of the famed Sitting Bull), the Sans Arc (known as Itzacpito), the Two Kettle (known as Oohhenonpa), and the Blackfeet (or Sihaspa). These people migrated westward from Minnesota, settling in the Black Hills region in the mid–1600s.

For the Lakota Sioux as well as other plains Indians such as the Algonquin-speaking Cheyenne and Arapaho, the Black Hills was Mecca; Paha Sapa was the Holy Land, a place of reflection and spiritual invigoration, a land of serenity, a horn of plenty: "…Before the Great Invasion, everything the Indians desired could be found in the Black Hills. They believed that the Black Hills was the very heart throb of the Earth Mother…." [Steiger, p. 151]

Paha Sapa provided home to elk, deer, antelope, mountain goats, bighorn sheep, prairie dogs, eagles, and hawks, all of whom provided sustenance and resources for the Lakota tribe. It was also the northern home of the American Bison or Buffalo, with whom the Lakota would always be associated.

The Lakota believed in the *Wakan-Tanka*, called *Manitou* by the Cheyenne, the Great Spirit, the Mysterious One, said to dwell in Black Hills for eternity. The Lakota not only believed in the Great Spirit, but believed everything on earth embodied an extension of the Great Spirit. Every rock, every tree; every blade of grass, every petal of flower; every bird of the sky, and every creature on earth, had a soul, a connection to Wakan-Tanka — the collective soul — very real and very involved in the life of everything. The Lakota would sing *Mitakuye Iyasin*, which means "All Our Relations." They treated all images as fellow beings, as relatives belonging to a vast family of nature. The mantle between life and death is stretched so thin, the Lakota would say, that the dead affect the living, ancestors influenced the lives of their descendants.

A deeply spiritual people, the Lakota constantly aspired toward greater closeness to the natural world, whose cycles determine the significant events of life. They sought wisdom and spiritual awareness, through various rituals and practices designed to develop their relationships with Wakan-Tanka, and the family of spirits. Rituals of purification and isolation occurred at significant events: birth, puberty, harvest, war, and death. These sacred liturgies would often transpire in the sweat lodge, which was constructed of thick branches forming a dome and covered in animal skins. A strong fire would be built, which would roast rocks, upon which water would be poured, creating a thick cloud of steam and heat. Among rituals of prayers and songs, herbs and self-inflicted pain, the Lakota would sweat, purifying themselves spiritually and physically. Lakota used other rituals before and after hunts, seeking courage and stamina beforehand, wishing to appease and even apologize to the animals' spirits afterwards.

One of the most noted spiritual rituals is the Vision Quest. Like Moses' sojourn to Sinai, like Buddha's contemplation under the bodhi tree, the Vision Quest brought the young man or woman from the protection of his or her people, into the wilderness in the midst of Wakan-Tanka. In seclusion, the Questor would engage in fasting and exposure to the elements; the ingestion of tobacco or hallucinogens; endurance of self-flagellation. These actions would combine to overexcite the nervous system and deprive the senses, inducing a heightened state of revelatory insight. The youth often sought direction and divine energy through an animal guide, who would pave the path toward adulthood. The Vision Quest served as the beginning of a lifelong search for knowledge and wisdom; these rites would be repeated during subsequent periods of confusion and trouble, as a means of regaining guidance and meaning.

The shaman served as the spiritual guide for the community; the medicine man, the holy man. The shaman held the post as the top visionary, a woman or man of special gifts, reputed to be in direct contact with the realm of the souls. The shaman guided the tribe toward the delicate balance between the natural and supernatural. The mantle of shaman would be passed from generation to generation through heredity or apprenticeships. The shaman foretold the future through rituals, seeking supernatural guidance for decisions made by the elders. The shaman possessed gifts in the healing arts, which would entail practices of herbology, and the smoking of tobacco and hallucinogens. The hallucinogens, however, were normally employed in certain manner, to enhance a particular ceremony. They provided a means toward heightened spiritual awareness, rather than escape from life's dilemmas. The medicine man or woman would also employ techniques of massage, dance, and face painting. Chanting and song would synchronize the soul to the rhythms and sounds of the Great Spirit. Sacred objects and art work — including Medicine Wheels resembling the sacred Tibetan mandala — helped to focus the mind and soul on the Center of Life.

Perhaps the most famous shaman in the history of Native Americans was the small-in-stature, dark-complexioned Oglala Lakota medicine man known as Crazy Horse. Born in approximately 1840, he made his Vision Quest to the Paha Sapa while still a youth, at which time he apparently achieved a particularly potent relationship with the Wakan-Tanka. Reportedly modest and retiring in nature, Crazy Horse attained reverence of the Lakota as a powerful and mysterious holy man, called "Strange One" even by his own people. He reportedly wore his hair knotted in the center top of his forehead, from which a single eagle feather — denoting spiritual height — waved from his locks. All descriptions of him rely on the memories of story tellers, for throughout his life Crazy Horse refused to allow his image to be recorded on white men's film.

Alongside his reputation as a powerful mystic, Crazy Horse is regarded by many as the greatest war leader in American Indian history. In less than two weeks in June of 1876, he dealt General George Crook — called by many the greatest Indian fighter of all time — the only defeat of his career. Eight days later, commanding the same band of Sioux, Cheyenne, and Arapaho Warrior, Crazy Horse led the massacre of the 7th Cavalry under the arrogant General George Armstrong Custer. Perhaps attesting to his special kinship with Wakan-Tanka, it is said Crazy Horse had his horse shot out from under him in battle eight separate times — but never once was injured.

Reputed as a man of integrity, Crazy Horse would become furious at the apparent deception on the part of United States representatives. He considered himself above men who negotiated with such treachery and duplicity. When approached about a treaty to relinquish some Lakota land to the U.S. government, he reportedly said, "One does not sell the land on which one walked." (Matthiessen, p. 11) When encouraged to accompany his fellow Oglala tribesmen Red Cloud and Spotted Tail to Washington to meet the Great White Father (President Grant), he assured them he was already with his Great Father (Wakan-Tanka), and certainly needed no intermediary. Regarded as the "last stronghold of a weakened and all but subjected nation," Crazy Horse never once compromised his position with the whites; he refused to wear the white man's clothes, or to adopt the white man's ways. He was stabbed in the back allegedly by Lakota police, fellow natives employed by the U.S. government, in September 1877, after having surrendered to authorities at Fort Robinson, Nebraska. He is buried at an unknown site above Wounded Knee Creek, near the Pine Ridge Reservation in southwest South Dakota.

One of the roles of the shaman, along with the elders of the tribe, was to lead the communal ceremonies. Practiced for the provision of necessary resources, these rituals also provided protection for warriors, the restoration of health, the success of childbirth, and victory in war. Rites invoked in the communal ceremony included the beating of drums, and chanting of songs which depicted ancient mythological stories. There would be great feasting, and the sacred pipe containing tobacco would be smoked. Holy objects would be incorporated into the communal celebration. Bird feathers, denoting special powers which enabled birds to soar with the spirits, would be used to create sacred ceremonial cloth and special ritual instruments. Often the Lakota ceremonies would include members of several of the seven tribes, whose leaders would direct the chanting, the rituals, and most of all, the dancing.

The Sun Dance, often continued for eight or nine days, included rituals of rhythm, chanting, and movement. Dancers would work themselves into a fevered spiritual pitch, seeking the altered state of consciousness which so often accompanied spiritual revelation. Other dances included Scalp Dances, War Dances, Rain Dances, and most famous of all, the Ghost Dance, called *wana ghi wa chipi.*

A Southern Paiute medicine man named Wovoka apparently developed the Ghost Dance in the 1880s. Wovoka's theology quickly spread among the tribes of the western United States, all of whom by then had been relegated to a repressive and impoverished life on the reservation. Wovoka preached rejection of the Anglo way of life, particularly in the use of alcohol, which he considered the scourge of the Native American. The Ghost Dance provided a ritual of hope, as the participants believing it would eventually cause the white man to vanish, the buffalo to replenish, and the ancient way of life to return, as the tribes had known it less than two hundred years previously.

So threatened were the Anglos by the potentially powerful unifying force of this ritual and other religious practices, that in 1883 Secretary of Interior Henry M. Teller — with the backing of several Christian churches — established so-called "courts of Indian affairs," tribunals created to eliminate what Teller considered "heathenish practices" on the reservations. One of the "Rules of the Court" spoke directly to the issue of dances:

> Any Indian who shall engage in the sun dance, scalp dance, or war dance, or any similar feast, so called, shall be deemed guilty of an offense, and upon conviction thereof shall be punished for the offense by the withholding of his rations for not exceeding ten days or by imprisonment for not exceeding ten days... [Utter, p. 89]

Despite the admonitions of these courts, the Ghost Dance continued to work its way east. By November 12, 1890, the practice of the Ghost Dance had reached the remnants of the Sioux tribes in southwest South Dakota, just east of the Black Hills. Near the Pine Ridge Reservation, at the edge of a north-to-south running creek called Wounded Knee, the Indians gathered for the dance. Though there is some debate about how the dance was actually performed, it is believed the participants formed a huge circle encompassing the entire tribal membership. The elders beat out the rhythm on the drums, and sang a song evoking memories of ancestors and the earth. The great ring swayed left to right, overcoming many of the dancers with great spiritual and emotional exhilaration. Several even fell unconscious.

In their fear of the ritual, government agents sent for 3500 U.S. troops to secure the Pine Ridge Reservation. The presence of such a large number of frightened, armed, bigoted white men precipitated the December 29, 1890 massacre at Wounded Knee, in which soldiers' guns killed more than 250 Teton and Yankton Sioux.

The massacre at Wounded Knee proved a culmination and magnification of the tug of war between Indian and Anglo over the lands surrounding Paha Sapa. At Fort Laramie, Wyoming, in a treaty signed in November 1868, the U.S. government guaranteed the Sioux exclusive and unfettered use of Black Hills — which the Sioux had retained for more than 200 years. But by then, white prospectors had been venturing into the sacred mountains for more than thirty years, searching for coveted veins of gold. Despite the government's assurances, six years later in August 1874 Colonel George A. Custer led a huge reconnaissance expedition of more than 1000 soldiers into the Black Hills. Custer's reputation with Indians had already been severely tarnished for his vicious attack on a peaceful Cheyenne camp at the Washita River in 1868. He would receive his due in 1876, in the face of Crazy Horse's mounted warriors. Meanwhile, Custer's reconnaissance opened the flood gates, as white men swarmed among the sacred Black Hills like locusts, in direct violation of the Ft. Laramie agreement.

In 1875, the United States government sought relinquishment of the Black Hills through treaty. Neither Crazy Horse nor Sitting Bull of the Hunkpapa would attend. After Custer's devastating defeat at Little Big Horn on June 25, 1876, the United States government — whose numbers and weaponry overwhelmed the tribes — began rounding the Lakota people into reservations. In September 1876, Red Cloud signed a treaty relinquishing Black Hills, under threat of starvation for his captive people

Today, the most famous landmark of the Black Hills is Mount Rushmore, sculpted by Gutzam Borglum. It depicts the faces of George Washington, Thomas Jefferson, Theodore Roosevelt, and Abraham Lincoln on a granite slab of mountain near Keystone. But currently, the completion of another landmark is nearing — the 600 foot long and 563 foot tall mountain statue of Crazy Horse, pointing toward the horizon. Dwarfing the presidents, the likeness of the Oglala medicine man — which will no doubt be a subject for contention, since he was supposedly never photographed — will be the largest sculpture in the world. A just tribute, perhaps, to the man, the people, and the beliefs raised in the shadow of Paha Sapa.

Sources

Matthiessen, Peter. *In The Spirit of Crazy Horse.* 1991, The Viking Press.

Steiger, Brad. *Indian Medicine Power.* 1984, Para Research, Gloucester, Massachusetts.

Storm, Hyemeyohsts. *Seven Arrows.* 1972, Harper & Row Publishers, New York.

Terrell, John Upton. *American Indian Almanac.* 1994, Barnes & Noble Books.

Utter, Jack. *American Indians: Answers to Today's Questions.* 1993, National Woodlands Publishing Company.

HOLY TRINITY

("Old Swedes Church")

Affiliation: Swedish Lutheran
Location: Wilmington, Delaware
1647

When the New Sweden Company settled along the banks of the Delaware River in 1637, several countries had already laid claim to the valleys along the Hudson and Delaware. The French had established colonies from Lake Champlain, north of the Hudson River, to Montreal. The Puritans of England had settled the Massachusetts Bay Company east of the Hudson River. Finally, the Dutch, through the West India Company, had founded the town of New Amsterdam on the island which would come to be known as Manhattan. Although the Swedish claim to the land would be brief, its impact would be considerable, affecting American life for decades to come.

Huguenot (French Protestant) Peter Minuit — the one-time director of the Dutch West India Company, who bought the Island of Manhattan for sixty guilders (24 dollars) worth of trinkets from the Mohawk Indians — led a small company of Swedish and Finn emigrants to the shores of the Delaware River. There, at the site of the present-day city of Wilmington, the New Sweden Church established Fort Christina, in honor of Sweden's queen.

At this time, Sweden remained entrenched in what would come to be known as the Thirty Years War. This was an attempt by Holy Roman Emperor Frederick II — with the aid of the Hapsburgs of Spain — to create a united Catholic Germany. If the Emperor succeeded, such a Germany, in combination with a Catholic Poland, would constitute a substantial threat to the newly reforming Sweden. In essence, it was the Roman Church's last ditch effort to halt the inevitable Reformation. Under King Gustavus Adolphus and later his daughter Christina, Sweden hoped to establish an outpost in North America, from which it could launch attacks against Spanish Catholic holdings — including Florida and the Caribbean Island — in the New World.

At first, little interest in emigration to the New World could be generated among the Swedes. Sweden had no surplus population, no overwhelming numbers facing hunger or poverty, no dissident groups seeking refuge in a new land. So desperate for volunteers had the New Sweden Company become, that it recruited a substantial number of Finns and Dutchmen among its members. For the first few years, the New Sweden Company succeeded in marginal sustenance along the shores of the Delaware, but could not expand much beyond Fort Christina.

After five years of watching the New Sweden Company merely flirt with success, the Swedish government, under Queen Christina and particularly her chief minister Axel Oxenstierna, decided to take a more vigorous involvement in the company. In 1642, Johann Printz, a physically huge, passionate and seasoned adventurer, arrived from Sweden to take charge of the colony.

By initiating a policy of fair dealing with the Indians — certainly a novel approach among many European settlers — Printz ensured a peaceful coexistence, helping to stabilize the Swedish colony. Gradually, the fur trade garnered increased profits. Soon the colony began drawing settlers from other countries, and more farmers and artisans emigrated from Sweden.

One of the greatest innovations brought by the Swedes to the colonization of America was a radically new style of dwelling place. To that point, when an immigrant family from Holland or England settled, they would fashion a crude dugout shelter in the side of a hill or mound, with walls constructed from bark or sod or thatch. The familiar A-frame, wooden homes often identified with the colonial period could not be constructed until there were enough neighbors and working hands to complete the structure. But in their native forest home, the Swedes had perfected a kind of house a solitary man could build to completion with just a pick-ax.

This newfangled home was built of logs cut from newly felled trees, the bark still covering the wood. Deep notches were cut at either end of the log, on both the top and the bottom. The builder then stacked the logs, one on top of the other, in a perpendicular fashion, with the end notches interlocking to form the walls of the dwelling. Each wall of stacked logs interlocked with other walls, forming a square. With the square of the house shaped, a door could be cut from the center of the front wall, and a roof could be formed out of thatch or bark. Stones would be assembled for the chimney and fireplace. A clay or moss mixture could

be used to fill in the cracks between the logs.

This classic log cabin could be built without the use of nails, saws, or hammers. The bark from the logs created a natural insulation, which provided a warm, relatively air-tight environment. The design proved so successful that it quickly spread from the Swedes to the Dutch and Germans, and even in some measure to the English. The log cabin became a staple form of housing for the pioneer, as the colonization of America spread west.

Before long, Johann Printz had established additional posts for the colony up and down the Delaware River shores. The expansion drew the attention of Dutch New Amsterdam director Peter Stuyvesant. Stuyvesant, a stoic Calvinist minister, viewed the growing Swedish Colony as a threat to Dutch commerce and lifestyle. When the Swedish colonists took control of Dutch Fort Sasimir in 1655, Stuyvesant sent Dutch troops to retake the fortress. The Dutch victory closed Swedish expansion along the Delaware River, and for all practicality, ended the regime of the New Sweden Company.

However, in addition to the log cabin, the 18 years of Swedish colonization brought another distinct and important contribution to colonization of North America: The introduction of the Lutheran Church.

In the 16th century, Martin Luther (1483–1546) began writing dissertations challenging many of the practices of the Roman Catholic Church. He questioned the propriety of papal indulgences, often granted for financial considerations rather than contrition and repentance. Luther asserted as well that salvation came from God's grace alone, rather than whatever works an individual might perform; that is, God granted salvation, which could not be earned. Luther questioned the doctrines of papal primacy and infallibility, pointing vigorously toward the corruption and hypocrisy of the Roman Church. Luther proposed the doctrine *sola fide*, or "justification by faith alone." He stated only by faith in Christ — and not by any initiatives on the part of Man — can humans be justified in the eyes of God. Most importantly, he asserted knowledge of God through the scriptures should be accessible to all people, with or without the interpretation of the priests.

Holy Trinity or "Old Swedes" Church in Wilmington, Delaware. (Photograph by Lisa Nichols, courtesy Holy Trinity Church.)

Luther's doctrines appealed greatly to the masses, who appreciated his divergence from many of the Roman practices. Through Luther's eyes, the common Christian need not buy or bribe his way to heaven, but would be blessed solely through belief in Christ. His literary works spread throughout his native Germany, and throughout Scandinavia. By the 17th century, the Lutheran faith had become the preeminent church in Finland, Denmark, Norway, and particularly, Sweden, one of the earliest to accept the teachings of Luther on a national scale.

The formal conversion of Sweden to the Lutheran teachings, and of the Swedish Church to the Reformation, began during the reign of King Gustav Vasa (1495–1560) in the 1520s. At the time, a considerable interest in the teachings of Luther had swelled among the Swedish people. They delighted in the access to God which Luther's treatise offered to the common human — without the intervention of priests, bishops, cardinals, or popes. King Vasa felt personally attracted to Luther's writings concerning church and state, especially the assertion that it was the state's duty to reform the church, since it seemed the church was uanble to do it itself. The king had been disappointed in the lack of support the Swedish Catholic Church offered his administration. Knowing he had the support of the populace, he convinced the nobility to allow him to take control of the Swedish Church lands. In 1527, Sweden formally renounced its allegiance to Rome. By the reign of Vasa's son, Charles IX in 1603, the majority of Swedes had become followers of Martin Luther.

As Sweden made its foray into the new world, the fledgling Lutheran Church followed. In 1640, the Reverend Reorus Torkillus arrived, becoming the first Swedish and Lutheran minister in North America. For the first time, Fort Christina hosted regular religious services for members of the Swedish Lutheran Church. In 1647 Swedish settlers, under direction of the Reverend Lars Lock built a wooden church at Transhook (Cranehook) on the south bank of the Christina River. At the same site, 51 years later, the stone-hewn Holy Trinity "Old Swedes" Church emerged under the pastorate of Swed-

ish missionary Eric Bjork.

The stone church is 60 feet long by 30 feet wide, with walls 20 feet high. Its stone construction is three feet thick at the base, and 2.5 feet at the window ledges. One large window behind the altar, and four smaller windows along the sides originally invited sunlight into the sanctuary. A wooden gable with wooden shingles comprised the original roof, over a vaulted ceiling, plastered walls, and a brick floor. Many changes to the church occurred over the years, most significantly the bell tower, constructed in 1803. Before the belfry, the 35-pound church bell hung from a walnut tree outside the west end of the chapel. The floor is constructed of herringbone brick, and the ceiling is vaulted. The black walnut pulpit was constructed by Philadelphia cabinet maker Joseph Harrison and is the oldest known to be in existence in the United States.

For almost 100 years, the old stone church served as the spiritual center for Swedish Lutherans in Wilmington. In 1791 the church was transferred to the jurisdiction of the Protestant Episcopal Church. However, Holy Trinity Lutheran Parish continued to worship in the church until 1830, when a new Lutheran Church was constructed. However, a small fraction of the church remained at "Old Swedes" Church. It underwent renovation in 1899, and in 1926 the crown prince and princess of Sweden — Gustav Adolph and Louise — visited the venerable sanctuary, presenting the congregation with a Swedish flag.

Holy Trinity is the oldest American church which stands as originally built, and is still used for regular religious services. The church yard includes a small cemetery, used as the burying ground for Fort Christina.

In 1938, 300 years of Swedish presence in Delaware was celebrated at the Old Swedes Church. The Old Swedes Church stands as a testimonial to the brief but influential early American Swedish colony.

Sources

Bishop, Peter, and Darton, Michael. *The Encyclopedia of World Faiths: An Illustrated Survey of the World's Living Religions.* 1987, Facts on File Publishers, New York.
Blow, Michael. *The American Heritage History of the Thirteen Colonies.* 1967, American Heritage Publishing Co., Inc.

Hawke, David Freeman. *Everyday Life in Early America.* 1988, Harper & Row Publishers, New York.

Oakley, Steward. *A Short History of Sweden.* 1966, Frederick A. Praeger, Publishers, New York.

Pomfret, John. *Founding the American Colonies, 1583–1660.* 1970, Harper & Row Publishers, New York.

Simon, Edith. *The Reformation.* 1966, Time Incorporated, New York.

Tunis, Edwin. *Colonial Living.* 1957, Thomas Y. Crowell Company, New York.

ST. ANNE'S SHRINE

Affiliation: Roman Catholic
Location: Isle Le Motte, Lake Champlain, Vermont
1666

Samuel de Champlain, two French soldiers, and a war party of 60 Algonquin and Huron Indians paddled canoes south along the Iroquois (Richeleau) River in 1609. The boats glided toward the lake which the Indians called Patawaboute, which means "alternate between land and water." Champlain and the two Frenchmen carried an early form of the shotgun, called "harquebus." The war party anticipated attack by the dreaded Iroquois tribe known as the Mohawks, who had been raiding and destroying the Canadian Indians' camps for decades.

Samuel de Champlain was born around 1570 in Brouage, France, the son of a sailor and a trained navigator. He had been commissioned by King Henry IV of France as principle geographer for the exploration and colonization of northern North America. King Henry sought sources of wealth for France (and, of course, himself) through the burgeoning fur trade of northern North America. He also hoped to find the fabled Northwest Passage, which would open the trade market between Europe and Asia via North America.

By 1603, Champlain had five years of navigation experience through the French army, and from voyages on a French trading ship to the West Indies, Mexico, and Panama (he reportedly was one of the first to cultivate the idea of a canal across the isthmus). In 1603, Champlain sailed down the St. Lawrence River, becoming one of the first Europeans to witness the splendor of Niagara Falls. He helped found Port Royal in Nova Scotia in 1605, and in 1608 established a fur trading post on the east bank of the St. Lawrence, at a site the Indians called "Rebec," meaning "narrowing of the waters." Champlain renamed it Quebec, the first important French settlement in New France (Canada).

The Iroquois had long tormented the Algonquins and Hurons in attacks along the Richeleau and the St. Lawrence Seaway. Both the Algonquins and Hurons, also known as the Wyandots, belonged to the Algonquin linguistic family of American Indians, indigenous to the northeast United States and Canada. The Iroquois, on the other hand, were comprised of five related neighborhood tribes — the Mohawks, the Cayuga, the Oneida, Onondaga, and the Seneca — which made up the renowned League of Five Nations. The Iroquois, who were known as "bad snakes" by other tribes, had developed a confederation among the related tribes, to cultivate cooperation and augment prosperity among them. They attacked the Hurons and Algonquins to display their political superiority, add to their growing territory, and contribute to their flourishing economic base. In particular, the Iroquois and the Hurons fought furiously, each inflicting horrendous tortures on warriors captured from the other tribe.

As Champlain ventured into New France, he befriended both the Algonquins and the Hurons, who were willing to trade beaver and martin pelts for tools from the Frenchmen. The Hurons, believing his introduced technology would overwhelm the Iroquois, insisted Champlain accompany them on their attack on the Iroquois. Not willing to abandon the alliance which was supporting his establishment of the French fur trade, Champlain reluctantly joined the Indians.

As the party meandered south, the Richeleau River suddenly widened to a girth of more than five miles. The canoes passed slowly to the west of a series of four islands, the first of which stood seven miles in length, and two miles in width. The Hurons sought possession of these islands, often used by the Iroquois as war camps.

Several days later, while approaching the southern end of the Patawaboute, Champlain's detachment suddenly encountered a large fleet of Iroquois war canoes, probably on the northwest shore of Lake Champlain. As Champlain's party came ashore, arrows and spears buzzed in both directions, and Champlain's force seemed greatly outnumbered. But suddenly Champlain and the other two Frenchmen raised their harquebuses and, with a thundering crack, fired into the advancing Iroquois force. The Mohawk warriors froze, and reportedly to a man suddenly turned and sprinted furiously back into the woods in a terror-stricken retreat. The horrified Iroquois had never encountered firearms before. The Canadian natives and the Frenchmen won the day, and several Huron warriors danced for victory at the occasion.

Unfortunately, Champlain's raid on the Iroquois resulted in the extension and acceleration of violence between not only the tribes, but between the French and the Iroquois as well. Says John Upton Terrell in his *American Indian Almanac*:

> The enmity which the Iroquois always held for the French may be traced to (this) single event... This was the first time the Iroquois had come up against the firearms of white men. ...but far from achieving its intended purpose the clash marked the beginning of a hundred years of vicious warfare between the French and the Five Nations, and it made the Iroquois the friends of both the Dutch (who traded them firearms) and the English.
>
> In later conflicts between the French and the English the Iroquois took the side of the English and were in a large part responsible for their final victory. Subsequently all but one of the Five Nations, the Oneida, fought against the American colonists, and in 1779 met their final defeat at the hands of the new nation's frontier troops. [Terrell, pp. 203, 204]

Little did Champlain know what the venture down the Richeleau had wrought. The lake he had paddled into would be named Lake Champlain, as it has been known ever since. The first island the war party skimmed past at the north end of the lake would be named Isle Le Motte, for Captain Pierre de St. Paul, Sieur de Le Motte. He eventually established Fort St. Anne, the first European settlement in the future state of Vermont. Within the rampart and chapel, also dedicated to St. Anne, would be erected the initial version of a sanctuary that would watch over the Isle Le Motte for more than three centuries.

The first missionary to the Isle Le Motte was Jesuit Father Isaac Jogues, who initially journeyed among the Iroquois nation in the summer of 1642. Jogues and his companions, which included several converted Hurons, tried to explain the Catholic faith and convert the Indians. The Hurons received the message with a less than enthusiastic response. The Indians captured the priest in August 1642, subjecting him to tortures as horrible as having his fingernails ripped from his hands. For 13 months the Mohawks held him in slavery, until he escaped in the fall of 1643. But whether due to faith, a sense of mission, or mere compulsion, he returned to the Iroquois in 1646, determined to continue his outreach. A Mohawk tomahawk to the skull ended his life on October 18, 1646.

For the next 20 years the residents of Quebec suffered invasions from the Iroquois, who would sail up the Iroquois River from the west shore of Lake Champlain. To stem the tide of attacks, the French decided to establish a series of fortresses at the mouth of the lake, including Fort St. Anne on the Isle Le Motte.

The fort on Isle Le Motte stood 96 feet in width and 144 feet in length. A bastion, stationed at each of the four corners, offered soldiers a solid armory from which to fire upon the marauding Iroquois outside. The fort quartered 60 soldiers, plus a scattering of New France citizens and Huron converts. The construction of the fort included the original Chapel of St. Anne, the first Christian place of worship in what would become the 14th state. From this chapel, Fr. Francis Dollier administered to the devout Catholic residents five of the seven sacraments, the staple of Catholic ritual:

Baptism

Dollier baptized the newborns of the newly converted Huron natives. In Catholic tradition, baptism is administered to infants, who, according to tradition, still carry the stain of original sin from Adam and Eve.

Communion

Fr. Dollier celebrated the mass at the Chapel of St. Anne, which was built particularly to accommodate the mass. Holy Communion was distributed at each mass, as a remembrance of the Last Supper. Catholic tradition believes in transubstantiation, asserting the bread and wine of communion is actually transformed into the body and blood of Christ. Therefore, the tradition further asserts, Christ's body and blood actually enter and become part of the body and blood of the believer.

Confession or Reconciliation

Soldiers at Fort St. Anne reportedly set up confessionals in small, dark booths called confessionals, in which repentants could confess their sins in private. The repentant made his or her confession to the priest, who would assign a penance for the repentant to perform. Recently, many Catholic churches have altered the sacrament to include face to face interaction between priest and repentant, and reconciliation ceremonies performed in groups.

Confirmation

This is a reaffirming of the baptismal ceremony, performed among older Catholics who have been educated in the faith and, presumably, are able to consciously renew their lifelong commitment as Catholics. This sacrament would traditionally be performed among eighth graders, raising the question of whether 13 years provides one enough years or experience to make such a commitment.

Last Rites

During the scurvy scourge in the winter of 1666 — in which 40 of the 60 soldiers were stricken due to ingestion of spoiled meat and flour — Fr. Dollier offered the last rites to the sick and dying. Traditionally, the last rites enable the faithful to make a final confession and receive the priest's blessing before death to greater ensure the believer's entrance into heaven. Due to illness and the skirmishes among the Indians, the last rites were a crucial part of the spiritual life at the fort.

Fort St. Anne probably did not witness the practice of the other two Sacraments, Matrimony and Holy Orders (the vow of Priesthood), as no women or seminarians resided at the fort.

Fort St. Anne, enveloping the chapel of St. Anne, probably remained an active fortress until around 1690. By then, the French had achieved a truce with the Iroquois, which curtailed the invasions. For the next 180 years the Chapel of St. Anne remained intact but abandoned. Various Lake Champlain travelers passing by the Isle Le Mott would often stop by the fort ruins, and perhaps meditate before the chapel of St. Anne. Finally, the chapel and most of the fort fell into disintegration. Meanwhile, St. Joseph's Church was established to serve the small Catholic population on the Isle, as the community of the Isle Le Mott developed.

Over the years, this tiny little island, with a population of scarcely more than 500, has been the centerpiece for several important historic events, affecting not only Vermont, but the United States as a whole:

- In February 1776, the Continental Congress appointed a delegation of commissioners to Canada, led by Benjamin Franklin. It is believed Franklin and his colleagues passed time on the Isle Le Mott, on the way to and from their diplomatic treks to Canada

- The fleet commanded by General Benedict Arnold which fought the Revolutionary War Battle of Valcour Island against the British in September 1776 was anchored off Isle Le Mott. More

St. Anne's Shrine, Isle La Motte, Vermont. (Courtesy St. Anne's Shrine.)

than 1000 sick or wounded soldiers were sheltered and treated at the Isle.

- A battery of six 18-pound cannons was stationed at Isle Le Motte during the War of 1812, to protect Lake Champlain from invasion by the British. The presence of the American fleet, commanded by Captain Thomas Macdonough, drove the British away from the Isle. The ruffian shore leave behavior exhibited by the American fleet — including the murder of a Vermont resident critical of the fleet's conduct — eventually caused the state of Vermont to drive the fleet out as well. Macdonough would later lead the American Fleet to victory at the Battle of Plattsburg Bay.

- It is a belief long held among Isle Le Motte residents that famed marching band composer John Philip Sousa composed his immortal "Stars and Stripes Forever" while visiting at the Isle's Reynolds Estate in 1897.

- On September 6, 1901, Vice-President Theodore Roosevelt was the principle speaker at a Vermont Fish and Game League convention, held at the Isle Le Motte estate of former Vermont lieutenant governor Nelson W. Fisk. It was here that Roosevelt first received word of the assassination of President William McKinley by Leon Czolgosz, at the Pan American Exposition in Buffalo.

In 1893, Bishop Louis de Goesbriand spearheaded the erection of a shrine to commemorate the original chapel and fort. He arranged for the purchase of an area of land called Sandy Point, where Fort St. Anne once stood. Parishioners from St. Joseph's gathered to clear the land, and erect a 36-foot high cross to mark the spot where the original chapel of St. Anne stood. The wooden replacement chapel, 13 feet long and nine feet wide, was built nearby. The chapel perched upon a 20-foot-square wooden platform, three steps off the ground. A plaster statue of St. Anne — who in Catholic tradition is known as the mother of the Virgin Mary, mother of Christ — was placed above the red cedar altar in the shrine. A relic of St. Anne resides in a small silver case within the shrine.

An open air pavilion was quickly added in front of the shrine, to accommodate the crowds, often as large as 3000, that have come to visit St. Anne's Shrine. Each year — for the following 100 years — as many as 50,000 faithful Catholics and other curious visitors have made pilgrimages to the Isle Le Motte, to pray and meditate before the venerable St. Anne's Shrine.

Sources

Berger, Josef. *Discoverers of the New World.* 1960, American Heritage Publishing Co., Inc., New York.

Kerlidou, the Rev. Hoseph, Couture, the Rev. Joseph N., Boucher, the Rev. Maurice. *St. Anne's Shrine.* c. 1980.

Terrell, John Upton. *American Indian Almanac.* 1994, Barnes & Noble Books.

Tumacacori Mission and Tubac Presidio

Affiliation: Roman Catholic, established by Jesuit missionary, run by Franciscans
Location: Arizona, 58 miles south of Tucson,
in Santa Cruz Valley along Santa Cruz River
1691

The Mission San Cayetino de Tumocacori and the adjacent Presidio at Tubac, Arizona, could easily bear the title "Seven Flags Over Tubac." During its 300+ years of European-American occupation, the adobe and tile-roof buildings overlooking the Santa Cruz River Valley of southern Arizona have flown the banners of seven separate nation-states: Spain, Mexico, Territory of New Mexico, Confederate States of America, Territory of Arizona, State of Arizona, United States of America. Had the various Indian nations — which have resided in this valley as early as 10,000 years ago — had colors to wave, the roster of flags would be even greater. Under each flag, a separate and distinct culture developed along the Santa Cruz River Valley. With each community, the face of southern Arizona changed, adding to the complex design which eventually became the forty-eighth state of the United States of America.

Native Populations

The valleys of southern Arizona — from the Salt and Gila Rivers to the Santa Cruz River at the Mexican border — are home to 10,000 years of Indian culture. The greatest of these cultures is the Hohokam. The name, translated into English, means *those who have gone.* The Hohokam developed a civilization long-lived and sophisticated enough to rival the great societies of the "Ancient Ones" (the Anasazi). The traditions and lifestyles continue today, through the descendants of this ancient people.

Much of the Hohokam culture may have emerged from some of the great ancient civilizations of southern Mexico, such as the Mayans or the Aztecs. Around 600 A.D., practices and customs commonly found in southern Mexico had emigrated to southern Arizona, and the Hohokam Society. For example, the Hohokam played a game of ball, on marked clay courts, in precisely measured dimensions, similar to a game played among the Mayans. A rubber ball, found no where else in North America, was found among Hohokam artifacts, and resembles similar balls found in the Mayan ruins.

The Hohokam may have been the first people to practice irrigation in prehistoric North America. They constructed dams, built reservoirs, and dug canals to divert the Gila River for agricultural and domestic use. They

Tumacacori Mission in the Santa Cruz River Valley of southern Arizona.

became elaborate artists and intricate artisans, creating ornaments, decorations, figurines, pottery of high quality and beauty; they even developed a form of etching unique to that period of North American history.

They practiced cremation, and buried offerings in special pits where the ashes were laid. They believed a hooting owl foretold impending death, and that owls carried the souls of dead to next world. They practiced polygamy; that is, a Hohokam man could have as many wives as he could reasonably support. They smoked cane cigarettes, and some possessed copper bells cast in southern Mexico.

Today, remnants of the Hohokam survive through the Pima, whose culture continues in and around the San Xavier Indian Reservation, north of Tubac. The early Spanish padres assumed "Pima" as the name of these people, since they heard these Indians utter the word on a frequent basis. The word actually means "no"; the Pima call themselves *A-a'tam kimult,* meaning "river people." They are aptly named,

for they have carried on many of the ancient beliefs and agricultural customs of the Hohokam in their ancestral land, in the valleys encompassing the Salt and the Gila River, as wells as the Santa Cruz River. Archaeologists refer to the Pima as "River Hohokam."

The close kin to the Pima are the Papago. Papago means "bean people," and suggests a staple diet of the people. Like the Pima, the Papago maintained many Hohokam customs, but lived a traditionally nomadic lifestyle. They roamed the hot desert stretching from present day Tubac to the Sonoran Desert in Mexico. They are known as "Desert Hohokam."

The other Indian tribe which has dwelt in the deserts of southern Arizona actually originated in southern Colorado, but spread its terror to Texas, New Mexico, Arizona, and northern Mexico. The tribe calls itself "Dineh" meaning "the people." They are better known by the derivation of the Zumi word meaning enemy, "Apachu." Like ravaging packs of wolves attacking domestic sheep, the Apache spread fear among all men: Spaniards, Mexicans, Pima, Papago, Americans alike. Like the wolves, the Apache did not raid for revenge or revolt, but simply as a way of life. They stole horses from the Spanish and in 1725 began to sell the animals to the Indian tribes to the north, forever changing the balance of power between the plains and the plateau tribes. They grew few crops, were not skilled in crafts or art and they shunned the sedentary life of the Pima. They wandered, scavenged, and preyed upon the weak and vulnerable. Under the leadership of the great chief Cochise, they exercised a reign of savagery scarcely equaled in the annals of the American West.

Spain

Jesuit Father Eusebio Francisco Kino was born in the Tyrolean Alps of Italy in 1644. Admitted to Society of Jesus 1669, Kino was educated and became skilled in mathematics, astronomy, surveying, and cartography. He arrived in Mexico in 1681, and after unsuccessful attempts to colonize Baja California, he moved to southern Arizona. In 1691 he built a visita, or temporary building, at the site of Mission San Cayetino de Tumacacori, five miles south of present-day Tubac. He also founded Mission Guevavi east of Tumacacori, and Mission San Xavier del Bac, south of Tucson.

Legends say Kino wandered about the lands without military escort. Although he taught his religion, he also introduced agriculture and various European fruits and grains to the Pima, Papago, and Yuma (Colorado River vicinity) tribes; Kino was pragmatic enough to understand evangelism is better received on a full stomach. His love for the Indians appeared sincere; Father Kino once rode 62 miles nonstop to advocate for a Yuma Indian sentenced to be whipped to death for a minor crime. All the while, Kino continued his cartographic projects. His 1710 Map of Baja California was circulated as the exemplary map of Baja in the 16th century.

Father Kino died in Magdalena, Sonora, Mexico, in 1711. But the Jesuits followed his lead, and by 1730 a mission ranch developed in Tubac, with Jesuits and other Spaniards directing the work of Indians.

By 1751, however, the Pima Indians had begun to tire of the Europeans. They resented the Spaniards claim of the mission lands, and objected to the cruelty by which Jesuits treated wayward or noncompliant Pima. Also, Luis Oacpicajua, Chief of Pima, felt he was not properly recognized by the padres. On November 20, 1751, Luis led a revolt by the Pima, killing more than 100 people, including several padres, among the three mission sites.

In response to the revolt, the Spanish government in Mexico City sent Captain Jose Diaz del Carpio to quell the uprising. Carpio arrived at the Indian village named Tubac, three miles north of Tumacacori, on March 7, 1752. He immediately sent scouts to the Santa Catalina Mountains, north of present Tucson, where Luis Oacpicajua had fled. Carpio offered the chief the choices of peace or war. Luis chose peace, and returned to Tumacacori to negotiate on March 18.

Carpio then set up a permanent Presidio set up at Tubac, central to the locations of Tumacacori, Guevavi, and San Xavier missions. By 1757, a population of 411 occupied this small town of Tubac, making it the first permanent European settlement in Arizona, and one of the oldest towns in North America.

In 1759, 36-year-old Juan Bautista de Anza of Fronteras, Mexico, replaced Carpio as Captain of Tubac Presidio. For the next 15 years, he and Father Francisco Garces (famous for his work among Yuma Indians) planned and dreamed of an overland passage from Mexico to Monterey, Alta California. In 1774, they forged a trail from Tubac through southern Alta California to Mission San Gabriel near present-day Los Angeles. One year later, on October 22, 1775, Anza led one of the most incredible journeys in the annals of North American exploration.

Following the overland trail he and Garces had blazed just a year earlier, Anza led a party of 234 poor residents from Culiacan, Mexico to a better life in Alta California. He was accompanied by Garces and the cantankerous Fray Pedro Font — whose comprehensive journals thoroughly documented the venture for historians. Traveling more than 800 miles in six months, Anza led the party across rivers, over deserts, and through mountains to the Presidio of Monterey, Mission Dolores, and the Presidio of San Francisco.

On the second day of the expedition, October 23, 1775, a Culiacan soldier's wife named Senora Felix died during childbirth. The child survived, and friends of the mother took care of the infant for the remainder of the trip. Miraculously, Senora Felix' mother proved to be the only fatality of the entire adventure. In fact, 244 persons actually arrived at Monterey, as several babies were born en route.

In November 1775, Anza and his party crossed the treacherous Colorado River with the help of Yuma Indians and their Chief Palma. Palma had befriended Anza and Fr. Garces during earlier travels, and Garces would remain with the Yuma while the rest of the expedition continued on to California. The Yuma's charitable nature would soon end, however, due to indiscretions and atrocities practiced upon them by Spanish soldiers in the coming years. Soon, the Yuma would turn their back on the Europeans altogether; in the end, no Spanish Mission was ever allowed to be built in Yuma territory along the Colorado River.

In December 1775, the Anza party's trail dipped into Baja California, then crossed the bitterly cold Coyote Canyon between the Salton Sea and the Vallecito Mountains. On a snowy Christmas Eve, Salvador Ignacio was born, reputed to be the first immigrant child given birth in Alta California.

San Gabriel Mission welcomed the expedition in January 1776. The families rested at the mission, which had yet to feature its Moorish-style buttressed facade, while Anza joined soldiers in San Diego in an attempt to quell the revolt of Hokan Indians. From San Gabriel, the party journeyed north along the Santa Barbara Channel. They encountered the Chumash tribe, who amazed the sojourners with their skills in fishing and boatmanship.

In March 1776, the Anza party passed through the missions at San Luis Obispo, San Antonio de Padua, and finally landed at the Presidio at Monterey, near the Mission San Carlos Borromeo. From Monterey, Anza and a smaller party set out to discover the sites for the San Francisco Presidio, Mission San Francisco de Asis, and Mission Santa Clara to the south. Finally, on June 17, 1776, the rest of the Culiacan settlers left Monterey and established the mission and Presidio on June 27, 1776. In completing the expedition, the Anza party secured San Francisco Bay for the Spanish Empire, and completed the overland route from Mexico, which over the years would bear the footsteps of countless immigrants.

Mexico

The Spanish government blamed the 1751 Pima revolt on the Jesuits; in conjunction with the government's disappointment with the Jesuit efforts in Baja California (plus rumors of jealousy on the part of the secular church in Spain) the Jesuits were eventually exiled from New Spain in 1767 by Pope Clement XIV. The Franciscan Order, already present in the Mexican colonies, took up where the Jesuits left off.

Construction of the mission church began under Franciscan Narciso Gutierrez in 1800, but lack of funds delayed the project several times. The original plan called for a series of vaulted barrel domes crowning the naves and the transepts of the cruciform church. Financial difficulties required scaling back the blueprint design, however, and the domes were confined to above the altar. The dome designed to top the reredos, or belfry to the right of the columned Romanesque facade never met completion, which accounts for the jagged, incomplete appearance the Mission Tumacacori bears today.

The interior featured a 75-foot nave with cobblestone flooring and a choir chamber loft high above the vestibule. The baptistry was placed under the reredos, and a rich tapestry of baroque Catholic images in bright native colors beckoned to the eye and imagination of the potential convert.

When the Franciscans took over the missions in the New Mexico Territory and established the missions of Alta California, they had originally planned to administer the missions for ten years, training the neophytes (baptized Indians) in the management of the lands. At the end of the ten years, according to the master plan the padres would turn the mission lands over to the neophytes, who would divide and work the land perpetually. Unfortunately, the Indians did not convert as numerously and completely as planned, and it took the padres longer to assimilate them into the European style of life than they had first anticipated. When New Spain revolted in 1810 as the Republic of Mexico, the new Mexican government required the padres to sign loyalty oaths. Most of the Franciscans refused to do so, left the New World, and the Indians and the Missions were left to fend for themselves. They did not do well.

Left in a limbo between their traditional way of life and the culture imposed by the padres, the neophytes at Mission Tumacacori and Tubac became easy prey to the raiding Apache. Raids were nearly continual for the next forty years, attacking neophytes and Mexicans alike. Tubac became a ghost town of adobe ruins from after 1821. Tumacacori and the other missions were officially secularized in 1834, and they were all but abandoned shortly thereafter.

In 1848, at the Treaty of Guadalupe Hidalgo following the Mexican-American War, the United States — for the paltry sum of $15 million, obtained the territory that would include California, Nevada, Utah, western Colorado, western New Mexico, and all but southern Arizona. The Gasden Purchase, executed on June 30, 1854, claimed the rest of New Mexico and Arizona. Named for James Gasden, the senator who negotiated with Mexican President Santa Anna for the territory, the treaty separated Arizona & New Mexico (making the Territory of New Mexico) from Sonora and Chihuahua, Mexico. The Mexican government made $10 million in the deal, with Santa Anna reportedly skimming a quarter of the sum off for himself. With the Gasden Purchase, the U.S. had cleared a railroad thoroughfare from the Rio Grande to the Pacific Ocean. Needless to say, the territory was ripe for speculators.

Territory of Arizona

In August of 1856, Charles D. Poston, a printer, bureaucrat, and land speculator from Kentucky, joined forces with German surveyor Herman Ehrenberger and Cincinnati's Major Samuel P. Heintzelm, a veteran of the Mexican-American War, who was stationed at Fort Yuma. The three entrepreneurs moved into the old Presidio and mission buildings of Tubac and Tumacacori. With funding from Ohio Railroad developers, they opened the headquarters for the Sonora Exploring and Mining Company. Ehrenberger sketched the first map depicting the Gasden Purchase, and Poston promoted the Gadsen Purchase lands in east coast and San Francisco newspapers.

Within the next four years. the Sonora Exploring and Mining Company opened eighty mineral claims, attracting attention and investors from all over the United States. Tumacacori and Tubac soon teamed with adventurers, speculators, and prospectors burned out from the disillusioning California Gold Rush. Two Mexican brothers opened the Heintzelm silver mine (named for the mayor) 20 miles west of Tubac. The mine was soon supplying silver for Tiffany's of New York

Charles D. Poston claimed the title "Alcalde of Tubac." He printed his own money; performed marriages for the community, and virtually became "the government." On March 3, 1859, he published the first edition of *The Arizonian,* the first newspaper in Arizona territory.

Early Arizonians, particularly Poston, relished in the idyllic time and setting. The Alcalde once recalled, "We had no law but love, no occupation but labor. No government, no taxes, no public debt, no politics. It was a community in a perfect state of nature" (Faulk, p. 90).

Poston grew quite rich. Among other wealthy entrepreneurs, he began lobbying for the creation of a Territory of Arizona, separate from New Mexico.

Just before the Civil War, an incident known as "the Bascom Affair" occurred, further straining the already thread-bare ties between Americans and Apaches.

One January evening in 1861, alcoholic rancher John Ward got drunk and beat his step-son, Mickey Free, who then ran away. Ward, rather than accepting the responsibility of his behavior, accused Chiracaua Apaches, led by the great Cochise, of stealing both the boy and several head of cattle.

The cowardly Ward reported the "abduction" to a naive Lt. George N. Bascom, stationed at Fort Buchanan at Apache Pass. Apparently determined to make a name for himself (unfortunately he succeeded), Bascom led 54 soldiers to Cochise's camp to "bring him to justice." They captured Cochise, but he quickly escaped. Both sides took hostages. Americans sent more soldiers after Cochise, who fled into the mountains, but killed his hostages. Bascom had his Apache hostages hanged from the gallows.

From that point on, Cochise escalated war against the Americans, killed hundreds, and destroyed thousands of dollars worth of property. Among the casualties was John Poston, brother of Charles, killed at the Heintzhelm silver mine. The Apaches enjoyed particular success in southern Arizona, as the Civil War drew men and supplies to the east, leaving the remaining residents particularly vulnerable to the raids.

Confederacy

Arizona leaned toward the Confederacy when the South ceded from the Union in 1861. Not only did the region fall below the Mason-Dixon line, but Arizonians sympathized with the secessionists. They felt snubbed by the Republican North, which vaguely referred to Arizona as simply the western half of the New Mexico territory. Also, Arizona expected a business boom from an anticipated railroad, which would link the Southwest with the Southeast.

With the Civil War, soldiers and supplies ventured east to serve the Confederate army. While the war waged on, the weakened Santa Cruz valley fell victim to extensive Apache raids, and the area suffered in a manner from which it has yet to fully recover.

Meanwhile, on February 14, 1862, confederate Lieutenant Colonel John R. Baylor conquered Fort Fillmore on the Rio Grande. He established the Confederate Territory of Arizona, and came to Tucson to raise the Texas (a Confederate state) flag.

In response, the Union Column from California, under Col. James H. Carleton, captured Tucson for the Union May 20, 1862. Carleton had little opportunity for military glory, however; Captain Sherod Hunter and Confederate Texas troops had anticipated their approach, and had fled the week before. Nevertheless Carleton, under martial law, took control of the city, and proclaimed himself governor of Tucson. Arizona was a Union possession, and on February 24, 1863, Abraham Lincoln signed the law creating the Arizona Territory of the United States.

Territory of Arizona, State of Arizona and USA

In 1862, a troop of Union cavalry settled into Tubac, which delighted the remaining citizens so much they allowed the soldiers to quarter in the old Presidio for free. They remained until the end of the Civil War, and they helped stave off the Apaches.

The Civil War and the Apaches — plus a series of disastrous floods and changing economic times, which would see residents of Tubac move to other areas — took a permanent toll on Tubac's prominence in Arizona. By the time statehood came to Arizona in 1912, the chief population centers had moved to Tucson and Phoenix.

Nevertheless, the Mission Tumacacori and the Tubac Presidio have managed to survive and thrive in different ways. In 1885, a teacher named Lillie Mercer opened the first Arizona school at Tubac. Life continued quietly for the next sixty years when, in 1945, an art school opened. Before long artists and artisans returned to the Tubac area, just as in the days of the Hohokam.

To commemorate the importance of the mission and the Presidio to Arizona and the southwestern United States, Tubac is now a state historic park, and Tumacacori enjoys the status of a National Historic Monument.

Sources
Faulk, Odie B. *Arizona: A Short History.* 1970, University of Oklahoma Press.
Fireman, Bert M. *Arizona: Historic Land.* 1982, Alfred A. Knopf, New York.
Riley, Frank. *DeAnza's Trail Today.* 1976, A World Way Publication, Los Angeles.
Terrell, John Upton. *American Indian Almanac.* 1994, Barnes & Noble Books.
Young, Bob, and Jan, Anza. *Hard Riding Captain.* 1966, Golden Gate Junior Books, San Carlos, California.

FRIENDS' GREAT MEETING HOUSE

Affiliation: Society of Friends
Location: Newport, Rhode Island
1699

No group has enjoyed greater, longer-lasting influence on social justice activism in the Unites States than the Society of Friends, also known as the Quakers. Since the formation of the first Friend's colony at Newport, Rhode Island, in 1657, the impact of the Quakers on American movements for civil and human rights has been both far reaching and profound.

The American Quakers were among the first to practice decent regard and treatment of the American Indian. Recognizing the "Inner Light" of each person, they called the Indian "brother," they paid him fairly for the land obtained, and they refused to give him alcohol, the scourge of many an American tribe. The reason why Quakers were consistently able to live peacefully alongside Indians so easily: they treated them as Children of God, rather than depraved, godless savages.

Quakers fought for the rights of African Americans long before it became fashionable. Quaker William Lloyd Garrison published a notorious abolitionist newspaper called *Liberator,* which fueled the cause of radical abolitionists. Friends regularly endured imprisonment rather than comply with the Fugitive Slave Act, and became instrumental in the construction of the Underground Railroad, the pathway to the free north for many runaway slaves. Isaac Hopper, a Quaker tailor in Philadelphia, habitually used his body as a shield between frightened slave and the merciless slave hunter. Lucretia Mott reportedly once turned aside an entire mob of angry slave owners preparing to tar and feather a fellow outspoken abolitionist. Levi Coffin, known as the President of the Underground Railroad, reportedly ushered more than 2000 slaves to freedom between 1826 to 1846. And during the 1860s, Quakers engineered the Philadel-phia streetcar boycott—in favor of the rights of African Americans to ride the rails—one hundred years before the advent of the Montgomery Improvement Association bus boycott.

Quakers marched at the forefront of the women's suffrage movement of the 19th and 20th centuries. Recognizing the Inner Light within women as well as men, the Friends early encouraged full participation of women as ministers, citizens, and church members. Abby Kelley Foster was one of the first Quaker women to refuse to pay taxes on her farm, claiming "taxation without representation." Lucretia Mott helped Elizabeth Cady Stanton plan the 1848 Women's Rights Convention in Seneca Falls, New York. Susan B. Anthony voted illegally in 1872 to protest her lack of enfranchisement, and which eventually led to a nonviolent protest during the Centennial celebration, to declare the Women's Bill of Rights. In 1913, Alice Paul led a hunger strike in front of the White House to protest the lack of women's voting rights.

During the Revolutionary War, Civil War, and World War I, Quakers were among the first to declare themselves what would become known as conscientious objectors—unable to accommodate the active participation in war with the peace-loving message of their faith. The effect of the Quakers' practices led to a provision for conscientious objectors during World War II, which assumed an even more prominent role during the Vietnam Era.

The American Friends Service Committee (AFSC) was formed during World War I, to bring aid and comfort to the wounded on both sides of the war in Europe. The tradition continued during the Vietnam Era when the AFSC, despite the heated objection of the U.S. military leadership, shipped medical supplies to both North and South Vietnam. At the Quaker aid center in Quang Ngai, a sign on the door reportedly read, in Vietnamese and English:

NO WEAPONS PLEASE:
Ninety Percent of the Patients in this center have
suffered injuries caused by weapons.
PLEASE LEAVE YOURS OUTSIDE

In 1942, Gordon Hirabayashi, a Quaker of Japanese ancestry, and a conscientious objector, chose to go to prison rather than face internment during World War II, the fate of thousands of Japanese-Americans during a uniquely tragic episode of paranoid American policy.

Conscientious objectors, civil disobedience, passive resistance, nonviolent protest: almost 300 years before these practices gained popularity in the 1960s, the Society of Friends commonly employed them for the protection of what they call "The Inner Light" inside every man, women, and child on earth. The Quakers have been front runners in the advocacy of such social movements as religious liberty; tolerance for the poor and the ignorant, rights for the Jew and the American Indian, Equal Rights for Women, abolition of slavery; prison reform, moral aid to prisoners, arbitration for settling of conflicts.

The influence of the Society of Friends upon America began in 1657, long before the conception of anything such as a "United States." In June of that year, eleven Quakers sailed from Bridlington, England aboard a tiny vessel called the *Woodhouse,* considered far too small to safely cross the Atlantic Ocean. Robert Fowler, a novice seaman, apparently cast off without compass or charts. Reportedly relying solely on divine guidance, the *Woodhouse* first landed at a creek at the west end of Long Island, near the Dutch settlement of New Amsterdam. Leaving five Friends at Long Island, the little ship continued through the pass known as Hell Gate, and arrived in Newport, Rhode Island. Rhode Island had been founded by former Puritan Roger Williams as a haven for religious freedom. Newport became the first colony of the Society of Friends in the New World, and the center for Quaker activities in America for the next 25 years. By 1661

the colony had grown large enough for yearly meetings, and George Fox, the founder of the Society of Friends himself, visited the Newport Society in 1672.

After more than three decades of meetings in private homes and business establishments, the Newport Society of Friends built the Great Meeting House in 1699. It is the second oldest Quaker meeting house in the United States, preceded only by the Meeting House in Flushing, New York. A massive structure built in the typical A-frame, New England colonial style, it featured a towering roof with forty-five foot girders, crowned with a single cupola. Rows of rough wooden benches faced the back wall, against which the benches for the elders were situated. Balconies rose above the meeting house floor, providing additional seating for the congregation.

This additional seating apparently proved insufficient for the growing community, as additions to the Great Meeting House were made in 1729, and again in 1807. A two-story north meeting room was added first, which included a compartment known as "the Ship Room," regularly used for the women's business meetings. The north meeting area eventually became the regular meeting place for the Newport Society of Friends, which reserved the Great Meeting House for quarterly and yearly meetings, which encompassed Friends from a greater geographical area. A south meeting area was added in 1807 for the still swelling membership. The Great Meeting House served the Newport Friends until 1905. It was restored to its original 1699 design in 1974, and is serviced and maintained by the Newport Historical Society.

The most famous member of the Newport Society of Friends was a woman named Mary Dyer. As a bride of 18, she traveled to Boston with her husband William. She befriended and followed antinomianist Anne Hutchinson to Aquidneck Island, after Hutchinson had been banished from Boston for challenging the authority of the Puritan Church. During a trip home to England in 1652, she became a Child of the Light, eventually forming the nucleus for the Newport Quaker colony.

After welcoming the *Woodhouse* group to Rhode Island, Dyer returned to Boston,

Friends' Great Meeting House, Newport, Rhode Island. (Photograph by Jay Walters.)

determined to convince Puritans of the error of their ways. She was imprisoned and released in 1657, after which she returned to Newport. Despite an increasingly hostile Boston, which welcomed transgressing Quakers with beatings, torture, and executions, Dyer returned to Massachusetts in 1659 for the final time. On the grounds of the State House in Boston stands a statue, whose inscription reads:

> Mary Dyer, Quaker.
> Witness for Religious Freedom
> Hanged on Boston Common, 1660

The origin of the Society of Friends can be traced to 17th century England, a time and place of great spiritual and religious revolution, as the British sought alternatives to the obligatory Church of England. The Society founder, George Fox, was born in 1624, in Fenny Drayton, Leicestershire. Apprenticed as a shoemaker and shepherd, Fox had little formal education, but reportedly possessed ample stores of energy, charisma, and curiosity. In 1644 Fox left home in pursuit of spiritual an-

swers. Despite extensive interaction with a variety of ministers and sects, he could not find a path through any specific religious denomination to give him comfort. Finally, Fox concluded that no religion or authority could bring contentment, but only direct, personal experience of the Light of Christ.

By 1647, Fox began openly confronting members of the other religious, a custom which landed him in prison eight separate times during his life. Fox began recruiting followers seeking a simpler means toward spiritual contentment. He set up headquarters in the home of Judge Thomas and Margaret Fell in 1652 at Swartmoor Hall in Ulverston. His followers began traveling two by two throughout England and eventually to the New World, to challenge the existing sects, and to encourage them to follow the Children of the Light, as the Quakers were becoming known.

At the heart of the Friends' philosophy is the inner light which dwells within each man, woman, and child on earth. A spark of divinity resides within each human, the Friends say, and therefore the task in life is to live in harmony, fairness, charity, and justice with every other human being on earth. It is the essence of social justice.

Because the inner light shines within each person, the Friends see no need for clerics, denominations, or doctrine to guide the individual toward God; as a matter of fact, they would say, these things provide a distraction rather than inspiration. At a typical Friend's meeting there is no minister, there is no prayer book, there are no shared recitations or songs. Scriptures are rarely employed. Instead, the gathered sit and wait in silence, examining and anticipating the inner light within each of them. Only when divine inspiration causes one to speak is the quiet broken, and a spiritual revelation is shared by a member.

The Quakers sought to model themselves after what they perceived to be the lives of the primitive Christians, living a pure and simple life, as close to the example of Christ as possible. The early Quakers — though many emerged from wealthy families — rejected elaborateness, shunned glamour and luxuries, abstained from liquor and tobacco, and avoided art, music, and dance. They rejected religions of conformity, and sought environments which accepted the idea that Christ could speak in every person. Since they believed the light of Christ shone equally in each human, the Quakers refused to bow or remove their hats before earthly authorities, and opposed the payment of tithes in church. They would not accept marriage by ministers, and they refused to take oaths of any kind — particularly oaths of allegiance to church or state.

These practices made the Quakers particularly dangerous and annoying in the eyes of the Church of England and, later, the Puritan Church, which (ironically) was established as a means to "purify" the Anglican Church. Both institutions relied on the loyalty and obedience to the authorities, while their economies relied on the tithings of the congregation. For these reasons, the Society of Friends faced severe persecution both in England and in Massachusetts, where Quakers were regularly imprisoned, exiled, beaten, tortured, and even executed for matters of conscience. In England, between 1652 and 1689, an estimated 15,000 Quakers faced jail sentences; however, unlike in Boston, no Quakers died at the hands of the persecutors.

Unfortunately, the Quakers seemed to do little to quell the tide of resistance and persecution they met in England and America. Zealous and confident in their newfound convictions, Quaker missionaries would habitually march into Protestant churches during Sunday services and denounce the memberships' participation. Other proselytizers would mix among revelers in open air markets and fairgrounds, deriding them for their frivolity and excesses. Roger Williams, the founder of Rhode Island, found the Quakers to be arrogant and contemptuous. His wrangling with visiting Friends founder George Fox is quite well documented.

Despite the confrontations, hardships, and persecution, the Society of Friends continued to spread among the colonies, with settlements springing up in Long Island, Maryland, and North Carolina. These settlements included the colony of Pennsylvania, founded by William Penn, and eventually known as the Quaker State. By the start of the Revolutionary War, there were an estimated 50,000 Quakers in a total colonial population of 1.5 million — nearly 3 percent of the colonists. For the next two centuries, the Society of Friends continued to work diligently to fuel the inner light within themselves, and to protect and to reveal that light within their persecuted fellow American.

Today, the Society of Friends makes up only about .006 percent of the United States population, approximately 120,000 members. Yet, they carry on the proud tradition of activism that first landed on the shores of Newport in 1657. Wherever there are incidents of civil disobedience, conscientious objectorship, nonviolent protests, or passive resistance for the cause of social justice, there are likely to be Quakers in the fray; or at the very least, those who have borrowed from the Quaker tradition.

Sources

Bacon, Margaret Hope. *The Quiet Rebels: The Story of the Quakers in America*. 1985, New Society Publishers, Philadelphia.

Nenn, Daisy. *A Procession of Friends: Quakers in America.*

1972, Doubleday and Co., Inc., Garden City, NY. Newport Historical Society. *The Great Meeting House at Newport, Rhode Island.*

Weigley, Russell F. *Philadelphia: A 300 Year History.* 1982, W.W. Norton & Co., New York.

FIRST MEETING HOUSE

Affiliation: Baptist
Location: Providence, Rhode Island
1700

Rhode Island, the smallest state in the union, bears the aura of a staid bastion of American tradition and history. One of the original thirteen colonies, it was the first to declare independence from Great Britain, yet the last colony to ratify the U.S. Constitution. It is a land of old New England prosperity, colonial architecture, F. Scott Fitzgerald, Ivy League colleges, and eighteenth century churches, as well as one of the oldest, most revered jazz music festivals in the country. Yet, as hard as it is to imagine, "Little Rhody" began as an asylum for religious radicals, and a hotbed for outrageous, liberal thought.

The original purveyor of radical thought in what would become the 13th state of the union was a London-born exile from the Massachusetts Bay Colony named Roger Williams. He arrived in Massachusetts in 1631, fresh from rejecting the Church of England as a newly avowed Puritan. An early friend of Colony Governor John Winthrop, Williams could have enjoyed the cozy position of pastor of a Salem Church. But gradually, Williams, a highly personable but outspoken individual, began expounding upon the controversial ideas which would navigate his life's journey. He encountered increasing criticism and opposition in Boston. Finally, after five years, the General Court of Massachusetts Bay Colony voted to exile Williams, and deport him back to England. But Williams fled the Colony, to find a safe haven for his revolutionary concepts.

Many of Williams' most important ideas were laid out in a doctrine he called "Soul Liberty." Williams firmly believed that civil authorities had absolutely no jurisdiction in matters of religion and personal conscience. He believed those same authorities should allow for "...a free and absolute permission of the consciences of all men ... not the very consciences of the Jews, nor the consciences of the Turks or papists, or pagans themselves excepted." (Polishook, p. 5) He advocated for an absolute division of church and state, saying an individual required complete freedom of choice to develop his own perception of God and a moral lifestyle. Of course, the success of the Massachusetts Bay Colony, and the financial comfort of its leaders, depended on the adherence of its members to the church hierarchy; any assertion which caused individuals to believe they could achieve salvation without such allegiance simply could not be tolerated.

The final straw for the Colony, however, broke when Williams called the King of England's right to give away colonial land a "solemn public lie." Williams reasoned since the king never purchased the land from the Indians — the owners, in Williams mind — the king (and therefore the Colonial government) had no right to grant it to the colonists. In this statement, Williams both validated the Indians claim to the land, and called into question the land titles granted by the Colony government. Both assertions challenged the economic basis of the Massachusetts Bay Colony, a challenge that could not be abided.

Finally, in 1635, Massachusetts Bay Colony authorities apprehended Roger Williams. By the General Court of the Colony, Williams was tried and convicted of sedition, heresy, and failure to take an oath of allegiance to the colony — the same oath of allegiance which drove Thomas Hooker to Connecticut. Williams was ordered banished to England, but in February 1636, he escaped and fled to Narragansett Bay, which was home to the Wampanoag tribe, a close lineage to the Narragansett tribe of Indians speaking an Algonquian dialect.

Roger Williams remained among the Wampanoag through the rest of that bitter winter, where he further developed his already considerable appreciation of the natives. Something of a spiritual nomad, Williams seemed in many ways more at home with the wandering, gathering native societies than in the structured, conservative, regulated, static New England townships. He developed true friendships among the Narragansetts and the neighboring Algonquian tribes, such as the Pocomtuc, Niantic, and the Massachusetts. His experiences with the Indians became the basis for a book he wrote in 1643, called *A Key into the Language of America*, intended as a dictionary of the Indian language, and a chronicle of Indian life.

(A year after the Massachusetts Bay Colony had banished him from their midst, Governor Winthrop had the nerve to call upon Williams to help stave off a war between the colony and the neighboring Algonquin tribes, one in which the tribes surely would have emerged victorious. Single-handedly, Williams reportedly entered hazardous Indian territory and convinced the tribe to spare the New Englanders. Even after virtually saving the lives of the colonists, he received neither an invitation to return to Massachusetts, nor even a thank you note from Governor Winthrop.)

In the spring of 1636, Roger Williams landed on a plot of earth on the Seekonk River granted by the Narragansett Indians. Williams and some companions from Salem established the site he called "Providence," in honor of "God's merciful Providence" toward him.

By 1638, Williams — the ex–Anglican, ex–Puritan, and ex–Separatist — had become a Baptist. He adhered to the central theme of the Baptists, derived from the 16th century "Anabaptists," from the Greek term "to baptize again." The Baptists asserted only adults who can consciously state a belief in Christ can be baptized into salvation. This tenet, known as "Believer's Baptism," directly opposed the notion of infant baptism. Baptists believed infant baptism — practiced by the Catholic, English, and Puritan churches — merely ensures membership in and authority to the institutionalized churches at an early age. That year, Williams and his followers established the First Baptist Church in America, the oldest Baptist congregation in the United States.

Two churches preceded the current representation of the First Meeting House. The congregation met in individual houses and public meeting areas until 1700, when pastor Pardon Tillinghast erected the First Meeting House several blocks north of the present-day structure. As the Baptist congregation increased in Rhode Island as well as throughout the colonies, the community constructed a larger second house to accommodate the swelling host of attendees. Finally, under the direction of pastor James Manning, the current beautiful First Baptist Meeting House was completed in May of 1775.

Actually the construction of the church benefited from the Colonial unrest taking place 50 miles north in Boston. Britain responded to the Boston Tea Party in December 1773, by passing the Coercive Acts in the spring of 1774. While Parliament designed these so-called "Intolerable Acts" to prevent further subversive "parties" from erupting in the future, the Acts only fueled sympathy in colonies outside Massachusetts. Unfortunately, it also closed off the port of Boston, which left a legion of carpenters and ship builders without work. These skilled laborers journeyed to Providence, where they completed the meeting house in less than a year. The artisans completed the great steeple in less than four days, the only steeple remaining in Providence which has not yet fallen to the ravages of wind, snow, rain, or lightning. A plaque on the wall of the foyer of the meeting house declares the building is "For the Publick Worship of Almighty God, and Also for Holding Commencement in."

Designed by architect Joseph Brown, and patterned after Georgian Architecture churches found in Great Britain, the Meeting House is one of the largest religious structures ever built in Colonial America. The main auditorium

section of the church is 80 feet long and 80 feet wide, each column hewn from a single oak tree. The stark, pearl white interior features a massively brilliant Waterford crystal chandelier, imported from Ireland and installed in 1792. The four-story steeple and spire towers 185 feet in height, and can easily be distinguished among the surrounding Providence skyline. Inside the steeple hangs a bronze bell, cast in London and weighing more than 2500 pounds. The meeting house accommodates 1400 persons, and is used each year for the commencement activities of Brown University.

Roger Williams determined that his new home for the Baptists would become a haven for all those he termed "distressed of conscience." He eventually sought and obtained a patent of civil incorporation from England's Parliament, and established the colony of Rhode Island in 1644. After ten years of repeatedly defending the merits of the colony to its detractors in England, Williams served as governor of Rhode Island from 1654 to 1657. He guided the establishment of a representative colonial government adhering to the principles of complete religious freedom.

From the outset, Rhode Island offered shelter for religious groups ostracized elsewhere. Not only the Baptists, but communities of Jews, Catholics, and Quakers found homes in Rhode Island. Regarding the Quakers, even Williams apparently found their ways and attitudes difficult to accept. Williams regarded the early Society of Friends to be a rather outspoken and unruly lot, trying even his long-standing patience. But, true to his credo — and despite several personal efforts to convince them to voluntarily renounce their practices — Williams supported their continued residence in Rhode Island.

One of the most noteworthy of the religious sects to settle in Rhode Island were the Antinomians, led by a newly banished former Puritan, 36-year-old Anne Hutchinson. The Antinomians believed established moral law to be of no consequence, since salvation was obtained by faith in Christ alone. Hutchinson had been convicted of heresy and sedition for the weekly women's meetings hosted in her Boston home. Attended by as many as 60 women at a time, Hutchinson used the meetings to discuss the weekly sermon and study the Scriptures, something Puritan women were not encouraged to do without the guidance — or, rather, dictation — of their husbands. Hutchinson's meetings became a forum in which the women could compare and contrast the Colony's "Covenant of Works" with Hutchinson's profession of the "Covenant of Grace." Hutchinson asserted those blessed by God's grace were not bound by human law, were in no need of guidance and intervention by the established church, and could determine their own religious practice for themselves.

Perhaps more than the threat she imposed toward the theological and economic bases of the Colony, as a strong, nimble-minded woman Hutchinson challenged the male dominated Puritan Society, which traditionally relegated women to roles of servitude and silence. Like Williams, she was tried, convicted, and banished by the General Court; in March of 1638, she followed Williams to the religious haven of Rhode Island, where she, her family, and several followers lived on Aquidneck Island (near present-day Portsmouth) for five more years. She then moved to Pelham Bay in New York, where she was killed in an Wappinger Indian raid in 1643.

For his own part, Roger Williams continued his spiritually nomadic lifestyle. Despite the fact he helped to found the oldest Baptist community in America, the community which eventually built the great First Meeting House, Roger Williams could apparently tolerate the confines of the Baptist Church no more than any other institution. He concluded Christianity had been irrevocably spoiled when Roman Emperor Theodosius declared Christianity the state religion in 390 A.D. Once Christianity became institutionalized, Williams believed, it fell subject to the same corruptions and hypocrisies plaguing all government systems. A life patterned after Christ could only be obtained through individual conscience and practice.

Williams left the Baptist church in 1639.

Opposite: *First Meeting House, Providence, Rhode Island. (Photograph by Susan Findley.)*

He became a Seeker, finding all sects and religions corrupting and limiting to his spiritual journey, which he apparently undertook, unsatisfied, for the remainder of his days. He died in 1683, on a date and in a place that remain unknown.

The legacy of Roger Williams is Rhode Island, now a community of tradition and history, but then the first colony to fully incorporate the values of religious freedom. These ideals are manifested in the First Baptist Meeting House, built by the community Williams helped to establish. The First Baptist Church in America continues as the longest-livedBaptist community, and one of the oldest church communities of any kind, in the United States.

Sources

Bishop, Peter, and Darton, Michael. *The Encyclopedia of World Faiths: An Illustrated Survey of the World's Living Religions*. 1987, MacDonald and Co., Ltd., London and Sydney.

Corbett, Scott. *States of the Nation: Rhode Island*. 1969, Coward-McCann, Inc., New York.

Jennings, John. *Boston: Cradle of Liberty*. 1947, Doubleday & Co., Inc., Garden City, NY.

Polishook, Irwin H. *Roger Williams, John Cotton, and Religious Freedom: A Controversy in New and Old England*. 1967, Prentice-Hall, Inc., Englewood Cliffs, New Jersey.

Rogers, Jay. *America's Christian Leaders: Anne Hutchinson*. 1997.

Steinberg, Sheila, and McGuigan, Cathleen. *Rhode Island: An Historical Guide*. 1976, Rhode Island Bicentennial Foundation, Providence.

Terrell, John Upton. *American Indian Almanac*. 1994, Barnes & Noble Books.

MISSION SAN ANTONIO DE VALERO (THE ALAMO)

Affiliation: Roman Catholic
Location: San Antonio, Texas
1718

"Remember the Alamo" is a phrase that fires the hearts and imaginations of students of the history and folklore of Texas and the United States. Characters such as Davy Crockett, Jim Bowie, General Santa Anna, William Travis, Sam Houston, General Cos, and Steve Austin played prominently in the first act of the drama called the Statehood of Texas. This drama has been replayed in countless books, articles, and films, the most famous of which was the 1960 rendering, starring John Wayne and Richard Widmark.

But exactly what was "The Alamo," and what was it doing in the heart of Texas? More importantly, how did it become such an integral part of the drama?

When I first saw the Alamo in 1845…it was a veritable ruin, partly from the destruction caused by the battle, but mostly from its long abandonment as the adobe of man. No doors or windows shut out the sun or storm; millions of bats inhabited the crevices in the walls and flat dirt roofs, and in the twilight the bats would pour forth in myriads. It was a meeting place for owls; weeds and grass grew from the walls, and even the cacti plant decorated the tumble-down roof of the old building that flanked the church…In the south wall (of the chapel) was a breach near the ground, said to have been made by Santa Anna's cannon. We boys could run up the embankment to the outer wall and onto the roof of the convent building — it was a famous playground. [Long, p. 335]

The Alamo, it seems, was never originally intended to serve as such a famous battlefield in Texas history. And even in the course of the history, the structure could never quite fulfill the role of the embattled fortress which would be its destiny. It possessed neither the design nor the endurance of a true fortress, lacking the massive walls or towering bastions that normally provided protection. Both Texans and Mexicans had considered it a superfluous possession, more than once mulling the temptation of leveling it to the ground.

The true name for the Alamo was Mission San Antonio de Valero, founded May 1, 1718. The Alamo chain of missions included San Antonio de Valero, Nuestra Señora de la Purísima Concepción de Acuna (1716), Mission San José y San Miguel de Aguayo (1720), San Juan Capistrano (1716), and Mission San Francisco de la Espada (1716), all founded in and around what is now the modern city of San Antonio, Texas.

San Antonio de Valero took its name from the viceroy of New Spain, Marquis de Valero, who had designated its establishment. San Antonio de Valero's founder was Franciscan Father Antonio de San Buenaventura y Olivares, who established the mission while Don Martin de Alarcón served as Spanish governor of Coahuila and Texas. The mission emerged as a joint project of the state and the church, built alongside the Presidio San Antonio de Bexar, which eventually grew up to be the city of San Antonio. The Spanish government regarded the missions as strongholds of the vast lands and resources they had claimed in the New World; the church, on the other hand, viewed the missions as a vehicle to evangelize and "civilize" the native peoples.

Founded on the banks of the San Antonio River, near San Pedro Springs, the design of the mission followed the typical quadrangle Spanish style. An adobe wall surrounded the mission plaza, to protect the residents from marauding Apaches and Comanches. These Indians did not particularly appreciate the padres' intentions, but coveted the mission's supplies and tools. In the southeast corner stood the chapel, with its now famous stone, columned facade. Construction of this Tuscan-style sanctuary actually began in 1744, situated alongside the mission convent, and the quarters for the padres. Adobe houses for soldiers, neophytes, and visitors stretched along the northeast, north, and west walls. The quadrangle included a cattle pen behind the convent, plus a well, a granary and several workshops for handicrafts made by the Indians. An irrigation ditch reaching the San Antonio River surrounded the quadrangle, while agricultural fields and cattle ranges stretched beyond the ditch, providing some sustenance for the mission community.

Indians speaking various dialects under the Caddoan linguistic family came to the Mission San Antonio, curious about the newcomers, their articles and manners. The Indians lived as hunters and food gatherers, not farmers (at least, not until agriculture was introduced to them by the missionaries). They hunted and trapped deer, antelope, javelina, rabbits, reptiles, birds, and insects. They also encompassed a variety of plant life in their diet, including cacti, mesquite beans, nuts, sotol, and agave.

From the padres' point of view, it must have appeared as if they were doing the Indians a great favor. After all, in addition to the salvation of their souls, the natives learned crafts, agriculture, animal husbandry, the Spanish language. The priests afforded the natives the rare opportunity to sing, dance, read, and write, all in an exotic language and culture. The missionaries provided food, clothing, and shelter for the Indians—most of which had been built or cultivated by the Indians' hands. The padres succeeded in creating devout Christians, good craftsmen, farmers, ranchers, and loyal citizens of Spain among a nominal number of native Texans.

The flip side of the Franciscans' good intentions was the decimation of the Indian culture. The Spanish regarded the Indians as barbarians, with seemingly little interest in understanding or supporting the native way of life. In many instances the missionaries (or the soldiers, or both) treated the Indian with stringency and cruelty. And, unfortunately, European-bred diseases such as measles and smallpox, as occurred in the epidemic of 1739 around the San Antonio Missions, devastated the native populations. In 1739, the Indian population which had grown to more than three hundred quickly fell to 185 from the effects of these diseases. Many Indians must

A 1910 photo of Mission San Antonio de Valero (today more commonly known as the Alamo), San Antonio, Texas. (Courtesy Daughters of the Republic of Texas Library at the Alamo. Gift of Heber P. Crocker CN95.37.)

have instinctively realized they were helpless before these scourges; those who had not actually fallen from the maladies quickly fled from the Mission, taking refuge in their own wilderness, where they had suffered no previous knowledge of such plagues.

Those Indians who did not flee San Antonio due to illnesses would leave simply because the mission lifestyle differed so vastly from their own. The Indians did not assimilate well to the Spanish system of labor. The Spaniards characterized the Indian's hunter-gatherer lifestyle as laziness. Often, the missionaries would follow the Indians into the wilderness to bring them back to the plaza. Governor Alarcon's idea of evangelism became chasing Indians

down with soldiers, and dragging them back to the mission at sword point.

By 1793, it had become evident the mission program had failed as a method for assimilating native populations into the Spanish Empire. Indian residents at San Antonio de Valero had fallen from 300 to only 57 by 1793. The decline of the missions forced the King of Spain to secularize them, selling the vast land holdings to civilians. Mission San Antonio de Valero became a military post against raiding Apache war parties. The mission and the villa housed the Second Company of San Carlos de Parras, which originated in the town of El Alamo in the Mexican state of Coahuila. This may be the origin of the nickname "The

Alamo"; a second theory is the name comes from the cottonwood or "alamo" trees, which grew abundantly in the vicinity.

Following Mexican independence from Spain in 1810, Mission San Antonio fell under several occupations and purposes, most of them renegade armies fighting for control of San Antonio and central Texas. Over the years the mission and villa fell into physical and financial ruin. In 1824, partially through the lobbying of Stephen Austin and his Texas colonists, the territories of Texas and Coahuila joined as one self-governing state.

Over the next 12 years, Texas marched steadily toward independence. When General Antonio Lopez de Santa Anna, newly elected President of the Republic of Mexico, banned immigration from the United States in 1833, the push towards secession from Mexico intensified. The Texas rebellion gathered fuel from volunteers and mercenaries from the southern United States, seeking easy land and room to spread the institution of slavery. Finally, after an uprising of residents in nearby Gonzales in 1835, General Santa Anna sent troops to stabilize the region.

Often forgotten, the Texas rebels were not the first occupants of the Alamo to face siege and invasion. In the fall of 1835, General Martin Perfecto de Cos, brother-in-law of President Santa Anna, commanded a company of men facing a ragtag army of Texas rebels led by Stephen A. Austin. From November 3 to December 4, under a steady stream of cannon fire, the Texans bottled up the Mexicans within the mission's adobe quadrangle. On December 5, the rebels invaded the villa San Antonio de Bexar building by building, until they forced their way into the Mission quadrangle. Due to poor planning, supplies, training, and leadership, the 1100 soldiers under General Cos surrendered to less than three hundred Texans on December 13, 1835. The siege and attack upon the Texans, under the command of Santa Anna three months later, occurred at least partially in retaliation for the humility suffered by his brother-in-law.

The Texans' bombardment of the mission had left the stone church collapsed, and the barracks in ruins. During their occupation, the Texans converted as much of the mission

for battle as possible, under the direction of lawyer and engineer Colonel Green Jameson. Jameson fortified the dirt mound and platform which General Cos had constructed inside the chapel, and mounted two 12-pound cannons facing the southeast. Jameson mounted 18 cannons along the barrack's roofs at the west, north, and south walls. A huge 18-pound cannon guarded the southwest corner.

The southern section of the old convent became a hospital, while a powder magazine occupied a sacristy along the north wall of the chapel. The western barracks became the officers' quarters, while the eastern adobe houses sheltered the soldiers. The rebels gouged a drainage ditch through the center of the plaza, connecting to the outside irrigation canal for a water supply.

The north adobe wall remained the weakest point of the quadrangle, crumbled by severe bombardment which the Texas rebels themselves had engineered three months earlier. Although the Texans tried to reinforce the wall, their work was cut short when the Mexican siege began. Over this weak link the massive sea of Mexican soldiers would finally flow into the Alamo.

On the second day of the siege, Texan commander Colonel William Travis dispatched one of the most dramatic messages in United States history, pleading for Texans and Americans alike to send help in this most desperate of hours:

> Fellow Citizens and Compatriots — I am besieged by a thousand or more Mexicans under Santa Anna...I call on you in the name of liberty, of patriotism, & everything dear to the American character, to come to our aid with all dispatch...If this call is neglected, I am determined to sustain myself as long as possible & die like a soldier who never forgets what is due his own honor & that of his country. VICTORY OR DEATH." [Haley, p. 51]

Despite the bulletin's heartfelt and heroic wording, it managed to scare up only 32 more men, bringing Travis' total to 183.

Some historians argue the 13-day siege, implemented on February 21 when Santa Anna overran the adjacent town of San Antonio de Bexar, served as a stall tactic by the Mexican commander-in-chief, while he waited for what he considered a sufficient number of soldiers and armaments to arrive. As it was, he had gathered between 2000 and 4000 troops, plus 21 cannons, 1800 mules, 37 wagons, 200 carts. Still, for an army which outnumbered the enemy more than 20 to one, Santa Anna's army suffered outrageous casualties. With all the fortifications Jameson had added to the Alamo, the Mexicans themselves apparently provided their own greatest obstacle.

General Santa Anna — who fancied himself the Napoleon of the New World — could have easily used his superior cannon fire to further weaken and possibly destroy the Alamo walls before charging. Instead he chose to "surprise" them with a full-scale, all-out charge. Sprinting out long before dawn, the Mexican army tripped and stumbled through the unfamiliar terrain under the darkened sky. The noise and confusion emitted by the Mexicans alerted the Texans to the assault. By far the biggest impediment, however, was the shower of bullets raining down on the backs of the unfortunate invaders from their own comrades' guns. Some estimates say seventy five percent of the Mexicans killed at the Alamo fell under friendly fire, as they desperately struggled to scale the walls of the old mission.

Despite the shortsightedness and apparent ineptness of Santa Anna's army, their numbers proved simply too overwhelming. By 8:00 A.M. on March 6, 1836, three days after the Republic of Texas declared its independence from Mexico under the leadership of Sam Houston, the Alamo had fallen. In the end between 600 to 1500 Mexicans died invading the Alamo, suffering up to eight deaths for every one for the Texans. Among the Texans, 178 out of 183

died in the attack. Five were captured and executed on the spot, former Tennessee Congressman Davy Crockett among them. Jim Bowie, bedridden from either typhoid, tuberculosis, or pneumonia before the Mexicans forged the wall, died of a bullet wound to the head. Lieutenant Colonel William Travis, commander of the Alamo force, also died from gun shot to the skull. Only three individuals survived: a woman named Susanna Dickinson, her 15-month-old son, and a slave named Joe. The Alamo once again belonged to the Mexicans.

A clear example of winning the battle but losing the war, the Alamo would mark the beginning of the end of the Mexican rule of Texas. At the Battle of San Jacinto in April 1836, under the impassioned cry "Remember the Alamo," a small Texas army commanded by Sam Houston routed Santa Anna's much more formidable troops. Texans almost immediately ratified their new constitution, naming Houston president of the New Republic. Within 12 years, the United States would win the war with Mexico, and Texas would join the Union as the 48th state.

Sources

Davis, Kenneth C. *Don't Know Much About History*. 1990. Avon Books, New York.

Haly, James L. *Texas: An Album of History*. 1985, Doubleday & Company, Inc., New York.

Long, Jeff. *Duel of Eagles*. 1990, William Morrow & Company, Inc., New York.

Terrell, John Upton. *American Indian Almanac*. 1994, Barnes & Noble Books.

Daughters of the Republic of Texas. *Alamo Chronology*. 1997, San Antonio.

CHRIST CHURCH
(The Old North Church)
Affiliation: Anglican, Later Episcopalian
Location: Boston, Massachusetts
1723

The mention of Christ Church in Boston draws little attention from the average American. The use of the name "Old North Church," however, suddenly brings images of patriotism, the Revolution against the British, and a harried lone rider on a moonlit night. The Old North Church served as the catalyst for what is no doubt the most famous equestrian ride in American history, at the heart of a chilling legend in a period filled with legends.

The Old North Church is widely recognized for its role in the fabled poem by Henry Wadsworth Longfellow:

> He said to his friend, "If the British march
> By land or sea from the town to-night,
> Hang a lantern aloft in the belfry arch
> Of the North Church tower as signal light —
> One if by land, and two if by sea;
> And I on the opposite shore will be,
> Ready to ride and spread the alarm
> Through every Middlesex village and farm,
> For the country-folk to be up and to arm."

Longfellow's poem "Paul Revere's Ride" fancifully recalls the events of the evening of April 18, 1775. Yet little is known about the church in the tale: What was the North Church? What is its history in relation to the city of Boston? And how did it come to play such an integral role in one of Colonial America's greatest dramas?

There is some question as to whether Christ Church was actually the "North Church" identified in history books and in Longfellow's verse. Some scholars have asserted the church from which the signal beamed was actually a church located at nearby North Square. In her notes from *Paul Revere: The World He Lived In,* Forbes says:

> Paul Revere, in the account he wrote for the Massachusetts Historical Society (1798), says the lanterns were hung in "North Church Steeple" and yet, in 1775, Christ Church was popularly Christ, and the church at North Square "Old North." After the latter was pulled down in 1776, the nickname "North" and "Old North" was transferred to the oldest church in North Boston, which was Christ. Although the North Square Church has been put forward as a candidate for the lanterns, it could not have been so used. Its spire was so "stumpy," lights hung in it would not have been seen in Charlestown. Copp's Hill lay between. Paul Revere, in calling Christ "North Church," was using the nomenclature common at the time in which he wrote, instead of when he rode.

Silversmith and Son of Liberty Paul Revere must have harbored some nostalgic thoughts as he waited in north Boston for the appearance of the lamps in the massive steeple of Christ Church. Revere had attended Christ Church as a boy with his mother Deborah and his father Paul, Sr. (born Apollos Riviore). Paul, Jr., was one of a society of seven North End boys who were paid a stipend to share the task of ringing the bells of the church. These boys faced rigorous training concerning how and when to ring these bells, which were regarded as the "best and sweetest bells" in America. Eight bells in all (the largest weighing well over 1500 pounds) hung from Christ's steeple and could clearly be heard at Harvard in Cambridge, across the Charles River. The first bells ever cast in England for the colonies, the bells were shipped to New England in 1748.

Reverend Timothy Cutler founded Christ Church as an Anglican Church in 1723. It opened for worship on December 29 of that year, built by the hands of Ebenezer Clough and his associates out of a reputed 513,654 bricks. The walls of the church are six inches thick, and the storied bell tower reaches 191 feet into the Boston sky. A magnificent work of Georgian architecture, the interior includes chandeliers with the dove of peace perched on the pinnacle of each which were constructed in Bristol, England, and first lit on Christmas in 1724. The casing from an organ built in 1759 remains in use at Christ Church.

Christ is the oldest church and the oldest standing building in the Massachusetts capital. The only Church of England in Boston at its dedication, Christ Church apparently enjoyed a surprisingly peaceful existence within the Puritan colony, which claimed the purification of the Church of England as its original purpose. Revere and his wife Rachel and children attended Christ Church, as did several generations of descendants to follow, all who became pew holders at the Old North Church. Today, the church houses the second Episcopalian Congregation in Boston.

Despite the implications of Longfellow's verse, the signals in Christ Church's steeple did not appear for Revere's edification alone. Revere, his friend John Pulling, and Colonel

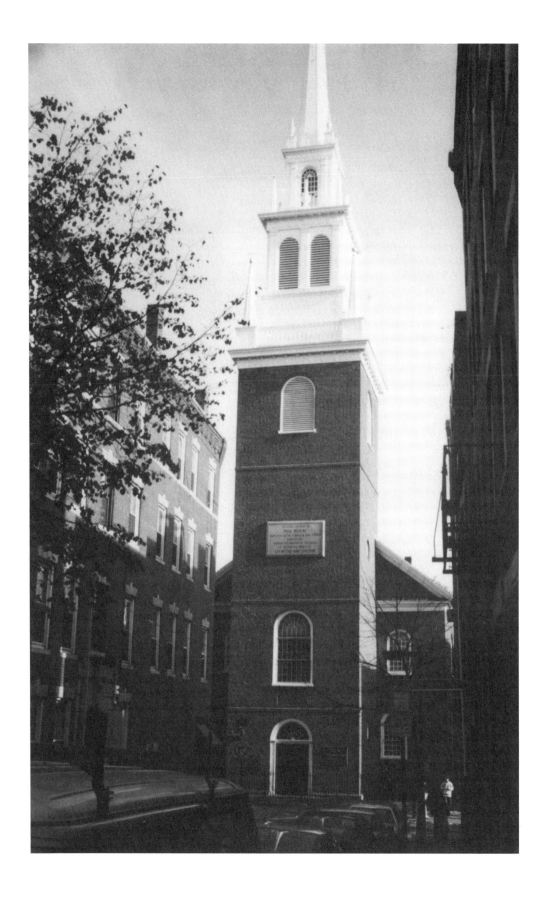

William Conant (a prominent citizen well regarded in colonial military circles) intricately worked out the code well ahead of time: "…if the British went out by water we would show two lanterns in the North Church steeple and if by land one as a signal…" (Taylor, p. 138). But the lanterns were meant to warn all Charlestown residents of the approaching British troops. Revere's task was to gallop beyond the limits of Charlestown, and warn colonists all the way to Lexington about the advancing British armament. Certainly, much of the Charlestown populace had anticipated the warning signal emitted from the Old North Church.

The lamplighter was a man named Robert Newman, who was then sexton (or property manager) at Christ Church. At a little past ten o'clock on April 18, 1775, word reached Newman and Captain Pulling—a vestryman at Christ Church—of the advancing Redcoats. Newman and Pulling stole to the Old North Church. After Newman entered the steeple, Pulling locked him inside, to prevent the possibility of British intervention. Newman lit two lamps, allowing them to flicker only a moment at a time, to escape British detection. Newman then apparently shimmied out of a window on the right side of the church, and ran off to safety, his task complete.

Generally unknown is the 13-mile ride between Charlestown and Lexington Paul Revere had traversed two days previous to April 18. Some historians feel this first trip was actually more crucial than the second, more heralded one. By the first week of April, 1775, it was commonly known among Boston's patriots that the British would soon move on Lexington, where a small arsenal, along with food stuffs and medical supplies, stood. "When?" and "How?" remained the unanswered questions. Revere rode out to the Lexington home of Reverend Jonas Clark on Easter Sunday, April 16, 1775. Samuel Adams and John Hancock—leaders of the rebel movement in the colonies—had attended a convention of the Provincial Congress between March 22 and April 22, and were lodging at Clark's house during the recess. Upon Revere's warning, Hancock and Adams arranged for the disbursement of the munitions and supplies throughout the countryside surrounding Lexington. Even if the British hit Lexington the next day, "…they would have (only) their march for their pains." (Taylor, p. 137)

Paul Revere was actually one of three messengers dispatched to warn of British advancement that April Tuesday night. William Dawes, an ardent patriot active in the rebellion for years, left first. He rode out to Lexington by way of Roxbury, a route four miles longer than Revere's. A second messenger, Ebenezer Dorr, took the Roxbury course as well. A third man, a Solomon Brown, apparently made the journey on his own, as a volunteer. Obviously, the rebels could not risk sending only one messenger; if a lone courier failed in his ride, the tide of history may have been severely changed.

Revere's April 18 sojourn actually began in Boston. When rebel intelligence first detected the British movement, Joseph Warren—head of patriot activities in Boston—quickly notified Revere. The silversmith remained in north Boston long enough to verify the appearance of lights in Christ's belfry. Then, Revere and two compatriots—at much personal peril, since such crossings were forbidden by the British guard—crossed the Charles River at 9:00 P.M. Revere mounted a small Narragansett pacer owned by Deacon John, son of livery owner Samuel Larkin, and headed immediately for Lexington.

At 11:00 P.M. Revere left Charlestown (modern-day Somersville) with the moon lighting the trail to Lexington. From Charlestown his pacer galloped along the Mystic River, crossing a plank bridge at Medford. After raising the alarm at Medford, Revere continued on to Menotomy (modern-day Arlington), awakening the minutemen there. At midnight Revere reached Lexington. With Lexington awakened, Revere met up with William Dawes, and the pair continued another six miles to

*Opposite: **Christ Church in Boston, widely believed to be the "Old North Church" made famous in the poem "Paul Revere's Ride." (Photo by Jay Walters.)***

Concord. He and Dawes were arrested outside of Concord by a British patrol, which confiscated the silversmith's horse, ending his midnight ride.

But the effect of the sprint soon became evident.

Meanwhile, several hours later in Lexington, 77 ragtag minutemen engaged the advancing 700-strong British army on a field of grass. From somewhere a shot rang out; the British broke ranks, and suddenly gunfire volleyed across the green. Within moments, eight minutemen lay dead on the Lexington green. This was the "the shot heard round the world," the beginning of the American Revolution.

Six years later, on October 19, 1781, General Charles Cornwallis surrendered his 8000 troops to General Marquis de Lafayette at Yorktown. The American Revolution had essentially ended. At the north end of Boston, the best and sweetest bells in America pealed out the news from the old steeple at Christ Church.

Sources

Buchanan, Paul. *Famous Animals of the States*. 1996, McFarland and Company, Inc. Jefferson, North Carolina.

Davis, Kenneth. *Don't Know Much About History*. 1990, Avon Books, New York.

Forbes, Esther. *Paul Revere & The World He Lived In*. 1962, Houghton Mifflin Company, Boston.

Taylor, Emerson. *Paul Revere*. 1930, Dodd, Mead, & Company.

ST. LOUIS CATHEDRAL

Affiliation: Roman Catholic
Location: Jackson Square, New Orleans, Louisiana
1727

In the heart of old New Orleans—flanked by St. Peter and St. Ann streets—a small niche of the historic city called Jackson Square is located. At the head of the square, offering itself as backdrop to the bronze monument to the mounted General Andrew Jackson, stands the oldest active cathedral in the United States. A church named for the famed sainted King of France, Louis the IX, has stood on this ground since 1727. The current, majestic three-steeple cathedral, named a minor basilica in 1964, has stood since 1852. In whatever form, the 270 year history of the Parish of St. Louis has been intricately entwined with the 280 year history of New Orleans, witnessing some of the most significant moments in the city's history commemorated in pageants passing through the Square.

New Orleans has been steeped in a multicultural amalgam since Jean Baptiste Le Moyne, Sieur de Bienville, declared the island at the mouth of the Mississippi River "La Nouvelle Orleans" in 1718. The French occupied New Orleans until 1762, at the end of the Seven Years War. Louis XV donated Louisiana (little valued by France at the time) to his cousin, Spanish King Charles III, after the Spanish had relinquished Florida Territory to the English. Spain occupied Louisiana for forty years, and then returned it to the French in 1803. To fund his campaign in Europe, Napoleon Bonaparte sold the territory to the fledgling United States in the Louisiana Purchase, solidifying America's growth and stature on the world stage. Thus the combination of French and Spanish culture combined with the traditions of African slaves, plus Choctaw and Chickasaw Indians, gave New Orleans a style and substance unlike anywhere else in North America. A more relaxed, romantic, cosmopolitan feeling pervaded this city, unlike the mostly Puritan-influenced settlements of 18th-century North America.

In particular, the mixture of French and Spanish created a New Orleans sub-culture, the Creoles. The Parish of St. Louis served as the center for French, Spanish, and Creole Catholic culture in New Orleans. St. Louis Church provided the only Catholic sanctuary in town, until the English-speaking parish of St. Patrick's emerged in 1833.

St. Louis Cathedral, New Orleans, Louisiana. (Photograph by Father Frank Montalbano, O.M.I., courtesy St. Louis Cathedral Gift Shop.)

The first Church of St. Louis' dedication took place on Christmas of 1727. Designed by French engineer Adrien De Pauger, the church stood 112 feet long, 32 feet wide, and 24 feet high. Box cruciform in shape, its most distinguishing features included its Romanesque facade, depicting the all-seeing Eye of God at its apex; and its single, small belfry, housing two church bells and a clock. The church provided eighteen pews for worship for the Catholic community. The church was incinerated on Good Friday, March 21, 1788, in a New Orleans fire which destroyed 856 buildings.

The first St. Louis Cathedral officially replaced the devastated church in 1794. Designed by Don Gilberto Guillemard, a French soldier in the service of Spain, the original Cathedral of St. Louis dwarfed the original church. Constructed of brick, it featured bell-capped, hexagonal towers flanking either corner of the Romanesque facade. Marble-hued paint adhered to the exterior, while the interior sanctuary featured a true marble floor and a magnificent altar, adorned by ecclesiastical sculptures and paintings.

The cathedral that stands today, dedicated December 7, 1851, is actually a reconstruction of the original cathedral, masterminded by architect Benjamin H. Latrobe, who also designed St. John's Church at Lafayette Square in Washington, D.C. The focal point of Jackson Square, the cathedral rests between two other masterpieces from New Orleans architectural heritage: the Cabildo and the Presbyter. The cathedral's fabulous, gleaming white-washed facade, with its three towering steeples, (the middle spire more than 140 feet tall), faces the dynamic statue of General Andrew Jackson on horseback, at the center of the square. French clock maker Stanislas Fournier designed the cathedral clock, at the center of the facade below the middle spire. Three of St. Louis' seven bells are attached to Fournier's clock; the other four are rung separately on special occasions. The interior is a beautiful intermingling of Roman and Baroque styles, highlighting murals, statuary, and inscriptions. Ten pillars support the balconies and ceilings of the sanctuary, which is 160 feet long and 80 feet wide. The magnificent high altar features the three feminine figures of Faith, Hope, and Charity. Below the mural depicting Louis IX initiating his crusade, reads an inscription drawing attention to the Eucharistic celebration "Ecce Panis Angelorum," which means " Behold the Bread of Angels."

The parish commemorates St. Louis, King Louis IX, who reigned over France from 1226 to 1270. Idealized by the Roman Catholic Church as the archetypal Christian King, Louis IX is known for repelling the English invasion of Henry III, and for leading the sixth crusade.

Two characters who could regularly be found about the cathedral expertly illustrate the colorful culture of 18th and 19th century New Orleans. The "Praline Vendor," usually an elderly African-American woman, often spoke both French and broken English. On a table covered in fresh, clean linen, she displayed pralines, coconut, pecans, or pistachios roasted in boiling sugar. She sold pralines along the cathedral fence, to the hungry parishioners leaving mass, heading home for breakfast.

The second character was the "Suisse" or beadle, who apparently helped maintain order and solemnity at the cathedral until 1913:

> This dignitary always precedes the bishop and the priests in the church processions, or paces up and down the aisles during the service — his approach announced by the thump of his spear — seating strangers and keeping order throughout the congregation. His uniforms consists of dark blue trousers, scarlet coat, gold-laced shoulder scarf, decorated with the Papal coat of arms; on his head a cocked hat trimmed with gold lace and black plume; in his hand he bears a gilded spear. [From "Old New Orleans" in *Leslie's Illustrated Weekly*, 1887]

Significant moments in the history of New Orleans, Louisiana, and America itself, can be marked by the processions passing the great doors of the Cathedral of St. Louis:

January 23, 1815

The Treaty of Ghent, officially ending the War of 1812, was signed by representatives of Britain and America in Belgium on December 24, 1814. But by then, a massive British fleet assembling at Jamaica had yet to receive word of the treaty. General Andrew Jackson, in response, prepares the island city of New Orleans for attack. In one of the great defensive military stands in American history, American and British forces fought the Battle of New Orleans.

The British leave Jamaica on December 2, determined to capture the port city of New Orleans, blocking the Mississippi trade route, and effectively crippling the American economy. Commanding a hodgepodge army made up of "Kaintucks," Choctaw Indians, Free Blacks, and Pirates, General Jackson's 5000 troops clash with Sir Edward Pakenham's army of 14,000, many of whom had participated in the sacking of Washington D.C. four months earlier. For 14 days, Jackson's troops continually pound and confuse the more powerful British army, scoring moral victories and sufficiently hampering Pakenham's invasion of the city.

Finally, on January 8, at Bayou Bienvenue outside New Orleans, Jackson draws the final line. As columns of the 1800 British infantrymen marched stubbornly toward the enemy, Jackson's riflemen, many using new Kentucky long barrel rifles for distance and accuracy, line up in rows four men deep. Each line fires at the British as the preceding line reloads, producing a steady, continuous barrage toward the Red Coats. American cannons bombard the British troops, one ball killing 200 soldiers by itself. At the end of four days, 700 British perish, 400 suffer wounds, and 500 fall captive; for the Americans, 13 dead, 39 wounded. The Battle of New Orleans ends, the city remains intact, two weeks after the War of 1812 had officially concluded.

On January 23, 1815, a victory pageant without parallel parades past the Cathedral of St. Louis. Spectators fill the windows and balconies of the surrounding buildings, as well as the entire acreage of what would become Jackson Square. Historian Charles Gayarre describes the scene:

> From the arch in the middle of the square, to the church, at proper intervals, were ranged young ladies, representing the different states and territories composing the American Union, all dressed in white, covered with transparent veils, and wearing a silver star on their foreheads. Each of these young ladies

held in her right hand a flag inscribed with the name of the State she represented, and in her left a basket trimmed with blue ribbons and full of flowers. Behind each was a shield suspended on a lance stuck into the ground, inscribed with the name of the State or territory...

> General Jackson, accompanied by officers of his staff, arrived at the entrance of the square, where he was requested to proceed to the church by the walk prepared for him. As he passed under the arch, he received the crown of laurels from the two children... [Huber, p. 19]

For many years following, the Cathedral of St. Louis holds solemn services commemorating the Battle of New Orleans.

December 19, 1824

A special commemorative "funeral" service is held this day to remember the Emperor Napoleon Bonaparte, who died in 1821. French parishioners celebrate their heritage and the pageantry of the "Little Emperor." Within the black-draped cathedral, admirers of the Emperor prepare a multi-leveled catafalque adorned by symbols and trinkets commemorating the life of Napoleon. A French troupe provides singers, and Judge J. F. Canonge gives the oration at a service officiated by the beloved Père Antoine.

January 22, 1829

Five years after the "funeral" for Napoleon Bonaparte, the parishioners of St. Louis, and the citizens of New Orleans pay their last respects in a pageant for the late Fray Antonio de Sedella, known about town merely as "Père Antoine." Thin, irascible, easy going, and widely popular, Père Antoine roamed about his parishioners of New Orleans, dressed only in a coarse monk's robe with a thick cotton cord at his waist, and a large broad-brimmed black hat on his head. He lived meagerly in a small hut behind the cathedral. He regularly arranged provisions for the poor with the local butcher and baker in the neighborhood. He was sensible and benevolent, an eloquent preacher, and the beloved spiritual leader of the French/Spanish/Creole Catholic culture. His courage was unquestioned. He had formed the bucket brigade which saved the Ursaline convent and the Royal Hospital during a 1788 fire which destroyed the original St. Louis Church.

But the stubborn Capuchin priest bore the label of firebrand, a thorn in the side of his ecclesiastical superiors. He constantly butted heads against his diocesan bishops and administrators, ignoring their directions, and steering less orthodox, more pragmatic roads among the parishioners he knew best. He served as pastor of St. Louis from 1781 to 1790, when he was suspended by Bishop Cirillo. Reinstated in 1795, he ran into Episcopal troubles again in 1805, when Diocesan administrators tried to remove him from his pastorate. In an extraordinary gesture of their loyalty, the trustees and parishioners virtually "elected" Père Antoine pastor, over objections of the diocese. (It must be remembered that in 1805, the American government did not as yet recognize the Catholic Church as a legal entity. Any legal jurisdiction over the parish of St. Louis, had to be held by trustees of the church.)

Years later, William DuBourg (the Sulpician priest who, in 1809, established Elizabeth Seton at the House on Paca Street on St. Mary's College campus in Baltimore) was named Bishop of New Orleans by Archbishop John Carroll of Baltimore. DuBourg also had trouble with Père Antoine. At one point DuBourg interdicted the church, and suspended Père Antoine's pastorate. But due to the outrage from parishioners and trustees, Diocesan authority once again acquiesced to the will of the people, reinstating Père Antoine as pastor.

Reflecting the faith of those people who loved him, Père Antoine receives one of the largest funeral services ever held in New Orleans. His body lies in state in Cathedral Rectory for three days while thousands pass the casket in mourning. On the morning of January 22, cannons fire to announce to the city the beginning of the services. Four pallbearers surrounded by eight close friends of Père Antoine bear the coffin through the streets of New Orleans. Following behind are members of the Louisiana Legion, as well as the local Catholic clergy. Other attendees included physicians and church trustees, as well as the governor of Louisiana, president and members of the Senate and House of Representatives,

Supreme Court justices, foreign consuls, the mayor, as well as thousands of mourners, Catholic or not. The march through the city ends at the Cathedral of St. Louis. The doorway is draped in black, above which a memorial plaque with the inscription in Latin read:

> Sacred to Father Antonio de Sedella
> Although you have fallen, full of years
> Yet you have left our hearts
> Filled with mighty sorrow.

July 26, 1834

New Orleans pays tribute to the Hero of Two Hemispheres, General Marie Joseph Paul Yves Roch Gilbert de Motier, Marquis de Lafayette (1757–1834).

The wealthy French Aristocrat who came to America at the age of 19, seeking fame and adventure, offered to serve under George Washington in the American Revolutionary War without pay, in exchange for a major general's rank. Lafayette and Washington became close friends, and Lafayette convinced Louis XIV to lend 7000 French troops to the 9000 Americans. The two armies combined to overwhelm the 8000 British troops under Charles Cornwallis at Yorktown, Virginia. On September 28, 1781, the allies implemented a siege, compelling the British forces to surrender on October 19. The campaign at Yorktown became the decisive victory of the Revolution, effectively ending British hopes for victory. Louisiana's first governor might have been Lafayette, but the Frenchman turned down the opportunity offered by Thomas Jefferson.

The memorial parade for General Lafayette wanders from the State House, down Chartes Avenue, to the entrance to the Cathedral of St. Louis. The casket is accompanied by military escort, followed by the American and French flags combined and covered with crepe. The governor of the state and the French consul, are followed by a line of veterans from the Revolutionary War. A bust of Marquis de Lafayette rides in a funeral canopy, trailed by a parade of 24 mourning citizens, representing the current states of the United States. The full extension of the procession reaches from the cathedral to the State House on Canal Street, more than ten blocks in the distance.

A solemn memorial service commences at the cathedral, where the altars and walls are covered in black. The ten sanctuary pillars and the supported balconies are also draped in black, and trimmed with decorations and inscriptions depicting Lafayette's most famous deeds and life events. A huge mausoleum occupies the middle aisle, bearing the brass urn holding the cremated remains of the Marquis de Lafayette.

January 8, 1840

Former U.S. President Andrew Jackson returns to New Orleans for the 25th Anniversary of the Battle of New Orleans. The city raises $5000 for Jackson, who is welcomed as a guest of the state. Jackson arrives by steamboat, greeted by an immense throng at the port of New Orleans. In an elaborate carriage drawn by four horses, Jackson is escorted by the Louisiana Legion and the Washington Battalion, which pass the cheering crowds down Canal Street. He meets old comrades at the State house, and conducts a military review in the Place d'Armes.

After a week of almost continual celebration, a practice in which New Orleans is quite well versed, on January 14 Jackson attends the St. Louis Cathedral, where he is greeted by Bishop Antoine Blanc and cathedral clergy. An oration is delivered in his honor, and in the Public Square before the cathedral, the cornerstone of the monument to be erected in his honor is laid. Jackson is driven by carriage to the port once again, where he boards the steamboat *Vicksburg,* as thousands wave farewell.

December 1847

Zachary Taylor, hero of the Mexican War, is hailed in yet another fanciful procession by the people of New Orleans. Taylor's victories at Monterey, Saltillo, and Buena Vista, Mexico, helped assure American victory in this little war, "won quickly and at relatively little expense." The War with Mexico added more than 500,000 square miles of territory to the United States through the Treaty of Guadalupe Hidalgo. Taylor's role assured him a place in the White House in 1849. (He died after serving a little more than a year in the executive office.)

More than 40,000 people crowd the Place d'Armes, and the surrounding streets and rooftops to catch a glimpse of the famed General. Reminiscent of the carnival held for Andrew Jackson seven years earlier, Taylor arrives by steamer as a 100-gun salute roars from various parts of the city. A special service is held at the cathedral by Bishop Blanc, and the adoring crowds cheer "Ol' Rough and Ready" as he rides his War Horse through the city to the St. Charles Hotel.

September 12, 1987

Hailed by many as the most important event in the history of the cathedral, New Orleans hosts a 14-hour visit by Pope John Paul II. The Pontiff addresses a gathering of more than 1000 clergy and religious at the Cathedral of St. Louis. Afterward, his pontifical motorcade, featuring the popularized "Pope Mobile," tours through the heart of the city, where John Paul II is beheld by tens of thousands of the faithful, the onlookers, and the curious. After addressing jubilant gatherings of youth, educators, African-American Catholics, the Pope celebrates mass for 200,000 at the shore of New Orleans' Lake Pontchartrain.

The Cathedral of St. Louis IX had been designated a Minor Basilica by Pope Paul VI on December 9, 1964, long before Pope John Paul II visited New Orleans. The title is bestowed by the Vatican upon cathedrals of particular historical or spiritual significance. The Basilica of St. Louis, King of France, as it is now known, remains the oldest active Cathedral or Basilica in the United States, poised to watch the procession of New Orleans' future, just as it has its past.

New Orleans continues to commemorate its heroes.

Sources

Davis, Kenneth C. *Don't Know Much About History.* 1990, Avon Books, New York.

Dufour, Charles L. *Ten Flags in the Wind: The Story of Louisiana.* 1967, Harper & Row, Publishers, New York.

Greenblatt, Miriam. *America at War: The War of 1812.* 1994, Facts on File, New York.

Huber, Leonard V., and Samuel Wilson, Jr. *The Basilica on Jackson Square.* 1989, St. Louis Cathedral, New Orleans.

Kane, Harnett T. *Queen New Orleans*. 1949, William Morrow & Company, New York.

Kane, Joseph Nathan. *Facts About the Presidents*. 1996, Ace Books, New York.

Meltzer, Milton. *Andrew Jackson and His America*. 1993, Franklin Watts, New York.

FIRST PARISH CHURCH

Affiliation: Church of Christ
Location: Brunswick, 23 miles northeast of Portland, Maine
1735

The long and illustrious history of First Parish Congregational (later United Church of Christ) Church has included, since the turn of the 19th century, a close legal and spiritual tie with Bowdoin College in Brunswick, Maine, including ongoing maintenance of the church on college land. College commencements were held annually in the sanctuary from 1806 to 1964, and convocation and baccalaureate ceremonies are celebrated there to this day. This relationship between college and church has brought some of the most famous and inspirational thinkers and orators to the pulpit and pews of First Parish Church. Of particular note and interest are two of the most important figures in American literary history.

A Vision Shakes a Nation

A bright but gentle beam of sunlight streamed through the arched window at the First Parish Congregational Church on March 2, 1851, and seemed to fall on the seated, quiet figure of a woman. Small in stature, she was poised in prayer at Pew 23 as the communion service commenced. The sermon of Dr. Adams, the minister for the service, focuses on the Revelations passage "...I am the Alpha and the Omega...." But, for some reason, the words from the Book of Matthew appeared in the woman's mind: "Inasmuch as ye have done it unto one of the least of my brethren, ye have done it unto me."

Gradually, as a mist spread over a verdant valley, a scene began to materialize in her mind's eye. Before her she saw the image of a large African-American male, stretched out over a damp pile of straw, inside a dank, dark

stable. His face, battered and laced with bruises; his body and limbs ached, covered in blood. Outside the barn stood the stout, angry figure of a white slavemaster, lash in hand, face twisted in anger. The son of his former owner knelt beside him.

> "Hush, Mas'r George — it worries me! Don't feel so! He an't done me no real harm, — only opened the gate of the kingdom for me; that's all!"
>
> At this moment, the sudden flush of strength which the joy of meeting his young master had infused into the dying man gave way. A sudden sinking fell upon him; he closed his eyes; and that mysterious and sublime change passed over his face, that told the approach of other worlds.
>
> He began to draw breath with long, deep inspirations; and his broad chest rose and fell, heavily. The expression of his face was that of a conqueror.
>
> "Who, — who, — who shall separate us from the love of Christ?" he said, in a voice that contended with mortal weakness; and, with a smile, he fell asleep.

According to her biographer, the woman became so affected by the vision that she wept out loud during the reading. That afternoon, she retired to her room and locked the door. From the inspiration of the vision she had seen from Pew 23, she reportedly wrote the entire scene, the death of Uncle Tom, virtually as it appears in her book, *Uncle Tom's Cabin*. This scene, apparently, became the cornerstone for the entire book, which would ultimately shake the seams of the nation.

Over the years, *Uncle Tom's Cabin*, as well as the character of Uncle Tom itself, has fallen into extensive derision, for the seemingly sim-

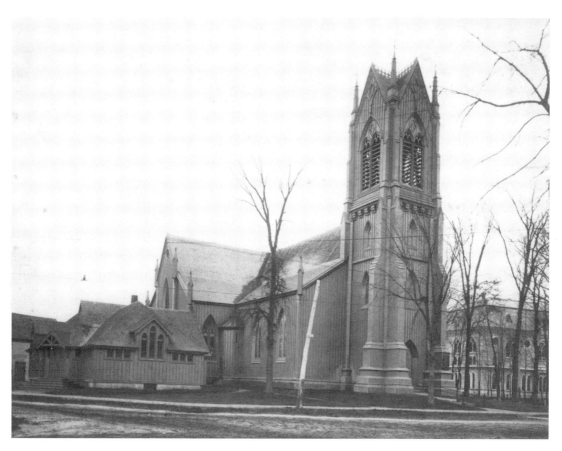

First Parish Church, Brunswick, Maine. (Courtesy First Parish Church.)

plistic way it portrayed African Americans in their plight as slaves in the early 19th century. Uncle Tom has become a caricature of the poor, ignorant, black man who turns the other cheek toward the white man far too often in the face of injustice and inequality when he should instead turn and fight.

Yet no other book in the history of the United States has had as much of an impact on its generation as *Uncle Tom's Cabin* by Harriet Beecher Stowe (1811–1896). Within a year it sold 300,000 copies in an era without paperbacks or huge franchise bookstores. To a general public without access to mass media as it has come to be known, it opened the nation to the plight of slavery as nothing else ever had or could. Its impact fostered the abolition movement, and pushed a nation unwilling to face up to its most dire hypocrisy ever closer to Civil War. Abraham Lincoln has been

quoted, during a visit by Beecher Stowe to the White House, as saying, "So you're the little woman that wrote the book that made this great war!"

Harriet Beecher Stowe was married to Calvin Ellis Stowe, a minister who graduated from Bowdoin College in 1824. The Stowe family began attending First Parish Church in 1850, and Calvin Stowe preached from the pulpit at First Parish many times.

The 19th Century Muse

A standing-room-only audience packs the graceful, hallowed interior of First Parish Church. Facing forward, the assembly listens intently to the highly anticipated commencement oration. An elderly gentleman, with long flowing white hair and beard, and stern, gruff expression, hunches over the large pulpit on the altar. It is July 8, 1875, and the occasion

Interior of First Parish Church. (Courtesy First Parish Church.)

is the 50th anniversary of the graduation of the class of 1825. The speaker, the most prominent member of the class and perhaps the most famous poet of the 19th century, addresses the assembly.

Ah me! the fifty years since last we met
Seems to me fifty folios bound and set
By Time, the great transcriber, on his shelves
Wherein are written the histories of ourselves
What tragedies, what comedies are there;
What joy and grief, what rapture and despair!
What chronicles of triumph and defeat,
Of struggle, and temptation, and retreat.
What records of regrets, and doubts, and fears!
What pages blotted, blistered by our tears!
What lovely landscapes on the margins shine,
What sweet, angelic faces. What divine
And holy images of love and trust,
Undimmed by age, unsoiled by damp or dust!

Whose hand shall dare to open and explore
These volumes, closed and clasped forever-
more?

Not mine. With reverential feet I pass;
I hear a voice that cries, "Alas! alas!
Whatever hath been written shall remain,
Nor be erased nor written o'er again;
The unwritten only still belongs to thee:
Take heed, and ponder well what that shall be.

These verses come from the poem "Moritori Salutamus," written by Henry Wadsworth Longfellow (1807–1882) for the 50th anniversary of his graduation from Bowdoin College, celebrated at First Parish Church. Born in 1807 and raised in Portland, 30 miles to the southwest of Brunswick, Longfellow remained a longtime resident of New England. Although Unitarian, Longfellow regularly attended services at First Parish Church until 1830, when a Unitarian community began to develop in town.

He had graduated from Bowdoin in 1825 with classmate novelist Nathaniel Hawthorne, having already decided on a career in verse and letters. Longfellow had spent the first six years of his academic career as a professor at Bowdoin. From there, after traveling extensively in Europe, gaining fluency in French, Spanish, German, and Italian, he returned to the United States. He spent 18 years as a professor of modern language at Harvard University, before settling into a career as perhaps the first poet in American history to earn a living *solely* as a poet.

Along the way, Longfellow penned some of the most famous and influential verse in American literary history. These include "The Song of Hiawatha," "Paul Revere's Ride," "Voices of the Night," "The Courtship of Miles Standish," and the lovely "Cross of Snow." Longfellow had set a standard for verse for at least the next 100 years; and now he was returning to his classmates, to revel in the passage of the years.

Longfellow apparently detested writing verse to order, and hated public speaking even more. But when he realized the girth of the pulpit of First Parish Church could shield most of his body from the audience, he reportedly relented, saying "Let me cover myself as much as possible; I wish it might be entirely."

First Parish originated with a riverside service conducted by the Reverend Joseph Baxter on the banks of the Androscroggin River on August 24, 1717. James Woodside served as its first resident pastor. The parish and the town of Brunswick survived a raid by Penobscot Indians in 1722, and built the first of its meeting houses in 1735. One of the meeting house galleries served as town arsenal during the Revolutionary War. A second meeting house emerged in 1808.

The present day cruciform church was designed and built by architect Richard Upjohn, and dedicated on March 18, 1846. From 1848 until 1866, a 30-foot spire towered high above the present belfry. This spire could be seen throughout the village of Brunswick, until it was toppled by a violent rainstorm in October of 1866. Inside the church, sunlight from the massive diamond-shaped windowpanes of the gothic-style windows delicately illuminate the lovely wood grains among the wall panels, pulpit, pews, railings, and pillars.

According to church historian Mildred Jones, one of the reasons the church attracted so many illustrious speakers, particularly during the 19th and early 20th centuries, is due to the reputation and character of Dr. George E. Adams, pastor of the church from 1829 to 1870. Adams attained praise as one of the most respected and celebrated ministers in the Northeast, so much so that First Parish Church was more often referred to as "Parson Adam's Church." So great became Adam's influence, that he was able to draw prestigious orators to the echoing halls of First Parish Church.

A much more pragmatic factor, however, further explains the appearance of so many famous persons at the church: through the 1800s and early 1900s, the college lacked a large facility in which to house a substantial audience, while First Parish Church could seat several hundred people at a time. Therefore, the college would use the church for its commencements and special programs, and the large crowds they would draw.

Nathaniel Hawthorne (1804–1864), author of *The Scarlet Letter* and *The House of Seven Gables*, graduated with Longfellow in 1825.

General Ulysses S. Grant (1822–1885) received an honorary LL.D (Doctor of Laws) degree from Bowdoin College on August 2, 1865, and attended that year's commencement at First Parish Church.

Brigadier General Joshua Lawrence Chamberlain (1830–1913), who was a hero at Little Round Top hill at Gettysburg, graduated from Bowdoin College in 1852, taught at Bowdoin until 1862, won the governorship of Maine in 1866, and served as President of Bowdoin College from 1871 until 1883. All the while, he remained an active and leading member of First Parish Church congregation.

William Howard Taft (1857–1930), who became the 27th President of the United States, and afterward became chief justice of the Supreme Court — the only man ever to hold both posts — spoke at First Parish Church on January 9, 1920, on the subject of the League of Nations.

Sir Wilfred Grenfell (1865–1940), English physician and missionary responsible for establishing hospitals and schools in Labrador and Newfoundland, spoke at the June 19,

1929, commencement, and received an honorary LL.D. degree.

Eleanor Roosevelt, (1884–1962), spoke on the subject of the British War effort on December 12, 1942, at the invitation of the Delta Epsilon Fraternity.

The Rev. Martin Luther King, Jr. (1929–1968), spoke in the church on May 6, 1964, on the topic "Are we making real progress in the field of race relations?" His appearance before a political issues forum was in conjunction with the opening of the program "The Portrayal of the Negro in American Paintings."

Sources

Ashby, Thomas Eldridge. *The History of the First Parish Church in Brunswick, Maine.* 1969, First Parish Church.

Davis, Kenneth C. *Don't Know Much About History.* 1990, Avon Books, New York.

Longfellow, Henry Wadsworth. *The Poetical Works of Longfellow.* 1975, Houghton, Mifflin, & Co., Boston.

Stowe, Harriet Beecher. *Uncle Tom's Cabin.* 1952, Dodd, Mead, & Company, New York.

ST. JOHN'S CHURCH

Affiliation: Episcopal
Location: Richmond, Virginia
1741

The political elite of Virginia met in St. John's Church in Richmond on Monday, March 20, in the stormy year of 1775. Relations between the colonies and Mother England quickly approached the edge of collapse, and now the Virginians assembled to decide how far past the brink that affiliation should be pushed. Among these founding fathers of Virginia and the United States sat two future presidents, as well as representatives of the aristocracy from the Colony's Golden Age. They listened with rapt attention to the stirring words of a 39-year-old self-taught attorney, whom they regarded as the leader of revolutionary thought in the colony.

The second Virginia Convention convened to ratify the resolutions proposed by the First Continental Congress held in Philadelphia in October of 1774. The Congress, with Richard Henry Lee, George Washington, and Patrick Henry among those representing Virginia, had gathered to garner colonial response to the increasing control the British Parliament attempted to legislate. While Congressional delegates concluded that Parliament should maintain authority over colonial commerce, the Congress professed opposition against the so-called Intolerable Acts, which England had implemented largely in response to the November 1773 Boston Tea Party. These measures, officially called the Coercive Acts, levied strict controls over political and economic life in Massachusetts. In response, Virginia and other colonies held a day of fasting and prayer in observance of the rebel Tea Party. The First Continental Congress created an association to boycott British goods, and passed ten resolutions delineating the rights of colonies and their assemblies.

In 1775, the factions comprising Virginia consisted largely of the plantation-owning gentry, their slaves, and a growing number of small farmers setting roots in the western half of the colony. The delegates of this second Virginia Convention emerged largely from the first faction: the best educated and wealthiest members of Virginia society, their estates thriving primarily on the all-encompassing tobacco plant, and the slave labor cultivating it. These delegates included some of the most prominent names in Virginia, as well as the whole of the American colonies. Forty-three-year-old George Washington, hero of the French and Indian War, traveled from his plantation home at Mt. Vernon to attend the convention in Richmond. Thomas Jefferson,

Opposite: St. John's Episcopal Church, Richmond, Virginia.

who would attend the Second Continental Congress in May of 1775 and author of the Declaration of Independence in 1776, also sat in attendance. Richard Henry Lee representing the most prominent family in Virginia, from which General Robert E. Lee would descend, would become one of the signers of Jefferson's fabled prose. Benjamin Harrison, Thomas Marshall, Canton Braxton, Robert Carter Nicholas; the names read like a roll call from Virginia's Aristocratic Age, and 120 of them gathered in St. John's Church to determine the uncharted course the colony would follow.

Since the end of the French and Indian War in 1763, England appeared to wage a concerted campaign to assert more authority and control over the American colonies. In addition, Parliament, whose constituents had become burdened with heavy English taxes, hoped to shift some of the financial weight onto the shoulders of the colonists. Reflective of its purpose, Parliament passed the Stamp Act of 1765, the Declaratory Act of 1766, and the Townsend Duties of 1767. Of these, the Stamp Act is the best remembered today for the part it played in American history.

The Stamp Act, as another example of the Mother Country assigning subservience and financial culpability to the colonies, excised a tax on all newspapers, custom documents, licenses, college diplomas, legal documents, and other published material. The British legislature felt the colonies had ample, if indirect, representation in Parliament, and felt justified imposing the levy upon the New World subjects. But the Americans saw the Stamp Act as another example of taxation without representation, England's further attempt to limit the colonists' self-governing intention.

Expectedly, the Stamp Act incurred the volatile wrath of colonists in Virginia and elsewhere. In the House of Burgesses, Virginia's lower legislative house, Patrick Henry proposed the seven Stamp Act Resolutions, which affirmed the colonists' rights as English citizens, renounced taxation without representation, and government without the consent of the governed. The House of Burgesses easily adopted the first four. Likewise, it adopted the fifth resolution, which professed only the leg-islature of Virginia would have the right to levy taxes, until timid conservative members managed to lead its overturn. Nevertheless, Royal Virginia Governor Francis Fauquier angrily dissolved what he perceived as the dissident House of Burgesses at the passage of the four resolutions.

But Fauquier's dissolution came too late; Henry's resolutions had already begun circulating among the other colonies. By the end of 1765, eight other colonial assemblies had adopted similar resistive measures to the Stamp Act. Local protests became violent disturbances in Boston, Newport, and Maryland. In Virginia, Richard Henry Lee led a procession with an effigy against George Mercer, the state stamp distributor. (Actually, Lee had applied for the position, but was passed over for Mercer.) Such public protests eventually led to the resignation of Mercer, and similar officials throughout the colonies.

Colonial protests became so defiant that Parliament repealed the act in March of 1766. Although Parliament found other measures by which to levy the colonist and assert its authority, the precedent had been set: The colonists knew they could effectively protest against and defy Parliamentary authority.

The author of the Stamp Act Resolutions was a 29-year-old, fiddle-playing Scotch descendent from rural Hanover County, northwest of Richmond. Born on May 29, 1736, raised near the woods of northern Virginia, Patrick Henry received his early education from his father, John Henry and himself. Henry grew up tall, lithe and lean, reportedly not handsome in appearance, but pleasant in personality. Although he failed at early attempts at mercantile and bartending, Henry managed to pass a law exam in Williamsburg in 1760, and opened a private practice in Hanover County courthouse. Thomas Jefferson regarded Henry as mentally lazy and uninformed, an inferior as a student of the law. But he also conceded Henry's consummate knowledge of the human heart, and powerful skills as an orator, one who used his theatrical gifts to stun audiences and sway juries like no other barrister in the colonies.

Normally amiable in humor and disposition, Henry became a fiery advocate for dissension and nonconformity, colonial autonomy and self-government a century after Thomas Hooker professed it in Connecticut. He advanced his legal reputation at Hanover County courthouse in the 1763 case called Parson's Cause, involving the so-called Twopenny Act passed by the House of Burgesses, and later vetoed by King George III. Henry publicly proclaimed the House's authority to pass laws beneficial to the people, and the impropriety of England's church and state ignoring or overturning such laws. Henry labeled George III a tyrant, declaring he deserved the disloyalty and disobedience of his subjects. Henry's resulting acclaim led to his election to the House of Burgesses, and appointment as a delegate to the Continental Congress. In 1776, he would be elected Virginia's first governor. But in 1775, he joined his fellow Virginians at the Church on Richmond Hill, to ratify the proposals of the first Continental Congress.

St. John's Episcopal Church is the oldest house of worship in the Virginia capital. First known as the church of the Parish of Henrico, short for Henricopolis, the region surrounding the church was named in 1611 for Prince Henry, eldest son of King James I of England. The parish originated in 1634, under the direction of Reverend Alexander Whittaker, who gained fame as baptizer of Pocahontas. Founded as an Anglican Church, it became an Episcopal Church after the American Anglican Church became the Protestant Episcopal Church in 1789.

The second Virginia Conventioneers chose St. John's for their meeting simply because, in 1775, it provided the largest meeting hall in Richmond. First constructed in 1741 on land donated by William Byrd II, the original church stood 60 feet long by 25 feet wide, with a 14-foot ceiling. The chancel and pulpit moved from the east wall to the south, when the parish added a 40-square-foot gallery to the original navel. The three-tiered square tower replaced the short belfry in the 1820s. In its various forms, St. John's has presided over the capital of Richmond for nearly three centuries. It became a National Historic Landmark in 1966.

The doors of St. John's opened for the second Virginia Convention on Monday, March 20, 1775. The Tuesday and Wednesday sessions proceeded in an uneventful manner, as the Virginians quietly adopted the proposals of the Continental Congress. Thursday's assembly seemed destined to continue with the same gentility, until Patrick Henry, possibly growing impatient with the passive discourse, decided to address the body.

In response to Parliament's increasing impositions, Patrick Henry proposed an independent militia to be immediately established in Virginia, for the defense of the rights and liberties of the colonies. Conservative convention delegates, from loyalist families which once comprised Virginia's oligarchy, tried to sway the gathering toward moderation, apparently longing for return of the happy, halcyon idyllic days of their Virginia youth. Many of the members felt they retained a civil rapport with Parliament, and loathed to invite the wrath of England, which would inevitably lead to complete conquest and martial rule.

In rebuttal, Henry delivered what is surely one of the most famous speeches in the annals of American history. He told the gathering no hope exists for peace and reconciliation with England, and questioned why, if England was so concerned with love and reconciliation, had it amassed such an extensive armory among the colonies. "Has Great Britain an enemy in this quarter of the world," questioned the exuberant Henry, " to call for such an accumulation of navies and armies? No sir; she has none..."

The barrister continued to remind the assembly that other methods of negotiation had been attempted: petitions, remonstrations, supposition, "We have prostrated ourselves before the throne," Henry admonished fervently. "There is no longer any room for hope." Standing before the transfixed assembly, punctuating each remark with impassioned expressions and gesticulations, he challenged his audience, telling them if they wished to be free, they would have to fight for their freedom:

> It is in vain, Sir, to extenuate the matter. Gentlemen may cry peace, peace; but there is no peace. The war is actually begun. The next gale that sweeps from the north will bring to our ears the clash of resounding arms. Our brethren are already in the field.

Why stand we here idle? What is it the gentlemen wish? What would they have? Is life so dear, or peace so sweet, as to be purchased at the price of chains and slavery? Forbid, Almighty God! I know not what course others may take. But as for me — give me liberty, or give me death! [Willison, pp. 266–267]

Henry's imageries of chains and slavery are particularly ironic today, as most of the Convention delegates either owned slaves or supported the institution. The effect proved irrefutable, however, as the Convention delegation reportedly responded in awed silence, as the power and consequence of Henry's words seeped into their hearts. The conventioneers did not rush out in the heat of conversion, drawing sword to attack any Tory in sight. Many conventioneers still feared the idea of revolution, and hoped for reconciliation with England, not independence as a nation. Yet, Henry's words tipped the hopes and imaginations of the delegates toward the reality of the situation: the colonies could not meekly remain under the subjugation of England

Over the two weeks of the convention, the delegates agreed to Henry's original proposal: the establishment of militia in Virginia. They based the authority for the act on a 1738 Act allowing creation of militia. Each county in Virginia would create, arm, and train a company of infantry of 60, plus a cavalry troop of 30. These militia, inevitably and eventually, would participate in the revolutionary war, would forever sever the strained umbilical between the colonist and their mother. Through his emotional and timely words, Patrick Henry succeeded in his struggle to whip "a gathering of quietly unhappy Englishmen into a band of militant Americans." (Hume, p. 116)

Each summer Sunday in Richmond, Virginia, visitors are welcomed to St. John's Episcopal Church, to view the reenactment of that fateful Thursday in 1775. Adorned in period costume, in the reconstructed 18th-century Anglican sanctuary once actually occupied by mythical characters of American history, local actors and history buffs recreate the scene of Patrick Henry's most famous discourse. Audiences sit and watch, and imagine they are witness to the formative days of the American Revolution.

Sources

Davis, Kenneth C. *Don't Know Much About History*. 1990, Avon Books, New York.

Dowdey, Clifford. *The Golden Age: A Climate for Greatness, Virginia 1732–1775*. 1970, Little, Brown, and Company, Boston.

Hume, Ivor Noel. *1775: Another Part of the Field*. 1966, Alfred A. Knopf, New York.

Willison, George F. *Patrick Henry and His World*. 1969, Doubleday and Company, Inc., Garden City, NY.

Prince William's Parish Church and Sheldon Church

Affiliation: Anglican
Location: Sheldon, Beaufort County, South Carolina
1757

South Carolina has been the setting for some of the most savage and infamous military maneuvers ever undertaken on American soil. The cities of Charleston and Camden fell under assaults lead by British Major General Sir Henry Clinton during the Revolution, while General Nathaniel Greene and his commanders defeated the British at the Battle of

Cowpens. Fort Sumter, outside Charleston, provided the site for the inaugural battle of the Civil War, while much of the South Carolina countryside fell victim to Sherman's March as the war's end neared. These famous combats, alongside encounters not so well known, have inalterably affected the landscape and mind-set of this small state in the southeast corner of the country.

Bearing witness to the destruction meted out during the country's two great homeland wars, from a uniquely intimate South Carolina vantage point, are the rust-tinted, weatherbeaten brick ruins of the once auspicious Prince William's Anglican Parish Church. Prince William's Church fell during the Revolutionary War, arose like the firebird as the Sheldon Episcopal Church, only to be decimated again during the Civil War. Today, slumbering among the moss-covered, twisted oaks in lowland Beaufort County, the Sheldon Church ruins stand as memorial to the devastating military calamities which befell the county during its first hundred years.

Prince William's Anglican Parish Church was formed on May 25, 1745, fifteen miles northwest of the town of Beaufort in present-day Beaufort County, South Carolina. Actual church construction commenced sometime between 1745 and 1757, the year of the church's dedication service. The church emerged on acreage donated by Edmund Bellinger, land which bordered the Sheldon Plantation, owned by the prominent Colonel William Bull family. The parish built a smaller chapel for the parish in McPhersonville, just to the northwest of the church.

Prince William's Church was a stately structure, reputed to be one of the earliest American attempts to duplicate the classic form of the ancient Greek temple. Rectangular in shape, the church featured colonnaded walls more than a yard thick; the bricks adhered in a Flemish bond. Seven Tuscan columns, each more than 30 feet high, flanked the outer wall on either side. An equestrian statue of namesake Prince William of Orange (1650–1702), son of King George II, stood before the church portico. With its classic facade and beautifully ornamented interior, Prince William stood for at least 20 years as perhaps

the loveliest place of worship in South Carolina.

But in 1778, three years into the Revolutionary War, Major General Henry Clinton, newly appointed supreme commander of British Forces in North America, received the advisory from London to focus the war effort to the southern American colonies. The war had not gone well in New England and the north, the hotbed for revolutionist organization and activity, from which the Continental army could draw a wealth of resources and enthusiasm to employ against the British. In the south, on the other hand, a greater proportion of Loyalists resided, with a greater reluctance to revolt against the King. The British hoped to draw from that loyalist support, and establish a stronghold for the English south of Virginia. They hoped to eventually establish the southern border of the colonies at the Potomac River, thus reducing the Thirteen Colonies by three.

In early 1779, under the command of General Augustus Prevost and with the aid of the British navy, the city of Savannah fell to the Redcoats, who took control of the whole of Georgia. Continental General Benjamin Lincoln and Admiral d'Estang of the French navy led a poorly executed campaign to extract Savannah from the English. But when the allied effort failed, d'Estang withdrew his ships and men. General Clinton took the opportunity to establish British control of the southern colonies.

While Clinton sent warships to the north of Charleston Harbor, Prevost led his troops north through the Carolinas, toward the impending fall of Charleston. During this "March on Charles Town" from March to May, Prevost pillaged and burned the Carolina countryside, catching Prince William's Anglican Church in the destructive path.

The nearby William Bull plantation served as an arms depot for the storage of firearms and artillery for the Continental army. The plantation also provided land used in drilling exercises for the colonial troops. Prevost's army destroyed any building in the vicinity that might be used to store supplies, arms, or men. These included churches, which were often among the best constructed buildings in the

Ruins of the Sheldon Church, Sheldon, South Carolina. (Courtesy St. Helena's Episcopal Church.)

area. Quickly reduced to smoking rubble, Prince William's Parish Church, along with most of the records and documents depicting the community members and activities, disintegrated in the blaze. As a result, little information concerning the original parish of Prince William is available. At the end of the razing, only the brick walls and columns of the stately Church of England remained. Local lore names the captain of the British company which burned the church as Andrew DeVeaux, a cousin of one Stephen DeVeaux, who was wounded at the Battle of the Beaufort, South Carolina, on February 2, 1779.

Charleston, South Carolina, fell to the British on May 12, 1779. A year later Camden, 100 miles to the northwest, succumbed as well. Total British conquest of the southern colonies seemed inevitable. But under the command of the understatedly brilliant General Nathaniel Greene, the badly outnumbered American troops scored an unexpected victory at the Battle of Cowpens in northwest South Carolina in January 1781. From that point, the Continental army, implementing the guerrilla tac-

tics employed at Cowpens, slowly released the British stranglehold on South Carolina. Southern Loyalist support failed as the force London counted on; this became a crucial overestimation leading to the ultimate British defeat in the southern colonies, and in the Revolutionary War.

In 1815, the Reverend Christian Hackel conducted a commemorative service among the crumbling fragments to which the British had reduced the once glorious Prince William's Church. One of the gathered later described the scene:

> The building was in ruins; the walls and columns of the portico alone were standing — sad monument to the violence and lawlessness of those times. The forest had resumed its sway, and the interior was filled with a large growth of trees which had to be cut down by one of the parishioners. Boards were placed on the stumps for seats, and with no covering but the clear blue sky on a balmy spring day, the man of God proclaimed to a large and respectable audience the glad tidings of salvation. [*Historic Review*, p. 77]

The rebuilding of the church began in 1825. The dedication as Sheldon Church of Prince William's Parish followed in 1826. Since South Carolina ceased as a Province of England, the church could no longer be considered part of the Church of England. Instead, Sheldon Church became a member of the Protestant Episcopal Church of the United States, founded in 1789 as the American outgrowth of the Church of England. Both the Church of England and the Episcopal Church are considered part of the Anglican Communion, as they recognize the leadership of the Archbishop of Canterbury. Many of the beliefs and practices of both the Anglican and Episcopal Church are similar to the Roman Catholic Church. A primary difference is the renouncement of papal jurisdiction, initiated by King Henry VIII in the sixteenth century.

By the mid–19th century, South Carolina had reemerged as a land of vast plantations and beautiful homes with lush gardens, maintained proudly through generations, often within the same family. Unfortunately, slavery, for those who could afford it, provided the ugly foundation of this pristine, agrarian lifestyle; the maintenance of the mansions made possible through the inhuman toil of the slaves. Unfortunately, the paradise would be lost, due in a large degree to the devastating breed of war waged by the Yankee often vilified by Confederates above all others: General William Tecumseh Sherman.

> Poor, bleeding, suffering South Carolina! Up to that time she had felt but slightly — away from the coast — the devastating effects of the war; but her time had come. The protestations of her old men, and the pleadings of her noble women had no effect in staying the ravages of sword, flame, and pillage…. [Davis, pp. 393–394]

Union troops eyed South Carolina with particular malice as the first southern state to secede from the Union at Fort Sumter, the setting where the war's first shots rang out. Many Yankee soldiers identified South Carolina as the birthplace of the Civil War, and the cause of all their troubles.

Sherman's notorious March to the Sea began on July 14, 1864, with the occupation of Sheridan, Mississippi. Marching through the heart of Georgia, Sherman watched the burning of Atlanta on November 16, 1864, and then conquered Savannah on December 22, 1864. From Savannah, Sherman's Army of the West continued north to Columbia, which fell on February 15, 1865. Charleston followed, but it might have been Confederate troops who ignited the fire there, to keep supplies from the Yankee regiments. Fayetteville, North Carolina collapsed on March 11, 1865. Finally Sherman met General Grant's army at the siege of Petersburg, on April 3, 1865. Within two weeks, on April 14, 1865, the Stars and Stripes rose over Fort Sumter once again.

Sherman's troops destroyed railroads, raided agricultural fields, burned houses, and destroyed any building which could be used in the Confederate cause. A massive juggernaut of 60,000 Union soldiers, on a 40-mile wide swath, marched through the heart of South Carolina, joined by hundreds of fugitive slaves seeking direction and protection, even in the meager form the army often provided. Along the way, Sherman's army faced only token resistance from Confederate troops, which seemed to dissipate further with each mile that passed.

Sheldon Church met its destruction after the evacuation of Pocotaligo by the Confederates, sometime between January 14 and January 20, 1865. The actual torching is believed to have been by a detachment of the 15th Corps of Sherman's army under the command of General John A. Logan. The small chapel in McPhersonville, which had been used by the Confederates as a smallpox hospital, was also reduced to smoldering ashes. Sherman's army obliterated all structures that might be used for storage, shelter, medical needs, or command headquarters. Sheldon Church's leaden statue of William of Orange disappeared, but probably at the hands of the Confederates rather than the Yankees. The Rebels no doubt melted the figure down, using the lead to supplement their dwindling supply of bullets.

During the March, Sherman insisted his troops forage exclusively off the land. He later argued it would have been impossible to adequately supply the troops for that kind of expedition, anyway. However, Sherman may have held a second agenda. By forcing his men to live off the bounty of the enemy, he made each soldier's personal livelihood directly dependent on his ability to seize, control, consume, and destroy. The destruction became a personal necessity, which no doubt increased its ferocity, towards Sherman's ultimate end: the final paralysis of the Confederate military cause.

A movement surfaced in the early 1900s from several southern Episcopal churches, insisting the United States government reimburse congregations whose property was destroyed in Sherman's March. The Sheldon Parish laid claims for both the Sheldon Church and the adjacent McPhersonville chapel, saying Sherman had destroyed them unnecessarily. The claim for the chapel was rejected, since it was used as a military hospital. The Sheldon Church exaction was dropped as well because, although it can easily be assumed to have been leveled by Logan's army, apparently no actual eye witnesses survived. Although other southern parishioners apparently received some compensation, the Sheldon Church received nothing. After the war, Sheldon Church parishioners moved to churches in surrounding communities. The ruined church would never resurrect again.

The horrific, intrusive desecrations endured by South Carolina through both of America's two great home wars may go far to explain the special rebel spirit exhibited by generations of South Carolina residents. Alongside its traditional simplicity, the southern temperament

for geniality and hospitality, lies the spark of rebellion, the fire of mistrust for an authoritative government, and the memory of a time which seemed — at least on the surface, for a small portion of the population — to harbor a gentler, more civilized lifestyle.

These violations are manifest in the Sheldon Church ruins, which remind the visitor of the complexity, courage, and horror of America's first century. Every spring, on the second Sunday after Easter, commemorative services are conducted by St. Helena's Episcopal Church from Beaufort. The faithful gather among the crumbling ruins and sad brick walls, "the towering columns, semicircular bastions and durable arches, in a cathedral-like setting of oaks with mourning veils of Spanish moss." (*Historic Resources*, p. 77) They gather in silence to contemplate, to pray, to remember.

Sources

Bishop, Peter and Darton, Michael. *The Encyclopedia of World Faiths: An Illustrated Survey of the World's Living Religions*. 1987, MacDonald and Co., Ltd., London and Sydney.

Davis, Kenneth C. *Don't Know Much About the Civil War*. 1996, William Morrow and Company, Inc., New York.

Dupuy, Col. Trevor Nevitt. *The Military History of Revolutionary War Land Battles*. 1970, Franklin Watts, Inc., New York.

Hutson, Francis M. "Prince William's Parish Church," *News and Courier*. Charleston, SC, May 12, 1957.

Ketchum, Richard M. *The American Heritage Book of The Revolution*. 1958, American Heritage Publishing Company, New York.

Low Country Council of Governments. *Historic Resources of the Lowcountry: A Regional Survey*. 1979.

TOURO SYNAGOGUE

Affiliation: Judaism
Location: Newport, Rhode Island
1763

In family therapy, the identified patient (or I.P.) is the individual within the family upon whom the cause of the family's problems are projected. The I.P. is the scapegoat, the black sheep, the root of the family's sufferings. Without a doubt, the Identified Patient

of Western religion has been the Jewish people.

> The Jews make a handy scapegoat for everyone's pain, for everything that goes wrong; France tries to expel them in 1252, later forces them to wear distinctive badges, later strips

them of their possessions, later tries to expel them again; Britain tries to expel them in 1290 and 1306; Cologne tires to expel them in 1414; blamed for the Black Death whenever and wherever it arrives, thousands are hanged and burned alive; Castile tries to expel them in 1492; thousands are slaughtered in Lisbon in 1506; Pope Paul III walls them off from the rest of Rome, creating the first ghetto. [Quinn, p. 269]

Christians over the centuries have justified their hatred, resentment, and persecution of the Jews by labeling them the murderers of Christ. Yet the Christian religion has its roots in the Jewish faith. Jesus himself was a Jew. Many of the rituals and practices found in various Christian worship services have their origins in ancient Judaic practices. The Scriptures include and are founded upon the Torah, the first five books of the Old Testament. Indeed, many characteristics of Christian worship, particularly the Roman and Orthodox Catholic services, are extremely reminiscent of Jewish practices. Judaism is the predecessor of Christianity; with no Judaism, there would be no Christianity.

Although Spain is generally thought of as a wholly Catholic nation, Jews have played an integral role in the history of the Iberian Peninsula for centuries. They are known in Hebrew as the *Sephardim,* or *Sephardic Jews,* which means the Jews of Spain. As late as the 13th century, the Jews participated in a mutually beneficial coexistence with both Catholics and Moslems, each sect finding its own particular and important niche within the economic picture. But by the end of the 15th century, the same religious bigotry and greed which drove the Moors from all of Spain save the southern state of Granada, permanently altered the position of the Jew. The growing Christian autocracies resented the relative success the Sephardim enjoyed within the multicultural structure. Suspicion and prejudice replaced the once open, tolerant, and inclusive Iberian society.

With the ascension of Ferdinand and Isabella to the throne in the late 15th century — and the accompanying Inquisition and approaching 16th century counter reformation wars — Spain assumed the role of the protectorate nation of Catholicism. Thousands of Sephardic Jews faced death and expulsion from Spain and Portugal. Those Jews who wished to stay were forced to publicly relinquish their ancestral faith, becoming *convertos* or *marranos* (Jews converted to Catholicism). By the 17th century, Spain's glory years had all but passed, and whatever financial benefits reaped by the Sephardims seemed to fade with the Spanish economy. Facing relentless persecution, many of the Sephardims began to seek refuge elsewhere: North Africa, the eastern Mediterranean, eastern Europe, and finally, the New World.

During the reign of Phillip IV, grandson of Phillip II, under whom Spain established the first settlement at St. Augustine, Florida, a conclave of Sephardic Jews left their homes in Spain and Portugal. In 1658 they sailed westward across the Atlantic, landing in the newly established colony of Rhode Island. Roger Williams, himself an exile from the Massachusetts Bay Colony, had established the Rhode Island colony 14 years earlier as a haven for freedom of conscience and religion. Word of this new haven had reached the Iberian Peninsula via sailing ship, where many Jews eagerly awaited the taste of religious freedom in America.

The new Jewish congregation disembarked at the coastal settlement of Newport. With no synagogue in which to meet, they gathered in private homes and rented meeting halls, for both worship and religious education for the children. A sacred cemetery, in which the Jews could be entombed according to their traditions, was established in 1677. Still, without the proper sanctuary in which to practice their faith, the community could not feel complete.

In the meantime, the new settlers lent their age old skills and knowledge as merchants, financiers, shippers, and craftsmen, to the booming pre–Revolution Newport economy. As Newport entered the 18th century, the Jewish community prospered and expanded. More Sephardim, escaping the tragic 1755 Lisbon earthquake, joined their brothers in faith at Newport. *Ashkenazim* Jews who had settled in central and eastern Europe joined the Newport congregation as well. Most significantly, a rabbi from Amsterdam named Isaac Touro arrived in Newport, destined to become the first spiritual leader of the Newport congregation.

As the fold enlarged, members realized they would need a permanent place of worship. The Newport Jews received generous contributions from numerous congregations worldwide, including the *Shearith Israel* (Remnant of Israel) Congregation in New York, the only American Jewish congregation older than Newport's. With its newfound treasury, Touro's congregation retained the services of architect Peter Harrison. Considered by many the finest architect of Colonial America, Harrison's works included King's Chapel in Boston and the Redwood Library in Newport. Now, he would design what would be regarded as his masterpiece, the Touro Synagogue.

Ground was broken for the synagogue in 1759, and dedication commenced at its first service on December 2, 1763. The synagogue followed design characteristics of Georgian architecture, popularized during the reigns (1714–1830) of British kings George I, II, III, and IV. The Georgian style borrowed symmetry and balance of ancient Roman architecture; Harrison, in turn, incorporated the Georgian motif in a design appropriate and accommodating of the Jewish rituals.

Located on quiet Touro street, with a plain, brick facade, the simple exterior belies the grace and beauty of the sanctuary. The interior is delicate and ornate, featuring finely tapered railing and beautiful chandeliers. During worship services, the congregation faces eastward, toward the city of Jerusalem, and toward the Holy Ark which holds the sacred Torah. (Torah, translated, means "to teach.") Twelve Ionic columns topped by twelve Corinthian columns supporting the roof represent the Twelve Tribes of Israel. The *ell*—where the Jewish children received their religious training—is situated to the side of the main meeting area. Five massive brass candelabra, donations from members of the congregation, dangle from the ceilings. The Eternal Light, symbol of Divine Presence, hovers suspended before the Holy Ark.

With its beautiful synagogue complete, the congregation took on the name *Yeshuat Israel*, which means Salvation of Israel. During the remainder of the prewar years, the Yeshuat Israel community, along with the entire city of Newport, enjoyed something of a golden age. With a proper facility for worship, the Yeshuat Israel could accommodate the full congregation in worship, religious education, and sanctified burial services, the three essential sacred functions of Jewish life. Yeshuat Israel enthusiastically celebrated Passover, Yom Kippur (the Day of Atonement), and Hanukkah at their impressive new synagogue.

Judaism is often regarded as a religion of action, rather than a specific doctrine. Incorporating beliefs into action and ritual is an integral part of Judaism. Although Jews point to the Torah as the foundation of their faith, there are many interpretations and manifestations of the Word of God. Maimonides' Thirteen Principles of Faith are often pointed to as a just synopsis of the Jewish beliefs. Still, there are those who refer to the Book of Micah, Chapter Six, Verse 8, as a summation of the essence of Judaism: "He hath shewed thee, O man, what is good; and what doth the Lord require of thee, but to do justly, and to love mercy, and to walk humbly with thy God?"

Newport's golden years quickly tarnished with the coming of the Revolution. British troops occupied Newport during the war, driving townspeople (Christian and Jew alike) from the coastal city. Many of the Yeshuat Israel moved to New York and elsewhere, reducing the congregation to a dwindling number. During this low point, ironically, the Newport synagogue received one of its most significant visitors.

It is important to remember that while the Jews of Newport were allowed to worship freely, they could not vote on community issues. In August of 1790, Touro Synagogue received a visit from President George Washington, accompanied by Declaration of Independence author Thomas Jefferson. They had come to Newport to promote the newly evolving federal government. During the visit, Washington listened to an address by Moses Seixas, warden of the synagogue. In his presentation, Seixas expressed the congregation's appreciation of the potential of the new nation:

Touro Synagogue, Newport, Rhode Island. (Photograph by Susan Findley.)

Deprived as we heretofore have been of the invaluable rights of free Citizens, we now (with a deep sense of gratitude to the Almighty dispenser of all events) behold a Government erected by the Majesty of the People — a Government, which to bigotry gives no sanction, persecution no assistance — but generously affordens to all Liberty of conscience and immunities of Citizenship... [*Touro*, p. 4]

Profoundly moved by the warden's sentiments, Washington replied by letter several days later, echoing many of the words he had heard from Seixas.

It is now no more that toleration is spoken of, as if it was by the indulgence of one class of people, that another enjoyed the exercise of their inherent natural rights. For happily, the Government of the United States, which gives to bigotry no sanction, to persecution no assistance, requires only that they who live under its protection should demean themselves as good citizens, in giving it on all occasions their effectual support.

May the Children of the Stock of Abraham, who dwell in this land, continue to merit and enjoy the good will of the other Inhabitants....

May the father of all mercies scatter light and not darkness in our paths. [*Touro*, p. 5]

Washington echoed the hopeful intent of the new government. However, religious acceptance was only a federal proposition, which would not be accepted by individual states for many years. The Jewish people would continue to suffer religious persecution, even in the "land of the free."

Unfortunately, even following Washington's visit, the declining years of Newport and the Touro Synagogue continued. Finally, the congregation known as Yeshuat Israel closed, and the title and deed of the synagogue passed to New York's Shearith Israel. For a brief time, the synagogue was used for the Rhode Island General Assembly, and later for the Supreme Court of Rhode Island. Finally, the synagogue closed completely. The building deteriorated, eventually overcome by weather, decay, and bats.

Meanwhile, Isaac Touro had moved to Jamaica, where he died in 1784. But his sons, Abraham and Judah, remained in Newport, becoming very successful businessmen, and generous philanthropists. Upon their deaths, the Touro brothers left more than $20,000 toward the preservation and continued maintenance of the synagogue. The Touro Jewish Synagogue Fund became one of the earliest bequests left specifically for the preservation of a historic site. It is probably in appreciation of the Touro Fund, as well as in memory of the first rabbi, that Touro Synagogue was so named.

Although the synagogue had occasionally been used for special services in the 1820s, it was not permanently reopened until 1883. A new Jeshuat (a respelling of Yeshuat) Israel congregation, comprised of Ashkenazim Jews, moved into the synagogue, continuing to follow the Sephardic traditions.

Today, the Touro Synagogue remains the first and oldest synagogue in the United States. In 1946, Touro Synagogue received the designation of National Historic Site, which enables the National Park Service to lend technical support towards its continued preservation.

A goal of family therapy is to remove blame from the Identified Patient, and to spread responsibility evenly among all family members. The Touro Synagogue is a reminder that, while the family of Western religion has made great progress in removing blame from the Jews, the process is far from complete.

Sources

Bishop, Peter and Darton, Michael. *The Encyclopedia of World Faiths: An Illustrated Survey of the World's Living Religions*. 1987, MacDonald and Co., Ltd., London and Sydney.
Grunfield, Frederic V. *The Kings of Spain*. 1982, Stonehenge Press, Chicago.
Himelstein, Rabbi Dr. Shmuel. *The Jewish Primer*. 1990, Facts on File, New York.
McKendrick, Melveena. *The Horizon Concise History of Spain*. 1972, American Heritage Publishing Co, Inc. New York.
Quinn, Daniel. *The Story of B*. 1996, Bantam Books, New York.
Touro Synagogue, National Park Service. US Department of Interior, 1996.

NISKAYUNA

Affiliation: United Society of Believers
Location: Seven miles north of Albany, New York
Circa 1774

One of the most unusual and successful of the American utopian societies emerged from an enclave of enthusiastic believers who landed in New York from Manchester, England in August of 1774. Known early as the Shaking Quakers, they had little actual affiliation with George Fox's sect in either England or America. They eventually called themselves the United Society of Believers in Christ's Second Coming, but today they are best known as the Shakers. Their unique brand of firebrand theology has uniquely colored the landscape of American religion for more than 250 years.

Although the Shakers eventually developed 19 separate self-sustaining communities east of the Mississippi River, the first settlement of Believers emerged seven miles north of Albany, New York. Not as well known as the Shaker Villages at Canterbury, New Hampshire, or Sabbathlake, Maine, Niskayuna nevertheless represents the first important foothold for the Shaking Quakers in the New World.

The founding force behind the Shakers in America was a willful and charismatic English woman named Ann Lee. Born in Manchester, England, on February 26, 1736, Lee toiled in textile shops as a youngster, never learning to read or write. Compelled into a prearranged marriage to Abraham Standerin, Ann Lee gave birth to four children, all of whom died at an early age. As Lee's religious avocation matured, her relationship with Standerin disintegrated into threats and sexual intimidation, eventually ending in permanent separation.

While living in Manchester in 1769, Ann Lee became affiliated with an enthusiastic religious sect led by James and Jane Wardley from Bolton, England. Influenced by a range of flourishing sects including the Quakers, French Enthusiasts, and the Methodists, the group became known as the Shaking Quakers. Like other radical sects of the time, the Shaking Quakers advocated deviation from the Church of England, which they saw as corrupt and self-serving. They challenged the Anglican Church and its members by incorporating confrontational tactics, preaching openly to locals, flagrantly violating state religious mores, and denigrating both laity and clergy. Lee became a devoted and effective disciple; as such, she came under persecution from the conservative church, subject to harassment, beatings, and imprisonment. In one episode of incarceration, she reportedly spent time in a tiny, decrepit cell, deprived by her keepers of both food and water. Reportedly one of her earliest and most loyal followers, James Whittaker, smuggled a straw into her jail cell. She stayed alive by sipping broth Whittaker secretly held at the keyhole during visits.

Already admired for her courage and resolve, Lee reportedly experienced her first mystical experience in 1770, a vision of Jesus. Her clairvoyant gifts drew more disciples to her side when, in 1774, she decided to come to North America. She boarded the sailing ship *Snow Maria* in Liverpool with eight followers including Whittaker and her brother William Lee. They landed in New York City in August. Lee and her followers remained relatively unnoticed in the New World over the next five years.

Perhaps due to Ann Lee's illiteracy and her resulting embarrassment at her inability to read and write there appear to be few records of life at Niskayuna during Lee's leadership. Reportedly they purchased 200 acres of land north of Albany in the name of sect member John Hocknell. The swampy, forested terrain bore the Iroquoian name Niskayuna (which may mean "big cornfield"), while the Dutch called it Watervliet. Originally eight followers came to Niskayuna with Lee from England. They built a primitive log cabin in which they dwelt for the first three years. Eventually three family dwellings plus a larger meeting house for worship services replaced the original house. In time, the first colony grew to more

than two dozen, forcing the little enclave to begin restricting new recruits to the settlement, reinforcing the need to establish settlements elsewhere.

Today, none of the original buildings exist; the structures occupying the Shaker Village at present-day Colonie, New York all originated in the 19th century. Only the fruit orchard, and the cemetery in which Ann Lee and her brother were buried, remain at the original settlement.

At Niskayuna, in isolation from other New York communities, the American Shaker movement formed and fermented. Ann Lee apparently accepted the mantle of leadership, regarding her followers perhaps as the children she could not raise herself. Charismatic and quiet, tender and disciplined, compassionate and firm; Ann Lee's followers called her "Mother Ann."

By 1780, the tenets of the Shaker gospel in America began to emerge.

The Shaking Quakers believed soundly in the necessity of confession, the authority of spirit, the condemnation of sin, and *most significantly*, the possibility of perfection — given the proper disciplines and activities. They anticipated the impending Armageddon, and sought the perfection of body and spirit which would earn acceptance into Eternal Life. They sincerely believed the Spirit of Christ became manifest in sincere Believers, particularly in a heartfelt and fervent manner of worship.

The spontaneous, frenetic movements which characterized the worship ceremonies — particularly under the guidance of Mother Ann — gave the Shakers its name and reputation. In the midst of their high energy ceremonies, the Shakers would drive themselves into spiritual and emotional ecstasy, which they claimed as the manifestation of the Spirit. During an age when most Christian sects considered dancing in any form sinful, one observer described a typical scene of worship at Niskayuna:

> There was no public prayer or preaching and little reading. By contrast, of singing there was abundance; some songs were with words and some without, some words known and some unknown. The gifts of the new "spiritual dispensation" including shaking and singing,

hopping and turning, smoking and running, groaning and laughing. The Believers viewed all these actions as manifestations of divine power and union with God...The noise of the night meetings was heard two miles away.... [Stein, p. 17]

The curious and the spiritual seekers alike journeyed to Niskayuna to witness the Shaker practices, and to hear the message of Mother Ann. As the enclave of Believers at Niskayuna grew, overwhelming the site's available accommodations, Mother Ann decided it was time to bring the Shaker gospel to the world. Accompanied by her brother William, who was an accomplished singer, and skilled orator James Whittaker, Mother Ann embarked on a two year missionary tour of New England from May 1781 to September 1783. Fostered perhaps by her illiteracy, Mother Ann claimed a preference of personal testimony and conversion over written doctrine and dogma. Her goal for the missionary tour was to strengthen converts outside Niskayuna, and bring the Shaker message to a sinful and godless world. Her evangelical message, which publicly exposed sinful behavior, derided established churches, and divided families and communities between believers and the condemned, drew the ire of the local citizenry. These persecutions, of course, served merely to strengthen the Shakers' resolve and fervency, which drew more converts to their side. The Shakers suffered through attacks by both mob and local militia. They endured beatings, whippings, jailings, and harassment. The harassers objected not only to their strange ceremonies and militant sermons, but to three basic Shaker principles considered particularly radical for the times.

In the first place, the Shakers believed sincerely in the equality of the sexes, and practiced sincerely what they believed. Not only was their leader a woman, but they believed the female was actually more susceptible to divine inspiration than the male. In subsequently established Shaker colonies, authority would be divided equally between two male and two female elders. These practices offered a specific and frightening challenge to organized American religions, the vast majority of which (even among nonconformist sects) featured male dominated, female subjugating hierarchies.

The early Shakers also advocated absolute pacifism, completely rejecting the thought of war, no matter how noble the cause appeared. They preached resistance to the Revolution against the British. Because Lee and the original Shakers came from England, the entire group were labeled as British sympathizers, accused of treason. Many considered their peace-loving principles "a highly pernicious and of destructive tendency to the Freedom and Independence of the United States of America." (Stein, p. 13)

Finally, in the quest for the perfection they so ardently desired, and in their expectation of the imminent apocalypse, the Shakers practiced celibacy in their nonstop campaign to overcome the appetites of the flesh. This belief may have arisen from Mother Ann Lee's own experienced tragedy at childbirth. The sexes were kept separate in living arrangements, as well as meeting houses, and interactions between male and female were strictly monitored. It appears the resulting repressed sexual energy may have been converted into creative energy, accounting for the highly industrious nature that has so characterized the Shakers.

If indeed sexual energy became industrious energy, the Shakers must have harbored a great deal of libidinous vigor. Mother Ann reputedly composed the motto "Hands to Work, Heart to God," which became a theme for Shaker handiwork. The Shakers regarded their labors as prayer in practice, and their aim toward perfection could be seen no clearer than in the fruits of those labors. The Believers became known for their quality carpentry and architecture, creating buildings and furniture short on ornamentation, but long on sturdiness and functionality. They developed potent skills in weaving and sewing, and found success in selling seeds and herbal medicines. One particular concoction, "Syrup of Sarsaparilla" by Dr. Thomas Corbett, became popular throughout the country. The inventions of the clothespin, the circular saw, and the flat-edge broom are all attributable to the Shakers.

Ann Lee died on September 8, 1784, nearly a year after completing her New England missionary sojourn. The administrative center of the Shaker religion moved to New Lebanon, New York by 1787. Under the leaders following Mother Ann — including men and women such as James Whittaker, Joseph Meachem, Frederick Evans, and Anna White — literacy, order, and organization were added to the initial inspiration and dedication of Mother Ann. Geographic consolidation replaced itinerant evangelism, with an emphasis toward inward community stability over the recruitment of new members. Additional converts regularly replaced young Believers who could not bear the restrictions of celibacy and communal living; Shakers frequently welcomed orphans into the security of the Village.

In its 1840s heyday, the United Society of Believers boasted a membership of more than 6000. Nineteen villages accommodating an average population of 300 Believers were spread from Maine to Kentucky, from Massachusetts to Indiana. The roll of Shaker Villages included New Lebanon, New York; Canterbury, New Hampshire; Pleasant Hill, Kentucky; Sabbathlake, Maine; Hancock, Massachusetts; and Watervliet, New York, the new name for Niskayuna.

The decline of the Shaker Villages began chiefly in the dawn of the Industrial Age, after the close of the Civil War. The Believers' costly, intricate handicrafts could not compete with the cheap mass production and distribution of the factories. By 1910, many of the Villages had completely closed, with most remaining Believers finding their way into mainstream society.

Currently, perhaps a dozen or two Shakers live much as they had in 1840, awaiting the revival Mother Ann had predicted 70 years previously. New Hampshire's Canterbury Shaker Village, and Sabbathday Lake Village in Maine remain essentially as living museums. Visitors can tour the village structures and marvel at the simple beauty of the Shaker lifestyle and craftsmanship.

Meanwhile, seven miles northwest of Albany at Watervliet, much of the Niskayuna dwelling place has been converted into the Albany Airport. What remains of Niskayuna's structures have been purchased by private entities, or converted into the Ann Lee County Home, a residential home for the elderly. Only the original graveyard — marking the resting place of Mother Ann, her brother, and other noted Shakers — remind the observer where the Shaking in America began: at Niskayuna, the birthplace of the United Society of Believers.

Sources

Burns, Ken. *America*. "The Shakers: Hands to Work, Heart to God." 1989, Florentine Films.

Filley, Dorothy M. *Recapturing Wisdom's Valley*. 1975, Shaker Heritage Society.

Horgan, Edward R. *The Shaker Holy Land: A Community Portrait*. 1982, The Harvard Common Press, Harvard, Massachusetts.

Stein, Stephen J. *The Shaker Experience in America*. 1992, Yale University Press, New Haven.

CANE RIDGE MEETING HOUSE

Affiliation: Christian Church (Disciples of Christ)
Location: Bourbon County, seven miles east of Paris, Kentucky
1791

Future American religious historians may well look upon and remember the 1980s as the decade of the evangelist. Under the encouragement of a highly conservative executive branch, the American public became inundated by the images of a trove of television proselytizers: Jimmy Swaggart, on his knees, tears streaming from his eyes, paternity suits hounding his heels; Jim and Tammy Bakker, leading the videotaped congregation in spiritual hymns, while evading the IRS and its tax collectors — all the while, black mascara flowing down Tammy's chubby cheeks; Oral Roberts, recruiting viewers to his gospel university; Jerry Falwell extolling the virtues of his Moral Majority, which (in the view of many) was neither a majority nor particularly moral. Graham, Schuller, Scott, Bryant; the cavalcade gamboled on. Viewers could scarcely flip their remotes without images of these media ministers infiltrating the very soul of the true American pastime.

However, this cacophony of electronic evangelists — with all their accompanying effects, admonitions, hallelujas — cannot hold a candle to the spiritual spectacle which shook central Kentucky in the summer of 1801. Without the aid of editing and rewriting, of dramatic camera angles and studio audiences, there occurred an evangelistic extravaganza so exhilarating its effects can be felt to this day, among the Bourbon County canebrakes and far beyond.

In the flat green acreage surrounding the Cane Ridge Meeting House, eight miles southeast of Paris, Kentucky, in the humid summer days between August 7 and August 12, they came. Some were spiritual seekers, following revival after revival, chautauqua after chautauqua, on a quest to fill the religious void which empties their lives. Others considered themselves the faithful, who simply could not get their fill of the good news; who reveled in the fellowship of brethren believers. The curiosity seekers, who sought to discern the motives behind the revelry, joined in the festivities. Among them also roamed the hecklers, the jokers, the critics, and the loiterers, all of whom apparently had nothing better to do. They gathered in droves on these hot August nights, forming the largest revival in the great line of revivals presented during the Great American Protestant Awakening of the late 18th and early 19th centuries. Observers estimated anywhere from 10,000 to 30,000 people traveled from all over the East and Midwest, to attend the Cane Ridge Revival.

Ministers from the Presbyterian, Methodist, and Baptist churches preached before small conclaves of the multitudes: from rotting stumps, fallen tree trunks, horse-drawn wagons, and make-shift platforms, they sermonized and admonished, cajoled and exulted, often all at the very same time. The preachers expounded on the themes of fundamental biblical adherence, Christian unity, and heart-felt acceptance of the Holy Spirit. As many as 3000 to 5000 individuals reportedly made their confession of faith right there, many displaying involuntary physical convulsions as evidence of their heart-felt conversions: They jerked and twitched, barked and bayed, sang and chanted, cried like babies, and they fainted dead away, often remaining unconscious for hours on end. The revival persisted over six days, and might have continued longer, had the revivalists not run out of food to share, and the horses not stripped the meadows bare of grass.

In the end, thousands of Protestants had reaffirmed the vigor of their faith, and the members of the host Cane Ridge Meeting House prepared to transform their congregation into a new, fundamentally awakened Protestant Church.

One of the chief organizers of the Great Revival of 1801 was a man named Barton Wallace Stone. Born in Port Tobacco, Maryland, in 1772, Stone studied for the Presbyterian ministry as a young man. An introspective, independent thinker, Stone harbored developing doubts concerning the veracity of Presbyterianism, its organization and practices, even as he prepared for his calling. Nevertheless, Stone completed his ecclesiastical instructions, and accepted the call to the Cane Ridge Meeting House of the Springfield Presbytery in 1798. Even then, he reportedly informed the Kentucky Synod that he would abide by the Westminster Confession of Faith (*the* doctrinal statement of Presbyterianism) only as long as he agreed it remained consistent with the word of God.

The Cane Ridge Meeting House originated under the direction of North Carolina's Reverend Robert W. Finley in 1791, a decade after the Presbyterian congregation was founded at the site in present-day Bourbon County. The

Cane Ridge Meeting House, Bourbon County, Kentucky. (Courtesy Cane Ridge Preservation Project.)

meeting house, established in an area recommended by pioneer explorer Daniel Boone, lies among the canebrakes (wild, twig-like reeds) which grow along a 15-mile ridge in the lowlands of central Kentucky. The Meeting House, then and now, remains the largest one-room log structure built in the United States.

Blue ash logs comprised the Cane Ridge Meeting House, cut from the surrounding forest. It encompassed an area 50 feet long, 30 feet wide, and 15 feet high, with three huge, 16-inch-square timber girders supporting the ceiling. A boxed pulpit stood at the north alcove, elevated high above the sanctuary, adding an air of authority to the preacher as he sternly gazed downward upon the congregation. Dirt comprised the original floor; split

logs provided the original pews. The spaces between logs contained no chinking, enabling members to keep a watchful eye open for hostile Shawnee and Cherokee Indians, who resented the white man's intrusion into their ancient hunting lands.

After the 1801 revival, whatever doubts Stone held concerning the Presbyterian Church had grown into full-blown rebellion. At the same time, the controversial revival incited the Springfield Presbytery authorities to question the beliefs of Stone and his followers. The Presbytery's inquiries in turn further incited Stone to question his loyalty toward the church. Stone actually approached the Kentucky Synod to offer his resignation as minister of Cane Ridge. But so great was his loyal following at the meeting house, the congregation chose to join him in his departure from the larger church, rather than lose him as their leader and spiritual guide. In June of 1805, Stone and five fellow Presbyterian ministers involved in the revival withdrew from Presbyterian fellowship, and organized an independent church, the members of which they called simply "Christians." This Christian Church accepted principles of universal salvation, the Bible as the fundamental source of truth and guidance; baptism by immersion, open communion, local congregational self-rule, the eventual reunion of all churches, and the divinity of Christ.

As a testimony to their dissatisfaction with and departure from the Presbyterian Church, Stone and his followers wrote the "Last Will and Testament of Springfield Presbytery," on June 28, 1804. The document signaled the end of Cane Ridge Meeting House as a Presbyterian place of worship. The "Last Will" specified the ways in which the newly organized church would deviate from Presbyterian practices. The transformed congregation would endeavor to eliminate divisions between Christians; they would refuse to recognize the title of "Reverend," asserting anyone assuming fervent study of the bible qualified for the ministry. The new church would consult the simple Gospel for their spiritual guidance; they would govern their own church, without the benefit or intrusion of a larger organizational body. In short, Stone and his congregation declared emancipation from the Presbyterian Church: "We will that the Synod of Kentucky examine every member who may be suspected of having departed from the Confession of Faith, and suspend every heretic immediately; in order that the oppressed may go free, and taste the sweets of gospel liberty."

In 1807, Stone and his followers rebaptized themselves in their new faith, in Stone Creek near Paris, Kentucky.

In 1824, Barton Wallace Stone met Alexander Campbell. Scottish brothers Alexander and Thomas Campbell had started a similar movement away from the Presbyterian Church in 1809 in western Pennsylvania. The Campbellites followed the Baptist Church for a time, eventually veering in their own direction. In their 1824 meeting, Alexander and Stone rec-

ognized the similarity of their movements and convictions. They began a concerted effort to unite their congregations, toward the ultimate goal of unifying all who called themselves disciples of Jesus Christ. In 1832, at Hill Street Church in Lexington, Kentucky, the Stone Movement and the Campbellite Movement combined to form the Christian Church. Today, the church is known as the Disciples of Christ, which claims more than two million members.

Over the years, the Cane Ridge congregation modified the original log structure of the Meeting House in several ways. At its original construction, the Meeting House sanctuary featured an upper gallery located in the back, created for slaves, who would access the gallery by climbing a rickety wooden ladder. Although Cane Ridge became an abolitionist church in 1795, the gallery, which continued to separate blacks from whites, remained until 1829. The gallery was then removed to a nearby barn, where it was installed as a hay loft.

By 1882, the congregation of the log church enlarged the window openings, installing glass panes. Builders nailed weather boarding to the outside, and coated the inside walls with plaster. They installed the present floor and pews, and relocated the pulpit from the north alcove to inside of the main door. A pot belly stove now warmed the meeting house from the middle of the sanctuary, and a pipe organ accompanied the congregation's hymns for the first time.

In 1932, 100 years after the Stonite and Campbellite factions joined forces, the Meeting House returned structurally to its original 1791 form, including the replacement of the African-American gallery. In 1954, to protect the refurbished meeting house, a superstructure forged of local limestone was fabricated around the meeting house exterior, preserving it for ages to come.

Barton Wallace Stone moved in 1734 to Jacksonville, Illinois, his residence for the last ten of his 72 years. He died as he lived, engaged in a preaching mission in Hannibal, Missouri, in 1844. His remains and those of his first wife, Eliza Campbell Stone, were exhumed three years later, and moved to the little fenced graveyard outside the Cane Ridge Meeting House.

Today, visitors from around the country and the world come to view the Meeting House. They learn of the life and influence of Barton Wallace Stone, the development of the Disciples of Christ, and the Great Cane Ridge Revival of 1801, the tumult from which hum-bles even the most elaborate modern ministry telecasts.

Sources

Kleber, John E. *The Kentucky Encyclopedia.* 1992, The University Press of Kentucky.

McGuire, Franklin. *Cane Ridge.* March 1995, Cane Ridge, Kentucky.

Thompson, Rhodes. *Old Cane Ridge Meeting House.*

MOTHER BETHEL CHURCH

Affiliation: African Methodist Episcopal
Location: Philadelphia, Pennsylvania
1796

Richard Allen looked forward to his new assignment at St. George's Episcopal Church in 1786. An impassioned, eloquent preacher, he would lead morning and evening prayer services at the church. His articulate charisma had drawn a sizable following to his prayer services. His calling to St. George's fulfilled what had been his lifelong mission: to preach the Gospel wholeheartedly among his people. But before long, as he realized the gulf existing between the free African and true freedom, even this new opportunity would not be enough.

It had been a long road for Allen. Born on February 14, 1760, he was one of four children of slave parents belonging to a Benjamin Chew of Maryland. When Allen reached age four, Chew sold his family to a Mr. Stokely at a plantation near Dover, and Allen spent the remainder of his childhood in the area of Philadelphia and Delaware.

At the age of 17, Allen experienced a spiritual conversion, and soon joined the local Methodist society. Mr. Stokely, living within the influence of Quakers of Pennsylvania, regarded Allen with more leniency and tolerance than most slave owners. He allowed Allen to invite Methodist ministers to the plantation, and Allen began studying Methodist Christianity in earnest. He learned to read and write as well. He began visiting other slaves in the area, preaching and sharing his conversion episode among them. He converted his family, and met regularly with other African Methodists, both slave and free, in the forests and fields about the Dover countryside.

Methodism — named for its methodical manners of worship and ritual — particularly attracted African Americans of the 18th century, as well as other common people raised under the influence of the Episcopal (meaning "government by bishops") Church of England. Under John Wesley, a priest of the Church of England and a student of Oxford, the Methodist movement began in 1739, as an effort to bring the Church of England closer to the common people. Wesley, alienated by the ritual and pomp of the English Church, never intended to forsake the Church of England, but merely bring it "on the road" to the people.

The movement came to America in 1766 in the person of Philip Embury, a Wesleyan Methodist preacher from Ireland. The First Methodist Episcopal Church in America opened on John Street in New York City in 1768. In 1784, Methodism broke from the Church of England, when Wesley took it upon himself to ordain two deacons — something, according to the English Church, only the bishops could do.

As Allen was steeped in the Methodist manner, he did not rebel against Mr. Stokely. Instead, he became determined to show Stokeley how a Christian laborer could work harder and more efficiently than a non-believer. As a reward for Allen's efforts in 1777, Stokely allowed Allen to earn wages on the plantation, with which he could eventually purchase his freedom. By the end of the year, he did just that, for 60 pounds silver and gold, or approximately $2000.

As a free man, Allen worked as bricklayer, a wood chopper, a shoemaker, and a wagon driver in Delaware. He showed increasing signs of a mystical, spiritually fervent personality, spending much of his waking hours in prayer, meditation, and study of the Bible.

In 1783, Allen began traveling among the Africans of the area, preaching and leading prayer groups between Delaware and Philadelphia. Well versed in Methodism, Allen worked as "helper" for itinerant Methodist preachers. In those days, itinerant preachers received callings into service by "circuits" covering specific geographical areas. Accompanied by horses and helpers, the preachers traversed the highways, homes, farms, and fields of the circuit, in an effort to reach the ordinary people. Although Allen preached and led services alongside and in place of the minister, he never actually attained recognition as an ordained minister.

In 1784, Methodist Bishop Francis Ashbury tried to persuade Richard Allen to accompany him on an evangelical trip to Virginia and the Carolinas. Allen would be paid in food and drink, but would often be forced to sleep in the carriage, as accommodations for Africans in the south were difficult to attain. In his first act of advocacy for himself and his people, Richard Allen refused to accompany Ashbury without the recognition, pay, and proper treatment of a minister.

During his travels, Allen had preached in Radnor, Pennsylvania. The people of Radnor welcomed and admired him as a skillful, passionate, and influential preacher, and his services became known for the frequent demonstrations of faith and excitement among the participants. When one of the elders from the Radnor church became an elder in Philadelphia, he sent for Allen to preach in the city.

Finally in 1786, Richard Allen arrived at St. George's Methodist Episcopal Church in Philadelphia. He began his ministry sermonizing by appointment. Soon he preached at least twice a day, conducting prayer meetings for the Africans in the church. His meetings drew more and more followers, until he maintained a consistently large constituency. His large following concerned many of the Caucasian members of the church, who grew increasingly wary of gatherings of Africans.

In the 18th century, African Americans were referred to as Africans, just as Germans, Swedes, Irish, and Polish were known by those designations. The term Negro did not become popular until the 19th century. Largely through the influence of the Quakers, the treatment of Africans in Pennsylvania became considerably more humane than in other states. A substantial anti-slavery sentiment had developed within the Quaker State. The Methodists, as well, grew more staunch in their abolitionist stance. Methodism eventually outlawed slavery among preachers and members; John Wesley himself called slavery the "Sum of all villainy."

But while European Americans could easily advocate for African Americans slaves, free Africans presented another matter. As with other immigrant groups who had come to America, much of the prejudice experienced by free Africans was based on economics. Free Africans presented competition to residents for paying jobs, whereas slaves did not. By 1790, Africans constituted 20 percent of the Pennsylvania population; and although freed from the bondage of slavery, the tyrannies of fear and bigotry still held them fast.

Unfortunately, the bigotry spilled over into the churches, including St. George's Methodist Episcopal. Africans were often required to take seats in the rear or in the gallery, apart from the European members. They were made to wait to take communion until the Europeans finished. They were also prohibited from gathering for prayer and meetings independently of the Europeans, who grew increasingly paranoid of African conspiracies. Although

Window at Mother Bethel AME Church in Philadelphia honors the church's founder, Richard Allen.

Richard Allen and other Africans historically tolerated these injustices, the time would come when they would tolerate no more.

The time came sooner than expected, on a Sunday morning in November 1787. Richard Allen and a man named Absalom Jones, a successful businessman and prominent member of the Philadelphia African community and Methodist Church, joined a small group of African Americans for services at St. George's Church. Entering the sanctuary, they headed for the back of the church, where they customarily gathered in deference to the white members. Allen and his companions had not realized the church elders had changed the African's seating from along the walls, to the gallery above the church floor. As the men found their pews, the church sexton instructed them to move. The Africans assumed they should move to the front of the sanctuary, where they knelt down to pray as the service began.

Intent on his prayers, Absalom Jones suddenly felt a firm hand on his shoulder, which tried to pull him up off his knees. A pair of trustees ordered him and his friends to leave. Jones implored the trustees to wait until the prayer ended, but they would not. Humiliated before the whole of the church, Jones, Allen, and the other Africans left the church, determined to never allow such an incident to happen again.

This incident led to the establishment of the Free African Society in Philadelphia, founded by Jones and Allen for the purpose of lending emotional and economic support to the Africans of Philadelphia. Absalom Jones led part of the society to found St. Thomas Episcopal Church, in July 17, 1796. But Richard Allen, in order to pursue the Methodism he had studied and believed in for so many years, led his own followers to form a separate church. With money he saved from his shoemaking business, and other funds raised among his followers, Allen bought a plot of land on Sixth and Lombard streets in Philadelphia. He moved a blacksmith shop to the lot, converted it into a church, and named it Mother Bethel African Methodist Episcopal Church. It was dedicated on July 29, 1796. Mother Bethel Church became a center for worship and assembly, as well as a haven for Africans in Philadelphia. In October of 1796, the church opened "the African School for the free instruction of the Black people." Allen's belief in the necessity of education for African Americans would remain a staple throughout the development of the church.

Mother Bethel Church remained under the auspices of the Methodist Church for 20 more years. In January of 1816, a court ruling declared Mother Bethel's independence when a white preacher from St. George's sued the African church for not allowing him to preach at Mother Bethel against the will of the congregation. The Pennsylvania Supreme Court declared Bethel a separate entity, which could not be forced into a decision by the Methodist Church against the will of Mother Bethel's members.

By then other African Methodist Episcopal churches — including another named Bethel, established in Baltimore by Daniel Coker in 1801 — had formed throughout the country. They followed Mother Bethel's impetus and, gathering in Philadelphia in April 1816, they agreed to form the national African Methodist Episcopal (AME) Church, the first national church developed strictly for African Americans. Richard Allen was elected the first bishop of the AME churches, the first African American bishop of any denomination in the history of the United States.

Today, the African Methodist Episcopal Church boasts more than a million members throughout the United States and the world.

A second prominent figure in African Methodist Episcopal Church history became Bishop of Georgia in 1880, 64 years after the establishment of the national AME Church. However, unlike Richard Allen, this man would not be satisfied with merely a separate church for his people. Frustrated and embittered by a lifetime of injustice and humiliation, he campaigned actively for one of the most controversial and compelling ideas in the history of African Americans, and in the long, bitter struggle between black and white in the United States. He advocated for emigration to Africa, the return of the African to the homeland. The bishop's name was Henry MacNeal Turner.

While a young minister in training in 1858, Turner attended a special program at Bethel AME Church in Baltimore, Maryland. The speaker of the day was an AME missionary to Liberia, Africa, named Alexander Crummel. A fiery speaker often quoted in the white press, Crummel testified to what he considered a most essential endeavor: the emigration of former slaves to Africa, as a redemption for the soul and dignity of the people. The sermon captured the young Turner's heart and imagination, and fueled a spiritual fire which would burn the rest of his life.

By 1858, Liberia had been an independent nation on the west coast of Africa for more than twenty-five years. The American Colonization Society, established by and for former American slaves, organized the settlement in 1822, naming the capital Monrovia after the current President, James Monroe. Over the next two decades, other colonies of ex-slaves took root in Liberia as well. In 1847, the colonies amalgamated, and formed the first independent republic in Africa. When Turner heard this story, Liberia became for him the answer for all Africans suffering oppression in America.

Henry MacNeal Turner was free born in 1834, in either Georgia or South Carolina. He ran away from the cotton fields where he apprenticed, working side by side with slaves. He worked in various capacities, meanwhile learning surreptitiously to read and write, as it was illegal for Africans to attain literacy in the South. In 1858, while working in New Orleans, he discovered the African Methodist Episcopal Church, and trained for the ministry in Baltimore and Washington, D.C.

During the 1860s, Turner attempted to secure several prominent government positions, by which he learned the bitter realities of life for free Africans in America. In 1868, he won election to the Georgia state legislature, but he was disqualified because Africans could not legally hold office. He applied to be a United States minister to Haiti, but failed for unspecified reasons. He actually became the first African postmaster in Georgia, but faced dismissal under false charges of fraud and corruption. Frustrated by his attempts to work in the public sector, he retreated to a career with the AME Church.

As a minister, and a literate minister at that, for the AME, Turner soon received the assignment as manager of publishing concerns for the national church. Through this position, Turner gained access to a considerable readership, with whom he could share his radical views. He possessed a dominating personality, with a biting tongue and a pungent vocabulary, both of which became readily evident in his speaking and writing.

Turner's experiences in the workplace convinced him of the hopelessness of life for Africans in America. He felt the African could never rely on the whites for any advantage, but had to gain it for himself. But in order to gain any advantages, Turner knew the African would have to hold power, own businesses, administer the government. Such opportunities, Turner believed, could only develop in a nation such as Liberia, where Africans were respected as full citizens.

Henry MacNeal Turner conceded the United States as the white man's nation, and entreated Africans to leave the country, and return to the fatherland. He urged blacks not to trust whites, nor to fight in any war for a country which did not recognize their full rights as human beings. He equated the African emigration to Liberia with the Pilgrims' flight to America. He visualized Liberia as the true "American Dream," and pressed for 5000 to 10,000 emigrants to Africa per year. Critics, meanwhile, charged that the kind of Africans Turner wanted in Liberia were the same Africans needed to improve the situation in America.

In 1880, Henry MacNeal Turner became Bishop of Georgia for the AME Church, one of 12 bishops nationwide. For the next ten years he tirelessly championed the emigration to Africa until finally, in a culmination of his dream, the AME Church sent Turner on a good will tour of Liberia.

On the tour, Turner discovered the reality of West Africa. Liberians survived in a marginally subsistent economy, indebted to European powers, and unable to police its own borders. With a hot and humid climate, and low, swampy lands, plagues of malaria killed the natives as well as the American immigrants. The new nation was hardly the Utopia Turner envisioned, but a hard frontier which the settlers still struggled to tame.

Turner remained undaunted. Despite the hardships, the bishop continued to implore African Americans to come to Liberia. He reported the Liberian "has manhood, freedom, liberty; he feels like a lord, and he walks the same way."

Several attempts emerged to organize mass emigrations to Liberia, particularly in the 1890s. At one point, legislation appeared in Congress to finance such an emigration, but it never advanced beyond committee. The Liberian movement never caught on to the degree Turner hoped, until it all but disappeared in the 20th century.

Henry MacNeal Turner died in 1915, without seeing his dream realized. But through his life and efforts, he called attention to the horrific plight of African Americans. Like Richard Allen, he paved the way for future advocates in the African Methodist Episcopal Church for many years to come.

Sources

Bishop, Peter, and Michael Darton. *The Encyclopedia of World Faiths: An Illustrated Survey of the World's Living Religions.* Facts on File Publishers, 1987, New York.

Redkey, Edwin S. *Black Exodus: Black Nationalists and the Back to Africa Movement, 1890–1918.* 1969, Yale University Press, New Haven.

Wesley, Charles. *Richard Allen: Apostle of Freedom.* 1969, The Associated Publishers, Inc., Washington D.C.

MISSION NUESTRA SEÑORA DE LA SOLEDAD

Affiliation: Roman Catholic
Location: California, 3 miles south of Soledad, near King City
1797

Santa Barbara features the beautiful Queen of the Missions, with its majestic twin towers and pink Roman facade. The Great Stone Church and the legendary swallows draw thousands of admirers to San Juan Capistrano. Carmel cradles San Carlos Borromeo, the magnificent Moorish-style Basilica, the final resting place for Friar Junipero Serra. San Francisco has the Mission Dolores, which served as the cornerstone to the fiery, west coast city. San Diego features San Diego de Alcala, whose stark white facade commemorates the beginning of the Alta California era.

Nuestra Señora de la Soledad, in contrast, stands amid the lettuce fields and farm equipment of the sparsely populated, rural and agricultural southern Salinas Valley. Its closest significant neighbor is the infamous Soledad State Correctional Facility. For nearly two centuries the mission ruins stood isolated, desolate, forgotten, and ignored, the victim of a glaring sun and an unforgiving wind. Other

missions found fame and accolades as monuments to the past, and centerpieces to great communities. Yet, in many ways, Mission Nuestra Señora de la Soledad exemplified the true experience of the Spanish Alta California Franciscan Missions: projects of great hope, expectation, and salvation; outposts for a vast yet overextended empire, which eventually fell to years of revolt, ruin, and despair.

In the summer of 1769 a small party of men, including Father Juan Crespi, and Captain (soon to be Governor) Gaspar de Portola of the Spanish military, stopped to make camp in a brown, dusty, sun-baked valley, some 40 miles southeast of Monterey Bay. Looking about them, the men could see little in any direction but miles and miles of lifeless clay, with precious few trees dotting the landscape. While camped at the bank of the muddy Salinas River, the party was approached by a small band of Indians, who managed to forge an existence in this valley. One of the Indian women

Mission Nuestra Señora de la Soledad in California's Salinas Valley. (Photograph by Penni Thorpe.)

reportedly uttered to the Spaniards a word that sounded like "soledad," which is the Spanish term for "solitude." It seemed no site in California had ever received a more appropriate designation.

Looking to establish a midpoint between Mission San Carlos to the north and Mission San Antonio to the south, the Franciscan Fathers decided to erect a mission on this lonely site 21 years after Crespi and Portola found it. Father Fermin Lausen, compatriot and successor to Father-President Junipero Serra, founded Mission Nuestra Señora de la Soledad on October 9, 1791. It is the 13th Alta California mission, and is named for Our Lady of Solitude, one of the designations for the Virgin Mary.

Despite the unlikely location, the mission met with some success in its first years. The first thatch-roofed church originated in 1797, and was enlarged in 1805. The final mission building took the familiar mission quadrangle shape, complete with Indian work station, carpentry shop, blacksmith area, and padres' quarters. (The building that stands today is a recreation of the small chapel flanked by the long padres' quarters.) For more than a century, the mission stood as the only substantial building in the vicinity.

The Indians who visited the mission belonged to the Costanoan, Salinan, and Essalen tribes. Although none of the tribes lived in the immediate vicinity, they all seemed to visit the valley on a regular basis, perhaps to gather food or to trade among themselves. Despite a relatively small native population from which to draw, mission records claimed the padres attracted a neophyte (baptized Indian) population of 727 by 1805. Under the direction of the padres, the neophytes successfully channeled the Salinas River for irrigation, and a healthy array of crops sprung forth. The padres and Indians raised and tended horses, nearly 1000 cattle, and several thousand sheep. The neophytes supplied the labor for the construction of the mission buildings. They crafted and painted many of the beautiful icons and decorations used in the chapel. The bright, fervent colors of the church reredos and walls were formed through the use of berries, lichens, and other natural hues. By 1820, at the peak of its popularity, Mission Soledad boasted a convert population of 2000. But a series of catastrophes ensued, shortly leading to the desolation and decay of the mission.

Three times, between 1824 and 1832, rain poured over the flat Salinas Valley, causing the Salinas River to overrun its banks, and spread across the flood plain on which Mission Soledad stood. Each flood destroyed the mission chapel, ruined its crops, drowned its livestock; the final flood tolled the death knell for the mission.

At the same time, a scourge of European diseases created epidemics, decimating the Indian populations at Soledad and throughout Alta California. Nearly one third of the original Indian population (estimated at 300,000) along the Mission Trail died from measles, chicken pox, malaria, influenza, and other foreign-born viruses. With the sickness came fear and despair from the Indians, who could not believe the Christian god could be good if its priests could bring such terrible sorrow. The neophytes fled in fright, bringing an end to the gathered faithful. Those who did not flee suffered from hunger as the flood-ravaged fields, baked dry by the sun and the hot wind, no longer produced food.

Finally, in May of 1835, Father Vicente Francisco de Sarria, the beloved stalwart of the mission who had been named first Father-Comisario of the mission, fell victim to the tragedy the mission he loved had become. Unwilling to abandon his sacred post, Sarria died of malnutrition while saying Mass. He simply could not get enough to eat. His death marked the final blow. The remaining Indians scattered, and the mission was skeletonized.

The Republic of Mexico (formerly New Spain) revolted against Spanish rule in 1810, substantially ending the era of a Spanish Empire in North America. The Mexican government gradually took over much of the land in Alta California. Over the next two decades, secularization removed the missions from the hands of the Franciscans. Although the Franciscans originally hoped to leave the mission compounds to the Indians, under the Mexican government the land was sold to secular interests and more often than not, abandoned. In Mission Soledad's case, the roof was sold off immediately, to pay off debts borne by the Mexican government. Eventually the mission itself was sold in 1846 by the Mexican governor for $800. After serving as a ranch house for a few years, Soledad fell into disrepair. For 90 years, the crumbling adobe stood in the dust, alone, solitary, "soledad," a monument to an experiment gone awry.

Although each of the Alta California missions have been restored, the original purpose, to civilize the Alta California natives in preparation for the extension of Spanish Colonies, came to an abrupt end within a short four decades.

The Alta California chain of missions, most of which became the cornerstones of great cities and communities in California, began in 1769 with the establishment of Mission San Diego de Alcala, founded by famed Father Junipero Serra. Serra also founded the missions San Carlos Borromeo de Carmelo at Carmel (1770), San Antonio de Padua (1771), San Gabriel Archangel (1771), San Luis Obispo de Tolosa (1772), San Juan Capistrano (1776), San Francisco de Asis (1776), Santa Clara de Asis (1777), and San Buenaventura in Ventura (1782). The missions that followed Serra's death in 1784 include Santa Barbara (1786), La Purisima Concepcion (1787), Santa Cruz (1791), Nuestra Señora de Soledad (1791), San Jose (1797), San Juan Bautista (1797), San Fernando Rey de Espana (1797), San Miguel Archangel (1797), San Luis Rey de Francia (1798), Santa Ines (1804), San Rafael Archangel (1817), and San Francisco Solano (1823). In all, 21 missions were built along a 532-mile pathway known as the King's Highway, El Camino Real.

In 1988, Pope John Paul II granted Father Junipero Serra (founder of the Alta California Missions) beatification, the second step towards full canonization, the Catholic Church's full declaration of sainthood. With the impending prospect of a Saint Serra, the great wave of controversy continues to swell around the Alta California Mission Chain and the constructive and destructive forces that came to bear among them.

Mission supporters say Serra and his padres were holy and humble men, who fervently believed in the sacredness of this great mission:

to bring the knowledge of the church and Christ to the unfortunate, unenlightened natives. The Franciscans brought civilization to the west, along with all its advantages: agriculture, architecture, crafts, medicine and education; technology and world knowledge. The Alta California missions provided the cornerstones to the great community that would become California. Serra supporters beg critics to view the Alta California missions in context of the times, in which they point out that the treatment of the American Indians was more cruel under regimes other than those of the Franciscan Fathers. Actually, many blame the cruelty experienced by the Indians on the Spanish military, whose Presidios accompanied the establishment of mission after mission.

In dispute of these claims, critics simply offer the marked and unmarked graves of the Indians within their territories, such as the Costanoan community near Mission Soledad.

Among the Penutian linguistic family of Native Americans, the Costanoan Indians occupied the geographical area from Marin County to Point Sur, and east to the Salinas Valley, centuries before the Christian Era even began.

They fished, hunted, gathered food, and lived in earthen huts. They traded regularly among neighboring California tribes, such as the Maidu, the Miwok, the Wintun, the Patwin, the Wintu, and the Yokuts.

When the Spaniards arrived, the Indians provided most of the labor for the construction and art work going into the mission compounds and churches (all of which, by the way, have been designated as historical landmarks). But in return, say critics, the Franciscan missions served as a virtual penal system for the natives. Indians were denied food for minor infractions, endured corporal punishment for missing religious services, and were forbidden to leave the mission complex once they were baptized. Natives often faced severe torture for practicing traditional religious rituals; tortures included slow roasting over fires, or garroting, the practice of slow strangulation through the twisting and tightening of rope around the neck. White soldiers and settlers habitually stole supplies and food from the Indians, and raped and accosted the women of the tribes.

When Indians fled the mission in the wake of cruelty and/or epidemic, they were often hunted down by the military, and dragged back to the missions as captives. At one point the Costanoan population numbered more than 7000. Yet, in less than 75 years, because of the intrusion into their land and their lifestyle, the Costanoans disappeared.

Franciscan records tout more than 16,000 Indian converts among the 21 missions. Yet, it is highly likely the padres had often mistaken the uttering of creeds and the singing of hymns for the forsaking of an ancient way of belief and life. The sedentary lifestyle, agriculture, sin and salvation, heaven and hell, a hierarchical universe; these were foreign concepts to native people who revered mother earth, respected all creation as equal, enjoyed pleasure for pleasure's sake, and wandered as a means towards sustenance. As one of the friars at the time observed, the Indians "live well free but as soon as we reduce them to a Christian and

community life ... they fatten, sicken, and die." (People in the West, p. 3)

In 1954, concerted efforts began to restore the compound at Nuestra Señora de la Soledad. Today, the Mission chapel and padres' quarters are rebuilt, appearing much like the 1832 complex, while ruins from the actual mission buildings remain close by. But while others among the Alta California missions have been incorporated into the bustling cities now surrounding them, Mission Soledad continues to stand in solitude, a quiet reminder of an empire that passed, and an ancient people that are no more.

Sources

A Sunset Book, *The California Missions: A Pictorial History*. 1979, Lane Publishing Company, Menlo Park, California.
Terrell, John Upton. *American Indian Almanac*. 1994, Barnes & Noble Books.
Lifetime Learning Systems. *People in the West: Junipero Serra*. 1996.

MOTHER SETON HOUSE

Affiliation: Roman Catholic, Franciscan
Location: 600 North Paca Street, Baltimore, Maryland
1808

The year 1803 was not a good one for Elizabeth Ann Bayley Seton. She had traveled to Livorno, Italy, with her husband of 11 years, William Magee Seton, who sought refuge from illness among his Italian friends there. They had left four of her five young children in the United States with relatives, taking only the oldest, Anna Maria, age eight. William Seton's business affairs had all but crumbled, and the stress of his work seemed to inalterably affect his already frail health. By the fall of 1803 his body was overcome with tuberculosis, and he died on December 27.

Barely 30 years old, Elizabeth Seton was now alone to fend for herself and her children. This turn of events might have crushed the spirits of many women or men. But instead of an ending, her husband's tragic death proved a new beginning for Seton. As is often the case

on the spiritual journey, the depths of despair brought new revelation and direction for the young New York native. In the coming years, she would not only succeed in supporting her family, but she would found the first American Catholic school, as well as the first American religious order for women. Seton herself would go on to lead a life so exemplary that in 1975, Pope Paul VI canonized her as America's first and only saint.

Elizabeth Ann Bayley was born on August 28, 1774, in the Battery district of New York City. She was the daughter of noted physician Dr. Richard Bayley and his wife Catherine Charlton Bayley, who died when Elizabeth was three. Her step-mother, Charlotte Barclay, whom Dr. Bayley married in 1778, apparently never accepted Elizabeth as her own, and actually distanced herself from

Elizabeth as the years passed. Ironically Elizabeth (who was called "Mother" for most of her history) lived essentially a motherless life.

Richard Bayley gained fame for his research of the feared yellow fever, or malaria. He enlisted as a surgeon with the British army during the Revolution and was stationed at Newport, Rhode Island. After the war, much of his time was occupied with his work and research in quarantine stations in New York City. Bayley's passion for his practice isolated him from his family during most of Elizabeth's formative years. Not until 1789, when Elizabeth was 15 and could correspond by letter during Dr. Bayley's absence, did the father/daughter relationship seem to blossom.

Raised in a comfortable Episcopalian home with little parental support, Elizabeth had an often lonely and introspective childhood. Though Dr. Bayley's financial success afforded her a fine academic and cultural education, including studies in French and music, she often clung to her Bible as her emotional bedrock. She spent many hours by herself, studying the Scriptures, developing a spiritual relationship with what she perceived as God. Although often kind, affectionate, and high spirited, Elizabeth's mood could quickly turn melancholy, and she often found herself enveloped in primitive, meditative, spiritual states. Even as a young woman, she seemed to be drawn to the possibility of a cloistered life. Still, Elizabeth Ann had grown into a dark-haired, dark-eyed, vivacious young woman, full of intelligence, affection, charisma, and grace. With few choices open to early 18th century women, life in affluent New York society set Elizabeth on the "normal" path of materialism, marriage, and motherhood.

Elizabeth Ann Bayley, age 16, met William Magee Seton, age 22, in the fall of 1790. Eldest son of William Seton, Sr., a wealthy New York merchant and financier, William Magee attended school and traveled extensively in Europe. He would inherit the management of his father's successful transatlantic import and export business. Handsome, charming, worldly, and wealthy, William Magee also bore an unfortunate family disposition toward consumption, or tuberculosis. Nevertheless, Elizabeth married William on January 25, 1794, at Trinity Episcopal Church in New York.

Over the next seven years, Elizabeth bore five children: Anna Maria (1795), William III (1796), Richard (1798), Catherine (1800), and Rebecca (1802). Elizabeth developed close relationships with William's Episcopalian family. While William attended his father's business, Elizabeth opened a boarding school at the Seton home on Stone Street in New York. Although a meager affair, this school afforded Elizabeth experience for future endeavors in Baltimore.

Although life progressed relatively happily for the Setons for four years, Elizabeth's cocoon began to crumble in 1799. After William Seton, Sr., died in 1798, the Seton business began to fail, and the family fortune collapsed. On the brink of poverty, William and Elizabeth were forced to move to a smaller home away from the wealthy neighborhood to which they had become accustomed. The sudden change in Elizabeth's lifestyle seemed to push her further away from the worldly and materialistic, and further toward the spiritual and ecclesiastic.

The collapse of William's business world greatly impeded his health. Racked with consumption, he could no longer focus on the task of rebuilding his livelihood. In an effort to improve his health, William accepted the invitation for respite from the Filippo Filicchi family in Livorno, Italy. The Filicchis and Setons had been business acquaintances and friends for many years. A prominent Catholic family in western Tuscany, the Filicchis offered welcomed comfort and hospitality to William and his wife and daughter.

On October 2, 1803, William, Elizabeth, and Anna Maria boarded the *Shepherdess,* leaving the other Seton children with relatives in America. After seven weeks at sea, they were quarantined for a month in a *lazaretto,* or sanitarium, outside Livorno due to a yellow fever scare. Finally, the family was quartered in Livorno as guests of the Filicchi's. William Magee Seton died of tuberculosis on December 27, 1803.

The passing of her role as wife seemed to mark a renewal of spiritual exploration for Elizabeth. While in Livorno for the next six months, Seton befriended Antonio Filicchi, younger brother of Fillippo. Antonio and his

wife Amabilia introduced Elizabeth to Catholicism, for which she seemed to hold a particular fascination. The young widow seemed particularly enraptured by the mysticism and grandeur of the Italian Catholic Churches, presented to her by the Filicchi family. The antiquity and spiritual ambiance of the Roman sanctuaries seemed to touch Elizabeth on an elemental, unintelligible level.

On January 8, 1804, after a visit to Florentine church *La Santissima Annunziata*, Elizabeth Seton entered in her journal:

> passing thro' a curtain my eye was struck with hundreds of people kneeling, but the gloom of the chapel which is lighted only by the wax tapers on the Altar and a small window at the top darkened with green silk made every object at first appear indistinct, while that kind of soft and distant musick which lifts the mind to a foretaste of heavenly pleasure called up in an instant every dear and tender idea of my Soul, and forgetting Mrs. Filicchi and companions, and all the surrounding scene I sunk to my Knees in the first place I found vacant, and shed a torrent of tears at the recollection of how long I had been a stranger in the house of my God, and the accumulated sorrow that had separated me from it. I need not tell you that I said our dear service with my whole soul as far as in its agitation I could recollect....
> [Kelly & Melville, 1987]

In Livorno, Elizabeth began her path toward Catholic conversion, with Antonio Filicchi as her personal sponsor and benefactor. She and Anna Maria, in the company of Filicchi, returned to New York in June of 1804. Her struggle with conversion became heightened by the bigotry and animosity between American Catholics and Protestants in the early 19th century. Estrangement developed between Elizabeth and the Seton clan. Nevertheless, under the guidance of Bishop John Carroll, to whom Elizabeth was introduced by Antonio Filicchi, and several prominent priests of New York, Elizabeth Ann Seton was baptized on March of 1805 at St. Peter's Catholic Church on Barclay Street in New York. With her conversion, the contemplation of eventual religious life began to re-emerge.

For the next three years, Elizabeth Seton lived off the generous support of the Filicchis, and the paltry earnings from yet another boarding school in New York. In the meantime, her two sons, William and Richard, through intercession by Bishop Carroll, enrolled at a Jesuit School for Boys in Georgetown, Virginia. At Elizabeth's request, Carroll arranged for Fr. William Dubourg to accompany the Seton boys on a visit to their mother in New York. Dubourg, a French Sulpician priest who later would gain appointment as Bishop of New Orleans, served as president of St. Mary's College in Baltimore. Through subsequent visits, Dubourg arranged for the transfer of William and Richard to St. Mary's, and offered an opportunity for Elizabeth to open a boarding school for girls on the St. Mary's campus.

In June of 1808, with money from the ever-generous Antonio Filicchi, Elizabeth Seton moved into the house which stands at 600 North Paca Street in Baltimore. A two story, French-style, red-brick home which Elizabeth Seton amusedly referred to as her "mansion," the House on Paca Street stood in the French section of Baltimore, right next to the chapel of St. Mary's College. This would be the first Catholic school for girls in America.

In the beginning, Seton enrolled seven students; by December of 1808, they would number ten, each paying a $200 tuition. Seton enlisted the aid of several teachers from St. Mary's School. The first two members of her religious community, Cecelia Conway and Maria Murphy, joined the House on Paca Street within the year. Seton's school offered a curriculum of reading, arithmetic, English and French, as well as needlework, music, and drawing. Sulpician Fr. Pierre Babade conducted religious education, and provided spiritual direction for Elizabeth.

The daily schedule for the girls' school proceeded as follows: :

6:00 A.M. to 9:00 A.M.— Chapel
9:00 A.M. to 1:00 P.M.— Classes
1:00 P.M. to 3:00 P.M.— Dinner
3:00 P.M. to 6:30 P.M.— Classes
6:30 P.M.— Chapel

Opposite: *Mother Seton House, Baltimore, Maryland. (Photograph by David Traub, courtesy Mother Seton House.)*

As her school developed over the next twelve months, Mother Seton, as she now was addressed by her students, began formulating plans for the establishment of a new religious order for American women. Knowing a larger facility would be needed, Seton enlisted the support of Fr. Dubourg, and a wealthy St. Mary's alumni named Samuel Cooper. With the financial support of Cooper, on June 21, 1809, Seton moved her embryonic school and community to the village of Emmitsburg in St. Joseph's Valley in north-central Maryland.

Patterned after the French Daughters of Charity established by St. Vincent de Paul, Elizabeth Ann Seton officially established her American Sisters of Charity order in Emmitsburg, Maryland. On July 19, 1813, sixteen women, including Cecelia Conway (Maria Murphy died in 1812), took their vows as Sisters of Charity, with Elizabeth Ann Seton as their Mother Superior. The title of Mother Seton (which had been associated with Elizabeth Seton nearly all her adult life) never seemed more appropriate.

After 47 years of hardships and triumphs, despair and spiritual enlightenment, motherhood and widowhood, and an overfamiliarity with death — which took both her daughters Anna and Rebecca before her — Mother Seton herself passed on January 4, 1821.

Over the next century and a half, the Catholic Church's tremendously laborious process of canonization inched along in the following route:

- 1882: James Cardinal Gibbons of Baltimore initiates the steps toward sainthood by saying Mass at Seton's tomb in Emmitsburg, Maryland.

- January 15, 1936: The Sacred Congregation of Rites declares no obstacle exists against the Cause of Canonization for Elizabeth Ann Seton.

- February 28, 1940: The Cause is formally introduced in 1940.

- December 18, 1959: After nineteen years of research and documentation, Pope John XXIII declares Elizabeth Ann Seton "Venerable," the first major step towards sainthood.

- March 17, 1963: After reviewing two miraculous cures attributed to her intercession Pope John XXIII beatifies Elizabeth Ann Seton. Mother Seton is called "Blessed," the second major step toward sainthood.

- September 14, 1975: After the Holy See verifies a third miraculous intercession by Mother Seton in 1963, Pope Paul IV declares, "We assign for Inclusion in the catalog of saints in heaven ... Blessed Elizabeth Ann, Widow Seton."

Thus, through the controversial process of canonization, completed one hundred fifty three years following her death, the Roman Catholic Church declares Mother Elizabeth Ann Bayley Seton the only American-born saint in its history. Since that time, the House on Paca Street has been known as Mother Seton House.

Sources

Bunson, Margaret and Matthew. *Lives of the Saints You Should Know*. 1996, Our Sunday Visitor, Inc, Huntington, Indiana.
Dirvin, Joseph I. *Mrs. Seton: Foundress of the American Sisters of Charity*. 1975, Farrar, Straus, and Giroux, New York.
Kelly, Ellin, and Annabelle Melville. *Elizabeth Seton: Selected Writings*. 1987, Paulist Press, New York.

SOCIETY OF CHRISTIAN UNITARIANS

Affiliation: Unitarian
Location: Philadelphia, Pennsylvania
1813

The roots of Unitarian thought began growing in Eastern Europe during the 16th century with antitrinitarian movements following the Protestant Reformation. These roots stretched to England, developing into the full-fledged Unitarian Church of England in the 1800s. The term Unitarian did not officially reach the New World, however, until a remarkable theologian turned scientist brought it with him to the City of Brotherly Love. The congregation he would form would eventually become the First Unitarian Church of Philadelphia.

During the Reformation, antitrinitarian viewpoints had sprung up in various places in 16th century Europe. Nineteen-year-old Michael Servetus challenged the precepts of the Trinity in a publication he called *The Errors of the Trinity*. He called the doctrine a mad delusion, saying it had no foundation in the Scriptures. Both the Catholic Church and Martin Luther himself condemned the paper; in the fashion of the times, Servetus burned at the stake for his efforts at enlightenment.

The antecedents of Unitarianism can be traced to Transylvania in the 1560s, where renowned theologian Francis David (aka David Ferenc, 1520–1579) founded the first congregation to use the term Unitarian. During roughly the same period, the Church of Poland, under the direction of cleric Faustus Socinus (1539–1604), adopted many tenets of the burgeoning Unitarian theosophy. Members of the Polish church came to be known as Socinians. They opposed the Trinitarian doctrine of the Roman Church, agreeing with Sertevus about the lack of a biblical basis for the doctrine. The Socinians also down played the divinity of Jesus, emphasizing rather the importance of his teachings. The Socinians fostered the ideals of freedom, rationality, and

tolerance in religion. These liberal lines of thought caught on in Romania, Hungary, and Austria, establishing dozens of communities following the Socinian antitrinitarian philosophy.

The counter-reformation suppressed Unitarian thought, as well as other forms of alternative concepts, in the 16th and 17th centuries, causing the disbursement of the Eastern Europe communities. But the followers spread the idea northward to England, where such personalities as Isaac Newton, John Biddle, and John Locke found the concepts intriguing. The movement remained disorganized until the 18th century, coalescing during Britain's Age of Dissension. Resigned Anglican Minister Theophilus Lindsey celebrated London's first Unitarian services at an auction house on April 17, 1774, delineating the tenets of the Unitarian Church of England:

> That there is One God, one single person, who is God, the sole creator and sovereign lord of all things.
> That the holy Jesus was a man of the Jewish nation, the servant of this God, highly honored and distinguished by him; and,
> That the Spirit, or Holy Spirit, is not a person, or intelligent being, but only the extraordinary power or gift of God....

Within the London audience sat celebrated American Colonial scholar, inventor, and statesman Benjamin Franklin, and a 41-year-old minister turned chemist named Joseph Priestly.

Priestly's active mind and liberal perspective found their expressions through the fields of science and theology. Though he reportedly never took a science course in his life, his newly developed friendship with the eminent Franklin seemed to stimulate his deductive curiosity in chemistry. Over the next decade,

Priestly proceeded in his makeshift Birmingham home laboratory, to make the following important biochemical discoveries:

- In 1767, Priestly discovered that graphite conducts electricity. Graphite is made of carbon, the primary ingredient comprising modern electrical resistors.

- In Birmingham, Priestly's home stood next to a brewery. While observing the brewing process, Priestly determined the gas emitted from the brewery vats could extinguish wood chips, and weighed more than normal air. This discovered gas would later be called carbon dioxide.

- In 1770, Priestly ascertained India gum could be used to rub out pencil marks. He called the gum rubber, and invented the first eraser.

- Priestly devised a method for producing the heavy gas he discovered in his home laboratory. When he dissolved the heavy gas in water, it created an effervescent, refreshing drink. For his invention of soda water, Priestly was admitted to the French Academy of Sciences in 1772; he received a medal from the Royal Society in 1773.

- In 1772, while experimenting with green plant shoots, enclosed containers, water, and candles, he became the first person ever to observe the respiration of carbon dioxide and oxygen in plants.

- Again in 1772, Priestly's experiments produced a new compound — nitrous oxide, or laughing gas, the first surgical anesthetic.

- In 1774, in an experiment with mercuric oxide, Priestly misidentified an emitted vapor as dephlosticated gas. At that time, many mistakenly believed that during combustion matter lost a substance called phlogiston, which acted as an adherent of matter. When phlogiston disappeared, the matter would incinerate. Unwittingly, Priestly had isolated the compound French chemist Antoine Lavosier would call oxygen.

- Later that year, Priestly documented the process, now known as photosynthesis, of gas emerging from green plant material growing in his jars under sunlight.

While Priestly gained acclaim for his progressive scientific thinking, he attracted the ire of the conservative religious community of London. Priestly, along with Lindsey, had accepted and expressed many of the controversial Unitarian ideals which had trickled in from Eastern Europe over the previous 100 years. Born in Leeds in 1733 and raised in a strict Calvinist home, Priestly deviated from his conservative ministerial training to become a staunch supporter and propagandist for the Unitarian cause. He founded a small Unitarian community in the Birmingham suburb of London.

Priestly often expressed his radical, heretical ideas in a paternalistic, condescending manner, which further irritated the learned theologians with whom he contended. His radical proposals — supporting antitrinitarianism, the humanity of Christ, as well as radical political movements such as the American and French revolutions, increasingly offended the ears of conservative English Christians. On July 14, the offense exploded, as a firebomb destroyed his Birmingham home, library, laboratory, and Unitarian Chapel. He and his family barely escaped with their lives. Priestly remained undaunted, and in 1794 sailed across the Atlantic to the United States, where he hoped to spread the good news of Unitarianism among the newly established United States.

Joseph Priestly settled in Northumberland, Pennsylvania, but remained determined to witness the establishment of a Unitarian Community in Philadelphia, which at the time served as the United States Capital city. Priestly's celebrated scientific achievements held him in good stead with Philadelphia academia and intellectuals, which augmented his ecclesiastical pursuits. Shortly after arriving in Philadelphia, Priestly wrote to Lindsey in England, saying, "I have little doubt but that I shall form a respectable Unitarian society in this place. The alarm of Unitarianism has been sounded so long, that it has ceased to be terrific to many, and I stand so well with the country, in other respects, that I dare say I shall have a fair and candid hearing." (Geffen p. 22)

On February 14, 1796, Priestly delivered his first sermon in America on the subject of Unitarianism, based on concepts he and Lindsey had studied and developed in London. The discourse commenced at the newly established Universalist sanctuary on Lombard Street in Philadelphia. The audience he described as "a numerous respectable and very attentive audience, including a great portion of the members of congress." (Geffen, p. 20) Among the audience sat vice-president John Adams. This and subsequent sermons apparently struck a chord with some of the populace, while Priestly interacted with some of the most celebrated names of his day, including Adams, Franklin, Thomas Jefferson, and President George Washington.

Priestly's words inspired a group of 21 Philadelphia merchants and businessmen, who had emigrated from England precisely to find the freedom to pursue their collective interest in Unitarianism. Many of this group had known Priestly and Lindsey in Britain, and had followed him to Pennsylvania. On August 21, 1796, these English Philadelphians met in a classroom at the University of Philadelphia to establish the Society of Christian Unitarians of Philadelphia. This congregation, virtually transmuted from English Unitarianism, became the first American congregation to use the controversial term "Unitarian" in its name. The Society officially brought Unitarianism to America as the predecessor of the First Unitarian Church of Philadelphia.

By this time, congregations promoting Unitarian ideals had already existed in New England, where they had begun to flourish. But these churches were liberal derivatives of Congregational or Episcopalian communities. Only the Society of Christian Unitarians of Philadelphia first fully identified itself as a Unitarian church.

The Reverend William Christie dedicated the Unitarians' first church in 1814. Designed by Robert Mills, who claimed to be the first Native American trained as a professional architect, the first Unitarian Church stood on the corner of Tenth and Locust Streets. The brick building seated 300, and cost the congregation $25,000. The octagonal shape distinguished the Unitarian structure from the usual cruciform church of orthodox Christendom. The 1828 expansion of the church, which would accommodate another 700 people, took place during the early tenure of the Reverend William Henry Furness.

In the person of the Reverend Furness, the Philadelphia Unitarian Church found its first long-term, stabilizing influence from the pulpit. The Boston-born Furness came to the Unitarians at the fresh age of twenty, fresh out of Harvard theological department, seeking his first pastorate. He stayed with the Philadelphia Society 71 years: 50 as pastor, and 21 in an emeritus capacity.

A childhood school mate and lifelong friend of noted poet and philosopher Ralph Waldo Emerson, the Reverend Furness brought his handsome appearance, charming personality, and magnificent, enchanting speaking voice to the Philadelphia congregation. The Unitarian community expanded little in his tenure, a fact Furness regarded as of little consequence:

> He defined his own purpose as that of restoring the true spirit of brotherhood to all churches, to the end that one day there would be no further division among the various branches of the Christian faith...the aim to be worked for is that all denominations as such may disappear and all men eventually worship together as one family.... [Geffen, pp. 314–315]

Like many of his fellow ministers in 19th century Philadelphia, Furness felt the antagonism and controversy created over the issue of slavery. Much of the Philadelphia mercantile which comprised the Unitarian community maintained substantial economic and familial ties with the South, ties given up reluctantly even in the face of such a morally reprehensible system. Unlike many men of the cloth, however, Furness willingly spoke out in favor of abolition. Often a solitary voice in the wilderness, Furness encountered the anger and resentment of many in his flock, particularly during the midpoint of the 19th century. Not until the advent and passing of the Civil War did Furness' views on slavery become adopted by the larger society. The Unitarian community finally acknowledged his insight on the matter, and standing-room-only crowds returned to the Unitarian church to savor his inspiring discourses. Largely due to the endurance and persistence of Furness, the First Unitarian Church of Philadelphia survived and thrived through the past century into the present.

Finally the Unitarians replaced the original church with the building that stands on Chestnut Street today. Described as a Greek cross with a shortened transept, the current First Unitarian Church emerged from the creativity of Frank Furness, son of Reverend Furness, and Philadelphia's most prolific architect. The new Ruskinian Gothic church features elaborate stone-carved ferns, lead-forms in ironwork, fish-scaled roof vents, and rough-hewn masonry. An intricate wood-and-iron hammer beam roof truss system creates the massively spacious sanctuary, illuminated by magnificent stained-glass windows designed by Louis Tiffany and John LaFarge.

Despite the fact that the Philadelphia Universalists opened its sanctuary to Joseph Priestly's 1796 sermon on Unitarianism, these two close liberal theological cousins remained separate, rarely interactive entities for nearly two centuries. The Universalists primary tenet

refuted the traditional Christian concept of eternal damnation; Universalist leader Hosea Ballou, author of the 1803 Winchester Profession encapsulating Universalists views, wrote: "Is God any less intelligent than a parent? Would a parent see any point in punishing a child forever? Would that improve the child?"

However, Unitarians and Universalists both rejected the necessity of creed, and promoted the pursuit of truth through knowledge and intellectual examination. Unitarians and Universalists emphasized the dignity and goodness of humans, and the desire of God to see humanity improve itself through divine gifts of compassion and intelligence. To complete the inevitable synthesis, at a historic convention in Boston in 1960, the two communities merged to form the Unitarian Universalists.

Thus, from the Society of Christian Unitarians in Philadelphia the community inspired by Joseph Priestly to call themselves Unitarians — more than 1200 Unitarian Universalist congregations exists in America today.

Sources

Bishop, Peter and Michael Darton. *The Encyclopedia of World Faiths: An Illustrated Survey of the World's Living Religions.* 1987, MacDonald and Co., Ltd., London and Sydney.

Catholic Encyclopedia. 1913, Encyclopedia Press, 1996, New Athens, Inc.

Geffen, Elizabeth M.. *Philadelphia Unitarianism.* 1958, University of Philadelphia.

Mendelsohn, John. *Why Am I A Unitarian?* 1964, Thomas Nelson and Sons, New York.

HARMONIE VILLAGE

Affiliation: Harmonists or Rappites
Location: New Harmony, on the Wabash River, southwest Indiana
1814

Several places of worship had been constructed within the town limits of New Harmony, Indiana, since its inception. The original church, built in 1815, featured a 20-foot-high belfry crowned by a hexagonal clock, whose bells could be heard tolling the hour seven miles away. Unfortunately, the design

included no lightning rod, and a bolt destroyed it within a few years. The second church included a lightning rod, walls of brick, and was in the shape of a cross. A rail-enclosed balcony perched on the roof of the church, from which the town band and chorus could entertain the village on Sundays. Finally, more than a century after the original villagers left, a Roofless Church — a walled garden featuring a 50-foot dome made of laminated pine — emerged as a site for interdenominational ceremonies.

In truth, all these structures are superfluous. For, the true sanctuary of New Harmony was the town itself, named by the original occupants "new Harmonie." Built by, and for the exclusive use of, the Harmonists, this hamlet was constructed to specifically support and enhance its residents unique community way of life. Utopian, communistic, and chiliastic, the new Harmonie way of life most certainly qualifies as a form of worship.

By the time George Rapp and his associates chose this site along the Wabash River in the southwest corner of Indiana, Rapp had perfected his community formula, which enabled his loyal followers to literally "live in Harmonie." Rapp had been born in 1757, raised in Iptingen, in the southwest state of Württemberg, near Stuttgart, Germany. He worked in vineyards as a youth, and developed his considerable physical and mental stamina, making him vigorous and vital throughout his long life. He possessed a forceful voice, and loved to sing hymns. His formal schooling was short-lived. Rapp studied philosophy and theology all his life, particularly the works of Swedenborg, Jacobi, Schleiermach, and Johann von Herder.

A self-educated teacher and self-proclaimed theologian as a young man, Rapp quietly dissented from the state Lutheran Church. He considered the German church to be of the Devil, focusing far too much on secular rather than spiritual matters. He loathed how the church forced residents to attend state services and pay tithings to the church, and forbade them to attend "unauthorized" religious meetings. He believed church members had learned their catechism by rote, forgetting the true meanings of the Scriptures.

George Rapp quickly developed a personal doctrine to which he adhered all his life, and which drew many followers to "unauthorized" meetings at his home. Rapp, like Martin Luther, believed final authority lay with the Bible. Salvation and enlightenment comes directly to the individual through God and the scriptures, with no need for clerical interpretation. Rapp believed true Christians had no need of government, but judged many of the peasants were incapable, on their own, to adequately apply the message of the scriptures to their lives. The focal point to Rapp's beliefs and message was his adherence to chiliasm, the belief that the Millennium — the Second Coming of Christ predicted in Revelations — would arrive in his lifetime. Obviously, this brought an urgency to Rapp's life, which he vigorously conveyed to his followers.

More than all else, perhaps, George Rapp believed in the gifts of his own strong will and superior intelligence. No doubt ever entered Rapp's mind: his destiny was to lead the peasants to the right way of life, in preparation for the Kingdom to come.

Rapp led his followers in sessions of chiliast prophecies and inspirational song. Still, Rapp remained an undemonstrative rebel, rendering to Caesar what was Caesar's, and keeping his disagreements with the church to himself and his followers. Not until 1799, after being arrested for driving a swine herd through streets of Wurttemburg on Good Friday, did Rapp decide enough was enough.

On October 7, 1803, leaving his wife Christina and daughter Rosina behind, George Rapp left Wurttemburg, Germany, destined for Philadelphia, Pennsylvania. Accompanied by his 18-year-old son John, and his business manager Frederick Reichert (whom Rapp later adopted as his son), George Rapp found his way to Butler County, Pennsylvania, 26 miles northwest of Pittsburgh, 12 miles from the Ohio River. In the winter of 1803, he bought 4500 acres near Connoquessing Creek for the equivalent of $800. By September 1804, more than 630 disciples from Germany followed him to Butler County, to the town which he would call "Harmonie." Eventually, the town would grow to 7000 acres.

Father Rapp, as he was called by his followers, called his Harmonists to live as he believed it pleased God to live: in communion in preparation for the millennium. Harmonie became a communist community, in the truest sense of the term. He based this economic model on Acts 2: 44–45: "And all that believed were together, and had all things common; and sold their possessions and goods, and parted them to all men, as every man had need." The Harmonists lived in harmony with one another, each enjoying an equal status in life, with wealth and property possessed in common, under the supervision of Father Rapp.

In support of the philosophic base of this new community, Rapp and his associates drew up the Articles of Association for Harmonie in February of 1805; these basic community agreements remained constant through the history of the community. Each member of the community agreed to transfer all assets and property to Rapp, and to submit to rules and regulations set by Rapp for the community. In return, Rapp promised to dispense appropriate religious instruction, plus all material necessities of life for every member, regardless of health, age, or demeanor.

In 1807, at the urging of Father Rapp, the Harmonists adopted the practice of celibacy in 1807 to further purify themselves for the second coming of Christ. He found support for the practice in 1 Corinthians 7:32–38: "He that is unmarried careth for the things that belong to the Lord, how he may please the Lord. But he that is married careth for the things that are of the world, how he may please his wife." Rapp reasoned, with the Kingdom around the corner, there was no need for progeny and, therefore, no need for connubial relations. Without the distractions of sex, children and the personal needs of a home, the efforts and attention of each member could be focused on the community, and the success of the community would provide an example to the world.

In support of the ideals of celibacy, the women of Harmonie were, as one observer wrote, "made as ugly as it is possible for art to make them." Those among the Harmonists who were unmarried remained unmarried, and of course, chaste; those already married stayed married, but refrained from sexual intercourse. Although some children inadvertently arrived into the community (apparently every urge could not be suppressed), reproduction was certainly kept to a minimum. Offenders did not face punishment as such, but peer pressure seemed to motivate most to toe the line. Those

who could not abide by the practice of celibacy and chastity eventually left the community, taking their share of the community property with them.

As every parent knows, the presence of children very often means the absence of money. In other words, the community did indeed flourish, and Father Rapp's vision for success seemed to be coming true.

Father Rapp firmly believed the key to the Harmonist's success was diligence in industry; the idle hand represented his greatest fear. So in 1814, after all 7000 acres in Butler County had been developed, lending more leisure time to the community, Rapp decided it was time to move on, to establish a new Harmonie to the west. In the spring of 1814, Rapp purchased on behalf of the Harmonists 24,734 acres in southwest Indiana along the Wabash River for $61,050. Attesting to the success of the original Harmonie, the property in Butler County sold for $100,000, giving the community an $85,000 profit.

By 1817, New Harmonie encompassed more than 30,000 acres, including Illinois land across the Wabash. By 1818, nearly 900 followers of Father George Rapp called New Harmonie their home.

Basing their new operation on the original Harmonie, the Harmonists enjoyed even greater success in Indiana than Pennsylvania. With better weather and more plentiful land, the Harmonists enjoyed many more arable acres to sow, more than 2000 in all. They quickly cultivated 15 acres of vineyard, 35 acres of apple orchard, and several acres of peach trees. The Harmonists also grew potatoes, cotton, corn, and flax. They raised sheep for wool and mutton, chickens for eggs and meat.

The buildings and businesses established in town are listed in this inventory by Frederick Rapp:

> one large three-story water-powered merchant mill; extensive factory of cotton and woolen goods, 2 sawmills, 1 oil and hemp mill, 1 large brick and stone warehouse, 2 large granaries, 1 store, a large tavern, 6 large frame buildings used as mechanic's shops, 1 tanyard of fifty vats, 3 frame barns 50 × 100, with one thrashing machine; 3 large sheep stables, 6 two-story brick dwellings, 60 × 60; 40 two story brick

and frame dwellings; 86 log dwellings; all houses have stables and gardens; 2 large distilleries, 1 brewery. [Wilson, p.54]

The town formed a simple quadrangle in design. It featured a watchhouse, an apothecary, a hatter's shop, wagonmaker's factory, a hospital, a soap factory, and, of course, a church. With industrial zeal and the lack of dependents, Harmonists developed a number of technical innovations. They used steam engines to power a cotton mill and a threshing machine. Water power was harnessed for their flour and pressing mills. A large dog walked a circular treadmill, which pumped water for the brewery, producing 500 gallons of beer each day. The townspeople also perfected a greenhouse on rollers. When inclement weather rolled in, it was far simpler for a group of townsfolk to roll the greenhouse over the plants, than to laboriously move the plants by hand into the greenhouse.

Daily life in Harmonie meant each villager addressing the task at hand, working from after breakfast to after sunset. Father Rapp, robust and ruddy, his long white beard waving in the Indiana sun, roamed among the fields and factories, happily exhorting the laborers. Harmonists drank beer and wine at the tavern, but only according to the rationing of Father Rapp. They studied music, assembling a band and chorus for regular performances. Outsiders characterized the Harmonists interchangeably as humorless, thrifty, diligent, sullen, hardworking, peaceful, neat, sanctimonious, and most of all, rich.

Indeed, money poured into the community till. Flatboats from new Harmonie floated down the Wabash to the Mississippi, where the greatly demanded Harmonists' goods would be sold for profit in New Orleans. By 1820, the annual value of these goods exceeded well over $50,000. By 1824, Harmonie land holdings had grown by 20 percent to more than 30,000 acres. So great was Harmonie prosperity that the town reportedly provided a loan to the state of Indiana, at 6 percent interest.

In spite of the prosperity and serene image, the Harmonists — like any community, religion-based or otherwise — could not escape their share of gossip and dissension. Like any other community — but perhaps more so in celibate Harmonie — the number one topic of gossip and dissension was sex. In 1809, while the Harmonists still lived in Pennsylvania, a fellow non-member German named Jacob Schaal circulated a rumor that George Rapp had fathered the child of a prostitute, who miscarried. Rapp hauled him into court, sued him for libel, forcing Schaal to pay a fine of 40 dollars, and to henceforth hold his tongue. But the rumor persistently followed Rapp and the Harmonists over the years.

The most infamous rumor surrounded the death of Father Rapp's son, John, on July 27, 1812, at the age of 27. Theories on the cause of young Rapp's death abounded. Some said he was killed by a felled tree, while others said he ruptured himself in an industrial accident. The most damaging version, however, says Father Rapp caught his only son indulging in sexual improprieties (which in Harmonie, it would seem, could mean anything). In a fit of rage, Father Rapp castrated his son, to ensure he would never violate the community rule of celibacy again. John later died of the wound. (Although no actual evidence of the act has been uncovered, the possibility is intriguing; the history of social deviance certainly attests to the calamities which can result from repressed or unchanneled sexual energy.)

Another controversy which had nothing to do with sex involved a set of naked human footprints impeded in a limestone slab in the yard at Rapp's home in Indiana. Rapp supposedly told his followers the footprints belonged to the angel Gabriel, as evidence that the Second Coming was at the threshold. The story reveals Rapp actually purchased the slab in St. Louis, and brought it home in a desperate attempt to further guide his wavering disciples along the straight and narrow.

It is quite possible that such stories were promulgated by communities surrounding the Harmonists. For the most part, the Harmonists kept to themselves, sharing neither their wealth nor the secrets of their success with the surrounding communities. The Harmonists had two chief purposes: to make money for themselves, and to provide for their own salvation. Their isolationist policy may have added to the resentment already felt by the neighbors over Harmonie's prosperity.

Without a doubt, though, the community of New Harmonie enjoyed particular success in Indiana, where they accumulated more wealth and experienced less dissension or outside harassment than at any other site. This prosperity can be attributed to George Rapp and his aids, excellent and inspired leaders, followed by faithful, obedient, well-trained, and hard-working disciples. New Harmonie housed a homogeneous community consisting of families which had undergone the same religious experience. The community shared a common goal, with incentives kept fresh by moving three times in 30 years.

By 1824, Father Rapp saw the community in the same position as in 1814: All available land had been worked, and the community once again faced the dreaded "Idle Hands." With their additional leisure time, the Harmonists wanted to spend more money, drink more beer, listen to the gossip about new Harmonie from the neighbors. They began to ignore the imminence of the millennium, in which Rapp still firmly believed. In 1824, Father Rapp lead his community back to Pennsylvania. They purchased 3000 acres in Beaver County, 18 miles north of Pittsburgh, near the Ohio River. But instead of naming the new site Harmonie, they called it Economy.

The Harmonists sold their Indiana town to a Welsh industrialist by the name of Robert Owen. Brilliant, egotistical and industrious, Owen was a confirmed socialistic atheist. He worked diligently to increase production and implement more humane working conditions in his textile mill in New Lanark, Scotland, then the largest and most successful mill in the British Isles. He also advocated for an education system which encouraged childhood curiosity, self-direction, and exploration. Most of all, Owen advocated the abolition of all religion, and the inhibition and superstition it brought to young minds. When his views on religion incurred the wrath of his fellow Britons, Owen came to America, with the idea of developing a Utopian community, to prove his beliefs on education and religion could be manifested.

Owen teamed with Scottish geologist and philanthropist William MacLure to establish their Community of Equality within the old Harmonist buildings at New Harmony. Based on the tenet that a human is the result of his circumstances, the Community of Equality would be a social system where property would be shared as a community, and each member received credit for the contributions it made to the whole. Curiosity and initiative would be encouraged in children, and each man or woman would be left to pursue the endeavor or career of most interest.

In 1826, Owen brought to New Harmony his famous Boatload of Knowledge. Scientists and professors from disciplines ranging from zoology and entomology to chemistry, music, and art. This boatload was to lead the Community of Equality to its enlightened destiny.

Unfortunately, Owen, much more a fleeting optimist than a substantial pragmatist, issued a nationwide blanket invitation to interested individuals far before the community ever got off the ground. The crush of humanity, many of whose motivations and interests were not nearly as lofty as Owen's, so crippled the new Utopia that it never evolved much past the planning stage. Almost immediately, New Harmony experienced a shortage of housing and food, and a disgruntled residency gradually began to disperse. The burning idealism was quickly doused in the wave of day-to-day realism. Despite the substantial dose of intelligencia, New Harmony could never begin to approach the prosperity of the Rappites at new Harmonie.

In 1826, a rift arose between Owen and MacLure over money still owed to the original Harmonists, and by 1827, the community property of the Community of Equality fell into private hands. Despite the failure of Owen's experiment, the sparks of inspiration struck on the Boatload of Knowledge continued to influence the fields of education, geology, drama, and government for decades to come.

In the meantime, in Beaver County, it became clear the Harmonist of Economy Village would never again approach the peak of prosperity it had reached in Indiana. The Harmonists slowly faded away. The Millennium, of course, never came, and the longer the community waited, the less inclined it was to follow Father Rapp. In 1832, a charismatic European named Count Maximillian de Leon (aka Bernhard Muller, traveling salesman) paid a visit to the village of Economy. Calling himself "the great Ambassador and Appointed One of God," he mingled with the Harmonites, and persuaded many of them of the goodness of marriage and the necessity of procreation. In the end, the Count de Leon led one third of the Harmonist away from Economy, taking $105,000 of assets with them. They followed de Leon to a new community on the Red River in eastern Louisiana.

Shortly after the departure of the Count, Frederick Rapp, Father Rapp's beloved adopted son and business partner, died in the forest near Economy. From that point forward, Father Rapp assumed the countenance of the old mystic, alive in the dreamy past, but absent to the present. He died in 1847. By 1900, only a few Harmonists remained, and in 1905, the society dissolved altogether.

To the end, George Rapp never lost his conviction of the coming millennium. On his very last day, he is reported to have remarked, "If I did not so believe that the Lord has designed me to place our society before His presence in the Land of Canaan, I would consider this day my last." His millennium never came. But for ten years, on the shores of the Wabash River in Indiana, Father Rapp led a community which came as spiritually and economically close to the Utopian society, as misguided as it was, as any community in America. The community was the church and, indeed, the church was the community.

Sources

Wilson, William E. *The Angel and the Serpent: The Story of New Harmony.* 1964, Indiana University Press, Bloomington, IN.
Young, Marguerite. *Angel in the Forest.* 1945, Charles Scribner's Sons, New York.

ST. JOHN'S AT LAFAYETTE SQUARE
("Church of the Presidents")
Affiliation: Episcopal
Location: Washington, D.C.
1816

From the very earliest days of the nation, it seems the American president has always enjoyed being seen (or being acknowledged for being seen) in church. It has always seemed a most "presidential" thing to do. No matter what the chief executive's personal religious affiliation, code of ethics, or relative standard of morals, if the country knew he attended church, then perhaps other failings would be overlooked. Most likely, the church the president has been seen in most is St. John's at Lafayette Square, which has come to be known as the Church of the Presidents. For, since its founding in 1815, every president of the United

States — starting with the 4th administration of James Madison — has at one time or another attended services at St. John's.

There had been plans to build a second Episcopal Church in Washington, D.C. closer to the White House than Christ's Church on Capitol Hill as early as 1812. The August 1814, invasion of Washington by the British army delayed the project, as the British burned the capitol as well as many of the other official buildings. Finally, land was purchased for St. John's in the summer of 1815, north of the White House across what would later be known as Lafayette Square.

The cornerstone for St. John's was laid on September 14, 1815, with construction completed in September 1816. Architect Benjamin Latrobe — who designed and worked on the Capitol building, The White House, Baltimore Cathedral, and Dickinson College, as well as the final reconstruction of St. Louis Cathedral in New Orleans — designed a structure both simple and grand in its austerity. The sanctuary outline formed a Greek Cross, a rectangular structure with pillars and a saucered dome at the center of the roof. Latrobe reportedly once wrote to his son, "I have completed a church that has made many Washingtonians religious who had not been religious before" (St. John's, 1997). Reverend William Wilmer, the first rector, celebrated the first service at St. John's on October 17, 1816.

The following is a short review of the presidents who have visited the Church of the Presidents; their dates of birth and death, their term(s) of office, their religious affiliation, some notes about their administrations, and the known circumstances surrounding their visits to St. John's on Lafayette Square:

James Madison
(1751–1836; term: 1809–1817)

James Madison was the fourth president of the United States, and the last surviving signer of the Constitution. Three-quarters through Madison's first term, on June 18, 1812, the young United States declared war against Great Britain presumably over the continued impressment of American sailors by the British into its navy. He and his wife Dolly fled for refuge in Virginia on August 24, 1814, when British troops invaded and sacked Washington, D.C, destroying many of the governmental buildings, including the Capitol Building and the White House.

Madison was Episcopalian, and an active member of St. John's Church. Upon the church completion in 1816, the church vestry, as courtesy, offered President Madison his choice of pew, free of stewardship. Madison, in return, asked the governing body to choose for him. At that point pew 28 became the President's Pew. (Pew 54 later became the President's Pew, after a church reconstruction.)

Madison's lovely and charming wife, Dolly, raised in a Quaker household, returned to Washington D.C. after her husband's death in 1836. She became a confirmed communicant of St. John's.

James Monroe
(1758–1831; term: 1817–1825)

James Monroe is best known, perhaps, for the Monroe Doctrine. Delivered as part of a congressional address in 1823, the Doctrine acknowledged the increasing interaction between nations, and asserted the United States would tolerate no interference by European powers in the western hemisphere. Monroe's term included the *McCullough vs. Maryland* decision in 1819, in which the Supreme Court asserted its role as interpreter of the constitution. In 1820, the Missouri Compromise, struck a precarious balance by letting Maine in as a free state, and Missouri in as a slave state. It also forbid slavery north of latitude 36, 30'. Finally, former American slaves established the African nation of Liberia in 1822; they named the capital "Monrovia" for the 5th American president.

The Reverend William Hawley, rector at St. John's, presided over the wedding of Samuel Gouverneur and Maria Monroe, daughter of the president, on March 20, 1820. An active member of the church, Monroe donated a cannon captured from the British in the War of 1812. St. John's had the artillery melted down by Paul Revere's metal works in Boston. Revere fashioned it into a thousand-pound bronze bell, which would peal over Washington from St. John's newly constructed steeple for generations to come.

John Quincy Adams
(1767–1848; term: 1825–1829)

The son of the second president of the United States, John Adams, John Quincy Adams is the only son of a president to become president. He was in office during the initial construction of the famed Baltimore and Ohio Railroad.

A devout Christian, a self-proclaimed "independent Congregationalist," and an avid abolitionist (particularly after his administration), Adams regularly objected to the Rev-

St. John's Episcopal Church, the "Church of the Presidents," Washington, D.C. (Courtesy St. John's Episcopal Church.)

erend William Hawley's fire and brimstone approach to preaching. Still, Adams often visited St. John's for evening prayers, and regularly attended two church services per day. After his administration, Adams apparently held contention with the whole of the City of Washington, questioning its moral and spiritual standards in the growing face of slavery. Apparently, most of the ministers of Washington's churches — many of whose members harbored southern loyalties — felt reluctant to take a stand on the issue, something Adams considered an abomination.

Andrew Jackson
(1767–1845; term: 1829–1837)

Andrew Jackson was the hero of the Battle of New Orleans, and the first president born in a log cabin. He hated Indians. Through his role in the Seminole Wars and signing of the Indian Removal Act of 1831, Jackson became chief guide on the Civilized Tribes' Trail of Tears. He was president during the Battle of the Alamo. During Jackson's administration, Marcus and Narcissa Whitman established their tiny ill-fated mission in Oregon Territory.

During his administration, a scandal developed, involving Jackson's Secretary of War John Eaton and his wife, the former Peggy O'Neill Timberlake. Eaton and Timberlake apparently conducted an affair until Timberlake's husband, a naval officer, met his death at sea. Shortly after Jackson named Eaton to his cabinet, the couple married.

Much of Washington society ostracized Peggy Eaton over her "indecent" conduct. The young minister of the Second Presbyterian Church — which Jackson regularly attended — went as far as to publicly denounce the Eatons' behavior. The President, in defense of his secretary, called the minister into the White House, dressing down the Reverend, and renouncing his membership to the Presbyterian church. From that point forward, Old Hickory generally attended services at St. John's at Lafayette Square.

Martin Van Buren
(1782–1862; term: 1837–1841)

Martin Van Buren was the first president born an American citizen. He lived until 1862, to the ripe old age of 80, long enough to watch eight other presidents succeed him. He was president on March 17, 1837, when the Republic of Texas adopted its constitution.

Since there was no Dutch Reformed church in the city, Van Buren attended St. John's while in Washington, often enough to be memorialized by the church. A stained-glass window commemorating him hangs in the north gallery transept of St. John's.

William Henry Harrison
(1773–1841; term: March 4, 1841– April 4, 1841)

Harrison was the first president to die while in office, completing what would be the shortest term for the Chief Executive in history: 31 days.

Harrison was reportedly seen on March 28, 1841, outside St. John's Church on a chilly morning without overcoat. A week later on Palm Sunday, Harrison, 68, died of pneumonia. St. John's Rector William Hawley presided over the memorial. Was it Harrison's short-sighted decision to forego the overcoat on March 28 that led to the cold which eventually led to his demise? Harrison had reportedly expressed the desire to become a full communicant of the church, which would have taken place on Easter Sunday.

John Tyler
(1790–1862; term: 1841–1845)

John Tyler is probably best known because of the presidential campaign of 1840, and the popular phrase "Tippecanoe and Tyler, Too." Tippecanoe referred to William Henry Harrison, for his role as general in the 1811 Battle of Tippecanoe against the Shawnee Indians. The phrase was part of a campaign song for the presidential ticket of Harrison and Tyler. John Tyler was the first president to marry while in office. The wedding between Jule Gardiner and recently widowed Tyler took place on June 26, 1844, in New York City.

Tyler's cabinet had a hand in recruiting St. John's rector in 1845, the brilliant Reverend Smith Pyne. John Spencer, who became Tyler's secretary of war, had been familiar with Pyne's work while in New York. Spencer reportedly prevailed upon St. John's vestry to call Pyne to service in Washington, D.C.

James K. Polk
(1795–1849; term: 1845–1849)

Polk served as president during the Mexican War, a conflict pursued largely under the auspices of manifest destiny; that is, the widely popular conviction that divine providence destined the United States to stretch from the Atlantic to the Pacific. As a result of the Treaty of Guadalupe Hidalgo with Mexico, the United States obtained the territory including present-day California, New Mexico, Arizona, Nevada, Utah, plus parts of Colorado and Wyoming for the paltry sum of $15 million.

On July 19 and 20, 1848, the first Women's Rights Convention took place at a small Methodist chapel in Seneca Falls, New York.

A Presbyterian and later a Methodist, Polk apparently occasionally attended services at St. John's at Lafayette Square.

Zachary Taylor
(1784–1850; term: March 4, 1849–July 9, 1850)

Propelled by his heroics in the Mexican War, old Rough and Ready took office as the 12th president. He held the office for only 15 months. On July 4, 1850, he reportedly ingested a bowl of cherries and a pitcher of ice milk, a favorite combination of his. He contracted cholera morbus, a common gastrointestinal illness from eating stale fruit and dairy products. Taylor died on July 9, 1850, the second president to die while in office. Personally undecided over the issue of slavery, his death served to further polarize a country already divided over the issue.

Though Zachary Taylor never formally joined the church, he regularly attended services at St. John's. The Reverend Smith Pyne, rector for the church, conducted the funeral service for Zachary Taylor.

Millard Fillmore
(1800–1874; term: 1850–1853)

For better or worse, little distinguished Fillmore's administration, often cited as the embodiment of mediocrity. When offered an honorary degree of Doctor of Civil Law by Oxford University, Fillmore reportedly replied, "I had not advantage of classical education and no man should, in my judgment, accept a degree he cannot read." Ironically, he later lost the 1856 election for presidency as candidate of the "Know Nothing" Party, better known as the American Party. Abigail Powers Fillmore, the first lady and former school teacher, instituted the presidential library. Before that, President Fillmore apparently had owned no books, not even a Bible.

While Fillmore held office, California became the 31st state, following a gold rush which brought thousands of treasure-seeking immigrants from as far away as Europe, South America, and China.

Although he and Abigail eventually joined the Unitarian Church, an Episcopal minister married them in 1826. This brief tie to Episcopalianism apparently continued in Washington, D.C., where they occasionally attended St. John's Church.

Franklin Pierce
(1804–1869; term: 1853–1857)

A graduate (and classmate of Henry Wadsworth Longfellow) from Bowdoin College, his baccalaureate commenced at First Parish Church in Brunswick, Maine. His administration featured two distinctive legislative acts: (1) The Gadsden Purchase Treaty of June 30, 1851, which brought to the United States the remainder of the territory left out by the Treaty of Guadalupe Hilgaldo; and (2) The Kansas-Nebraska Act of May 22, 1854, which left the issue of slavery to popular sovereignty in those territories and, as a precursor to the Civil War, led the southern territory to be known as "Bleeding Kansas."

Pierce's first two sons died as children. When his third son, Bennie, tragically perished in a train accident, Pierce reportedly threw himself into his Episcopal faith, an apparently unsuccessful attempt to find solace for his grief. He attended St. John's regularly, and attended to prayers each morning. However, he did not accept formal baptism until 1865, at St. Paul's Episcopal Church in Concord, New Hampshire.

James Buchanan
(1791–1868; term: 1857–1861)

The only president to remain a bachelor throughout his administration, Buchanan became known more for what he failed to do, than what he did. In his attempt to steer clear of the issue of slavery, his inaction actually hurried the nation's march toward Civil War. The final straw may have been the Dred Scott decision, in which the Supreme Court of the United States, under Chief Justice Roger Taney, essentially reduced the rights of slaves to those of domesticated animals.

The decision drove an unretractable wedge between the North and the South, and on February 4, 1861, the Confederate States of America arose.

An apparent communicant at St. John's, Buchanan reportedly attended the church regularly, but was never baptized. Eventually following a presidency he happily departed, he was baptized in a New York Presbyterian church.

Abraham Lincoln
(1809–1865; term: 1861–1865)

Known as the Great Emancipator, Lincoln issued his Emancipation Proclamation on September 22, 1862. Throughout the bloody years of the Civil War, Lincoln considered the Proclamation only a by-product of his primary stated and desired goal: the preservation of the Union. The Emancipation Proclamation did not actually free all the slaves, but outlawed slavery in confederate states. The Thirteenth Amendment, ratified on December 18, 1865, finally abolished slavery in the United States.

Eight days before the presidential inauguration in 1861, a tall, lean gentleman dressed in black reportedly sat in the first pew with Senator William Seward, listening intently to Dr. Smith Pyne's discourse on 1 Corinthians 7:31. After the service, Seward introduced the stranger as president-elect Abraham Lincoln.

The great president never formally joined any church, but reportedly remained throughout his life a "Christian without a Creed."

Andrew Johnson
(1808–1875; term: 1865–1869)

Andrew Johnson was the first president against whom impeachment proceedings were brought. Against the wishes of Radical Republican senators, Johnson contradicted the Tenure of Office Act of 1867, by firing Radical Republican Secretary of War Edwin M. Stanton. These Radical Republicans wanted to see the South punished further after its defeat, and opposed the lenient policies carried out by Johnson. They tried to impeach the president, who gained acquittal by one vote.

Johnson's term was highlighted by ratification of the Thirteenth Amendment on December 18, 1865, which abolished slavery in the United States. The administration also featured the land deal known as "Seward's Folly," in which Secretary of State William H. Seward, on March 30, 1868, arranged for the purchase of Alaska from Russia for $7.2 million dollars.

Although adhering to no particular faith, Andrew Johnson often attended several churches, including St. John's. However, he reportedly found the Protestant practice of selling pews, allowing the rich to obtain the best seats, repugnant. He preferred the Catholic tradition of "first come, first serve." As president, he often defended the Roman Catholic church from critics, and became known as a champion of religious freedom.

Ulysses S. Grant
(1822–1885; term: 1869–1877)

The decisive and courageous commander of the Union army seemed ill-prepared for, and overwhelmed by, the tangled web of the political world. Scandals ranged from speculators cornering the Gold Market with the help of Grant's brother-in-law; to Grant's Secretary of War taking bribes from Indian Traders; to a conspiracy involving whiskey tax money. Grant's administration is generally regarded as the worst of the 19th century, and one of the worst of all time. One of the president's virtues may have actually led to his downfall, as his steadfast loyalty made it difficult for him to question the motives and actions of his so-called friends and aids.

During Grant's tenure as chief executive, the transcontinental railroad linking east to west joined at Promontory, Utah on May 10, 1869. And on June 25, 1876, Crazy Horse led his warrior Lakota Sioux and Cheyenne tribes in the massacre of General Custer and his 7th Cavalry at Little Big Horn, Montana.

During the campaign of 1872, Grant ran against the first woman presidential candidate, Victoria Claflin Woodhall, and the first African American vice-presidential candidate, noted writer and agitator Frederick Douglass, both on the Equal Rights Party ticket. An exact date cannot be determined, but is nevertheless assumed Grant, though a Methodist, attended St. John's Church at least once during his two presidential terms.

Rutherford B. Hayes
(1822–1893; term: 1877–1881)

The administration of Rutherford B. Hayes meant the end to the post–Civil War Reconstruction era, as federal troops finally withdrew from the South. On February 15, 1879, Hayes signed into law a provision allowing women to practice law before U.S. Supreme Court, striking an early blow against sexual discrimination. Hayes became the first president in office to visit the West Coast, stopping a the Palace Hotel in San Francisco on September 8, 1880.

A Methodist, it is nevertheless believed Hayes visited St. John's Church at least once during his presidential term. The exact date and nature of such a visit is unknown.

James A. Garfield
(1831–1881; term: March 4, 1881– September 14, 1881)

On July 2, 1881, Charles J. Guiteau shot James A. Garfield twice at the B&O Railroad station in Washington, D.C. Garfield lived for three more months with a bullet near his pancreas, finally succumbing to blood poisoning. He was the second president assassinated, after only six months in office. His short tenure did not leave room for many achievements. However, Clara Barton organized the American Red Cross on May 21, 1881.

Due to the brevity of Garfield's term, the exact date and nature of his presumed visit to St. John's is unknown.

Chester A. Arthur
(1830–1886; term: 1881–1885)

President Arthur may be as well known for his bushy sideburns as anything else. After the retirement of Rutherford B. Hayes and the death of James A. Garfield, Chester A. Arthur was the third president in 1881. In 1883 he signed the Pendleton Act into law, which has been credited with the creation of the modern civil service system.

Arthur's wife, Ellen "Nell" Lewis Herndon, died 15 months before Arthur assumed duties of vice-president under the Garfield administration. She had been an active Episcopalian in New York. After Arthur began his presidential duties following Garfield's assassination, he joined St. John's Church. In Ellen's memory, he donated the window on the south side of the church, which happens to face the White House across Lafayette Square. At night, from his study, President Arthur could gaze at the light shining out from Ellen's window at St. John's.

Grover Cleveland
(1837–1908; first term: 1885–1889; second term: 1893–1897)

Grover Cleveland, although regarded among the better presidents in history, is known more for his unusual relationships than his administrative abilities. In 1884, during his campaign for president, Cleveland was confronted with a paternity suit from Maria C. Halpin, with whom Cleveland had an affair in 1881. Cleveland accepted responsibility for the child, named Oscar Folsom Cleveland by his mother, and supported him all his life. From this episode emerged the chant, "Ma, Ma, Where's My Pa? Gone to the White House, Ha, Ha, Ha!" which became popular among his opposition in 1884.

Cleveland, a bachelor when he entered the White House, married his ward (daughter of a deceased law partner) Frances Folsom on

July 2, 1886. The ceremony took place in the Blue Room; he was 49, she was 21.

Grover Cleveland is the only president so far to serve non-consecutive terms. The Statue of Liberty was dedicated on October 28, 1886, during his first term.

Although baptized a Presbyterian, Cleveland could occasionally be seen at St. John's in the Presidential Pew.

Benjamin Harrison
(1833–1901; term: 1889–1893)

Benjamin Harrison was president between Grover Cleveland's unprecedented two non-consecutive terms. During Harrison's term, six states were admitted to the Union, more than in any other administration: North Dakota (1889), South Dakota (1889), Montana (1889), Washington (1889), Idaho (1890), and Wyoming (1890). In 1889, Dexter Avenue Baptist Church in Montgomery, Alabama, held its first religious services.

Although an active Presbyterian, Benjamin Harrison occasionally attended St. John's.

William McKinley
(1843–1901; term: 1897–1901)

William McKinley was the third president assassinated, and the fifth to die in office.

During his term the Spanish-American War was fought; through its victory, the United States added the Philippines, Guam, and Puerto Rico to its territories. Also, the McKinley administration accepted the annexation of Hawaii in 1898. This is something the Cleveland administration had opposed, due to the unscrupulous methods by which American interests in the islands had conspired to overthrow the Hawaii's Queen Liliuokalani. During his term, Japanese immigrants formed the Young Men's Buddhist Association in San Francisco.

McKinley, though a Methodist, served as a focal point for two specific ceremonies at St. John's at Lafayette Square. The first was a memorial service for the popular Queen Victoria of England, who died in 1901. The second service was a memorial for himself, after a bullet — which had been fired on September 6 at the Pan American Exposition in Buffalo — from the gun of anarchist Leon Czolgosz, finally killed McKinley on September 14.

Theodore Roosevelt
(1858–1919; term: 1901–1909)

At 42 years, ten days, Theodore Roosevelt was the youngest man ever to serve as president. An active, vigorous man who attained fame through his heroics at San Juan Hill in the Spanish-American War, Roosevelt won the Nobel Prize in 1906 for his diplomatic work on the treaty which ended the Russo-Japanese War. He was the first American ever to win the prize. During Roosevelt's administration, the United States, in a treaty with Great Britain, gained the right to construct and administer a canal across the Isthmus of Panama. Roosevelt was also the first president to openly advocate for the conservation of natural resources.

As a member of the Dutch Reformed church, Theodore Roosevelt reportedly attended St. John's Church sporadically. But his second wife, Edith — a devout Episcopalian — and their children (Theodore, Jr., Kermit, Ethel, Archibald, and Quentin), could be found at St. John's 28th pew on a regular basis. The Roosevelt children reportedly preferred St. John's to other churches due to the brevity of the services.

William Howard Taft
(1857–1930, term: 1909–1913)

William Howard Taft was the largest man to ever serve as president, reaching a top weight of 332 pounds. He was also the first and only president to serve as Chief Justice of Supreme Court, which he did from 1921 until 1930. On April 14, 1910, at National Park in Washington, D.C., at a game between the Washington Senators and the Philadelphia Athletics, Taft became the first president to officially open the baseball season by throwing out the first pitch.

Taft considered himself Unitarian and attended St. John's only rarely. His wife Helen "Nellie" Heron, however, was Episcopalian, and regularly accompanied the Taft children — Robert, Helen, and Charles — to St. John's at Lafayette Square.

Woodrow Wilson
(1856–1924; term: 1913–1921)

The cerebral Woodrow Wilson served as president of Princeton University in New Jersey from 1902 to 1910, three years before accepting the office of president of the United States. He served as president during the entirety of World War I; at the passage of the Eighteenth Amendment (1919), which prohibited the sale of alcoholic beverages; and the Nineteenth Amendment (1920), which extended the right to vote to women. In 1916, Wilson sent General John Pershing with 6000 armed troops into Mexico to attempt and fail to capture the elusive bandit Pancho Villa. On December 18, 1920, Wilson won the Nobel Prize for his work with the League of Nations.

In September of 1919, Wilson suffered a paralyzing stroke. From that point on, his second wife Edith Bolling Galt Wilson, essentially filled the role of chief administrative assistant. She had final word concerning which items from his cabinet would be brought to his attention. Perhaps singularly due to her help, Wilson was able to complete the second term of his administration.

As former president of Princeton, Wilson was a devout Presbyterian; as such, neither he and nor his family could often be seen at St. John's. However, in 1961 an organist at St. John's found a prayer book from 1858, on which was stamped the word "President's Pew." The church then invited the past and present chief executives to sign the book as a commemorative. Again, Mrs. Edith Bolling Galt Wilson acted on behalf of her husband. At the age of 89, she signed the President's Pew prayer book for her husband Woodrow, 37 years after his death.

Warren G. Harding
(1865–1923; term: 1921–1923)

It is said Warren G. Harding's father, George Harding, once told him, "It's a good thing you wasn't born a gal, cause you'd be in the family way all the time. You can't say no." That statement may indeed summarize the 29th presidential administration, which was probably the worst of all time. Extra-marital affairs, scandals, bribes, kickbacks, drug traf-

ficking, suicides, criminal activities: Harding's term saw it all, and in less than two years. Mercifully, for himself and the country, Harding died at the Palace Hotel in San Francisco on July 29, 1923, reportedly from food poisoning. Warren G. Harding was the 9th president to die while in office.

Given the nature and activities of his administration, it is not known exactly how much time Harding spent in church.

Calvin Coolidge
(1872–1933, term: 1923–1929)

Compared to his predecessor's, "Silent Cal's" administration was extremely silent. Normally of frail health, Coolidge customarily slept eleven hours a day, including a two-hour nap in the afternoon. Within the span of his administration was included the Scopes Monkey Trial in 1925, concerning the teaching of evolution in public school. On May 20, 1927, Charles Lindberg completed his historic transatlantic flight. Calvin Coolidge was also the first president to appear in the newsreels.

Coolidge was a Congregationalist. Although his visit to St. John's is assumed, the exact date and nature are unknown.

Herbert Hoover
(1874–1964, term: 1929–1933)

The name of Herbert Hoover will forever be linked with the Great Depression and Black Thursday. Although he obviously did not single-handedly cause the depression, he did little to convince the American public there was anything he could do about it. A particularly bleak episode involved the Bonus March of 1932. Thousands of World War I veterans camped outside the capitol, seeking the Bonus promised to them during the Coolidge Administration. As a response, Hoover sent armed soldiers to drive off the demonstrators, drawing widespread criticism, and adding greater tension to the already bleak depression. During his administration, the "Star Spangled Banner" was adopted as the national anthem, and W.D. Bard opened the Temple of Islam #1 in Detroit, Michigan. In 1932, the International Peace Garden opened on the border between Manitoba and North Dakota.

As a Quaker, he rarely attended St. John's Church. However, he belatedly signed the President's Pew prayer book in 1961, at the age of 87.

Franklin Delano Roosevelt (1882–1945; term 1933–1945)

Franklin D. Roosevelt gained election to an unprecedented four consecutive presidential terms, the longest period of any chief executive. Despite his disabled legs (a result of polio, contracted in 1921) which left him confined to a wheelchair, Roosevelt served for 12 years, before a cerebral hemorrhage killed him on April 12, 1945. His tenure in office saw the end of the Great Depression, and the advent of the New Deal. The 21st Amendment repealing prohibition was passed on December 5, 1933. On December 7, 1941, the "day that will live in infamy," a carrier-based squad of Japanese aircraft attacked the naval base at Pearl Harbor, Oahu, Hawaii. The attack hurtled the once-reluctant United States into World War II.

Franklin Roosevelt was an Episcopalian, who was seen at Episcopal churches as far west as Cheyenne, Wyoming. He worshipped regularly at St. John's. Roosevelt reportedly strolled across Lafayette Square to attend church services at the opening of both the 1933 and the 1937 terms. He also attended a special inaugural service on January 20, 1945, before his fourth swearing-in, to be held at the White House. The last service on Roosevelt's behalf proved to be his own memorial.

Harry S Truman (1884–1972; term: 1945–1953)

The administration of President Harry S Truman will always be equated with the only use of atomic weapons in warfare. Reportedly rather than risk American lives and prolong World War II in a proposed invasion of Japan, Truman ordered an atomic bomb dropped on the city of Hiroshima, Japan, on April 6, 1945, when Japan refused to surrender, and a second bomb was launched against Nagasaki, Japan, on April 9. Japan surrendered in less than a month. In contrast to this ominous decision, Truman's tenure will also be known for the birth of the United Nations, the charter of which was signed on June 26, 1945, in San Francisco. Both the Communist scare and the Korean War started under the Truman administration. The Baha'i House of Worship was dedicated in Wilmette, Illinois, in 1953.

Harry S (the "S" is just a letter; it stands for no name) Truman became a Baptist in 1902, and normally attended the First Baptist Church in Washington, D.C. His wife Elizabeth "Bess" Truman was Episcopalian, however, and the president sometimes joined her at St. John's. In 1969, at the age of 85, Harry S Truman signed the St. John's Presidential Pew prayer book.

Dwight D. Eisenhower (1890–1969, term: 1953–1961)

The presidency of Dwight D. Eisenhower, commander-in-chief of the Allied forces in Europe during World War II, is often regarded as an era of good feeling. But it was also a period dominated by the Red scare. On June 19, 1953, Julius and Ethel Rosenberg were executed as communist spies accused of selling atomic weapon secrets to the Russians. In 1954, Senator Joseph McCarthy was finally censured by the United States Senate, after four years of a public smear campaign that ruined the lives of many known or suspected communist sympathizers. Eisenhower's term was known for the Montgomery Bus Boycott and *Brown vs. Board of Education* decision (1954); the launching of Sputnik and the Space Race (1957); the admittance of Alaska and Hawaii to the Union (1959).

Baptized at the National Presbyterian Church in Washington in 1953, Eisenhower rarely attended services at St. John's. He did, however, sign the Presidential Pew prayer book in 1969.

John F. Kennedy (1917–1963; term: 1961–1963)

John F. Kennedy and his wife, Jacqueline Bouvier Kennedy, seemed to magically rule over the United States from the White House, nicknamed "Camelot," by the press after the mythical castle of King Arthur. The youngest man ever elected to the presidency, the young executive offered the country the hope of a

"New Frontier." Kennedy's administration featured the advent of the Peace Corps (March 1961), acceleration of the Space Race, the confrontation of Cuba through the Bay of Pigs fiasco (April 1961), and the Cuban Missile Crisis (October 1962). The Kennedy years also introduced the Warren Court and the popular notions of "civil rights" and "due process" to the nation. Frank Lloyd Wright's "Little Jewel" was dedicated in July 1961.

But the fairy tale came to a crushing end on November 22, 1963, when Lee Harvey Oswald reportedly shot the president from the window of a book warehouse in Dallas, Texas. Through four heartbreaking days, the nation watched the televised murder of the killer, the swearing-in of Lyndon Johnson, and the funeral procession of its fallen young leader through the streets of Washington D.C.

Kennedy's Roman Catholicism precluded him from attending services at St. John's. However, he did enter the sanctuary to welcome the new rector, John Harper, on March 10, 1963. He reportedly greeted the minister and the attending bishop, shook the hands of the vestry, signed the President's Pew prayer book, and quietly slipped out the door. Eight months later, the copper bell of St. John's steeple would toll in memory of the martyred president.

Lyndon Baines Johnson
(1908–1973; term: 1963–1969)

Although it actually started long before and ended long afterwards, the Vietnam War and the subsequent protest of a nation will always be identified with the Lyndon Johnson administration. Unlike previous wars, Vietnam was filmed and transmitted directly into the living rooms of the American people by television. Never before had a military conflict been so scrutinized by so many millions. The Johnson administration also featured the signing of the Civil Rights Act on July 2, 1966, and the appointment of the first African American justice of the Supreme Court, Thurgood Marshall (1967).

Although Johnson was baptized a Disciple of Christ in 1926, he attended several churches while in Washington. On one particular occasion of note, Johnson quietly slipped into St. John's for a moment of silent but fervent prayer. The date was November 23, 1963, the morning after President Kennedy was shot, as Johnson was about to undertake the duties of the chief executive. He signed the Presidential Pew prayer book later that year.

Richard M. Nixon
(1913–1997; term: 1969–1974)

Richard Milhouse Nixon, known by many as "Tricky Dick" since his days as Eisenhower's vice president, became the first president in history to resign from the executive office. Nixon faced the threat of impeachment after the revelation of his administration's involvement in the infamous break-in of Democratic National Headquarters at the Watergate Complex in Washington, D.C. After investigators discovered a web of intrigue, surveillance, and paranoia interwoven throughout the White House and campaign staff, Nixon resigned the presidency in disgrace before a national television audience on August 9, 1974.

The Watergate scandal and subsequent resignation notwithstanding, the Nixon administration was not without its notable moments. Neil Armstrong, commander of the Apollo 11 space mission, became the first human being to set foot on the moon on July 20, 1969. Nixon became the first president to visit the Republic of China in February 1972. Finally, after more than a decade of fighting which cost more than 48,000 American lives, the Vietnam War came to an end with the peace accord in Paris on January 27, 1973.

Raised a Quaker, Nixon nevertheless managed to visit St. John's during his years in Washington. In 1967, for instance, he attended the funeral service of Christian Herter, who had served as secretary of state while Nixon was vice president under Dwight D. Eisenhower. Nixon signed the Presidential Pew prayer book shortly after his inauguration in January 1969.

Gerald R. Ford
(1913–; term: 1974–1976)

Gerald R. Ford was the first vice president ever to serve as president following a resignation. Ford faced an avalanche of criticism after he decided to grant Richard Nixon a full pardon for "all offenses committed against the United States." Ford argued the pardon would allow the country to heal after the Watergate scandal, and rationalized Nixon's resignation as already more punishment than any prison term would mete. However, critics and Democrats condemned the pardon as merely a method to keep special prosecutors from a lengthy and devastating investigation for the Republican Party.

The aftermath of the Nixon regime left little time for many accomplishments during the two Ford years. However, eight days after he granted Nixon's pardon, Ford granted clemency to all Vietnam War draft evaders and deserters.

A baptized Episcopalian, Ford attended St. John's Church regularly with his wife Elizabeth "Betty" Anne Bloomer Ford. The newly installed President Ford reportedly had prayed for divine guidance at St. John's while mulling the decision whether to pardon Richard Nixon. Whether the requested guidance ever came remains a matter of debate.

James Earl Carter
(1924–; term: 1977–1981)

The Baptist peanut farmer from Georgia rose from virtual obscurity to the Oval Office. His administration featured the historic 1978 meeting at Camp David between Egypt's Anwar Sadat and Israel's Menachem Begin. Unfortunately, 66 Americans became hostages in Tehran, Iran, on November 4, 1979.

An openly religious man, Carter attended services at several Washington, D.C. churches, including St. John's at Lafayette Square.

Ronald Reagan
(1911–; term: 1981–1988)

The Hollywood actor who would be president, Reagan's Republican administration ushered in a new generation of conservative ideals and policies. Reagan's presidency featured Reaganomics and the Iran-Contra Scandal.

At 77, Reagan closed his second term as the oldest man ever to serve as president. A baptized Episcopalian, Reagan's occasional appearances at the Presidential Pew at St. John's

began January 20, 1981, the date of his first inauguration.

George Bush
(1924–; term: 1989–1993)

Ronald Reagan's vice president succeeded the conservative Republican administration for one term, becoming the first vice president since Martin Van Buren subsequently elected to the Oval Office. The 41st president proved unable to live up to his campaign promise of "Read my lips: no new taxes." However, Bush launched the quick and popular Gulf War in August of 1990. Following the invasion and annexation of Kuwait by neighboring Iraq, Bush stationed 400,000 American troops in the Persian Gulf to protect "American interests."

Both practicing Episcopalians, George and Barbara Bush attended St. John's Church on the date of his inauguration, and on subsequent occasions, both during and after his administration.

Bill Clinton
(1946–; term: 1993–)

President William Jefferson Clinton attended the memorial for Ron Brown, secretary of commerce, whose airplane crashed in Croatia in April of 1996. Bill Clinton is Baptist, and his wife Hillary Rodham Clinton, regularly attends Foundry Methodist Church in Washington D.C. However, it is known Clinton has a special fondness for the 8:00 A.M. service at St. John's, particularly on "good golf days."

Clinton scored the greatest Democratic election victory margin since LBJ in 1964, ending the 12-year Republican reign in Washington, D.C. In the process, 104 million American voters showed up at the polls for the November 3, 1992 election of Bill Clinton, the greatest number in the history of the United States. Six years later, Clinton became the second president to be impeached. He was acquitted by the Senate on charges of perjury and obstruction of justice in connection with his affair with White House intern Monica Lewinsky.

Sources

Davis, Kenneth C. *Don't Know Much About History*. 1990, Avon Books, New York.

DeGregario, William A. *The Complete Book of the Presidents.* 1984, Dembner Books, New York.

Green, Constance McLaughlin. *The Church on Lafayette Square, 1815–1970.* 1970, Potomac Books, Inc., Washington.

Kane, Joseph Nathan. *Facts About the Presidents.* 1996, Ace Books, New York.

EL SANTUARIO DE CHIMAYO

Affiliation: Roman Catholic, Franciscan
Location: Chimayo, near Santa Cruz River, 24 miles north of Santa Fe, New Mexico
1816

The region of land between the Santa Cruz River and the Sangre de Cristo Mountains in northern New Mexico has been considered sacred since time immemorial. The Tewa Indians — from whom the legendary Pope arose to lead the natives in a revolt against the Spanish padres and soldiers in 1680 — called this dry, hilly valley "the land of fire and hot water," and considered it holy ground. A hot spring geyser erupted regularly showering its reputed healing waters upon the grateful Pueblo-dwelling Tewa. Even the mud, which remained long after the hot springs subsided, is touted for its regenerative powers. Medicine men from the Tewa Tribes relied on its power for generations.

These legends of miracles have persisted through the years of Spanish invasion and conquest, and colonization by Mexico to this very day, perpetuated by a singular storied event: The miracle of the crucifix of "Our Lord of Esquipulas." Since then, the land has housed one of the most famous and unusual shrines in North America, visited by thousands of believers whose pilgrimages and demonstrations have intermingled with historically significant causes and movements throughout the decades.

According to one version of the tale, on a chilly Good Friday night in 1810, Don Bernardo Abeyta, with his compadres from La Hermanidad de Nuestro Señor Jesus Nazareno (The Brotherhood of Our Lord Jesus the Nazarene), gathered about a small but warming fire in the wilderness outside Chimayo near the Santa Cruz River. This brotherhood consisted of devout Catholic laymen who performed some of the ritual duties during priest-scarce time in northern New Mexico. These penitents commenced with carrying out the ritual praying, fasting, and physical penance customary for Good Friday.

Abeyta had wandered off by himself for a bit, and approached the bank of the Santa Cruz River, along the slope of a small hill. Suddenly, Abeyta saw brilliant light emanating from what appeared to be an opening in the ground. Abeyta rushed to the spot, and began digging with his bare hands into the spot from which the light shone.

Within seconds, Abeyta uncovered a large wooden crucifix, depicting "Our Lord of Esquipulas," better known as the Black Christ. The tradition of the Black Christ — carved from dark balsam wood — comes from the village of Esquipulas in eastern Guatemala in 1594, where a miraculous cure attributed to the dark crucifix created a huge devotional following in Central America.

Some believe the crucifix actually once belonged to a priest who had come from Esquipulas in Guatemala, as a missionary to the Tewa Indians. The priest was killed by the Indians, and both the body and the crucifix were buried along the banks of the Santa Cruz.

In any case, when Bernardo Abeyta found the crucifix, he immediately called La Hermanidad compadres to come and venerate the figure. A smaller group of the brotherhood rushed to the town of Santa Cruz, to fetch Fr. Sebastian Alvarez, the closest priest to Chimayo.

Upon hearing of Abeyta's remarkable discovery, Alvarez hurried with some people from Santa Cruz to Chimayo. The priest picked up the crucifix, and the small procession carried it back to the church at Santa Cruz, where it was placed on the main altar.

The following morning, the crucifix had disappeared from the main altar. After searching throughout Santa Cruz, the priest and a small party retraced their steps, and eventually returned to the shores of the Santa Cruz River. There, in the same hole where Bernardo Abeyta had originally found it, lay the crucifix of Our Lord of Esquipulas. The priest and the people returned the crucifix to Santa Cruz, only to discover it missing the next morning. Once again, the crucifix had mysteriously found its way back to the Santa Cruz River plain. The people decided that, indeed, this was where the crucifix belonged. Almost immediately, plans for a small chapel to house the "miracle" were designed, and by 1816, the chapel was completed.

The chapel, featuring twin bell towers and massive four foot adobe walls affixed by mud and timbers from the locality, surrounds the spot where Abeyta had discovered the crucifix. A small room surrounds the hole where the crucifix first reportedly appeared. The hole is filled with the sacred earth whose healing powers are touted. The crucifix itself is six feet high, stands on the altar, and is painted dark green and decorated with gold leaf.

Since its completion, and in response to a plea from Fr. Sebastian Alvarez in 1813, thousands of believers, an estimated 300,000 annually, have made the pilgrimage to what has come to be known as "The Lourdes of America." During Holy Week alone, typically 30,000 pilgrims make the trip; by foot (often more than 100 miles), bike, car, train, plane; from down the road, across the state and country, and from around the world. They seek the healing of the body and the replenishment of the spirit. Stacks of canes and crutches litter the chapel floor, left by pilgrims who attest to the healing power of the sacred earth of Chimayo. Many more who have not sought physical restoration, are said to have left the el Santuario de Chimayo refreshed, invigorated, contemplative, and at peace.

One of the most stirring pilgrimages took place in the spring of 1945. Troops from the New Mexico National Guard, many of whom were Mexican-Americans, had been sent to the Philippines to fight with the Allies against Japan in World War II. Many of these National Guard troops had been among the captured at Corregidor Island, and had constituted a high percentage of the poor souls fated to participate in the horrible Bataan Death March.

In April of 1942, 83,000 American and Filipino troops camped on Corregidor Island, on the tip of the Bataan Peninsula, at the mouth of Manila Bay. This was considered the focal defense point for the Philippines. General Douglas A. MacArthur had left Corregidor a month earlier, headed for Australia with his vow, "I shall return." He did not return soon enough.

Following a surprise air raid by the Japanese which all but destroyed Philippine air defense, the Japanese launched a massive invasion in April 1942, overwhelming and capturing all but 13,000 of the 83,000 troops. On April 9, 1942, the Japanese forced 70,000 Philippine and American troops, including those from the New Mexico National Guard, to begin the 100-kilometer march up the Bataan Peninsula, without food or water. More than 10,000 troops died from thirst, hunger, or execution, marking one of the cruelest campaigns in the Pacific theater. The march also marked the imminent fall of the Philippines to Japan.

Those who survived the march vowed to make a special Lenten Pilgrimage to El Santuario de Chimayo the following spring. On crutches, in wheelchairs, on their knees, many of the troops made the pilgrimage in thanksgiving for their lives. There are other annual pilgrimages as well.

Thirty-one miles west of Chimayo stands the village of Los Alamos, chosen as the site for the laboratory of the J. Robert Oppenheimer's Manhattan Project in 1942. Its isolation from large population centers, its tremendous open

El Santuario de Chimayo, Chimayo, New Mexico. (Courtesy Holy Family Church.)

space, its remoteness from the East and West coasts, and its access to water and power made it the ideal setting for the initial American testing of the atomic bomb, which was destined to be dropped on Hiroshima and Nagasaki three years later.

In 1982, John Leahigh of Albuquerque founded what has become an annual ecumenical event: the Prayer Pilgrimage for Peace. Hundreds of pilgrims process from Chimayo out to the chapel, where they pray and meditate before having lunch. From there, a car caravan heads west 31 miles for the Jiminez Mountains at Los Alamos, the birthplace of the atom bomb. There, Believers of all faiths participate in a Native American ritual to bless the earth, and protect it from the ravages of war. The Prayer Pilgrimage for Peace continues to be repeated each year, on the first Saturday after Easter Sunday.

In 1986, the first international Earth Run for Peace occurred, and the flame that lit the torch held by the runners found a permanent burning place at El Santuario de Chimayo. It is one of three sites in the United States where the inspiration flame still burns; the other two are the gravesites of John Fitzgerald Kennedy and Martin Luther King, Jr.

Recognized for its unique place in southwest history, El Santuario de Chimayo achieved designation as a National Historical Landmark in 1970 by the Department of the Interior.

Sources

Canto, Minerva. "Chimayo Walk Reaffirms Faith," *Albuquerque Journal North*. April 2, 1994, 4.

Davis, Kenneth C. *Don't Know Much About History*. 1990. Avon Books, New York.

Kunetka, James W. *City of Fire: Los Alamos and the Birth of the Atomic Age*. 1978, Prentice-Hall Inc, Englewood Cliffs, NJ, 1978.

Price, Jess. "On The Road to Chimayo," *New Mexico Magazine*. March 1989.

Wade, Will. "The Ghost of Battles Past," *San Francisco Examiner*. December 15, 1996.

St. Michael's Cathedral

Affiliation: Russian Orthodox
Location: Sitka, Baranoff Island, Alaska
1816

The colonial powers responsible for the initial exploration of North America are most often remembered as England, Spain, Holland, and France. However, from the mid–18th century through the mid–19th century, Russian fur hunters known as the *promyshleniki* managed to forge from the northeast tip of Siberia, across a narrow channel of Pacific Ocean, down from the tip of Alaska nearly to the San Francisco Bay. Russian influence and architecture can be found as far down the western North American coast as northern California, and throughout the coastal islands of Alaska. In particular, in the former Russian Capital of Sitka on Baranov Island, stands an especially impressive memento to Russian-American colonization: St. Michael's Russian Orthodox Cathedral.

Sitka became the governmental seat of Alaska in 1808, replacing the capital at Kodiak. The initial St. Michael's Church originated in 1816, was first replaced in 1830, and for the final time by the cathedral, which was designed and built by Ivan Veniaminov, later canonized as Innocent I, first Bishop of Alaska, the Apostle to America. The magnificent cathedral features a huge octagonal dome, an 84-foot bell tower, and a cruciform design. Its cornerstone was laid in 1844, and it was dedicated in 1848. Although Russia officially left

St. Michael's Cathedral, Sitka, Alaska. (Courtesy Alaska State Library.)

Alaska in 1867, St. Michael's remained the center of the Russian Orthodox Church, which still maintains a substantial following in Alaska.

The Eastern Orthodox Catholic Church broke away from the Roman Catholic Church in 1054 AD, at the Council of Nicene. The various Orthodox Churches, including Russian, Greek, Byzantine, Ethiopian, Serbian and others, are linguistic and cultural variations on a familiar theme. The Orthodox Christian Church is often referred to as the "Church of the Catacombs" because of its efforts to maintain the traditions and practices as closely as possible to the early Christians. Indeed, the dark, frescoed, candlelit church sanctuaries, resounding with the chanted liturgies, often create a cave-like ambiance for the congregation. The ancient, symbolic beauty of the icons, the pungent power of the incense, the physical prostration and bowing of the congregation, the echoing song of the choir, the flickering enchantment of the candlelight: the Orthodox service influences all the senses, and communicates to the soul in ways no sermon ever can. There is a great emphasis on mysticism, on the interplay between the natural and the supernatural.

In his book *The Russians*, Hedrick Smith muses,

> [N]o ancient smell is more vividly unforgettable than the exotic incense of an Orthodox mass and no institution more central to renascent Russianism than Orthodox Christianity. For centuries the Church has been a special guardian of Russian culture. Anyone who knows Russia understands that churches are her artistic glory.

At the same time, the Orthodox Church maintains a very corporate approach to the church, and the laity have a greater role in the body of the Orthodox Church than in the Roman Church. Each individual has a part to play for the salvation of the whole. Divine guidance intercedes throughout the whole church, and influences the laity's election of clergy.

Throughout its history, the Russian Church enjoyed a powerful and often luxuriant societal position. The Patriarch of the Church was viewed as the ruler of spiritual matters as much as the Czar ruled the corporeal. In turn, the church has historically preached subservience by the people to the state, a position that benefited both the state and the church. But in the 18th century, Peter the Great wanted the subservience of the church itself. The Czar abolished the office of Patriarch, placing control of the church under his command.

Far greater change occurred in 1917, when the Bolsheviks recognized the impediment the Orthodoxy presented to the people in accepting and understanding the new Marxist philosophies. The Communists propagated atheism, believing the acceptance of the idea of

God relegated the people to a weakened state, in which they could not attain its greatest potentials. The Party placed great restraints upon the church and the message it presented to its people, censuring the priesthood and its proselytizing.

So intricately interwoven is the church with the land and its people, however, that trying to eradicate it completely from the Russian heritage is like trying to remove the minerals from the soil. It has been said, in fact, that in Russia "the trinity is church, soil, and Mother Russia."(Smith, p. 24) Indeed, Joseph Stalin allowed a resurgence of Orthodoxy during World War II, knowing it would create the fervor of patriotism needed for the struggle. And, while the Party continued to preach atheism and the power of the people, state representatives and spokespersons continued to baptize their children, collect their icons, and bury their dead in Orthodox ceremonies. Now, as the walls of the Soviet State have been torn down, there is a resurgence of appreciation, as never before, for the hallowed place of the Church in Russian culture and history.

The eastward Russian march toward the Pacific Ocean actually began in earnest in the early 17th century, when the country's fur trade began searching for virgin territory with which to embellish its harvest, as the availability of sable pelts gradually declined. By 1628, explorers has reached the Lena River in central Siberia. By 1639, the push had extended to the Sea of Okhotsk, and the edge of the north western Pacific Ocean. In 1650, the Trans-Siberian Railroad had reached the City of Inkutcsh, north of Mongolia, which had been established as a commerce center for the fur and tea trade with China.

As Russian explorers and hunters pushed further east, communication and political ties with St. Petersburg became stretched beyond the point of usefulness. These pioneers found they could rely less and less on supplies and equipment from the homeland. They would have to find other sources of food and natural resources for its expanding empire, and they began to look seaward.

The final link to the New World occurred during the reign of Czar Peter the Great (1672–1725). Peter I is known as "The Enlightener of Russia," because he had introduced the otherwise progressively backward Russia to the customs and technical advances of Western Europe. Now, he would bring Russia to the Western Hemisphere. Ever watchful for opportunities to increase his power and wealth, Peter was determined to expand the borders of the Russian Empire and to acquire whatever riches lay eastward beyond its present coast.

Peter I commissioned Vitus Bering, a Danish sailor with the rank of Captain in the Russian navy, to lead the voyage beyond the shores of Russia. After initial sojourns along the eastern coast of Asia, Bering journeyed eastward in 1728 aboard the *St. Gabriel,* and sailed through the 68-mile corridor of sea that would eventually bear his name. He returned to Russia and, after several years of delays, Bering return to the strait in 1741, aboard the *St. Peter.* Accompanied by Captain Alexia Chirikov aboard the *St. Paul,* Bering sighted the peak of Mt. Saint Elias on the western coast of Alaska, and within months had established posts on the Aleutian Islands. Bering and much of his crew died of scurvy on Commander Island in December 1741.

Occupying the various islands when Bering and Chirikov landed were an ancient, seafaring people later to be called the Aleut, and for whom the Aleutian Islands were named. The Aleut had named the land "Alaska," meaning "Great Land." Living in grass-covered underground dwellings, the Aleut had braved the chilling waves and blinding fogs, living off the abundance of the sea, long before the first Russian state ever existed.

In line with other European adventurers to the New World, the subsequent Russian occupation of the Aleutian Islands devastated the native population. Those not assimilated into the Russian lifestyle, or decimated by small pox, tuberculosis, measles, or venereal diseases, were butchered by smoking muskets. Russians murdered 3000 Aleuts in one invasion of Attu Island; the harbor at this western Aleutian Island is aptly named Massacre Bay. It is estimated the Aleut population before 1741 numbered between 15,000 and 30,000; by 1864, less than 200 remained.

Many of those not killed were manipulated into service of the promyshleniki, whose success at fur trapping in Alaska can be attributed directly to the Aleut. The natives introduced the Russians to the fur-covered, single-occupant canoes known as kayaks. These vessels could maneuver the jagged, inlet-laid Alaskan coast much more efficiently than the trappers' clumsy wooden rigs. The Aleut had been harvesting these waters for generations untold. They virtually re-schooled the promyshleniki in hunting techniques, and introduced the tools on which their enterprise would depend.

While the trappers' financial success can be traced to the tutelage of Aleuts, their lives and livelihoods rested squarely on the backs — or more precisely, the pelts — of the sea otter and the fur seal. Naturally peaceful, and not yet fearing the onslaught of these new hunters, these marine mammals provided not only the furs to barter, but often the only food available. As with the sable in their own native Siberia, the Russians hunted the otter and the seal to the brink of extinction. It is fortunate, particularly for the sea otter, that the Russians never ventured as far south as Monterey Bay, where the last major colony of sea otter exist today. If they had, the California sea otter may well have already been pushed passed the edge of oblivion. The Russians did hunt as far south as the Farallon Islands. However, between 1820 and 1840, they nearly obliterated a population of northern fur seals which once numbered an estimated 80,000.

As Russians began carving a foothold in North America, they discovered other nations were focusing their entrepreneurial eyes upon the future Alaska as well. In 1774, the Spanish explorer Juan Perez extended Spain's investigation of the New World as far north as Nootka Sound, on the west coast of Vancouver Island. England's Captain James Cook had sailed into Norton's Sound on the central Alaskan coast in 1778. The British also had established a flourishing fur enterprise called the Hudson Bay Company at Hudson Bay, and the Americans and British had established a joint fur trade at Astoria in present-day Oregon. Under the reign of Czar Paul I in 1799, the Russian-American Company emerged, having been granted a monopoly on the Russian fur trade in the New World.

In the summer of 1783, three ships carrying 192 men landed on the shores of Bering Island, establishing a permanent settlement there. A year later, a second settlement was built on Kodiak Island. Russian traders called upon priests to train and educate the natives, and thus Russian Orthodoxy came to Alaska. With the 1790 arrival of Alexander Baranov, recently named manager of the Russian-American Company, Kodiak became the Russian Capital in Alaska.

In 1802, Russians established Fort St. Michael near present-day Sitka. This was not an entirely welcome event, as the native Tlingits sternly resisted the occupation of the Russians. The Tlingits occupied the coast from present-day Juneau to British Columbia. Unlike the Aleut, the Tlingits relied on the vast timber resources of the mainland forests, and built substantial wooded boats, houses, and ceremonial totem poles. The Tlingits attacked Fort St. Michael, killing the men and capturing the women as slaves. Two years later, Russians retaliated, reestablishing permanently the settlement at Sitka, which would eventually be named the capital.

The next 14 years would see the height of Russian influence in North America under the rule of the indomitable Alexia Baranov. Isolated from communication and support from St. Petersburg, Baranov continued to search for ways to supply and feed the settlers under his regime. Under Baranov's nearly autonomous reign over the Russian-American Company (many times it seemed his will alone kept the Russian-American Company afloat) explorers and fur traders would expand southwest to the Hawaiian Islands, and as far south as Ft. Ross in Sonoma County, California. The Russian-American Company conducted business with the Hawaiian Royal Family, with British traders in Astoria, Oregon, and with the Spanish colony at San Francisco Bay. Unfortunately, Russians could never establish a permanent colony in any of these places, nor develop the agriculture they would need to support the overall operations of the Russian-American Company.

With the death of Baranov in 1818, the Russian colonies slowly began to dissipate. Sea otter and fur seal pelts became increasingly difficult to find. Wars between Russia, Sweden, Turkey, and Britain drew the attention and resources of St. Petersburg away from Sitka.

Many of the 13 governors of Alaska following Baranov proved to be competent and accomplished administrators. Governor Baron Ferdinand Wrangell, for example, established the first comprehensive North American conservation program in 1830, designed to replenish the sea otter and fur seal stocks. But all 13 lacked the drive and impunity of Baranov. While they managed to live at Sitka in relative splendor, there was little they could do to save the ever-weakening Russian presence in Alaska.

Finally, in 1854, as Russia prepared to enter the Crimean War against Britain, talk of selling Alaska to the Americans began to arise. Russia's defeat in the war created additional debts, for which extra capital would be needed. Since Britain regarded Alaska as little more than frozen wasteland, Russia turned to the United States, ever eager to pursue its expansionist ideals.

On March 30, 1867, at a ceremony on Capital Hill outside Sitka, Ambassador Edouard de Stoeckle of Russia executed the sale of Alaska to the United States with Secretary of State William H. Seward. The final sale price of $7.2 million for the 586,400 square miles of land placed the actual cost per acre at a little less than two cents. At the time, and for three decades following, the sale was decried as "Seward's Folly," and Alaska would be called "Seward's Icebox." Not until the gold strikes in 1896 would America begin to comprehend the incredible wealth of natural resources Alaska would bring to its coffers.

Through the 20th century, Alaska and Russia continued their unique and precarious relationship, as the United States and the Union of Soviet Socialist Republics gradually maneuvered to opposing positions on the global stage. Particularly after World War II, through the paranoia and intrigue of the cold war, each stared warily at the other across the iron curtain along the 68-mile-wide Bering Strait.

Through it all and beyond, St. Michael's Cathedral has stood tall, and the Russian Orthodox Church has maintained its considerable influence on the history and culture of Alaska. In 1962, the Cathedral was designated a National Historic Landmark. Four years later, it was destroyed in the downtown Sitka fire. But the Russian Orthodox community, which had waned in recent years, rallied in a resurgence of faith. They saved many of the precious icons from the fire, and completely rebuilt the cathedral. Today, St. Michael's stands as an emblem to the days when Russia occupied North America.

Sources

Davis, Kenneth C. *Don't Know Much About Geography*. 1992, Avon Books, NY.

Goetzman, William H. and Glyndwr Williams. *The Atlas of North American Exploration*. 1992, Prentice Hall, New York.

Hoagland, Alison K. *Buildings of Alaska*. 1993, Oxford University Press, New York.

Naske, Claus-M and Herman E. Slotnick. *Alaska: A History of the 49th State*. 1979, William B. Eerdmans Publishing Company, Grand Rapids, Michigan.

Smith, Hedrick. *The Russians*. 1975, Quadrangle/ The New York Times Books Company.

Wheeler, Keith. *The Alaskans*. 1977, Time-Life Books, Alexandria, VA.

DWIGHT MISSION

Affiliation: Congregational
Location: Near Russellville, Arkansas
1819

The story from Pope County, Arkansas, concerns two teachers who came to the territory with two very different purposes. One was an eccentric, mixed-blood Cherokee dreamer known as the Cherokee Cadmus, who developed the written Cherokee language. The other was a stalwart Congregationalist minister sent by the American Board of Foreign Missions (ABFM) to Pope County to found and build the territory's first school.

The Cherokee nation began scouting new hunting lands west of the Mississippi as early as 1795. Their ancestral home along the thickly forested southern Appalachian mountains, including southwest Virginia, the western Carolinas, eastern Tennessee, northern Georgia and Alabama, faced increasing European-American development at the turn of the 19th century. The Cherokee searched for open territory again, and many turned, or were turned, toward the "Father of Waters."

The Cherokee has been numbered among the so-called "Five Civilized Tribes," which included Choctaw, Creek, Chickasaw, and Seminole. European-Americans called them "civilized" because they, more than most Native Americans, emulated many of the mores and customs brought from Europe to America, and incorporated them into their own lifestyle.

They built roads and schools. They adopted European costume and deportment, and Cherokees often intermingled with European-Americans. They also developed a representative form of government. The Cherokee accepted many of the white man's practices, as if attempting to find a way for both cultures to remain together in the Southeast. But with these new ways, the Cherokee also discovered the trickery, deceit, and broken promises by which the white man would eventually overrun the land.

Through the 1803 Louisiana Purchase, President Thomas Jefferson obtained from Napoleon Bonaparte's France the vast majority of what would become American states west of the Mississippi River. Jefferson's administration agreed to make available to the Cherokee lands in the territory of Arkansas, in exchange for prime territory in Georgia. Chief John Jolly, a Cherokee elder from Tennessee who favored emigration to new lands, became one of the first to emigrate to Arkansas. The Treaty of 1817 established a Cherokee Reservation between the White and Arkansas rivers, in the northwest section of the present state of Arkansas.

In response to the migration of the Cherokee, the American Board of Foreign Missions — the Protestant organization charged with sending evangelical missions to foreign territories — sent the Reverend Cephas Washburn to Arkansas Territory in 1819. A hardy Congregationalist, born and raised in Vermont, Washburn had previous experience preaching the gospel to Georgia Cherokees. Anxious to embark upon his work, Washburn left Savannah, Georgia in the fall with three other missionary families. Crossing the present states of Alabama and Mississippi, he arrived in Little Rock, where he claimed to have preached the town's first sermon. The missionaries finally settled at the Illinois Bayou, west of present day Russellville.

Dwight Mission was named for President Timothy Dwight of Yale University in Connecticut. The missionaries and their wives built the entire mission compound, including the cabin dwellings for themselves, the large barn-like meeting house, the shops, the mills, and the mission schools.

The Cherokee welcomed Washburn and his colleagues. By 1828, a total of eight missionary families, all from New England, had come to live and work at Dwight Mission. Under the direction of Washburn, the mission quickly became a self-sustaining operation, due mostly to necessity. What little money and supplies the AFBM contributed — often less than $1000 and a box of groceries per year — frequently became delayed or lost in transit. The mission boasted a plentiful garden, in which Indian pupils grew much of the produce used by the mission.

The consistent tenets of the Calvinist-based churches (Puritan, Presbyterian, Methodist, Baptist, or Congregational) included the important role of education in the conversion of the soul. John Calvin (1509–1564) believed by learning different aspects and disciplines of humanity, one could gain understanding of the scriptures and the Spirit. Thus, a mission school designed to educate the ignorant mind accompanied each mission church sent to save the savage soul. By 1822, more than 80 Cherokee boys and girls had enrolled at the mission school, the first school in the territory of Arkansas. The enrollment would eventually reach more than 100.

Typically, the school maintained a vigorous and stringent schedule: At daylight, the students, required to live and work at the mission compound, arose for their agricultural and domestic chores. At 7:00 A.M., they busied themselves in the practices of reading, singing, and prayer, and then breakfast. School opened after breakfast, with time for play, singing, and prayer. Instructors presented the daily chapter of the Bible, often followed by a quiz on the passage. Writing, arithmetic, agricultural arts, and sewing were all included in the curriculum.

Of the ultimate aim of the mission, Washburn reportedly said,

> True, there was ... a desire to elevate [the Indians] by intellectual culture and the introduction among them of the arts and uses of civilized life; but the paramount aim and effect was to make known to them the only way to be saved from sin and eternal woe...we labored long and prayed often, and with strong, crying, and tears.... [Ashmore, p. 38]

Although Washburn claimed the salvation of the Indians' souls as the mission's primary concern its true function, as in the case of many of these missions, meant assisting the assimilation of the intruding culture into the residing culture. Indeed, Washburn seemed to interpret the Indians' adoption of American clothing as a sign of mission success. Whether it is the intention of the missionaries or not, this assimilation of the intruding culture seems to be the result, at least for those of the residing culture who assimilate. For those who do not, the fate can be much worse.

Although there appears to be no documentation of an actual meeting between Cephas Washburn and Sequoyah, the most famous of the Cherokee, it is hard to believe such a meeting never took place. It is easy to imagine the sober Calvinist minister's befuddlement at the exotic Cherokee sage. Yet it is also easy to imagine the respect each might have had for the other and his accomplishments.

Sequoyah, known to the white man by the name George Gist, was born in Tennessee in 1770. Even as a child, he displayed the traits of a gifted artist and silver smith. As an adult he reportedly became an alcoholic, a womanizer, and something of a loafer. An introverted dreamer, he became even more introspect

Painting of Dwight Mission, near Russellville, Arkansas, by unknown artist (from Russellville Centennial 1870–1970*).*

when drunk. Although many, both European and Native American, believed him to be insane or even enchanted, his genius can scarcely be doubted.

Many Cherokees held a fascination for the ways of the European. Sequoyah's special interest lay with the written language. He marveled at the white man's ability to communicate through the "talking leaves." When a hunting accident in 1812 limited his physical abilities, Sequoyah found he had suddenly more time to contemplate and create. He set to work to give the Cherokee tribe its own talking leaves.

By the time Sequoyah followed Chief Jolly to Arkansas in 1822, he had completed the Cherokee alphabet, or more precisely, the syllabary. He created a distinct symbol for each of 86 distinct Cherokee sounds. He successfully taught the syllabary to his daughter, Ahyoka, and then to neighboring children and adults. Eventually he would present his invention to the Chiefs of General Council, who were so astonished they immediately adopted it as the official Cherokee syllabary.

Sequoyah brought to Arkansas a collection of his own letters and compositions including his first, an exposé on the territorial boundary between the Cherokee Nation and American State of Georgia. He began teaching the syllabary to Cherokee children in Arkansas. Within a short time, it became possible for nearly every Cherokee to read and write in the native language, proving the Indian, just like the white man, could "talk from a distance." Interestingly, Sequoyah — despite the fascination with the white man's language which inspired his amazing invention — never learned to speak, read, or write English.

Sequoyah became the first known individual in history to compose a written language for an entire people. At the same time, the Cherokee became the first Native American tribe to use a written form of language. The Chiefs of General Council awarded Sequoyah a silver medal in 1824. Within four years the Cherokee Tribe published its first newspaper, *Cherokee Phoenix*. Life in Arkansas treated Sequoyah well, but it would not last.

The Treaty of 1817 proved merely a tiny mist in the Trail of Tears. The land in Arkansas originally belonged to the warlike Osage tribe.

The American government simply removed the land from the Osages, and gave it to the Cherokees; a decades old ploy of pitting one tribe against another. This created animosity and bloodshed between the Osage and the Cherokee which lasted for many years.

Even though the Jefferson administration ostensibly granted the Cherokees the right to resettle in Arkansas in 1817, they actually had no legal deed to the land. When they arrived in Arkansas, the Cherokee often found white settlers had claimed land promised to the natives. Indians regularly lost the right to own land, as well as many other rights, based on their status as non–Christian; if they were Christian, they were denied because they were Indian.

Gradually, one "treaty" after another, pushed the Cherokees out of Arkansas, as they had been pushed out of the Southeast. Cherokee territory overlapped onto valuable cotton-growing lands coveted by the whites. Under the Jackson and Van Buren administrations the Indian Removal Act of 1831 relocated the Cherokee to Oklahoma. En route, more than

3500 of the estimated 17,000 Cherokees lost their lives. Similar woeful tales can be told of the Choctaw, Creek, Chickasaw, and Seminole Indians. Hence, the road from Georgia to Oklahoma became known as the Trail of Tears.

Dwight Mission followed the Cherokee to the Arkansas-Oklahoma border, where it continued to thrive until the Civil War. Washburn retired from Dwight Mission in 1840, and continued to preach the Calvinist doctrine in Arkansas. Sequoyah had moved west of the Arkansas border, and settled in present day Texas. He died in 1842, in a cave near a Comanche camp.

Sources

Ashmore, Harry S. *Arkansas*. 1978, W.W. Norton & Company, Inc., New York.

Davis, Kenneth C. *Don't Know Much About History*. 1990, Avon Books, New York.

Ehle, John. *Trail of Tears: The Rise and Fall of the Cherokee Nation*. 1988, Doubleday Books, New York.

Terrell, John Upton. *American Indian Almanac*. 1994, Barnes & Noble Books.

Waldman, Carl. *Encyclopedia of Native American Tribes*. 1988, Facts on File Publications, New York.

OAKLAND CHAPEL

Affiliation: Presbyterian
Location: Alcorn State University, Alcorn, Clairborne County, Mississippi
1830

The college campus surrounding venerable Oakland Chapel in Clairbourne County, rural southwest Mississippi, made a dramatic sociological turn-about during the 19th century. This same campus, forged by the hands of Mississippi slaves in 1830, became America's first fully government supported university for African Americans during the Reconstruction Era after the Civil War. The campus became the site for one of the finest institutions of its kind in the nation. Oakland Chapel has marked the slow and painful climb toward equal access to and opportunity for higher education for the African American, a climb which has yet to be completed.

Seven miles west of Lorman, 80 miles

southwest of Jackson, 45 miles south of Vicksburg, and 40 miles northeast of Natchez, Mississippi, Presbyterians in 1828 established Oakland College among the moss-draped oak trees of present-day Clairborne County, five miles east of the Mississippi River. The college, in all its manifestations, is now the second oldest undergraduate and graduate institution in the state. Chartered in 1830 as the "Institution of Higher Learning under the care of Mississippi Presbyter," its doors opened on May 14, 1830.

The curriculum of Oakland College (the name changed in 1832) was designed for the instruction of planters, physicians, lawyers, and ministers. College courses included:

Oakland Memorial Chapel on the campus of Alcorn State University, Lorman, Mississippi. (Courtesy Alcorn State University.)

rhetoric, moral and mental philosophy, Christianity, astronomy, political economy, mathematics, and English literature. Early campus buildings, built largely by the slaves of Mississippi Presbyterians, included the president's house, the professors' residence, 15 student cottages and, of course, Oakland Chapel.

Standing three stories high, 112 feet in length by 65 feet in width, Oakland Chapel remains one of the best examples of Greek revivalism architecture in America. A classic brick building with six gleaming white pillars at the facade, its belfry and clock tower reveals the time to all four corners of the campus. The exquisite wrought-iron stairs leading to the chapel came from the nearby antebellum home called Windsor Castle. The chapel contained "rooms for recitations, philosophical apparatus, laboratory, cabinet, library, and a hall sufficient to seat 900 persons (Posey, Appendix p. 21). Oakland Chapel provided a hall of prayer for Oakland College, as it does for the current institution.

A widespread custom in pre–Civil War days required slaves of the ministers and staff to sit in the balcony during services. These African ancestors, ensnared in the greatest hypocrisy of the "land of the free," probably never dreamed their grandchildren and great grandchildren would one day attend commencement exercises in the same grand chapel.

Presbyterian minister Jeremiah L. Chamberlain, born in the then-anonymous little town of Gettysburg, served as Oakland College's first president. During the stormy decade before the Civil War, pro-unionist Chamberlain died from an assassin's bullet at the gates of the College, killed by a Port Gibson secessionist over a dispute of slavery. Chamberlain and his family are buried on campus.

By the advent of the Civil War, Mississippi showed a census of nearly 800,000 people, African-descendent slaves comprising 55 percent of that population. But Oakland College welcomed neither Africans nor women of any background to its wooded acreage, enrolling instead more than 1000 white male students, adding 30 student cottages to the plant. But the war forced the closure of the college, and efforts to revive the Presbyterian college later failed.

On May 13, 1871, in the midst of the post–Civil War Reconstruction Era, the state of Mississippi purchased the Oakland College site from the Mississippi Presbyterian synod for $40,000. John L. Lynch, the leading black politician and speaker of the Mississippi House of Representatives, signed a bill creating a new college from the old site, designated for the education of black youth. Oakland College became Alcorn University, in honor of Mississippi governor James Lusk Alcorn. Governor Alcorn, regarded as quite the progressive thinker among Mississippi politicians, nevertheless favored separate but equal education for blacks, and harbored many of the common myths and prejudices concerning the education of African Americans:

> I myself was a slaveholder, and apprehensive that the restraints of reason would have been insufficient in the case of a people who had been held under lifelong restraints of force, I did not accept the facts of reconstruction without some lingering doubts. ... To set at rest that form of opposition to the great work on which the happiness of our fellow-citizens of all classes depends, and to assure you my judgment and conscience as to the wisdom of reconstruction, I have instituted investigations...of the capacity of the colored people for well-ordered freedom. [Posey, p. 4]

Tougaloo College and Shaw College, both founded in 1866, predated Alcorn University as higher learning institutions in Mississippi for blacks. But both Tougaloo and Shaw were private institutions, while Alcorn University — under the auspices of 1862 federal legislation called the Morrill Land Grant Act — became the first American land-grant, state-subsidized college exclusively for the use of African Americans. State legislation provided $50,000 over ten years for the establishment of the university, plus three-fifths of the proceeds from the sale of 30,000 acres of public land in Mississippi, scripted for agricultural use. In all, the state contributed $113,400 towards Alcorn University, expanding the campus size from 225 to 1700 acres.

In July of 1874, an advertisement describing the new Alcorn University appeared in Frederick Douglass' *The New National Era*:

> The location, far removed from the contaminating influences of city life, is high and

healthful; and the surroundings are agreeable and attractive in an imminent degree." Its commodious buildings all erected and furnished for academic purposes, are situated in a beautiful oak grove, gently undulating and clothes in a perennial dress of verdue pleasing to the eye and quietude. No discrimination is recognized by the institution on account of color, caste or other class distinctions. [Posey, pp. 10–11]

The most important personality in the development of Alcorn University was also one of the most compelling figures of the 19th century Reconstruction Era. Hiram Rhoades Revels was born on September 27, 1827, in Fayetteville, North Carolina. A descendent of free blacks, he attained ordination as a Methodist minister in 1845, and served as pastor for the African Methodist Episcopal Church in Baltimore. Revels actively urged escaped slaves to fight for their own freedom, organizing several black regiments for the Union army. During the early days of the Reconstruction Era he worked for the Vicksburg branch of the Freedman's Bureau, established in March 1865 by Congress for the purpose of rehabilitating the nation's four million slaves. Revels also organized a school for freed slaves in St. Louis, Missouri.

In 1866 he settled in Natchez, Mississippi, with his wife Phoeba Bass, who eventually bore six daughters. He rose to alderman of the town in 1868, and soon gained election to the Mississippi State Senate, representing Adams County. Impressed by Revels passion and oratory skills, state senators pushed for his 1870 election to the United States Congress. Despite Revels' election victory, Senators felt compelled to debate the admission of an African American into the "hallowed halls." The Senate held its own vote on the matter, which Revels won by a tally of 48 to 8. On February 25, 1870, Hiram Revels became the first African American United States Senator in history.

Senator Revels reportedly always felt ambivalent toward politics, but also felt he could better serve his people from the stump than from the pulpit. Nevertheless in 1871, he resigned his seat in the Senate to become the first president of the newly organized Alcorn University. Revels served until 1873, resigning over

political battles with the state governor. He resumed the position in 1875, completing his second term as Alcorn president in 1882, resigning due to of ill health. He died of a stroke in 1901, at a religious conference in Aberdeen, Mississippi.

During Revels' tenure as president, the University adopted the name Alcorn Agricultural and Mechanical College, which better illustrates the institution's purpose and curriculum. In 1878, Alcorn A&M had eight faculty, and 179 mostly male, black students.

It offered a three year primary course, a two year preparatory class, and a four year college course. Its curriculum consisted of English, Latin, and mathematics, but emphasized a range of industrial arts: agriculture, carpentry, blacksmythery, printing, painting, nurse training, sewing, domestic industries, and laundry. By today's university standards, Alcorn A&M College provided little more than a trade school for its students. Yet, these courses became the cornerstone for an institution which consistently expanded its mission and its scope over the decades, adding the classic arts, letters, and science studies to its vocational courses. With a reputation for excellence, Alcorn evolved into what has been widely regarded as one of the finest "black colleges" in the country, producing more than 20,000 alumni over its 127 year history.

Like other historically black universities, Alcorn University has had to struggle to maintain adequate funding from the state. Despite the bigotry and exclusionist tactics faced over the decades, Alcorn and the other black universities have shone as often lonely beacons to African Americans seeking equal economic opportunities in the "land of the free." As of 1993, these institutions have awarded nearly one-third of the 1.1 million undergraduate degrees earned by African Americans. Almost every African-American physician or dentist who has ever come from Mississippi graduated from Alcorn, which has placed alumni on the faculties of colleges and universities throughout the country. As the national media reflect a return of African Americans to the Deep South due to expanding social and economic opportunities, Alcorn and other traditionally black institutions may again find themselves at the center of the effort to bring educational and economic opportunity and advancement to all Americans.

Today, Alcorn State University boasts a faculty and staff of more than 500, and a student body of more than 3000. Sixty percent of the current student body are females, and the demography has become multicultural. Fifty percent of the current Alcorn students obtain post-graduate degrees.

Through all the transformations, from Oakland College to Alcorn University, from Alcorn A&M to Alcorn State University, Oakland Chapel has remained and endured. In 1888 the Chapel hosted the commencement for Beulah Turner Robinson, Alcorn's first female graduate, and the first black woman to graduate from a state-supported college in America. In 1989, it welcomed President George Bush to the commencement exercises.

Today, it provides space for prayer meetings, laboratory work, and classrooms for Alcorn's more than 300 multicultural, coeducational students. Fully renovated in 1959, Oakland Chapel entered the National Register of Historic Places in 1975, as landmark for the oldest land-grant college for African Americans in the country.

Sources

Carter, Hodding. *The Angry Scar: The Story of Reconstruction*. 1959, Doubleday & Company, Inc., Garden City, NY.

Davis, Kenneth C. *Don't Know Much About History*. 1990, Avon Books, New York.

National Register of Historic Places, United States Department of Interior. *Statement of Significance, Alcorn University*. 1975.

Posey, Josephine McCann *Against Great Odds: The History of Alcorn State University*. 1994, University Press of Mississippi, Jackson.

Vobejda, Barbara. "Blacks' Migration to South Accelerates." *San Francisco Chronicle*. January 29, 1998.

KIRTLAND TEMPLE

Affiliation: Church of Jesus Christ of Latter Day Saints
Location: Kirtland, 20 miles northeast of Cleveland, Ohio
1836

The site most associated with the Church of Jesus Christ of Latter Day Saints, is Salt Lake City, Utah. Brigham Young (1801–1877) established this utopia for the Mormons 17 years after the prophet Joseph Smith founded the church. On the shores of the Great Salt Lake, the Mormons spent 40 years building the fabulous Mormon Temple and Tabernacle out of Utah gray granite. Mormon missionaries reached out to the world, and continued to develop the building of worldwide membership; but always with an eye toward Salt Lake City, which now stands as the administrative heart of the church.

There is another place, however, quite a bit less known, but no less instrumental in the evolution of the Mormon Church and philosophy. On a small hill just south of the town of Mentor, overlooking the northeast Ohio village of Kirtland, stands the very first temple established by the Church of Jesus Christ

of Latter Day Saints. Under the direction of Joseph Smith, the Kirtland Temple was built by the members of the fledgling church as its first "…House of Prayer, House of Fasting, House of Learning, House of Glory, House of Order, House of God…"(Launius, p. 1)

Any story of the Latter Day Saints must begin with the story of its prophet, founder, and first president, Joseph Smith, Jr. Born in Sharon, Vermont, on December 23, 1805, Smith grew up during the Great Second Awakening, when Protestant sects throughout the western world underwent a revival in energy, enthusiasm, and expansion. Smith's family moved to Palmyra, New York, when he was ten. Then, between 1819 and 1827, Smith is said to have experienced his conversion, a series of revelations which led to the publication of the Book of Mormon, and the establishment of the new church.

Reportedly, some time between 1819 and

1821, Smith set out for a walk among the woods outside his Palmyra home. While contemplating spiritual questions troubling him, Smith claims to have encountered a vision of God and Jesus. In the vision Smith is warned not to join any existing church, as all churches fall short in knowledge and authority of God. Instead, the apparition tells him he will be the instrument of a reorganization of God's church on earth.

The next reported revelation takes place on September 21, 1823. An angel named Moroni appears to Smith, revealing gold tablets, the Scripture which provides the basis of the Book of Mormon. For the next six years, relying on revelations from Moroni and the gold tablets, Smith dictates the Book of Mormon to scribe Martin Harris. The Book of Mormon is published, as what Smith claims is an addendum to the Bible — God's attempt to further clarify the Bible for the modern, western age.

According to the Book of Mormon, in 600 B.C., before the Babylon invasion, a tribe of Israelites under the leadership of a man named Lehi set sail from Israel, across Indian and Pacific Oceans, landing upon the west coast of America. Over the next 600 years, the tribe multiplies, and divides into two conflicting communities: the Nephites and the Lamanites. After his crucifixion, Jesus Christ appears to the tribes, vowing to set a new order. Christ establishes a peaceful coexistence for the next 200 years. But again, divisiveness develops between the two groups, culminating with the destruction of the Nephites at the hand of the Lamanites, in A.D. 421. The last prophet of the Nephites is Moroni, whose father was named "Mormon." It is Moroni in his deified form who appeared to Joseph Smith. The Lamanites, according to the Mormon scriptures, are the ancestors of the American Indians.

Armed with the new Book of Mormon and the new inspiration, the energetic and charismatic Smith leads six of his followers to establish the Church of Jesus Christ of Latter Day Saints on April 6, 1830, in Palmyra, New York. From that point, the word of the new church begins to spread throughout the northeast.

Through the novice missionary movement, the new religion is well received in northeastern Ohio; so well, in fact, that Smith and the leaders decided to institute church headquarters there. Subsequently, Smith claims to have received a revelation to build a temple in Kirtland, with exacting details, dimensions, and features laid out in the vision. By 1831, Joseph Smith and his wife Emma move to Kirtland, joining a burgeoning Mormon community of more than 200. Temple construction commences in June of 1833.

Following the directions presented in his vision, the Mormons build the temple on a hill facing eastward, above the town of Mentor in northeast Ohio. A three-story building, the temple is 79 feet long and 59 feet wide. The single belfry and spire would rise nearly 100 feet above the ground. The three-story structure would be fashioned of native materials, including poplar, oak, and walnut from the forest, and sandstone from the nearby quarry. Its outer walls would be "rough cast," through a mixture of pebbles and sand with the plaster. The cost of the temple, estimated at between $45,000 and $70,000 in 1830 dollars, would be met through donations from growing church memberships in communities throughout the northeast.

The first temple floor would house the sanctuary for general community worship and rituals. On either end of the sanctuary elaborate pulpits for the Aaronic and Melchizedek priesthoods would be built. The Priestly Order of Aaron would include the younger priests, who would officiate over specific rites such as baptism. The Melchizedek order would include the elder, who would guide the direction of the earthly church.

The second floor of the church would contain the classrooms for the School of the Apostles, where priests (any faithful male church member is eligible) would receive their training. This school would compose the Doctrine and Covenants in 1835, which would be regarded as *the* defining church position on various matters of faith, based on the revelations of Joseph Smith, Jr. The Apostles would engage in study of a wide range of subjects, including history, geography, political science, foreign languages, and philosophy, as well as theology and religious history. Smith even ini-

tiated a course in Hebrew, conducted by a Jewish scholar. This tradition of the importance of education would continue through the history of the Mormon Church.

The temple's third floor would contain more classrooms, rooms for priestly quorum meetings, and offices for the management of the congregation and church. The entire structure would be illuminated by a series of 30 magnificent windows of various styles and sizes.

Some of the church's greatest early leaders participated in the building of the Kirtland Temple. Joseph Smith himself labored in the sandstone quarry alongside his brother, Hyrum Smith and served as foreman for the project. Young Brigham Young, skilled as a painter and glazier before joining the church, worked on the elaborate church interior. Emma Smith led the women's efforts in cooking and sewing for the laborers, which reportedly numbered no less than 100 at a time during the project.

Early in the course of temple construction, the Saints confronted the persecution from non-believers which would beset them throughout their history. At night, vandals would ravage the work site and knock down walls erected by the Saints. Even cannon fire threatened the project. Finally, the Mormons posted guards around the construction site, to protect the work in progress.

It is difficult to pinpoint exactly what about the Mormons so infuriated nonbelievers. Certainly, non–Mormons pointed to the practice of polygamy, which was actually practiced by less than 5 percent of all Mormons, as an abomination in the eyes of God, and used its termination as a rationalization for tormenting the Saints. But the Mormon Church did not acknowledge the practice of polygamy until the 1840s. (The practice was officially banned by the church in 1890, essentially in exchange for Utah's statehood six years later.) The persecution felt in the 1830s, therefore, cannot be explained by polygamy.

More likely, non–Mormons felt religious, economic, and political competition from the Latter Day Saints. Mormons customarily conducted business (often quite successfully) only with other Mormons; they voted as a bloc during elections, and they drew membership (and, therefore, tithes) away from established churches. As often occurs when faced with a new belief system, non-believers feared the Mormon faith as a threat to their own faith. Non-Mormons resented the challenge of the Saints' system of beliefs, especially when that system seemed to lead to greater levels of happiness and prosperity.

The dedication of the completed Kirtland Temple commenced before a gathering of more than 1000 on March 27, 1836. For weeks following the dedication, church members testified to revelations and visions which appeared to various members of the Kirtland Temple. During one such experience, Saints witnessed to the appearance of angels, and tongues of fire as in the Pentecostal scene from the Gospel of Luke. Another dramatic apparition involved the appearance of Jesus, followed by Moses, Elias, and Elijah, entrusting Joseph Smith and Oliver Cowdery with the new "holy priesthood."

The Latter Day Saints finally entered their first temple, which would be the center of the Mormon community in Kirtland. All important rites and rituals of the Mormon faith are performed for the community at temples such as Kirtland's. Mormon couples married at the temple are considered united for eternity, beyond even death. Children are believed to be incarnate souls which existed before birth and are baptized by Aaronic priests into the church customarily at the age of eight. Ordinances of death, including scripture readings and baptism, can be performed vicariously for souls of even those long dead. The study of genealogy thus becomes important, enabling relatives with firm knowledge of the deceased relative's life and character to accept the ordinances by proxy for the ancestor. By a faithful life and participation in the rituals, Mormons believed humanity could eventually achieve divinity, and be counted among the deity in a polytheistic afterlife with God the Father, the heavenly Mother, and Jesus Christ.

Kirtland Temple, near Cleveland, Ohio. (Courtesy Library-Archives, Reorganized Church of Jesus Christ of Latter Day Saints, the Auditorium, Independence, Missouri.)

Unfortunately, the original Kirtland community would not last. The economic depression called the Panic of 1837 forced the closure of the bank Joseph Smith had organized to add financial stability to the Kirtland community. The sudden foreclosure added debtors to the list of adversaries to Smith and his church, and forced many of the Mormons westward.

Most of the Mormons abandoned Kirtland by 1838 and true ownership of the Temple and other church properties remained a controversy for the next four decades. Since the Mormon Church had not yet been recognized as a legal entity, legal possession of the temple would have to lie with an individual or individuals, none of whom apparently held a clear claim to the property. In 1860, the probate court of Lake County took possession of the property, and began liquidating the holding to pay off debts owed by Joseph Smith, Jr., from the Panic of 1837.

Finally, the Reorganized Church of Jesus Christ of Latter Day Saints — an offshoot of the Mormon Church under the direction of Joseph Smith, III, sought a more conservative path than the one forged by Joseph Smith, Jr., in Navuoo — filed suit to claim possession as successor to the original church. In February 1880, the Court of Common Pleas named the Reorganized church as the "legal successor to the early Mormon organization founded by Joseph Smith, Jr., and heir to the rights and possessions of the early organization." Over the next 79 years the Kirtland Temple served the local Reorganized church, until the membership initiated a full scale renovation of the temple in 1959.

Meanwhile by 1838, the path of Joseph Smith and the early Mormon leaders had taken several decisive turns. Smith and his followers moved to Liberty in Jackson County, Missouri, in 1838. Unfortunately, the persecution followed them, leaving Smith jailed for six months in Liberty. In 1839, Smith escaped, and moved his church to Navuoo, along the shores of the Mississippi River in northwest Illinois. For a time, it appeared the Mormon Church, and in particular Smith, would enjoy a life of new abundance in Navuoo. The Saints built a new temple, and the city (often known

as "The City of Joseph") enjoyed an economic boom; with more than 10,000 residents, Navuoo became the second largest city in Illinois. Smith assumed positions of mayor of Navuoo, and commander of the city militia; he even announced his candidacy for the President of the United States in 1844. But the economic jealousy and hostility that followed Smith and his church finally erupted into a boiling cauldron over the topic of polygamy.

By 1843, Smith had apparently sanctified the practice of polygamy among a select group of his Apostles. Smith (who himself may have had as many as 50 wives) validated the practice by pointing to polygamous Biblical characters, such as Solomon; they justified polygamy as a way of propagating the pure genealogy of the Mormon priesthood. They also regarded it as a noble way of assimilating single women into the fold. Nonbelievers, of course, attributed the Mormon connubial custom to the lustful, degenerate natures of the Mormon leaders; tales of great orgies in the Mormon temples circulated among the non–Mormon rabble.

(The fact that polygamy indeed existed among the Saints points to the subservient role of women, particularly in the early church; there was no advocacy, after all, for polyandry in the church. Since the formative years, however, the role of women has been both improved and expanded.)

In any case, the controversy of polygamy fueled the fires of internal dissension within the Church of Latter Day Saints. Some dissidents spoke outwardly against Smith and his elders, hurling accusations involving a multitude of immoral sexual practices, including polygamy. These charges fueled the organization of non–Mormon vigilantes, dedicated to the eradication of the Mormon prophet and church. In response to the mob, Smith considered organizing his militia, in defense of himself and his church. Finally, to avoid an all out war, Smith and his brother Hyrum turned themselves into the authorities on June 26, 1844. The Smith brothers were confined to a two story jailhouse outside the city of Navuoo. The next day, a vigilante mob charged the jail, fatally shooting Joseph Smith, Jr., and his brother.

Three years following the death of the

prophet, Brigham Young led a huge wagon train of Mormons, perhaps as many as 12,000 trailing behind over 120 miles of prairie, to their new home in Salt Lake City, Utah. Between 1853 and 1893, the Mormons built their fabulous six-spired granite Tabernacle, with the statue of Moroni on its highest steeple. Other landmarks — such as the Beehive House, the Administration Building, the General Church Office Building, the Historical Department (containing the renowned Church Library-Archives and Genealogical Department), and the Relief Society — followed, along with Brigham Young University in nearby Provo.

Today, Salt Lake City, with an area population of more than one million, stands as the undisputed capital of activities for the Latter Day Saints, and the Mecca of Mormonism. Membership of the Latter Day Saints has doubled once every 15 years over the last century and a half. Today, the Mormons number more than 10 million worldwide, making it the most widespread and successful homespun religion in the history of the United States.

But as the Mormon Church prepares to enter the millennium as one of the world's major religions, the Latter Day Saints must gaze 1500 miles to the east and 161 years to the past toward the little town of Kirtland, Ohio. Here, in this village of 5880 inhabitants, prophet Joseph Smith, Jr., gained his first, stormy, ecclesiastic foothold. On a little hill above the village stands the Kirtland Temple, whose legacy is Salt Lake City and all its glory.

Sources

Arrington, Leonard J., and Davis Bitton. *The Mormon Experience*. 1979, Alfred A. Knopf, New York.
Bishop, Peter and Michael Darton. *The Encyclopedia of World Faiths: An Illustrated Survey of the World's Living Religions*. 1987, MacDonald and Co., Ltd., London and Sydney.
Doctrine and Covenants of the Church of Jesus Christ of Latter-Day Saints. 1973, Deseret Book Company, Salt Lake City.
Launius, Roger D. *An Illustrated History of Kirtland Temple*. 1986, Herald Publishing House, Independence, Missouri.
Lattin, Don. "Mormon Crusade Goes Global." *San Francisco Chronicle*. April 8, 1996.
Smith, Joseph, Jr. *Book of Mormon*. 1986, Church of Jesus Christ of Latter-Day Saints, Salt Lake City.

WHITMAN MISSION

Affiliation: Presbyterian
Location: Waiilatpu, near Walla Walla, Washington
1837

On the overcast evening of November 29, 1847, Roman Catholic missionary Father Broillet, on his way to visit the nearby Cayuse Indian Camp, came upon the normally bucolic compound of the Whitman Presbyterian Mission at Waiilatpu, outside what is now Walla Walla in southeast Washington State. This evening, however, the scene was anything but placid. Smoke trailed skyward from the smoldering blacksmith shop at the center of the compound. Broken windows could be found on all the mission buildings. Scattered among the buildings and fields lay the bodies of 12 European Americans, all of whom had been attacked and killed by members of the Cayuse Tribe. Dr. Marcus Whitman, physi-

cian and head of the mission, lay in the kitchen alongside his adopted son Jonathan Sager. Whitman's neck and shoulders had been butchered with a Cayuse tomahawk, his face slashed nearly to the point of non-recognition. Throughout the adobe house, windows and doors had been shattered, the cooking stove destroyed, books and papers scattered about, and utensils and clothing missing, all signs of the terrible anger and resentment which had harbored for 11 years within the Cayuse.

Outside, in a shallow pool of muddied water, lay the limp and lifeless body of Narcissa Whitman. A bullet wound penetrated her chest, and, like her husband's, her face had been slashed and mutilated. Of the 12 missionaries and hired hands that had been killed, she was the only woman. Cayuse rarely killed women; more often than not, they were assimilated into the tribe. Her death served as testimony to the pointed bitterness the tribe felt toward her.

Forty-seven injured, sick, and horrified survivors, many of them children, had huddled for safety in the bunk house used for emigrants passing to Oregon. Within two days, five Cayuse tribesmen, including the chief Tilokaikt, were rounded up and held responsible for the deaths of the missionaries. But clearly, the attack of the Cayuse upon the Presbyterian Mission had been supported by many in the tribe, and seen as a form of self-defense, to save the life and culture of the Cayuse. Within a month, all five were put to death. Tilokaikt was quoted as saying, "Did not your missionaries tell us Christ died to save his people? So die we, to save our people." Unfortunately, Tilokaikt and his brother Cayuse could not.

The story of Whitman Mission recalls the hopeful naiveté of the 19th century missionary movement. Though seemingly effective within homogeneous, European-American communities from which they came, these missions more often than not failed miserably in their ultimate goal, which was to Christianize the native population. Faced with the vast cultural gulf separating the missionaries from the "heathen," the missionaries rarely converted substantial numbers to Christianity, and in fact set in motion, often unwittingly, the sequences of events that would lead to the obliteration of the native culture. In the case of the Whitman's, the result was the destruction of the missionaries themselves.

The journey of Narcissa Whitman began in Prattsburg, New York, where she was born on March 14, 1808. She was the eldest of eight children of Clarissa and Stephen Prentiss, an esteemed entrepreneur and landowner in northern New York. She grew up in an upper-middle class home, in which she became accustomed to a comfortable, clean, orderly life, in which all her physical and material needs were easily met.

Her mother raised Narcissa from an early age to be strong, pious, and evangelical. Clarissa Prentiss believed saving souls provided the purpose of life for the devout Presbyterian. Narcissa loved and nearly idolized her mother and, determined to emulate her, she pledged herself to missionary work at age 15. With little opportunities open to women in the early 19th century, Narcissa saw missionary work as the only avenue toward "colorful adventure." She would read inspiring (and often unrealistic) portrayals of the missionary life in evangelical journals such as *Mission Herald*, in which the heroic "envoys of Christ" would open the eyes of the poor to the enlightenment of European-American Christendom.

Narcissa received her missionary training by working within church female organizations, and later teaching in church-based schools. Among men and women whose backgrounds and beliefs proved very similar to her own, she developed a reputation as a bright, forceful, and enthusiastic evangelist. She witnessed portions of the Great Protestant Revival of the early 19th century, in which fits of weeping, groaning, and shaking accompanied and validated conversion. These physical phenomena authenticated the "born again" experience. Narcissa grew to believe that all those truly converted to Christianity would experience the same involuntary experience.

Narcissa, through the model of her own mother and through the practice of church members, grew judgmental, openly critical of behaviors among church members which seemed less than appropriate. She believed justified chastisement to be an important component to the salvation of souls, the proper method for keeping fellow Christians on the narrow road to heaven.

By the 1830s, Narcissa hungered for missionary work, for the work of the Lord in some exotic locale among the spiritually starving. She naively believed the evangelical work she performed among the white, Anglo-Saxon, Protestant community of upstate New York had prepared her emotionally to enter the missionary field. Surely, she believed, all those who did not know Christ would respond in the same positive, grateful manner once the Gospel of Truth was revealed to them. In truth, her experience in homogeneous Prattsburg did little to prepare her for work among those whose appearances, lifestyles, histories, and belief systems differed so greatly from hers.

Marcus Whitman was born in 1799 in Steuben County in Western New York to Alice and Beza Whitman. His father died when Marcus was seven, and his mother seemed to reject him, sending him off to live with other family members in Massachusetts. The absence of close family ties seemed to create a restless character; throughout his life, he seemed to spend more time traveling between tasks than anything else. He was a man on the move, and like Narcissa he yearned for missionary work at an early age.

Instead of the ecclesiastic path, Marcus actually studied medicine in 1823. In those days, medicine did not hold the kind of status it enjoys today, and much of the medical arts involved trial and error as opposed to applied skill and knowledge. Nevertheless, Marcus apprenticed as a physician in 1825, settled in Rushville, and worked toward a career as a medical missionary. In 1832, he moved to Wheeler, New York, seven miles southeast of Prattsburg. Ill health, to which he was susceptible all his life, caused the rejection of his initial application to the American Board of Foreign Missions (ABFM) in 1834. But with recruits dwindling for American Indian Missions, the ABFM accepted Whitman's application in 1836.

Although Narcissa and Marcus had known each other through various social and religious functions, they formally met through Samuel Parker, a fiery congregational missionary wanting to move west to convert the heathen natives of western North America. Their marriage became one of pragmatism as much as passion. Both wanted to be missionaries, and the ABFM encouraged such couples to marry to preserve piety. After a year's engagement, in which they actually spent less than a week together, the two embarked on a life of missionary work together. They married in late February 1836. Within a month, they would be bound for the west and their missionary future.

The Whitmans, accompanied by several other missionaries headed for the same territory, traveled by boat from Pittsburgh to St.

Louis, and then by horse and wagon between St. Louis and Ft. Vancouver on the Columbia River. During the course of the trip, the Whitmans experienced their first contact with members of the Nez Percé, Flathead, and Pawnee Indian tribes. But this introduction to Indian culture did nothing to change their misconceptions; they remained inclined to regard the natives as novelties, and as spirit-hungry savages desperate for enlightenment from a stern but gentle missionary.

Despite the harsh and arduous conditions of emigration and the death of a traveling companion the Whitmans survived the journey. They arrived at Fort Vancouver on September 1, 1836, and finally settled 25 miles east of Ft. Walla Walla, in a place known as Waiilaptu. Here, they would begin their task of converting the heathen.

The object of the Whitmans' mission was a faction of the Shahaptin linguistic group of Indians known as the Cayuse. Closely tied in history, language, and customs with the more famous Nez Percé of Washington, Idaho, and Montana, the Cayuse had occupied the Walla Walla River Valley for thousands of years. Hunters and gatherers by nature, the Cayuse adapted when European settlers began to arrive in the northwest, becoming brave and skillful horsemen. Their tribal organization featured loose family ties, in which children were raised liberally and with few injunctions. Men held responsibility for the hunting, gathering, and defense of the tribe, while women maintained the tribal camp.

The Cayuse Indians initially agreed to allow the missionaries to settle on their land because they believed that participation in their European religious rituals would gain them access to the white man's technology and abundance. However, the Cayuse never intended to abandon their ancient ways and adopt Christianity, something the missionaries felt would be but a matter of time.

Within months, the Whitmans' expansive, two story adobe home became the center of missionary life at Waiilaptu. The home featured a large kitchen with cook stove and pantry, with bedrooms upstairs. It was furnished with household goods and furnishings Narcissa had picked up at Ft. Vancouver. Be-

Whitman Mission. (Courtesy National Park Service.)

hind the house a prosperous garden grew, in which the Whitmans raised potatoes, vegetables, and melons. Eventually, a dormitory and a blacksmith shop would be added to the compound.

Although Marcus Whitman was considered the administrator of the mission, and he generally led the Sabbath service held at the Whitman home, Narcissa actually directed the religious education for the mission. During the week she ran the mission school from her kitchen. At first Narcissa seemed optimistic and confident about her ability to transform the Cayuse. But over the months and years, the task grew much more daunting then she could have ever imagined.

No amount of missionary zeal could surmount the vast cultural gulf separating the Cayuse and the Whitmans. For 11 years the Whitmans, particularly Narcissa, since Marcus was often off providing medical treatment to missionaries, Indians, and settlers outside the mission, labored to transform the Cayuse, culturally as well as spiritually. The Whitmans

tried to introduce the Cayuse to agriculture. Although the Cayuse appreciated the abundance of food it produced, the Indians considered the tilling of the soil a violation of mother earth, and against the hunter-gatherer tradition. Narcissa tried to encourage the Indian women to give up their subservient roles in their tribal community, and entreated them to perform European-American chores the Indians considered beneath them. Narcissa never mastered the Indians' language well, and there were differences in dress, hygiene, parenting, and housekeeping which could never be surmounted. To worsen matters, Narcissa believed the transfer of worthwhile culture could occur in only one direction: Anglos to Indians. She thought it inconceivable for a white woman to learn anything from the Indian. In short, Narcissa Whitman tried to apply Christian love to that which she could not understand, trust, or even tolerate.

The most crucial cultural gap, however, involved the very heart of the mission's purpose: salvation of the Cayuse souls. For all the Whitmans' preaching and warning, proselytizing and prophesying, the Cayuse could not understand the concept of sin and eternal punishment. To the Cayuse all of life was good, and all its pleasures good. When Narcissa admonished the men of their tribe for their gambling, their horse racing, and their polygamy, the tribesmen could not accept it and eventually came to resent it. They certainly did not appreciate the foretelling of an eternity in the fires of hell. For Narcissa, however, such admonishments comprised her sacred duty.

Over the years the Indians' resentment grew. According to Cayuse custom, relationships were greatly based on the exchange of goods and services; if a man gave another man a gift, it was expected the second man would reciprocate. The Cayuse had initially agreed to accept the missionaries, and participate in their religious rituals because they believed they would share in the white man's technology and riches. But when they saw the Whitmans growing more prosperous, particularly as more white settlers came from the east, the Cayuse came to grudge their presence, and began to demand the missionaries either leave, or pay for the land.

By the mid–1840s, the Whitmans had all but given up on converting the Cayuse. Instead, they turned their attention to the growing wave of emigrants to Oregon Territory, and the Whitman Mission for all intents and purposes became a way station for weary travelers. Not unexpectedly, Marcus and Narcissa felt much more comfortable in the role of innkeeper for weary travelers, than they ever had as missionaries. The focus of the mission essentially changed from converting the heathen to Christianity, to replacing the heathen with white Christians. One way or another, it seemed the Walla Walla River Valley would become Christian land. As thousands of emigrants crossed the Walla Walla, many of them settled in the area, and the Cayuse watched as their beloved, ancient lands slowly disappeared. Soon, tensions between the Whitmans

and the Cayuse increased, and small but indicative incidents of violence erupted.

In 1847, as many as five thousand emigrants came to Oregon, many passing through the Whitman mission to rest and resupply. With them came the diseases, dysentery, malaria and, most particularly and tragically, measles. Between October and November of 1847, nearly half the Cayuse tribe had died from the disease; reportedly, the missionaries buried five or six Indian corpses every day. This proved the final blow. The Cayuse, who recognized Marcus Whitman as a healer with special spiritual powers, blamed his medicines for the deaths, and plotted for some time to kill him. Finally, for the sake of the health and safety of the tribe, the attack commenced on that cloudy November morning in 1847.

The bloody attack by the Cayuse only served to fuel the bigotry and hatred already felt by most of America toward the American Indian. Throughout the 19th century, and well into the 20th century, Marcus and Narcissa Whitman had been hailed as courageous and pious Christian Martyrs. But, in truth, the ultimate victims turned out to be the Cayuse Indians. By 1860, what was left of the tribe had been relegated to the newly established Ambitiously Reservation, along with Indians from the Ambitiously and Walla tribes. In the end, the effect of the Anglo culture and the Protestant religion, churches, colleges, schools, and meeting houses, can be found in a multitude of locations throughout the former Oregon territory. But the Cayuse struggled to maintain their identity, and retain the culture that they so proudly developed thousands of years before the white man arrived.

Sources

Confederated Tribes of the Ambitiously Reservation. *History and Culture of the Cayuse, Ambitiously, and Walla Walla Indians*. 1996.

Jeffrey, Julie Roy. *Converting the West: A Biography of Narcissa Whitman*. 1991, University of Oklahoma Press.

Terrell, John Upton. *American Indian Almanac*. 1994, Barnes & Noble Books.

THE GREAT STONE CHURCH OF KAWAIAHAO

Affiliation: Congregational
Location: Honolulu, Hawaii
1842

When the first Protestant evangelical mission settled on the shores of Oahu in 1820, little could have been known of its impact on the inhabitants of the Sandwich Islands. Yet, within 70 years, before, during, and after the construction of the Great Stone Church of Kawaiahao, offspring of these missionaries, known as "the mission boys," would contribute substantially to the inundation and overthrow of the Hawaii royalty, which had ruled the islands for generations. Eventually, the transformation would be complete, and in 1959 this tiny, autonomous paradise kingdom would become the 50th state of the United States of America.

Up until the last two decades of the 18th century, each of the Sandwich Islands (discovered and so named by British explorer James Cook in 1778) operated more or less as an independent sovereignty, interacting periodically during incidents of trade or war. But by the end of the century, Hawaii's greatest king, Kamehameha I (1779–1819), with the aid of acquired foreign technologies of shipbuilding and weaponry, unified the island chain through conquest.

Kamehameha planted a loyal governor on each island, keeping surveillance via courier-by-canoe. He invited high chiefs who might oppose him to reside at his palace at Oahu where he could keep an eye on them. Through a tax that extended throughout the island chain he filled the stores of the royal treasury with hogs, fruits, vegetables, firewood, salt, and fresh water. With these items, along with the offer of sexual favors from Hawaiian women to lonely sailors, Kamehameha accumulated a store of scissors, knives, mirrors, clothing, as well as firearms and ships, from the foreign merchant ships.

Unfortunately for the Hawaiian culture,

Kamehameha appeared to be the last truly self-assured, self-actualized monarch. The rest, like many of the Hawaiian people, became overwhelmed in the upheaval of language, custom, and belief. Not until Queen Liliuokalani ascended to the throne in 1891 did Hawaii claim a monarch who could hope to preserve the ancient ways of the native people. But by then, the tide of change had swelled so high, nothing could stop it.

After Kamehameha's death in 1819, many among the high chiefs' court began to question the old the *kapu* system — the Hawaiian system of taboos and privileges, which often threatened lawbreakers with punishment of death — which had helped keep the late King at the height of his power. As early as 1778, when Captain Cook's ships the *Resolution* and the *Discovery* anchored near the shores of Kauai, the Hawaiian ways felt the sway of the *haoles,* or outsiders.

As Cook and his crew seemed unaffected and unthreatened by the kapus, the old beliefs suddenly emerged within the light of doubt. New ideas, not the least of which was American Protestant Christianity, with all its precepts and mores, found their ways into Hawaiian culture and lifestyle. The Hawaiian native society, which three decades ago had been untouched by outside influence, faced brisk, radical change.

The concept of a Protestant mission of the Sandwich Islands moved forward when Samuel J. Mills, a leader of the American Board of Foreign Missions, heard the story of Opukahaia. This Hawaiian-born orphan came to New England with an American sea captain. Educated at Yale University, Opukahaia proved to be an exemplary convert to the Christian faith, which convinced Mills success awaited the mission established on the Sand-

The Great Stone Church of Kawaiahao, Honolulu, Hawaii. (Courtesy Hawaii State Archives.)

wich Islands (which have always been called *Hawaii* by the natives).

The first mission commenced in 1819 under Congregational ministers Asa Thurston from Vermont and Hiram Bingham from Boston.

With their wives and four converted Hawaiians, Thurston and Bingham made the 159-day trip from Boston, around Cape Horn in Africa, to Kailua, Hawaii where they arrived April 19, 1820. Thurston settled in with King

Liholiho, son of Kamehameha, in Kailua, on Hawaii, while Bingham and company moved to Honolulu, Oahu.

Liholiho directed them to build their mission at *Ka Wai a Haʻo*, or *Kawaiahao*, which means "fresh water pool of Haʻo." Ancient stories tell of how the chiefess Haʻo, queen of Oahu, used to bathe in the Ka Wai, or fresh water pool.

At first the Hawaiians regarded the missionaries and their activities with idle curiosity. Attendance at their services, let alone conversion to their faith, remained sparse at best. The Hawaiians resisted the kind of rigorous, superfluous daily work the New England Congregationalists encouraged, and could not comply with the missionaries' restrictive customs. On the other hand, the sensual and liberal attitudes of the Hawaiians regarding dress, sexuality, and comportment (such as incest within the royal family, thought to intergenerationally maintain the royal traits of the family) appalled the New Englanders. Thus for the first five years, the mission languished in isolation among the rest of the society, and its success seemed doubtful.

But when the unchristened King Liholiho and Queen Kamamalu succumbed to measles on a trip to London in 1825, the missionaries (who buried the king and queen at the mission) pointed to their fatal illnesses as an example to the Hawaiians of the fate of unbelievers. The frightened high chiefs began attending the Congregationalists' services and forbidding certain activities on the Sabbath.

Kaahumanu, the powerful sister of the governor of Hawaii, converted to Christianity when Sybil Bingham, the wife of Hiram, nursed her to health after a severe illness. The common folk soon followed the chiefs' example. Restrictive puritan injunctions replaced the ancient *kapus.*

Bingham began preaching in Hawaiian as well as English. Suddenly enrollment at the mission school blossomed, giving the missionaries the opportunity to influence the minds and beliefs of hundreds of Hawaiian children, including those of the chiefs and the monarchs. Nearly 3000 Hawaiians now attended services at Kawaiahao each Sunday; the simple thatched-roofed, Hawaiian-designed mission churches, of which there were four successive versions, quickly proved inadequate for such large congregations.

In 1827, plans were developed for the building of the Great Stone Church. The actual construction began in 1835 and was completed in 1842. At a length of 144 feet, a width of 78 feet, and a height of more than 50 feet, the Great Church required more than 14,000 stones which were extracted from the coral reef outside the Honolulu harbor. Natives transported some of the stones upon wooden platforms rolled over timber poles and dragged by five or six men. The mortar was made of sand and limestone cooked in smoking kilns at Kawaiahao.

Timbers from the Oahu forests formed the frame and rafters, and more than 100,000 wooden shingles covered the roof. Ten concrete steps led up to the Romanesque facade, featuring four distinct columns supporting the porch and bell tower, all of which were completed later that year. In 1845 builders added the town's first clock to the tower. Finally, the Great Stone Church of Kawaiahao opened to dedication on July 21, 1842, and served the converted royal family and local members for generations.

The native people in Honolulu provided most of the labor involved in the building of the Stone Church. The original cost of materials totaled $30,000, borne chiefly by King Kauikeaouli (Kamehemaha III). Over the years, the missionaries solicited funds from locals and from congregations back home in New England. Eventually these funds would provide the church with interior decorations and furnishings. The church, the first of stone on the Hawaiian Islands, became a portent to the changing times ahead.

Because it is impossible to indict the morals of a society without judging its system of government, the missionary influence altered both the chiefs' system of beliefs, and the islands' governmental structure as well. American Protestantism with its ideals of representative government and capitalism found its way into the Hawaiian political design. These American ideals eventually inspired the adoption of a constitution monarchy, severely curtailing the powers of the royalty.

The adoption of American Protestant ideals, which became policies, allowed American industrialists and entrepreneurs to buy up land and establish enterprises on the islands. The sugar industry skyrocketed during the American Civil War, when sugar from southern states became unavailable to the Union. Sugar cane became Hawaii's staple, its most important crop.

The plantation owners already anticipated annexation from the United States, which would provide a permanent, duty-free market for the sugar. Sugar plantation owners, some of whom were sons of the Protestant missionaries, contracted for immigrant workers to come from southeast China. These newcomers competed with native workers for labor in the fields and eventually in other employment arenas.

The natives abandoned many of the ancient Hawaiian artisan skills, responsible for producing some of the finest ceremonial clothing, basketry, canoes, and gourdwork in the world, in favor of strenuous manual and tedious clerical labor in a capitalistic agricultural and manufacturing economy. New England abolitionists who became plantation owners in the islands obtained cheap labor at the hands of the native and foreign workers. Those same abolitionists used Hawaiians and Chinese in the island sugar cane fields under conditions ironically similar to those besetting the Africans in American cotton and tobacco fields.

The infusion of foreigners into the islands affected the native people in a more primal way. Just as the introduction of feral dogs, cats, and pigs by Captain Cook wiped out the native nene, or Hawaiian goose, the introduction of foreign bacteria devastated the native human population. Far more than all the guns, cannons, ships, and swords combined, disease became the greatest danger facing the Hawaiian people.

Cook's crew introduced venereal disease to the native women. Typhoid and cholera hampered Kamehameha's conquest of Kauai. Overseas workers in the sugar and whaling trades spread small pox, which struck more than 6000 and killed more than 2000 natives between February 1853 and January 1854. Imported illness including alcoholism and opium abuse eventually wiped out an estimated 80 percent of the native Hawaiian population.

By 1842, Hiram Bingham had returned to New England, old, ill, and frail. But his legacy of the Great Stone Church, and the descendants and compatriots of the missionaries had become firmly entrenched in the Hawaiian Islands. The key figures among "the mission boys" included:

Sanford Ballard Dole

Son of Protestant missionary Daniel Dole, Sanford Dole was born in Honolulu in 1844. After studying law for two years at Williams College in Massachusetts, he returned to Honolulu to practice law.

Dole gained election to the Hawaiian Legislature in 1884 and 1886, and was appointed justice of the Hawaiian Supreme Court in 1887. An opponent of King Kalakaua, Dole greatly influenced the adoption of the Hawaiian Constitution in 1887. Not many years later he would become president of the provisional government which would overthrow Queen Lilioukalani in 1893.

During the McKinley administration, Dole became first territorial governor of Hawaii, and later was appointed to the Hawaiian Supreme Court.

Gerrit Parmele Judd

A physician born in Paris in 1803, and trained in New York, Judd became physician to the Sandwich Island Missions in 1827. As sole doctor for the Islands, Judd gained the confidence of many in royal lineage. Because of his significant skills in languages, Gerrit Judd became a translator and interpreter, and later an adviser to the king. He eventually joined the treasury board, and subsequently served as minister of foreign affairs (1843), minister of the interior (1845), and minister of finance (1846). He became a legislator in 1858.

An ardent Protestant and teetotaler, Judd swayed the royal family's acceptance of American Protestant principles which led, eventually, to the adoption of representative government policies.

Lorrin Andrews Thurston

Son of mission co-founder Asa Thurston, Lorrin Thurston was born in Honolulu in 1858. He attended Oahu College and studied law in Hawaii and at Columbia University in New York. He set up a law practice in Honolulu in 1883, and gained election to the Hawaiian legislature in 1886. An early and avid supporter of annexation, Thurston drafted the Constitution of 1887.

Writer, editor, and owner/operator of *Honolulu Advertiser* newspaper, Thurston would use his journalistic influence to spread pro–annexation, pro–American, and anti–Hawaiian propaganda among *haoles* and Hawaiians as well. He played an instrumental role in the revolution against Queen Liliuokalani, and the subsequent adoption of the provisional government.

The influence of the mission boys culminated in the Constitution of 1887, penned by the compelling Thurston. He and the other members of "the Hawaiian League," many of whom were missionary boys, maneuvered King Kalakaua into signing the document. The Constitution effectively limited Kalakaua's role to that of figurehead monarch. At the same time it relegated the right to vote to those who paid taxes, owned sufficient amounts of land, and swore allegiance to the new constitution — which included roughly barely one-third of all native Hawaiians.

When Kalakaua died of Bright's disease in 1891, his sister Liliuokalani inherited the throne. Artistic and aristocratic, the willful Lilioukalani intended to return power to the Hawaiian people, both the monarchy and the common folk. She planned to restore the vote to native Hawaiians only.

Much to the alarm of the mission boys, Lilioukalani advocated a national lottery and licensure of the opium trade. Both of these ac-

tions would create revenue for the Hawaiians independent of the *haoles'* interests.

Under the leadership of Dole and Thurston, and with help of United States Minister John Stevens and troops from the warship *Boston*, the mission boys apprehended Liliuokalani, and set up a provisional government with Sanford Dole as president. The provisional government, suddenly claiming independence from American interests, ignored protests from the Grover Cleveland administration in the United States. Under the charge that Liliuokalani committed treason by opposing the provisions of the Constitution, the new administration of "president" Dole placed Queen Liliuokalani on house arrest in the Iolani Palace.

The Cleveland administration — recognizing the clearly unscrupulous practices of the so-called revolutionaries — blocked annexation through the remainder of its term in 1898. But the supporters of annexation had enjoined too many allies in Washington.

Finally, on July 7, 1898, under the William McKinley administration, the Hawaiian Islands became annexed as territories of the United States. Many years later Hawaii would be granted statehood.

Today, there is a growing effort among Hawaiians to rekindle the ancient ways: the arts and crafts, the dress and language, the religion and the royal lineage of the island people. But there, too, stands the Great Stone Church of Kawaiahao — the edifice which, though built by Hawaiian hands, helped to usher in an American tidal wave of influence upon these peaceful islands of the Pacific.

Sources

Damon, Ethel M. *The Stone Church at Kawaiahao*. 1945, Honolulu Star-Bulletin Press, Honolulu.

Daws, Gavan. *Shoal of Time*. 1968, The MacMillan Company, New York.

Nakao, Annie. "The Flowering of Lili," *San Francisco Examiner*. January 27, 1997.

WESLEYAN CHAPEL

Affiliation: Methodist
Location: Seneca Falls, New York
1843

Wesleyan Methodist Church stood on Fall and Mynderse streets in Seneca Falls, in the region of upstate New York called "the Reform Belt" for the numerous humanitarian and libertarian causes which emerged there. As no original photographs of the structure exist, estimates of the chapel's actual appearance are based on church records and community reports appearing in the Wesleyan Chapel Historic Structures Report.

Historians conjecture a fairly modest, unobtrusive building. Built of brick, it stood two stories high topped with a gable-style roof, while the exterior extended 43 feet wide by 64 feet long. The interior reportedly featured 11 rows of wooden pews, with two stoves connected to chimneys flanking the altar and pulpit.

A gallery perched over the vestibule at the back, with stairways reaching down the east and west walls. Twenty-four windows permeated the east, west, and south walls, apparently filling the sanctuary with more than ample sunlight.

The Wesleyan Methodist Church was founded and dedicated in 1843. The Methodist church eventually abandoned the chapel, moving into a new church in 1871. Remodeled several times after its sale, the structure served many functions through its long life. Over the years it was a movie theater, apartments, an opera hall, an automotive garage, and a laundromat.

But in 1848, the simple chapel played host to one of the most unusual and progressive events, and introduced one of the most profound documents, in the history of the United States. On July 19 and 20, the first Women's Rights Convention took place at this Methodist church, bringing together under one roof two of the 19th century's greatest political activists. The highly significant chords struck during these two emotionally and politically charged summer days on the shores of Cayuga Lake have reverberated throughout America ever since.

In the mid–19th century, the political and social yoke upon the shoulders of women remained firmly in place. By 1848, American women still could not vote, could not will property, and could not earn money while married. They could not borrow money nor sell property without their husband's consent. In fact, in the matter of inheritance, the rights and needs of the children, particularly male children, came ahead of the wife and mother's. Married women had been considered essentially their husband's possessions, and single women, if fortunate enough to find work, paid taxes to a governmental system in which they had no say.

The system was firmly in place. So pervasive as to be nearly invisible, the oppression appeared impervious to question or challenge.

Volunteer work in the expanding Protestant missions provided one of the few political and social outlets allowed for 19th century American women, who labored about their Christian duty to aid and educate the destitute and "heathen." Many who worked among escaped Southern slaves became increasingly well informed concerning the Abolitionist movement, and the rights of the Africans as human beings. The work in the Abolitionist camps necessarily led to discussions about the rights of all humans, which, of course, included women.

The primary personality behind the 1848 Women's Rights Convention was a 33-year-old homemaker turned activist named Elizabeth Cady Stanton. Stanton had moved to Seneca Falls in 1847 to raise her children with her husband Henry Stanton, an active reformer, abolitionist, and political worker. He had helped to form the Free-Soil Party, and had been an executive in the American Anti-Slavery Society.

For a man in 1848, Henry Stanton seemed quite the progressive thinker. At their wedding in 1840, Henry supported Elizabeth Cady's decision to keep her maiden name, and to eliminate the phrase "to obey" from the vows. Yet, the demands Elizabeth Cady would make at the Seneca Falls convention would drive Henry to the verge of leaving house and home.

Elizabeth Cady was born on November 12, 1815, in Johnstown, New York, northwest of Schenectady. Her father was Judge Daniel Cady. It is said that an early episode involving the judge may have been a defining moment in shaping Elizabeth Cady's life and goals.

Apparently, a neighbor named Flora Campbell had come to consult with Judge Cady about her rights concerning some property. Campbell's husband had died, and willed the couple's entire farm — which Campbell had helped to pay for — to her wastrel son. Campbell had sought advice from Judge Cady about how to recover the farm.

To Flora Campbell's despair, Judge Cady informed her nothing could be done, because the law viewed her possessions as her husband's even if she had earned or inherited the money to purchase them. The judge told the unhappy widow a husband had the legal right to dispose of his wife's earning, her property, and even her children.

Her father's statement had so infuriated young Elizabeth Cady that she threatened with scissors to physically cut the offending laws out of the judge's lawbook. The judge, catching her in the act, admonished her to find a better way to handle her frustration and fury: she should work to change the laws she disagreed with as she grew older. Elizabeth Cady apparently took his advice closely to heart.

Elizabeth Cady graduated in 1833 from Troy Female Academy, the closest thing to an educational opportunity for females. After completing her schooling, she worked at a local Johnstown church to raise money for the ordination of an aspiring young minister. The effort was successful, but upon his return to the home church, the disdainful minister promptly delivered a Sunday sermon on the

divinely ordained subordinate position of women in society. In a shocking public display, Elizabeth Cady arose in the middle of the sermon and marched from the body of the church. It would not be Elizabeth Cady's last demonstration against a male-dominated Christian church.

Almost immediately upon moving to Seneca Falls, Elizabeth Cady Stanton took up the cause of women's rights, campaigning for the historic Married Woman's Property Act of New York State The act was passed by the state legislature in April of 1848. This act, for the first time, gave women the right to hold title to property independent of their husbands.

Riding the coat-tails of victory, Elizabeth Cady Stanton attended a July 1848 tea with famed Quaker abolitionist Lucretia Mott in nearby Waterloo, New York. Stanton had met Mott in 1840 in England while attending an antislavery convention with her husband. The women had been excluded from participating directly in the convention. Indignant, Stanton and Mott vowed that one day they would hold a women's rights convention in the United States to address exactly this kind of indiscretion and prejudice on the part of male-dominated society.

Therefore, on July 13, 1848, Mott, Stanton, and a small group of Hicksite Quaker women met to plan the Women's Rights Convention. The centerpiece of the convention would be the proposed Declaration of Rights and Sentiments, penned by Elizabeth Cady Stanton, and modeled after Thomas Jefferson's Declaration of Independence. The Declaration provided essentially a list of "injuries and usurpages on the part of man toward woman," along with ten resolutions for the restoration of inalienable rights to women.

As a meeting place they secured the use of Wesleyan Chapel, which was the only church in town which would allow so radical an event as a women's rights convention. For its progressive ideas, Wesleyan became known by some as "the Great Lighthouse"; by others, as "the Devil's Depot."

An advertisement in the *Seneca County Courier* appeared the following day. The *Courier* announced the convention would transpire at 10:00 A.M. on Wednesday, July 19, and Thursday, July 20, with women invited to the first day, and the general public welcomed the second.

When Elizabeth Cady Stanton and the other women arrived at Wesleyan Chapel on the morning of July 19, they found the front doors locked. Stanton's nephew had to crawl through a window to open the chapel. Within a few minutes the simple sanctuary was filled with nearly 300 attendees, including a large contingent of aggrieved female factory workers from Seneca Falls' growing industrial section.

(An interesting historical note: Among these workers sat a young glove factory worker named Charlotte Woodward. Woodward would be the only woman to attend the Women's Rights Convention in 1848 and live to see the passage of the 19th Amendment to the Constitution in 1920.)

The July 19 agenda focused on the reading and discussion of the Declaration of Rights and Sentiments, and its ten accompanying resolutions. Far from a skilled orator, Elizabeth Cady Stanton opened the convention with her first public speech. Delivered quietly and nervously, her message nevertheless left a profound impact upon the audience:

> We are assembled to protest against a form of government, existing without consent of the governed — to declare our right to be free as man is free, to be represented in the government which we are taxed to support, to have such disgraceful laws as to give man the power to chastise and imprison his wife, to take the wages which she earns, the property which she inherits and, in the case of separation, the children of her love...
> The world has never seen a truly great and virtuous nation, because in the degradation of woman the very fountains of life are poisoned at their source. It is vain to look for silver and gold in mines of copper and lead. It is the wise mother that has the wise son. So long as your women are slaves you may throw your colleges and churches to the winds....
> To have drunkards, idiots, horse-racing, rum-selling rowdies, ignorant foreigners, and silly boys fully recognized, while we ourselves are thrust out from all rights that belong to citizens, it is too grossly insulting to the dignity of women to be longer quietly submitted

to. The right is ours. Have it we must. Use it we will. The pens, the tongues, the fortunes, the indomitable wills of women are already pledged to secure that right. The great truth, that no just government can be formed without out the consent of the governed, we shall echo and re-echo in the ears of the unjust judge until by continual coming we shall weary him.... [Miller, p. 19]

Two tenets espoused fervently by Stanton, consent of the governed and no taxation without representation, also lay at the very heart of the American Revolution.

On Thursday, July 20, the convention reconvened, with more than 30 men in attendance. The most notable, especially from a historic standpoint, was Frederick Douglass, recently freed African American slave and eloquent editor of nearby Rochester's abolitionist newspaper, the *North Star*.

Douglass was born in February 1817, in Talbot County, Eastern Shore, Maryland. He never knew his white father, and his mother, whom he rarely saw, struggled in slavery some 20 miles to the south.

Douglass worked as a house servant and as a caulker at a shipyard. Among the years of hard labor, whippings, cruelty, and humiliation, Douglass managed to educate himself, often buying books with money he earned at odd jobs. Numerous measures employed by his owners and "Negro breakers" to subdue Douglass' spirit seemed merely to add to his resolve.

In 1838 he escaped north with borrowed papers from a free black man. After publishing his *Narrative of the Life of Frederick Douglass* in 1845, he purchased his freedom for $750 in 1846, and began publishing the *North Star*, the nation's longest running anti-slavery periodical.

By 1848, Frederick Douglass had emerged as one of the country's most distinguished and inspiring abolitionist writers and speakers. Douglass came to attend the Women's Rights Convention, realizing that the rights of women and African Americans were branches of the same tree.

The Resolutions which accompanied the Declaration of Rights and Sentiments stood as the issue for the Thursday meeting. The most controversial of the ten, proposed by Elizabeth Cady Stanton herself, was Resolution #9: "Resolved, that it is the duty of the women of this country to secure to themselves the sacred right to the elective franchise."

This proposition seemed so unthinkable that Henry Stanton threatened to leave his wife, and Judge Cady implored his daughter to retract her signature on the document. The contemporary press derided the proceedings, casting the beliefs and viewpoints expressed as a threat to the cores of social, religious, and legal foundations.

Nevertheless, Elizabeth Cady Stanton and her compatriots persisted, urging the audience to support the resolutions. But it was Frederick Douglass' speech which riveted the audience, and ultimately swayed the positive vote. He echoed his sentiments in a *North Star* article eight days later:

> We hold woman to be justly entitled to all we claim for man. We go farther, and express our conviction that all political rights which it is expedient for man to exercise, it is equally so for woman. All that distinguishes man as an intelligent and accountable being, is equally true of woman, and if that government only is just which governs by the free consent of the governed, there can be no reason in the world for denying to woman the exercise of the elective franchise, or a hand in making and administering the laws of the land. Our doctrine is that "right is of no sex." We therefore bid the women engaged in the movement our humble Godspeed.... [Miller, p. 53]

Thus, in less than 24 hours in Seneca Falls, both a woman and an African American spoke to the issue of consent of the governed, and equal rights — including the right of suffrage — for all human beings. Although Frederick Douglass was the only man at the convention to vote for Resolution 9, acceptance of all ten resolutions nevertheless passed by a majority vote.

Frederick Douglass appeared regularly at women's rights conventions from 1848 thereafter. He lent his considerable support to the cause of women's suffrage, even as black suffrage became constitutional in 1869, with the passage of the 15th Amendment of the United States Constitution.

This amendment actually caused a rift between Stanton and Douglass. Stanton believed suffrage for women should be included in the Amendment, and had hoped that Douglass would not support the amendment because women's rights were not addressed. Douglass, for his part, accepted the suffrage for black men as part of the list of rights he felt was due to African Americans. He was willing to support suffrage for women at another time; Stanton was not.

An eloquent and powerful advocate for universal equality, Frederick Douglass particularly championed the cause of the African American. He firmly espoused the belief that slaves and ex-slaves could not wait idly while white abolitionists gained freedom for them; he believed African Americans should personally fight for their freedom. Thus Douglass became one of the chief proponents of black enlistments for the Union army. Throughout the secession of the Confederate states, the Civil War, and the Reconstruction Period, Douglass consistently proved equal to his title "The Great Agitator."

Frederick Douglass died on February 20, 1895. The *Rochester Democrat and Chronicle* called him one of the nation's great men, "great in gifts, greater in utilizing them, great in his inspiration, greater in his efforts for humanity, great in the persuasion of his speech, greater in the purpose that informed it." (Miller, p. 68)

For Elizabeth Cady Stanton, the 1848 Women's Rights Convention proved the launching point for a brilliant and controversial lifelong campaign for Women's Rights. She remained on the cutting edge of the advancement toward equality for women, often alienating allies not so willing to push the limits. Stanton could not be satisfied with changing legal constrictions against the freedom; there existed plenty of social, cultural, and religious mores she believed had been designed to keep women "in their place."

For example, Stanton viewed the typical 19th century women's costume with its petticoats, frills, corsets, and long skirts as but another subtle but effective means of constraining female potential and physical power. In response, Stanton became one of the first women to wear "bloomers," long, baggy, knee-length trousers which allowed greater freedom of movement.

In 1851, Elizabeth Cady Stanton met Susan B. Anthony. The combination of Anthony's gritty organization and research abilities with Stanton's vision created a formidable political activist team. In 1852, Stanton gained election as president of New York State's Women's Temperance Society. In 1862, Stanton moved to New York City, five years later becoming the first woman to campaign for the United States House of Representatives.

After the disappointment of the 15th Amendment and subsequent political defeats for women, Stanton grew bitter over the rights continually denied to women but given to African Americans. Her sentiments gained her the label of an elitist. As a consequence, she became distanced from other activists.

Growing older and more isolated, Stanton turned inward, focusing her energies on the traditional Christian Church, which she continued to view as the great stumbling block in the attainment for rights for women. In 1895 she wrote *The Women's Bible*, a 19th century effort in politically correct prose. Stanton essentially edited the Bible to make its decrees more inclusive and fair for women, and to comment on how women had historically been depicted in the "holy book." *The Women's Bible* provided further challenge to the oppression of women Stanton believed lay at the very core of a society dominated by white males: in its patriarchal, organized Christian religion.

Elizabeth Cady Stanton died in October of 1902 in New York City.

Today, a National Park Service memorial stands at Fall and Mendyrne streets, occupying the space which encompassed the original Wesleyan Chapel. Other than the information in the Historic Structures Report, it is difficult to imagine precisely how the original Wesleyan Chapel appeared. On the other hand, it is easy to understand the eventual, lasting effect the Women's Rights Convention of 1848 had on the political and social landscape of the United States.

Sources

Faber, Doris. *Oh, Lizzy*. 1972. Lothrup, Lee, and Shepard, Company, New York.

Miller, Bradford. *Returning to Seneca Falls*. 1995, Lindisfarne Press, New York.

Newsome, Carol A., and Sharon H. Ringe. *The Women's Bible Commentary*. 1992, Westminster/John Knox Press, Louisville, Kentucky.

Yocum, Barbara. *Wesleyan Chapel Historic Structures Report*. 1992, National Park Service, U.S. Department of the Interior, Seneca Falls, NY.

JOSS HOUSE TEMPLE

Affiliation: Taoist
Location: Weaverville, California
1852

On the corner of Oregon Street and Highway 299 in the Trinity County hamlet of Weaverville, in the highly forested region of northwestern California, stands a peaceful cedarwood temple surrounded by a well-manicured lawn, by which trickles a quiet brook. The timber-constructed porch facade is painted in the pattern of sky-blue tile with pearl white mortar, but it is entirely made of wood. A red-hued cedarwood gate encloses the porch and temple door, over which hangs a gold sign with Chinese characters. The structure is called "Wom Lim Miao," the "Temple Amongst the Forest Beneath the Clouds." At the roof's pinnacle perch the forms of five symbols: the lotus flower, representing purity and perfection; two Chow Win dragonfish, which provide protection from floods; and two traditional, more elaborate dragons, to guard the temple from evil.

Through the gate and the great front door, a bright red spirit screen guards the entrance to the temple. It prevents evil spirits — who, by tradition, can move only in a straight line —

from entering the sacred sanctuary. Inside, flickering candlelight dimly lights the dark, rich wooden sanctuary. Slivers of sandalwood burn in the old iron stove to the right, filling the rafters of the honorable, ancient chamber with a soothing, introspective fragrance. The cedarwood floor, where worshippers kneel and bow, is set off by an altar railing. The railing is a new addition; in the old days, worshippers freely wandered about the altar. Elaborate, silk tapestry banners lean against the left wall, alongside the beautiful, cylindrical King's umbrella. Both the banners and the umbrella appear in parades and celebrations, such as at the beginning of the Chinese Lunar calendar, from January 19 to February 21.

On the temple's right side, to the left of the old iron stove, a drum and gong hang on its pedestal, poised to serve the offerer. When a worshipper burned an offering of temple money in the stove, he would pound the drum, and strike the gong, to alert the deity to the imminent offering.

Just ahead of the colorful main altar, a simple wooden offering table stands, where worshippers would offer gifts of fruit, candy, wine, or incense. These items could be purchased from the temple priest, who performed the tasks of temple caretaker. All around the main altar, proverbs stitched on richly colored tapestries hang from the walls and ceilings, reminding the worshipper of the ancient wisdoms.

The beautiful, ancient, elaborately decorated main altar is actually divided into three separate shrines, each clothed in gold leaf, candles, banners, and bright pictures. To the left, the Altar of Health features the figures of Cling Loy Goon (god of fortune); Toy Sing Goon (doctor of 10,000 herbs); and Uah Poe (god of medicine and surgery).

At the right is the Altar of Mercy. Residing here are Leong Mar, the goddess of voyage, to whom the worshipper would pray for an expectant return home. The worshipper might also pray to Kuan Yin, the goddess of mercy, known as "the one who listens," in whose name a quiet reflecting pool resides outside the temple.

Finally, at the center is the main altar, called the Altar of Decision. Petitioners offer gifts here to Kuan Ti, the god of knowledge and literature, and to Bok Ai, for protection in a strange new world, and to ward off disasters of flood or fire.

The Joss House Temple served as the spiritual center for the Taoist Chinese immigrants who lived in Weaverville in the late 1800s. The name Joss House is reportedly derived from a corruption of the Portuguese word "Deos" for "God." In addition to the temple proper, an adjacent side room functioned as quarters for the caretaker, as a hostel for Chinese travelers, and as judicial court for the Chinese, unrecognized by the American courts. Although occasional celebrations and group rituals took place at the table, it primarily served the solitary, individual Taoist worshipper, who entered the temple for moments of solitude, serenity, soothing recollections of home, and graces of fortitude in a hostile, strange land.

Joss House is a temple of Taoism, which at once is a religion and a philosophy. With influences from Buddhism, Confucianism, and nature worship, Taoism's roots stretch back more than 3000 years. The Taoist seeks the balance between *Tao* (the way) and *Te* (the power), represented in the popular symbol of the *yin* and the *yang*. The Taoist also seeks to balance the prolongation and elevation of human existence, while respecting and adhering to the forces of nature. Practices involving herbal medicine, physical health, yogic exercise, and keen self-awareness and cultivation have all grown out of the Taoist body of thought. The Taoist seeks the unchanging, transcendental Oneness underlying a world of conflict and change. Tao often poses more questions than it answers and, in truth, often renders answers irrelevant; the seeking is more important than the finding.

The Taoist tradition includes the identification of more than 30,000 deities. Many of these gods were actually ancestors, real human beings whose lives and actions earned veneration and worship after death. Taoists would pray and make offerings to these ancestors, believing their intercession in the course of events would bring fortune to the petitioner's life. In this way, the Taoist deities very much resembled the Roman Catholics' Communion of Saints. For, in the Catholic tradition, the saints

Joss House Temple, Weaverville, California. (Photograph by Penni Thorpe.)

were real human beings, who would intercede with God on the petitioner's behalf.

The 19th century wave of Chinese immigration to northern California had primarily one cause: the promise of gold in *Gum Sum* (Gold Mountain), the Chinese term for California. By 1850, the southeast Chinese provinces of Hong Kong, Canton, and Macao faced a plethora of natural and human-made disasters. A great famine had fallen across southeast China, and in 1849, the Xi Jiang River flooded its banks, killing more than 10,000 people. At the same time, the threat of war loomed in Canton. The Taiping Rebellion — which permanently weakened the ruling Quing Dynasty, eventually killed 20 million people, and drove countless others from their homes — added to the treacherous conditions of 19th century southeast China.

With the fabulous discovery of gold in California in 1848, the Chinese, like residents from countries around the world, hoped to travel to California, quickly make their fortune, and return home as soon as possible. Most of the Chinese were from middle class backgrounds: merchants, businessmen, farmers, clerks. Many would earn what they could, and send it back home; but some never made it home.

The migration to California was enormous. In 1852 alone, more than 20,000 Chinese immigrants passed through the Golden Gate of San Francisco. A good portion of them headed to the Trinity Alps area of northern California, where in July of 1848, Major Person B. Readings found gold on a sandbar on the Trinity River. The immigrants settled in places called Weaverville, Douglas City, Lewiston, Junction City, Quinby, and Don Juan Bar. The Chinese would often band together to work placer or water mines abandoned by whites, or construct their own flumes and dams. Through the meticulous, patient labor with which they were well familiar ,the Chinese frequently recovered substantial amounts of gold.

By the end of 1852, the Chinese population in Weaverville had reached an estimated 2500 (only 1000 less than the total population of Weaverville today). A "Chinatown" quickly emerged, including a bakery, hotel, restaurants, doctor's offices, as well as a gambling hall, brothels, opium parlors, and other means of helping foolish Caucasian miners spend their money.

In the center of Chinatown Joss House Temple arose, also in 1852. The Chinese planted a garden with pine and locust trees about the Temple. Destroyed in 1860 by fire, the temple was rebuilt, and again destroyed by fire in 1873. A third temple — taking two months to build, and dedicated on April 18, 1874 — is the same temple that stands today on the corner of Oregon Street and Highway 299.

The local Caucasian Christian residents taunted the Chinese and their "heathen religion," and referred derogatorily to the temple as "Josh House." The whites referred to the Chinese as barbarians; but actually, many of the tenets — charity, compassion, humility — the Taoist philosophy held in common with the values Christians purported to hold. Unfortunately, the Christians rarely showed these virtues toward the Taoists.

More than for their religion, the Chinese felt resentment from Caucasians for the economic competition they provided the miners. In 1850, the Foreign Miner's tax was levied in California. First aimed at Mexican immigrants, the bulk of the tax fell upon the Chinese. Forced to pay four dollars a month in tax simply for their foreign status, the Foreign Miner's tax met its objective: to curb Chinese immigration, with statewide numbers falling from 20,000 in 1852, to 4470 in 1853. The clearly vindictive tax would not be declared unconstitutional until 1870.

In true Taoist tradition, however, the immigrants endured. Like the water that gently wears away the rock, they sought to control through non-interference. Despite the animosity heaped upon them by jealous Caucasian miners, the Chinese continued to work, save, and prosper in and around Weaverville. Settling in Weaverville, the Chinese would form companies, comprised of individuals who had emigrated from the same specific prov-

inces of China. One company came from Hong Kong (called "Yong-Wa") and three from Canton (Se-Yep, Neng-Yong, Sam-Yep).

In April of 1854, the four groups opened a gambling hall in Weaverville. Out of the activities of this parlor sprung one of the most notorious episodes in Chinese Weaverville: The Tong War.

Apparently, one gambler from Hong Kong and one Cantonese player became embroiled in a dispute over a game of chance. Over the weeks animosity grew between the Hong Kong and Cantonese camps. Tempers continued to boil, until on July 15, 1854, the dispute escalated into actual battle. A Hong Kong force of 110 met a Cantonese army of 250, in a clearing outside the town. Armed with iron pikes and tridents forged at the local blacksmith shop, and surrounded by 2000 jeering, taunting Caucasian spectators, the two camps jostled and sparred, in a mostly ceremonial display. Finally, one agitated white onlooker fired a pistol. Suddenly, the two bands rushed at one another, leaving one Chinese dead, and 20 more wounded. The Anglo instigator who had fired the gun also died. The local sheriff quickly confiscated all the weapons, and the Tong War ended.

Relatively few such incidents actually occurred within the Chinese settlement of Weaverville. Compared to other areas of California, the immigrants actually received relatively civil treatment by Caucasians in Trinity County. Because the Chinese depended little on whites for their livelihood, and rarely interfered with white labor, the Chinese lived in comparative peace and prosperity. The whites, for their part, seemed to understand the stability and financial support, particularly through the Foreigner Tax, the Chinese provided the local economy.

Soon the promise of employment by the railroads, whose recruitment of Chinese laborers grew from 2000 in 1865 to 15,000 in 1869, drew many residents away from Weaverville. As gold production declined, more Chinese left the Trinity Alps. Between 1880 and 1931, the official census of Chinese within the town limits of Weaverville dropped from 494 to 16 individuals. Much of the original Chinatown disappeared through destruction or removal. Due to the efforts of Moon Lim Lee, son of Chinese emigrants born in Weaverville, the Joss House Temple was preserved.

In 1956, the Temple became an official California State Park. But worshippers continue to visit the Temple Amongst the Forest Beneath the Clouds, which remains the oldest continuously active Taoist temple in the state.

Sources

Bishop, Peter and Michael Darton. *The Encyclopedia of World Faiths: An Illustrated Survey of the World's Living Religions.* 1987, MacDonald and Co., Ltd., London and Sydney.

Parrinder, Geoffrey. *Religions of the Modern World, from Primitive Beliefs to Modern Faiths.* 1971, The Hamlyn Publishing Group, New York.

McDonald, Douglas and Gina. *The History of the Weaverville Joss House.* 1986, McDonald Publishing, Medford, Oregon.

OLD MISSION OF THE SACRED HEART

Affiliation: Roman Catholic, Society of Jesus, Coeur d'Alene Indians
Location: Outside Cataldo, Idaho
1852

The Old Mission of the Sacred Heart, in north central Idaho, enjoys a history unique among the Christian Indian missions of the United States. Small, self-contained, and successful, the mission's impact on the Coeur d'Alene Indians is felt to the present day.

During the late 18th and early 19th centuries, great epidemics swirled among the nomadic Indian tribes of the Northwest plateau. European diseases such as smallpox and cholera passed from French and English fur traders in eastern Canada to tribes such as the Huron and the Iroquois. As those tribes intermingled with tribes further west, for hunting, fishing, trading, etc., the diseases moved west as well. The ailments spread like wildfire among the nations. Tribes desperately searched for methods to combat the disease, methods which could not be found among traditional rituals and practices.

Stories tell of how, sometime between 1812 and 1830, a band of Iroquois Indians from northeast United States and Canada ventured southwest from Hudson Bay to circulate among the Salishan linguistic tribes, in the land which now comprises the states of Washington, Idaho, and western Montana. As the Iroquois intermingled and sometimes intermarried with the Salishan, they spread stories of strangers among the Flathead, Nalispel and Coeur d'Alenes. They called the strangers "Black Robes." The Iroquois spoke of the crossed sticks the Black Robes wore about their necks; the Great Prayer the Black Robes spoke; the rituals the Black Robes practiced. The tales told of the Great Spirit, and the Great Spirit's Son. They also spoke of how the Black Robes could resist the terrible epidemics inflicting the tribes. The Black Robes, they assumed, possessed a great power, a special knowledge of God.

For many years the Iroquois spoke of the advantages the Black Robes brought to the tribes they lived among. Finally, after years of consideration, four braves from the Flathead Nation from the Bitter Root Valley of southwest Montana set out in 1831 to bring the Black Robes to the Northwest. They traveled to the white settlement of St. Louis, and met with the Reverend Matthew Condamine, who promised to come to the Flatheads the next year. For reasons unknown, he never came.

The Flatheads sent more delegations to St. Louis in 1835 and 1837, again with the purpose of bringing the Black Robes back among them. Each time they were assured Black Robes would come out to teach them, but none ever did. Finally, in 1839 two more Flathead warriors, Ignace and Peter Gaucher, traveled to Council Bluffs, Iowa, to meet with Jesuit Priest Pierre De Smet.

Born in Termonde, Belgium, on January 31, 1801, De Smet had early developed an exceptionally strong physique and an enthusiasm for adventure. De Smet had attended seminary in 1821 in Mechlin, Belgium, where he had been inspired by stories of missionary work in the New World. He joined the Society of Jesus and was ordained a priest on September 23, 1827. He worked on the East Coast of the United States for 12 years, before embarking on his journey to the Northwest Plateau. By all accounts, De Smet enjoyed universal appeal among the Indians, and could safely walk among them even in times of greatest conflict.

After founding missions in Montana and Washington, De Smet wandered across the Bitter Root Mountains in the Spring of 1842, arriving at the beautiful valley of the Coeur d'Alene Indians. Coeur d'Alene chief Twisted Earth welcomed De Smet among his people. He told the priest how in 1740 his father, Circling Raven, had experienced a vision about the strangers in black robes who would come to the tribe. Chief Twisted Earth told De Smet how they had anxiously waited for the Black Robes to walk among them, and to tell them the stories of the Great Spirit. De Smet stayed with the Coeur d'Alene two days, sharing the New Testament and reciting prayers he had translated into the Salishan language. Upon leaving he promised to send more Black Robes, to live among them in their valley.

Father De Smet sent Father Nicholas Point, a talented artist, and Brother Huet, a skilled carpenter, to build the Coeur d'Alene mission on the St. Joe River in December of 1842. With the help of the Coeur d'Alenes, the Jesuits laid out a new village, a concept quite novel to the Coeur d'Alene's hunter-gatherer way of life. They felled trees, opened roads, sowed public fields, and erected a rough log cabin church. The mission remained in St. Joe valley for four years, until spring flooding from the river finally drove the villagers to higher ground. Pierre De Smet himself chose the present site for the mission in 1846, making Sacred Heart Mission headquarters of Northwest Missions. For the next 30 years, Sacred Heart's

success remained unparalleled among the Jesuit chain.

One of the reasons for the success of Mission Sacred Heart may be pure logistics. The Coeur d'Alene tribe of Indians had occupied the valley surrounding Coeur d'Alene Lake, upper Spokane River, and Clearwater River for perhaps thousands of years. Their Salishan speaking neighbors included the Nalispel, who lived north of present-day Spokane, Washington, and the Salish, who have become known as the Flatheads, occupied northwest Montana.

The Coeur d'Alene, whose name means "jagged heart," were so christened by early white trappers, such as Hudson Bay Company. These fur traders considered the tribe to be very "standoffish," especially concerning the foreigners' access to Coeur d'Alene women, and called them "the jagged hearts" for the prickliness of their natures. The Coeur d'Alene name for the tribe is "Scheechuumsch," which means "foundling." The origin is uncertain, but the names the Indians gave themselves often indicated something about the area from which they came.

Hunter-gatherers, the Coeur d'Alene lived off the elk, deer, and bear which occupied the area surrounding their native home. They fished in the lakes and rivers, and gathered berries and roots in the forests. Families sometimes shared lodges of tree limbs and bark, but more often dwelt in single teepees, constructed of elk or deer skin fastened around timber poles.

It is estimated there never existed more than 400 individuals who dwelt around St. Joe's River. Quite isolated in their river valley from surrounding tribes, the Coeur d'Alene seemed to mingle less than other Indians. With the smaller numbers and self-contained valley, the Coeur d'Alene, though never totally abandoning its traditional nomadic lifestyle, seemed to assimilate more easily to the agrarian lifestyle so crucial to the mission system.

Another reason for the success at Sacred Heart seems to be what might be termed "the Jesuit Style." Founded by Ignatius Loyola during the time of the Renaissance and Reformation, the Society of Jesus, or Jesuits, emphasized education, and seemed prepared to encounter and accept a variety of lifestyles, beliefs and customs. The Jesuits seemed to possess an understanding of the connectedness of body to soul, of spirit to nature, and did not try to separate and suppress one from the other.

Two important basic tenets of the Jesuit missions seemed to be assimilation and accommodation. The Jesuits lived among the tribes, learned and adapted to the tribe's way of life. Slowly, the priests would earn the Indians' trust, until they could slowly introduce concepts which, in the opinion of the Jesuits, would enhance the Indian's lives.

The Jesuits, as Europeans, transferred directly from the Old World, did not burn with the passion of Manifest Destiny; conquering the land, and opening the way for settlers. They did not seek to "Americanize" the tribe, but simply tried to make territory suitable for white settlement. Neither the government nor the military, with all the companion unsavory practices and diseases, both biological and social, accompanied the Jesuits on their quest.

The Catholic religion seemed to appeal to the Coeur d'Alenes, who enjoyed and understood the tactile, sensory rituals, which offered imagery and ideas resembling their own. Perhaps there existed an understanding of the mystical nature of the rituals; certainly, the music and the symbolism seemed more intriguing than austere, cerebral practices such as Bible studies and Sunday school. While it is difficult to say how many Indians the priests actually converted, it seemed many found solace and comfort in the ideas and ceremonies offered by the Jesuits. This enthusiasm for the religion seems to have manifested itself most with the construction of the Mission of the Sacred Heart Church. The project's director, Fr. Anthony Ravalli, came to Sacred Heart Mission for the very purpose of erecting the sanctuary. Born in Ferrara, Italy, on May 16, 1812, Ravalli entered the Jesuit novitiate in 1827. In addition to theology and philosophy, he studied mathematics, apprenticed in an artist's studio, and honed his skills as an engineer, architect, and mechanic.

The Jesuits were equipped with simple tools such as a broad ax, ropes and pulleys, and a pen knife. The church began to rise in the fall of 1848, with Ravalli guiding the Coeur d'Alene in felling trees and hauling rocks from the river. The Mission church was 90 feet in length, 40 feet in width, and 30 feet in height. The church uprights had been cut from neighboring pine trees. They were 18 inches square. The rafters were ten inches square.

With no nails (extremely rare and expensive in those days) available, Ravalli had the uprights and rafters joined by wooden pegs poked through holes bored into the wood. He secured the roof and walls by drilling cavities at the edges, and running willow saplings through the openings. Native craftsmen sealed the gaps between the wood planks with mud and leaves. Massive timbers comprised the sanctuary floor, and six wooden columns, carved from neighboring trunks, supported the porch and overhang. Amazingly, without a single shred of metal, the structure has stood for more than 120 years.

Inside the sanctuary, Fr. Ravalli hand-carved the delicate wooden figures of St. Joseph and the Blessed Virgin. Paintings of the sacred heart of Christ, of heaven, of hell, and of the Fourteen Stations of the Cross were all designed by Ravalli's hand. By 1853, the Church of the Sacred Heart was complete; the Indians squatted on the timber floor during services.

Despite the relative harmony within the mission village, all was not peaceable among the Coeur d'Alenes at all times. The late 1850s brought a particular anxiety among the Northwest Indians, fueled in no small part by the series of treaties, which confiscated literally thousands of square miles from the natives, exacted by Governor Isaac Stevens of Washington Territory. One celebrated battle which sprung from this tension became known as the "Steptoe Disaster."

By 1858, Fr. Joseph Joset had already been stationed at Sacred Heart for seven years, appointed as vice-provincial of the missions. A stout-hearted and earthy man, he lived and worked comfortably among the Indians, quickly gaining their respect as adviser and spiritual teacher. By this time, many of the Coeur d'Alene warriors shared the sentiments of neighboring Spokane and Palouse braves, who believed, prophetically, as it turns out, their land would be imminently overrun by

Mission of the Sacred Heart near Cataldo, Idaho. (Courtesy Idaho Historical Society.)

the white Americans. Rumors spread by other tribes, and stoked by an ongoing series of skirmishes between whites and Indians, agitated the warriors further. Despite efforts on the part of Fr. Joset to steer them toward a pacifist's path, the Coeur d'Alene braves vigorously prepared for what they anticipated would be a desperate fight for their homeland.

In May of 1858, a small company of 152 American troops led by Col. Edward J. Steptoe crossed north through the Snake River into Palouse territory in eastern Oregon, without first issuing notice, a common courtesy, to the Palouse tribe. When the Indians confronted him, Steptoe explained the expedition as a re-

connaissance to Colville, Washington, to quell an uprising between miners and Kalispel Indians. The tribal warriors did not accept the explanation. Despite diligent efforts on the part of Fr. Joset to prevent a battle, the Indians finally fell upon the soldiers. They killed seven, wounded 13, and drove the remaining troops south and back across the Snake River. Three Coeur d'Alenes also died in the skirmish.

The Steptoe Disaster, along with the Indians' rising fear of impending loss of their lands, led to a greater battle four months later, called the War of 1858. This outbreak pitted 720 U.S. troops under Colonel George Wright, against a combined war party of Coeur d'Alene, Spokane, Kalispel, Palouse, Yakima, and Pend Oreille Indians, greatly outnumbered by the troops. Although relatively few Indians actually lost their lives, Wright's army pillaged and destroyed Indian land and property, including more than 900 war ponies, in a concerted effort to suppress further hostilities among these tribes. Wright's mounted dragoons and howitzer guns frightened and scattered the warriors sufficiently to induce many of the Coeur d'Alene braves to seek refuge at the Sacred Heart Mission. They enlisted Fr. Joset's help in securing a peace treaty with the soldiers. An agreement was reached, and the War of 1858 ended barely two weeks after it began.

Wars, broken treaties, and disappearing Indian lands characterized the Northwest Territory of the late 19th century. Somehow through it all, the Jesuits and the Coeur d'Alene managed to maintain a continual relationship based on mutual appreciation and respect. Seemingly untouched by the calamity surrounding it, the Sacred Heart Mission remained the spiritual and social base for much of the tribe.

But it would not last forever. In 1877, under pastor Father Joseph Cataldo, the Coeur d'Alenes faced relocation from their beloved mission and valley, which was quickly being depleted of arable land for the tribe. The U.S. government had set the boundaries of their new reservation to the south, exempting the Mission of the Sacred Heart. The working mission was moved to De Smet, Idaho, within

the boundaries of the reservation, while the Old Mission Church structure remained behind. Augustine of the Coeur d'Alenes, reportedly protested, "Have we then to leave this beautiful church which we built with our own hands ... where the hungry were fed, the sick got medicine, and the poor got clothing?" (Cody, p. 40)

The abandonment lasted for 51 years. Finally, in 1928, a drive to rejuvenate the old mission began. After extensive restoration, the Mission church received honors in 1962 as one of few historical landmarks in the state of Idaho. The Mission of the Sacred Heart remains the oldest building continually in use in the state.

Each year, on the Feast of the Assumption of the Blessed Virgin into heaven, the Coeur d'Alene Indians return to the Old Mission. They erect teepees, celebrate tribal dances, share traditional foods, and remember their forefathers, and the coming of the Black Robes to the valley of the Jagged Hearts.

Sources
Burns, Robert Ignatius. *The Jesuits and the Indian Wars of the Northwest*. 1966, Yale University Press, New Haven and London.
Cody, Reverend Edmund R. Cody, M.A. *History of the Coeur d'Alene Mission of the Sacred Heart*. 1930, Cataldo, Idaho.
Kowrach, Edward J., and Thomas E. Connolly. *Saga of the Coeur d'Alene Indians*. 1990, Ye Galleon Press, Washington.
Terrell, John Upton. *American Indian Almanac*. 1994, Barnes & Noble Books.

MISSION ST. IGNATIUS

Affiliation: Roman Catholic, Jesuit
Location: 41 miles north of Missoula, Montana
1854

The Jesuit Mission of St. Ignatius enjoyed a wholly optimistic beginning. Father Pierre De Smet had been welcomed by Chief Big Face, or Long Face, of the Flathead tribes, after he and his tribe had awaited the coming of the Black Robes for years. The Flatheads had heard

of the Black Robes through the Iroquois in the 1830s, and hoped that the priests' religion and knowledge would bring them power and sustenance in the difficult times of disease and warfare.

De Smet agreed to accompany the Flatheads back to the Northwest, after they had come looking for a Black Robe to live among them. In 1842, De Smet established Mission St. Mary's near Fort Owen (present day Stevensville) in the Bitter Root Mountains in western Montana, and the Sacred Heart Mission in northern Idaho. De Smet then landed at the Pend Oreille River, in what is now northwest Washington state, in 1844. There, De Smet established the Mission of St. Ignatius, named for Ignatius Loyola, founder of the Society of Jesus, with a kindly, Dutch administrator named Father Adrian Hoecken.

Hoecken was born in Tilberg, Holland, and ordained a Jesuit priest in 1842. A man of ill health most of his life, Hoecken reportedly possessed a keen eye for natural beauty, and a close identification with and appreciation for the Indian ways. Cordial and kind to everyone, Hoecken had been especially beloved by his Indian parishioners, who revered him as a kind and dedicated father figure.

It has been thought that the Flatheads were so named because of their practices of flattening the soft skulls of their infants. In reality, according to Terrell, the Flatheads did not participate in the common practice forming the baby's skulls into an oblong shape: "They were called Flatheads because, unlike some of their congenitors who lived farther to the west, they left their heads in a normal condition, that is, flat on top, instead of deforming them by pressure to slope toward the crown." (Terrell, p. 352)

After four years of enduring annual spring floods in the Pend Oreille River Valley, the Jesuits moved Mission St. Ignatius to its present site, in a lush interior valley below Flathead Lake, at the foot of Mount McDonald in the Rocky Mountain range. The priests immediately erected a log cabin home, establishing the Mission St. Ignatius on September 24, 1854.

Within six months a bustling little hamlet had emerged against the back drop of the towering Rockies. The original mission compound included the log cabin priest home (which still stands), a log cabin chapel, blacksmith shop, carpenter shop, and a fair-sized chapel. Teepees and long houses, constructed by the Indians, surrounded the mission compound.

Higher in elevation than the Washington locale, the St. Ignatius Mission offered better soil for agriculture, a more remote location from burgeoning white settlements, and a more central gathering place to a greater number of tribes. Called *Sinieleman* (meeting place) by the Indians, the new mission drew tribespeople from several local camps: Besides the Flatheads, Kalispel Indians from the mission's old site on the Pend Oreille River; the Kutenais from the American-Canadian border; and the Pend Oreille (the name comes from the French, meaning "Earring") from the nearby areas surrounding Flathead Lake to the north. Along with Sacred Heart in the Coeur d'Alene lands to the west, St. Ignatius for a time held claim as the most successful of the Jesuit missions.

But, scarcely ten months following the building of St. Ignatius, Governor Isaac Stevens —first governor of newly organized (1853) Washington Territory, the far northwest corner of the continental United States— called for an Indian Council at Hell Gate, Montana. Located on the banks of Hell Gate River, the site stands seven miles northwest of present day Missoula, and 34 miles southwest of St. Ignatius. Though ostensibly Stevens called the meeting to present to the Indians how the government would help prevent raids of the Blackfoot Indians of the southern plains, actually the governor's primary objective was to situate the tribes to make way for the westward traffic along the Oregon Trail. The Hell Gate Treaty of 1855 effectively split the lands of the Pend Oreilles, Kutenais, and Flathead Indians, leaving them on a reservation barely one sixth the size of their original lands. The Hell Gate Treaty was a microcosm of the long history of negotiations between Native Americans and the United States government.

Governor Stevens recruited Fr. Hoecken to attend the council, hoping the priest's influence would ensure a smooth commencement. Stevens had overrated Hoecken's pull with the Indians. The tribes revered the priest, and often listened to him concerning spiritual matters, but the chiefs normally precluded his participation in tribal policy matters. Hoecken normally avoided such political entanglements, anyway; his personal priorities included the continuing development and maintenance of

St. Ignatius Mission, at the foot of Mount McDonald in Montana. (Courtesy Jesuit Oregon Province Archives, Gonzaga University [Neg. #114.1.1].)

the new mission, which had been inundated with a cholera epidemic at the same time as the Hell Gate Council. Against his better judgment, Hoecken agreed to come to Hell Gate, if for no other reason than to offer support for his parishioners.

More than 1400 warriors and chiefs from the Flathead, Pend Oreilles, and Kutenais attended the Council. Coined by the government "The Flathead Confederacy," the gathering was more accurately a loose assemblage of linguistically and geographically linked tribes. Although these tribes had intermingled and intermarried, each tribe clearly clung to its own interests and, particularly, their own land. Among the most prestigious of the Indian representatives were Head Chief Alexander, the 45-year-old chief of the Pend Oreilles, somber, without fear, outspoken, and honest; Chief Big Canoe, second in charge of the Pend

Oreilles, eloquent and passionate in speech; High Chief Victor, 80-year-old chief of the Flatheads, the first of the tribe to be baptized by the Jesuits; Chief Moses, subchief of the Flatheads, called Bravest of the Brave, reputed to be a superior horseman; and Head Chief Michael, stoic and silent, leader of the Kutenais.

Stevens offered one of two possible sites to which the three tribes could relocate, where supposedly they would enjoy greater isolation from white settlers, and protection from the marauding plains Indians. The first included several hundred square miles in the Bitter Root Valley, ancestral home to the Flathead Tribe. The second represented 2000 square miles in the Mission Valley, surrounding St. Ignatius in the lower section of Pend Oreille territory. In exchange, the Indians would lose more than ten times the land (roughly the western

half of the state of Montana) and move together into whichever reservation site was chosen.

Stevens also proposed the provision of
schools, blacksmith, carpentry, and a hospital
to the reservation, all at government expense.
The governor's offerings, of course, proved a
small piece of a larger agenda: to remove the
tribes out of the way of Stevens' growing political ambitions.

Apparently Stevens, a man neither used to
nor accepting of obstacles to his objectives,
naively expected the tribes to simply exchange
the lands for what he perceived to be a generous governmental offer. Unfortunately, Stevens
underestimated the chiefs' insight and their
ability to read the writing on the wall. He also
underestimated their integrity and their un-
willingness to part with ancient traditions and
beliefs. Finally, and most importantly, Stevens
simply did not comprehend the Indians' steadfast love for their lands.

The chiefs were dumbfounded that Stevens
expected them to give up so much land for so
little in exchange. Big Canoe reportedly told
him, "It is our land. If you make a farm, I
would not go there and pull up your crops. I
would not drive you away from it." (Burns, p.
100) True, the tribes needed help in control-
ling the plains tribes; and true, they could not
fight the overwhelming resources and wealth
of the U.S. government in the wake of western expansion. Still, the eastern Washington
Territory had been their tribal homes for centuries, a home they would not readily relinquish.

It is difficult to discern how much of the
Hell Gate Council became a comedy of errors
in communication and diplomacy, and how
much had been an exercise in gross manipu-
lation and distortion on the part of Governor
Stevens. In many cases, an apparent lack of
competent interpreters exacerbated the failure
of the process. Fr. Hoecken, skilled in the Flathead Confederacy languages, estimated all parties actually understood less than ten percent
of the ideas presented at the council. Stevens,
aware of the misunderstandings, would repeatedly twist words and meanings to gain his
own advantage in the talks. Consistent with
his apparent lack of regard for the Indians, the

governor often spoke in biting, sarcastic tones.
Condescending and haughty, Stevens remained quite convinced of the superiority of
his position, his power, and his skills.

The chiefs, however, possessed skills in
their own brands of negotiations. They questioned the government's ability to protect
them from the Blackfeet or any other tribe.
They clearly had no intention of giving up any
of their lands: The Pend Oreilles and Kutenais
refused to abandon their lands along the Canadian border from Washington and Montana;
the Flatheads would not leave their ancestral
home in the Bitter Root Valley.

The Council labored on for nine days, with
patience and tempers on all sides growing perilously short. The stalemate continued: The
Pend Oreilles and Kutenais would not relocate
south, and the Flatheads refused to move
north. In a moment of exasperation, the Flatheads' High Chief Victor finally declared he
would leave the Bitter Root Valley only if the
Great White Father (the president) himself declared the Bitter Root Valley the lesser of the
two possible sites.

Stevens reportedly jumped on the opportunity, purposefully misinterpreting Victor's
statement to mean if the president's representative (namely, himself) approved of the northern territory, Victor would agree. Stevens
arranged for an aide to survey the two lands
who, of course, found the northern site the
better of the two. The signatures of 18 Indians were applied, legitimately and otherwise,
to the treaty, although clearly none of them
fully understood what they were signing.

The end result had reduced the combined
territories of the Flathead, Pend Oreilles, and
Kutenais Indians to the present Flathead Reservation, about 2000 square miles. The United
States absorbed the rest of the lands, more than
23,000 square miles, of Northeast Washington Territory. In adherence to the promises,
the treaty provided the Indians schools, hospitals, a carpentry shop, and a blacksmithy on
the reservation. Unfortunately, only the Jesuits
provided these services, for but a limited
amount of time. The United States government, who had promised funding for these
provisions, never provided a cent to Fr.
Hoecken and the Jesuits.

For more than four decades the tribes of the Northwest Plateaus, many of whom resented the misrepresentation at Hell Gate, protested and fought the whites for what they saw as the robbery of their ancestral homes. The Hell Gate Treaty highlights the unfortunate litany of obstacles impeding just and understandable agreements between the tribes and the United States.

There were many reasons why negotiations between the United States and the Northwest Plateau Indians did not work well. Among the tribes of the Northwest, located between the Cascades and the Rockies, dwelt an estimated 125 separate groups, speaking 56 mutually exclusive languages. The tribes among the Salishan language groups (the Flatheads, the Coeur d'Alenes, the Pend Oreilles, the Kalispels) often shared common hunting-gathering grounds. They often formed alliances and trading partnerships, which could be built, broken, and built again in but a brief passage of time, given the winds of political change. All the Northwest tribes engaged in much intermingling, both biological and cultural. Thus, the theoretical boundaries and categories imposed by the white Americans proved much less absolute in practice. All political, territorial, cultural, and communicative boundaries proved much more fluid for the Indians than for the government. Given sufficient cause, unity could be strong among Indian tribes but also very informal, and subject to change, based on many fluctuating factors.

In negotiation, the white men did not take into account this informality of Indian political units. There was often an assumption that one village or one chief spoke for an entire people, when actual political allegiances would usually not extend beyond the village. The Indian concepts of time, territories, boundaries, and ownership varied among the tribes, and certainly differed and opposed the concepts among the whites.

The general regard or disregard for Indians felt by a majority of whites in the mid– to late–19th century also came into play. Although exceptions existed, most whites considered the Indian a nuisance to be avoided or abated. Under the banner of Manifest Destiny, the settlers felt predestined for the territory of the west; they certainly would not allow the natives to impeded their drive toward destiny. An unintroduced populace considered the Indian dirty, ignorant, savage, and, most importantly, in the way. Government-provided negotiators, however well intentioned, could not remain impervious to the feelings of the times.

The Jesuit priests often accepted the role of reluctant mediators, because they feared for the lives of the Indians in an all-out war with the United States. Outnumbered, outresourced, and outmatched, the Indians' chances were not good, and the Jesuits seemed to sincerely wish to protect the lives of the Indians among whom they worked. Unfortunately, the Jesuits often saved Indian lives at the cost of Indian lands, the nomadic lifestyle, and, most important, freedom. Once the Indians lost their freedom to wander their lands unencumbered, the reduction and extermination of the tribes was imminent. The wild hunter-gatherers could not be transformed into quiet, peasant farmers. They became, as one writer phrased it, "Americanized Indians in melancholy reservations."

St. Ignatius Mission continued its operation among the Flathead Confederacy for years following the Hell Gate Treaty, but its initial enthusiasm seemed dampened by the council's fallout. The first church at St. Ignatius emerged between 1856 to 1864 under the direction of Fr. Anthony Ravelli, the architect of the Sacred Heart Mission. The second and current church with its towering belfry and gothic buttresses was completed in 1891.

Fr. Hoecken attempted to develop a boarding school for Indian children in 1862, in adherence to the terms of the Hell Gate Treaty. It was soon closed, however, because the government never contributed the funds it promised. With the help of the Sisters of Providence and the Ursaline Nuns, a school for boys opened in 1888. When Congress cut off all government help to the mission school in 1896, it managed to limp along almost solely through charitable contributions.

Despite the lack of support from the U.S. government, Mission St. Ignatius reached its heyday between 1890 and 1896, with 320 children enrolled in the school. But in 1896, 1919, and 1922 devastating fires ravaged the mission and school. Today, St. Ignatius operates as a Catholic parish, serving a community of several hundred families of mixed ancestry: Flathead, Pend Oreille, Kalispel, and various European ethnicities.

Perhaps it is true that once the door of discovery to the New World opened to the European, the fate of the American Indian was sealed. The European diseases, both bacteriological and social, were brought to the Atlantic Coast, then swept across the continent, killing an estimated two-thirds of the native population. Indian immunities and practices fell helpless before these scourges, forcing the Indians to seek the white man's knowledge and cures, to combat the diseases. Once invited to dwell among the Indians, nothing could stop the advancement of the Europeans. Pandora's box sprang open, and the mix of European-

American and Native-American brought about predictable and tragic results.

It is interesting to contemplate what might have happened to our present day culture if the European-American spent a little more time trying to understand the Indians, rather than simply moving them aside. Although much of their land had been taken from them, the Indians do not allow the United States to wipe their existence from the collective memory. Monuments such as the Mission St. Ignatius encourage the memory.

Sources

Burns, Robert Ignatius. *The Jesuits and the Indian Wars of the Northwest*. 1966, Yale University Press, New Haven and London.
Terrell, John Upton. *American Indian Almanac*. 1994, Barnes & Noble Books.
The St. Ignatius Post and the Ronan Pioneer. "100 Years of Achievement." September 23, 1954, St. Ignatius, Montana.

WABAUNSEE FIRST CHURCH OF CHRIST
("Beecher Bible and Rifle Church")
Affiliation: Congregational
Location: Wabaunsee County, Kansas
1857

One of the most insidious and shortsighted bills ever passed in the United States Congress was the Kansas-Nebraska Bill of 1854. Spearheaded by Democratic senator Stephen Douglas, who held interest as a railroad director and a land speculator, the bill nullified the long standing Missouri Compromise, which set the line between slave and free state at the southern border of Missouri. Douglas' bill, which he penned in concession to southern supporters, opened the territories of Kansas and Nebraska to settlement and eventual statehood. It also deferred the question of slavery in the territories to popular sovereignty. That is, the will of the people residing in the territory would allow or prohibit slavery. Es-

sentially, the issue would be decided by which side of the slavery question held more votes in the territory.

The race for "Bleeding Kansas" was on.

By the mid–19th century, Connecticut had become a national center for progressive political and social thought. Many suffragists, prohibitionists, and abolitionists served as links for the famous Underground Railroad and made their homes in the fifth state.

At the same time, the most prominent Protestant preacher in the United States was the charismatic pastor of Brooklyn's Plymouth Church, Henry Ward Beecher. Born in Litchfield, Connecticut, in 1813, Beecher was the son of noted Congregational minister Lymon

Beecher, and the brother of *Uncle Tom's Cabin* author Harriet Beecher Stowe. With ruddy complexion, waving red hair, and a deep, compelling voice, Beecher regularly packed the balconies of Plymouth Church, as worshippers gathered to hear his stirring orations on God's word and social conscience.

Beecher regarded slavery as a religious matter. He preached about the institution of slavery as a system for "the animalization of three millions of men in the bosom of a Christian land, under the cover of democratic institutions." (Hibben, p. 157) He believed people to be "inherently vile and could be counted upon to embrace vice every time unless restrained by legal or moral considerations — preferably both." (Hibben, p. 157) The Missouri Compromise, which provided such a legal and moral barrier, had been eliminated. But until 1854, Beecher seemed to take a rather moderate view towards the eradication of slavery, believing it would disappear with moral development, rather than legislative injunction. Like many of his day, Beecher greatly preferred the institution of slavery over the obliteration of the Union, the separation of the South from the North.

But the moderate view of Beecher disappeared when he decided to speak up at a March 1854 abolitionists' fundraising meeting at the North Congregational Church in New Haven, Connecticut. Members of the church had decided to form an enterprise called the Connecticut-Kansas Company, under the direction of one of New Haven's leading citizens, Charles B. Lines. The company would travel to and settle in Kansas to help tip the balance of the new territory's populace toward free statehood.

During the course of the meeting, which was called for the purpose of raising money for the Company's sojourn, a Yale University professor named Silliman pledged to donate the $25.00 cost of a Sharps Carbine Rifle, a new style of firearm manufactured by Christian Sharps in Hartford, Connecticut, to the Connecticut-Kansas Company. Silliman correctly anticipated the usefulness of such a weapon in the new territory. The minister of North Church added a similar pledge to the professor's.

Apparently unwilling to be overshadowed in his devotion to the cause, Henry Ward Beecher zealously offered a pledge on behalf of Plymouth Church. He pledged the cost of 25 Sharps rifles, "to promote the just and peaceful settlement of the Kansas issue," and challenged the New Haven congregation to match the offer. The congregation equaled the offer with $675, two rifles more than Beecher. The deal was done. Word of the famous preacher's commitment spread. The irony of Reverend Beecher's vow did not escape the American press and public; soon the Sharps Carbines became known as "Beecher Bibles." Interestingly, one of Beecher's Plymouth parishioners, not the preacher himself, donated 25 bibles to accompany the rifles to Kansas.

Thus at midnight on March 31, 1856, 60 residents of New Haven led by Mr. Lines, left their homes, families, and neighbors for the 1500 mile journey westward. From New Haven they crossed the Long Island Sound to New York by steamship. Leaving New York City they traveled by train to St. Louis, Missouri. From St. Louis on the Missouri River, they took a steamboat named *Clara* across the state to Kansas City, Missouri. In Kansas City, Lines and Company purchased oxen, wagons, farming supplies, and equipment, and headed down the Oregon Trail through Lawrence, Topeka, to Uniontown, near present-day Willard. They crossed the Kaw River, and settled in Wabaunsee, some 30 miles northwest of Topeka.

Wabaunsee, in the language of the local Kaw tribe, means "Dawn of Day." When Charles Lines and his Connecticut-Kansas Company reached the land their scouts had recommended for them in April of 1856, a pristine frontier awaited:

> a vast ocean of tall prairie grass, under the ever changing skies. To the north lay the Kaw River, crowning the bluffs beyond. A few miles to the east stood hills of spectacular beauty, and the prairie rolled gently away toward the south and west. The silence was broken only by the winds or by the song of the meadowlark, and at night by the music of the prairie wolves. The land belonged to the Indians, to the roving herds of buffalo and antelope, and to the great flock of migratory birds. [Beecher, p. 1]

This new land called Kansas was in for quite a shock.

Almost immediately, the Connecticut-Kansas Company erected a tent city, the precursor to the "New Haven of the West." The newcomers divided the land among themselves, and would establish the First Church of Christ of Wabaunsee in June of 1857. Almost immediately, their courage, as well as their Beecher Bibles, would be put to the test.

The Connecticut-Kansas Company journeyed simultaneously with thousands of other pioneers from New England and other northern cities, seeking to control the vote in Kansas for the antislavery faction. In response, residents of Missouri flooded the territory, determined to ensure Kansas joined Missouri among the other slave states. These "Border Ruffians" from Missouri facilitated an illegal and bogus election, in which the pro-slavery forces won the vote. But the antislavery constituency recognized the skullduggery, refused to acknowledge the election results, and set up their own provisional and illegal government in Topeka.

President Franklin Pierce ill-advisedly denounced the government in Topeka, which seemed to provide an excuse for the Border Ruffians to act. In what many historians consider to be the true inaugural battle of the Civil War, Border Ruffians attacked the free-state town of Lawrence, Kansas on May 21, 1856. Eight hundred Ruffians, armed with five cannons, stormed through Lawrence, killing one man, burning buildings, and destroying an antislavery newspaper office. In retaliation four days later, the fanatic and undoubtedly psychotic abolitionist John Brown led a retaliatory attack at Pottawatomie Creek, murdering five settlers with broadswords. (The Pottawatomie Creek "campaign" would be a foreshadowing of Brown's famous fevered assault on Harper's Ferry, Virginia three years later.)

Counterstrike followed counterstrike, as hostilities on both sides escalated recklessly. The New Wabaunsee settlers and their Beecher Bibles joined in the savage violence, as Kansas chaos inched dangerously close to the brink of anarchy. Within six months, more than 200 people died in the war for Bleeding Kansas.

The bitter hostilities plaguing Kansas continued well into the Civil War. Far west from the main theater between the organized Union and Confederate armies, guerrilla warfare flourished upon the broad meadows of Kansas, Missouri, and Arkansas. The combatants ignored commonly accepted rules of war, rarely took prisoners, and made the massacre a common occurrence.

The best known of these "jayhawkers" was Captain William C. Quantrill, considered by some the bloodiest man in American history. Eventually achieving the Confederate commission of Colonel, he commanded an army of up to 450 men, including Bloody Bill Anderson, Jesse James, and Cole Younger. Quantrill engineered a series of vicious attacks against civilians, including the slaughter of 180 Lawrence, Kansas settlers in August of 1863. Quantrill's terror spread east until June of 1865, when he was killed by a Union patrol in St. Louis.

Meanwhile, despite the upheaval prevailing in Kansas, the members of the First Wabaunsee Church of Christ managed to build their sanctuary, which would come to be known as the "Beecher Bible and Rifle Church." After two years of raising funds from New Haven, construction of the hardy stone church commenced in 1859. Parishioners quarried local limestone and transported it on a sledge pulled by the oxen purchased in Kansas City. Builders mixed the mortar with which to cement the stone by hand and, with crude masonry tools, formed the shakes which give the church its shingled texture. Straight-backed wooden pews divided the sanctuary with a column down the center; the men sat on one side of the column, and the women sat on the other. A ladder stretched upward from the rear balcony to the inside of the forty-foot belfry. The congregation employed coal stoves to heat the sanctuary in the winter, and hitching posts for the horses during services. Dedication of the new church came in May of 1862. By that time a large portion of the Wabaunsee population had vacated the town, as the men left home to join the Union army.

Wabaunsee never blossomed into the great city the New Haveners had envisioned. Many of them eventually left, but those that stayed helped to develop a thriving farming commu-

First Wabaunsee Church of Christ, known as the Beecher Bible and Rifle Church, Wabaunsee, Kansas. (Drawing by D. J. Stith, courtesy First Church of Christ, Wabaunsee.)

nity, and the First Church of Christ became one of the largest and most influential Congregational churches in Kansas. It continues to hold Sunday services to this day.

Meanwhile, Henry Ward Beecher continued his astounding career as a minister, despite the reproach he received over his "Beecher Bibles." He remained one of the most influential preachers in America until in 1875, when he was sued for adultery by his best friend. Theodore Tilton accused Beecher of an affair with his wife, Elizabeth. Although a hung jury acquitted the reverend of the accusation, the American public never fully exonerated Beecher, and the incident hounded him the rest of his life. He died in 1887.

As a fitting tribute to the Connecticut-Kansas Company, the Beecher Bible and Rifle Church became the first interracial Congregational church in Kansas. The fact that it did not occur until 1950, however, points to a basic hypocrisy which plagued many of the antislavery Northerners: although they dearly wished to free the African Americans from the bondage of slavery, they balked at their integration into mainstream society. They feared their racial and ethnic differences, and the competition they might present in the local economy. Although Northern whites considered slavery a blight, actual freedom for the blacks all too often proved an inconvenience.

Nevertheless, the monument erected by the Kansas State Historical Society a few blocks to the north of the church provides a fitting salute to the First Church of Christ in Wabaunsee: "In Memory of the Beecher Bible and Rifle Colony, which Settled this area in 1856, and helped make Kansas a Free State. May Future Generations Forever Pay them Tribute."

Sources

Davis, Kenneth C. *Don't Know Much About the Civil War.* 1996, William Morrow and Company, Inc., New York.

Davis, Kenneth C. *Don't Know Much About History.* 1990, Avon Books, New York.

Flayderman, Norman. *Flayderman's Guide to Antique American Firearms and their Values.* 1977, Follett Publishing Company, Chicago.

Hibben, Paxton. *Henry Ward Beecher: An American Portrait.* 1927, George H. Doran Company, New York.

Monaghan, Jay. *Civil War on the Western Border, 1854–1865.* 1955, Little Brown, and Company, Boston.

Van Dusen, Albert. *Connecticut.* 1961, Random House, New York.

The Beecher Bible and Rifle Church. 1963, Wabaunsee, Kansas.

ST. MARY'S IN THE MOUNTAINS

Affiliation: Roman Catholic
Location: Virginia City, Nevada
1860

The deep red spire atop the pure white belfry of St. Mary's in the Mountains Church towers over the 19th century town of Virginia City, Nevada. Now maintained by 700 residents to provide tourists a glimpse into a way of life a century ago, this ghost town had once been a booming city of 30,000, at one time the wealthiest community in North America. St. Mary's in the Mountains is integrally linked to the story of the community, and in the life of its most prominent citizen.

Not the broad, horizontal town as depicted in the popular television series *Bonanza*, Virginia City is a tiered community perched on a series of hills in western Nevada, between Carson City and Reno. Beneath the city more than 560 miles of tunnels run, beginning at the lower east end of town. These tunnels are the legacy of the gold and silver mines which at one time made Virginia City the greatest boom town in America. In the latter half of the 19th century, miners extracted more than $400 million in gold and silver ore. Virginia City's great success virtually bought Nevada's way into statehood. Although Nevada lacked the required 60,000 in population needed to join the Union, President Abraham Lincoln worried about obtaining the one additional state vote needed to ensure ratification of the thirteenth amendment, which would outlaw slavery in the United States. He also coveted the Nevada territory's gold and silver as a means for funding the Civil War effort. Lincoln therefore lobbied Congress to secure Nevada's entrance into the Union, which took effect October 31, 1864.

Virginia City reportedly received her name on behalf of an early miner named James Finney, whose nickname "Old Virginny" commemorated his home state. The town is also known as "Queen of the Comstock Lode," coined after Henry Comstock, a fast-talking con man. Comstock, beginning in 1859, managed to finagle his way into ownership or co-ownership of nearly every mine in and around Virginia City. Unfortunately, Comstock spent his riches as fast as he gained them, and in a few short years had lost his entire fortune. He took his own life with a revolver.

In 1858, a year before the arrival of Henry Comstock in Virginia City, Reverend Joseph Gallagher offered the first Catholic mass to the local Irish residents in Nevada. Two years later Gallagher's brother, Reverend Hugh Gallagher, started the first Catholic church in Nevada. A simple wooden structure, it reportedly blew over in a bout with the fierce northern winds of Virginia City known as "The Washoe Zephyrs."

In 1862, a 37-year-old priest from County

Kilkenny, Ireland, arrived in Virginia City. Patrick Monague (1831–1895) had worked as a miner in the California gold mines for seven years, accumulating enough money to underwrite his seminary training in France. He returned to the western United States, and served as both priest and bishop for most of the remainder of the century. His fame, however, rests with the construction of what would become known as "the Bonanza Church," which served the poor and sick of Virginia City throughout the silver strike era.

St. Mary's in the Mountains is a magnificent structure, whose gothic design clearly dominates the otherwise humble skyline of Virginia City. The red brick sanctuary is crowned by a pearl white belfry and a brick red spire, the combination of which stretches more than 140 feet toward the heavens. Twin brick minarets flank the belfry, each reaching 60 feet skyward. Over the stained glass rose window at the center of the facade reads the sign: "This is no other than the House of God and the Gate of Heaven (Genesis 34)."

The ornate interior features pews and columns hewed from California redwood, and a baptismal font which is reportedly the largest single block of pewter in the United States. Paintings, donated by the Daughters of Charity, depict Christ in Gethsemane, the Blessed Mother, and St. Patrick. The sanctuary also features a statue of St. Anthony and the Stations of the Cross, both imported from Italy. These artifacts, along with the silver used to forge the church bell, came from the generosity of the church's most famous of its predominantly Irish parishioners, John W. Mackay.

John Mackay had been the biggest of the quartet known as the "Bonanza Big Four." The Big Four included James Fair, mine superintendent and future U.S. senator; two saloon keepers turned stockbrokers, James Flood and William O'Brien; and Mackay. Mackay was born in Dublin, Ireland. He arrived in Virginia City in 1859 in the wake of the California Gold Rush, after unsuccessfully working the California mines for seven years. Mackay carried a reputation as "the only one of his kind in the history of the lode … a sturdy, slow-thinking, slow-speaking, methodical Irishman

… he did not drink, smoke, or gamble." (Ostrander, p. 9)

Mackay started his career in Virginia City working the mines at four dollars a day, the fair wage rate formally established in 1861 by the first miner's union in the country. Gradually, Mackay worked his way up to the position of timberman at six dollars a day, then to contractor for a share of the mining certificates. His first success as a mine owner came with the Kentuck mine, which he and a partner bought in 1862. The Kentuck produced $5 million in gold and silver in the next three years

In 1869, the thoughtful, sober Mackay teamed with the fast-talking, hard-drinking James Fair, purchasing the Hale and Norcross mine for $16,000, the majority of the capital coming from Mackay's already flourishing mining business. They elected San Francisco-based stockbrokers James Flood and William O'Brien as directors of the Hale and Norcross. With Fair appointed as superintendent (although as much of the credit is attributed to Mackay as Fair), mine productivity increased tenfold in two years.

In 1871, the Big Four purchased the Consolidated Virginia mine for $11,500; in January, 1872, they bought up the Gould and Curry mine for $50,000. Mackay built a mansion two blocks south of St. Mary's in the Mountains, from which he managed his operations. The stage was set for the strike which would shake the world.

The frenzy created by the California Gold Rush fueled Nevada's mining era. Prospectors, either heading to or returning from the Sierra foothill gold country, stopped over in western Nevada to test their luck. Mining involved painstaking, backbreaking work. Workers toiled underground both day and night, contaminating their lungs with "miner's consumption," resulting from constant exposure to the toxic ore fumes. Under the earth, protected from the wooden shafts bracing the tunnels, the miners would strip away handfuls of bluish clay to pick out the precious gold nuggets. Before long, however, the miners recognized the bluish clay as silver, the amounts of which far surpassed gold in the Virginia City hills.

For months, Mackay, Fair, and their min-

ers struggled fruitlessly in the dark tunnels, some reaching more than 500 feet below the center of Virginia City. Finally, in March of 1873, the mining crew struck a thin vein of ore, a mere trickle of mineral which would eventually develop into the greatest gold and silver strike in the history of the world. The "Big Bonanza" eventually produced $135,000,000 worth of gold and silver, an amount worth more than $2 billion today. Company stock sold wildly in San Francisco, assuring the fortunes of the Bonanza Big Four.

William O'Brien took his $12 million and moved to San Francisco, where he lived the remainder of his life as a gambler. James Flood also relocated to the City by the Bay, investing his $12 million in the building of the most opulent mansions in the West. James Fair earned $15 million in the Big Bonanza, and used it to finance a successful campaign for U.S. senator.

John MacKay remained in Virginia City, becoming the richest man in town, worth more than $100,000,000 when he died. In addition to his mining interests, Mackay also founded the Postal Telegraph Company, an early rival to Western Union, which pioneered the first transatlantic and transpacific telegraph lines in the world. A parishioner at St. Mary's since his arrival in Virginia City, Mackay's wealth proved to be one of the church's greatest assets. More than any other factor, Mackay saved St. Mary's in the Mountains from obliteration in the fire of 1875.

On October 26, 1875, a miner, severely intoxicated after a long day of labor in the pits, knocked over a kerosene lamp illuminating his room at the northwest end of town. The Washoe Zephyrs, the same winds that destroyed the original St. Mary's church in 1860, caught sparks from the rooming house fire, and scattered them among the brittle wooden buildings throughout the north wing of Virginia City. Soon, the entire wing roared with flame, headed southeast toward St. Mary's. To keep the fire from spreading further, city leaders agreed to dynamite the church, hoping the inferno would stop there. Ever the benefactor, Mackay vowed to personally finance the re-

building of his beloved parish. As always, Mackay remained true to his word. Although there have been subsequent renovations and repairs, St. Mary's in the Mountains stands today largely due to the generosity of John W. Mackay.

Perhaps the most celebrated ceremony involving St. Mary's in the Mountains had been the funeral for one of the Queen of the Comstock Lode's most notorious and beloved citizens. In Virginia City of the 1870s, prostitution had become almost as big a business as mining. As in most mining towns, women practicing the world's oldest profession followed the miners to cash in on their success. As few professional opportunities availed themselves to single women in the late 19th century, many turned to prostitution to survive and, in some cases, to become rich. One of the most successful courtesans in Virginia City was Julia Bulette. Born of French parents in England in 1832, Bulette came to Virginia City via New Orleans in 1863. Legends say Bulette became rich and famous through the establishment of "Julia's Palace."

In addition to the connubial comfort offered to numerous miners, bankers, or cattlemen, Julia's Palace reportedly brought a touch of class and refinery to the otherwise blustery mining town. Grateful clients reportedly bought Bulette furs, champagne, jewels, and fresh flowers. She hosted fanciful dinners featuring fine imported wines and French cuisine, a far cry from the miners' usual hard tack and whiskey. She brought out the best in her clientele; hard-fisted, soil-covered prospectors would bathe, dress in their Sunday best, and employ their most gracious manners when coming to call at Julia's Palace. Julia Bulette donated to charities, fed the poor, and even earned distinction as the only honorary female member of the volunteer fire department.

Unfortunately, Ms. Bulette's impact on the "Queen of the Comstock Lode" would not last. On the morning of January 20, 1867, she was found strangled and beaten in her bed, her belongings missing from her room. The "respectable women" of Virginia City rejected any notion of a memorial for this "notorious

Opposite: *St. Mary's in the Mountains, Virginia City, Nevada. (Photograph by Penni Thorpe.)*

woman." But the volunteer fire department donated a silver-handled casket, and 2000 grieving men of Virginia City reportedly filed in a lavish funeral procession from St. Mary's in the Mountains to her gravesite on a hill above the city, where her headboard marked her grave.

The most famous resident of Virginia City was a young Samuel Clemens. He had obtained employment on the editorial staff of *The Territorial Enterprise*. Here, Clemens first employed his pen name Mark Twain, and took the first steps on the road to his celebrated literary career. Twain worked as the apprentice to a reporter named Dan DeQuille (aka William Wright). Through *The Territorial Enterprise*, DeQuille expounded upon the exploits of the Comstock Lode. The worldwide press picked up his reports; soon Virginia City became a household synonym for wealth, gold, silver, and the wild, wild west.

Those wild west days of Virginia City have long since passed. Driving north on Route 341, there is at first little to alert the visitor to the approach of the ghost town turned tourist attraction. But suddenly, against the horizon of rolling hills beyond the valley to the east of Mt. Davidson, the red and white steeple of St. Mary's of the Mountains appears. Eclipsing the skyline, the Bonanza Church heralds the visitor, and bids welcome to the Queen of the Comstock Lode.

Sources

Bucchianeri, Virgil. "St. Mary's in the Mountains: Nevada's Bonanza Church." *Northern Nevada Catholic*. Summer 1997, Diocese of Reno.

Ostrander, Gilman M. *Nevada: The Great Rotten Borough, 1859–1964*. 1966, Alfred A. Knopf, New York.

Reno-Tahoe Speciality, Inc. *Virginia City*. Historical Nevada, 1997.

Smith, Grant H. *The History of the Comstock Lode, 1850–1920*. 1943, University of Nevada Bulletin, July 1, 1943.

BRADFORD CONGREGATIONAL CHURCH

("The Little Brown Church in the Vale")

Affiliation: Congregational
Location: near Nashua, 40 miles southeast of Mason City, Iowa
1864

In a wooded glen against a backdrop of drooping oaks, towering pine trees, waving grasses, and verdant rolling hills, a small chapel greets the visitor with a tranquil and humble welcome. Not the site of social unrest or political transformation, of cultural conquest or spiritual emergence, the church's legacy is the simplicity of a song. This song has floated from the lips, and alighted upon the ears of music lovers over six generations from around the world.

The song is called "Church in the Wildwood." It was written in June of 1857 by a young music teacher named William Pitts. Pitts traveled by stagecoach one summer

morning from McGregor in southeast Wisconsin to Fredericksburg, Iowa, to visit his beloved fiancée, Ann Elise Warren. His coach stopped near Bradford, outside what is now Nashua, six miles to the west of Fredericksburg.

During the lunch break Pitts took a stroll down a path along the Cedar River, in the area surrounding the stagecoach stop. A poet as well as a children's music instructor, Pitts' creative process often entailed imagining verse which could touch a young heart. As he wandered about the lovely countryside, enraptured in thoughts of his beautiful bride-to-be, he happened upon a small clearing amongst a knoll of trees. The clearing seemed the perfect size for a small, simple church, sheltered by the protective branches of the surrounding forest.

The picture of the chapel came to Pitts' mind: small, unassuming; the breeze echoing through the windows, the pine needles gently massaging the simple brown structure. A small belfry reached above the church roof toward the tree tops.

Pitts could imagine himself as a child, approaching the shelter the small chapel provides. He felt the serenity and security a boy would feel within its shadow, and he could almost hear the comforting sounds of the church bell, ringing softly from the belfry, calling whoever might be near, perhaps even the animals and birds in the forest, to come and pray within the chapel's cozy walls.

Slowly, then with increasing speed, the words of a poem began to form in his mind:

> How sweet on a clear Sabbath morning
> To list to the clear ringing bell
> Its tones so sweetly calling
> O come to the church in the vale.
>
> There's a church in the valley by the wildwood
> No lovelier spot in the dale;
> No place is so dear to my childhood
> As the little brown church in the vale.

The phrases rolled over and over in his mind. As soon as he arrived home and could find some paper, he wrote down the words of his poem. Some time later, he added the sweet melodic tones, and the result was his beautiful song.

The song remained a private work for several years afterward.

Meanwhile, Reverend Ozias Littlefield had founded the First Congregational Church of Bradford, near Nashua, Iowa, in 1855. The congregation met in restaurants and log cabins for Sunday service, as a church for the community had yet to be built. But in 1859, J.K. Nutting, a spirited preacher and amateur architect, became pastor of the First Congregational Church of Bradford. He arrived determine to change the course of the congregation.

Nutting quickly organized the Bradford Academy, featuring a school for music for the children of the town. Next, he fostered a drive to build a church in Bradford. The economic life of Bradford thrived that year, and Nutting began gathering donations of money and manpower. Mrs. Joseph Bird donated the land for the church, a quiet clearing in a forest on the banks of the Cedar River, close to the stagecoach stop.

The pastor drew up plans for the building, the construction of which commenced in 1860. The project continued for two years, until the Civil War and its call to arms halted the work. Production quickly resumed, however, and completion drew near in 1863.

Despite the recession of the times, logs, stone, lumber, and labor became available, donated by local church members who were eager for a church to be built in their midst. Other Congregational churches donated money for other needed materials. Thomas Cole, a local Pittsfield businessman, donated the bell that hangs from the 45-foot-square belfry.

The church would be painted in plain brown Ohio "mineral paint," the only color of paint the struggling congregation could afford. Upon completion, the tiny church would seat only 125 people.

By then, William Pitts had settled in Fredrickburg with his bride. He happened to land a job with the Bradford Academy, teaching young people music. One day, while traveling by wagon to his position at the Academy, Pitts passed by the clearing which had so inspired him seven years before. Overcome with astonishment, Pitts found the frame of a little wooden church newly erected at the very spot he had walked upon that June afternoon. The vision that inspired his song had somehow blossomed into reality. His song would be private no more; indeed, it would go on to tremendous popularity.

In 1862, before a gathering of his pupils that included Reverend Nutting, William Pitts publicly sang "The Church in the Wildwood" for the first time. At the dedication of the recently completed little church in the spring of 1864, Mr. Pitts directed his music school choir, who led the congregation in the words of the chorus:

> Come to the church in the wildwood
> Oh, come to the church in the dale;

Bradford Congregational Church, known as "the Little Brown Church in the Vale," near Nashua, Iowa. (Courtesy the Little Brown Church in the Vale.)

> No spot is so dear to my childhood
> As the Little Brown Church in the Vale

From then on, the First Congregational Church of Bradford would be known as the Little Brown Church in the Vale.

William Pitts sold his song to H. M. Higgins Company of Chicago for $25. This money helped fund his education, by which he earned his medical degree. He set up his practice in Fredericksburg, while raising his family and continuing to teach music to the children of the area. Although Dr. Pitts would compose many other songs, nothing else would leave the impact of "The Church in the Wildwood."

By the turn of the century, both the church and the song had fallen out of public recogni-

tion. But at the outbreak of World War I, both experienced a sudden revival.

The song had been resurrected by a quartet named the Weatherwax Brothers from Charles City, Iowa, 11 miles north of Bradford. The most popular singing quartet of their era, the Weatherwax Brothers appeared at chautauquas and outdoor gatherings of various sorts throughout the United States and Canada. The brothers would reportedly end their concerts the same way each night: telling the story of the Little Brown Church in the Vale, and ending their performance by singing the song.

Another group called the Fiske Jubilee Singers toured the country with the song, and reportedly performed it before the royal courts of Europe. The lyrics were translated into several languages, and became popular in Australia, Russia, France, and Germany. In Japan, the church is regarded as something of a shrine.

Thus "The Church in the Wildwood" gained acceptance as one of the great Protestant religious songs, appearing in hymnals, tapes, and recordings throughout the world.

There is debate as to whether "The Church in the Wildwood" would be considered a hymn or a secular song. There is certainly a religious feeling to the song, and it has appeared in numerous nonsectarian hymnals over the decades. Yet, there are those who would not consider it a proper hymn, since there is neither a scriptural nor a liturgical theme to it. There is no doubt, however, about the spiritual power of the song, which speaks to the longing of the human soul for serenity.

What makes music such an important part of religious practice and ritual? Some say the vibrations of the music affect the participant on a cellular level, recreating and transforming the self on an elemental plane. Others believe the melodies and lyrics touch the soul at an emotional depth unreachable by mere words or doctrine.

A third idea, however, may be that music is the language by which one expresses the inexpressible. In immersing oneself in the rhythms and sounds of the ceremony, the celebrant conveys the unconscious, soulful understanding of the Divine. In the realm of the metaphysical, of course, such understanding resides at the heart of every individual's spiritual journey.

The revival of the song focused attention back on the Little Brown Church itself. As the congregation rebuilt, the church began attracting engaged couples, who saw the chapel's pastoral setting an ideal locale for their wedding ceremony. Since World War I as many as 800 couples a year have been married at the Little Brown Church, sometimes with as many as 18 weddings performed a day. According to current pastors Bob and Linda Myren, an estimated 68,525 couples have been wed at the Little Brown Church.

Each year in August the Little Brown Church conducts a reunion of couples who have been married in the humble. In 1977, at the 25th anniversary of the "Celebration of Marriage," more than 1200 couples attended. Thirty-four of those couples had been married more than 50 years, and some had traveled as far as southern California to attend. Some couples had wed in the presence of their parents and grandparents, all of whom had been married at the Little Brown Church in the Vale.

As many as 150,000 people per year visit the Little Brown Church in the Vale each year. Although Bradford is now a ghost town, the Church is tenderly maintained by a local group dedicated to ensure its survival into the millennium. All the care and attention afforded the church over the years would never have come, however, without "The Church in the Wildwood" by William Pitts. It moved and lifted the hearts of thousands of churchgoers around the world, and inspired a wedding shrine in the wildwood of northern Iowa.

Sources

Raffensperger, Gene. "Ringing Endorsement for Pastor." *Des Moines Register,* October 14, 1981.

Simbro, William. "Loving memories revived at Little Brown Church." *Des Moines Sunday Register.* August 14, 1977.

"The Little Brown Church in the Vale" and It's Composer. *Kansas City Star.* October 30, 1918.

"The Origin of the Song: The Little Brown Church in the Vale." *The Palimosest.* March 1921.

ST. MARK'S CHURCH

Affiliation: Episcopal
Location: Cheyenne, Wyoming
1868

St. Mark's Episcopal Church in Cheyenne is undoubtedly one of the most historic buildings in the Cowboy State. The first church edifice of any denomination built in the present state of Wyoming, it was founded under the direction of Reverend W. Cook, an Episcopal missionary from St. Mark's Church in Philadelphia. Reverend Cook came to bring Episcopalian civility and religion to the wild and woolly west. With a donation of $1000 from the Pennsylvania church, 19 original Cheyenne parishioners erected the first church building on land donated by the Union Pacific Railroad. The parish dedicated the sanctuary on August 23, 1868, 22 years before Wyoming achieved statehood.

The parish of St. Mark's is firmly intertwined among some of the more historic events of the 44th state. For example, former Pinkerton detective Tom Horn, suspected of several murders of sheep ranchers in Wyoming and Colorado, was convicted in November 1903 of killing 13-year-old Willie Nickel in the Laramie Mountains. Horn had apparently mistaken the boy for his father, sheep rancher Kels P. Nickel, at an ambush in the Iron Mountain section of the Laramies. Rumors flew alleging that Tom Horn had been hired by cattleman John C. Coble to kill the elder Nickel, who had reportedly injured Coble in a previous knife fight.

One of the most publicized judicial decisions in its day, the Horn trial brought severe pressure on the shoulders of acting governor Fenimore Chatterton to commute Horn's sentence. Politicians, cattle barons, and the general public threatened the safety and political health of Chatterton, who nonetheless held his ground and insisted that Tom Horn would be put to death as his sentence decreed.

St. Mark's assistant pastor John Watson called on Horn in his jail cell the night before the execution. Watson visited Horn, accompanied by members of the church choir, who reportedly brought the convicted killer to weeping tears with their rendition of "Jesus, Lover of My Soul."

The next morning Tom Horn swung from a rope outside the Laramie County Jail, mere blocks away from St. Mark's Church. Several of St. Mark's parishioners witnessed the execution, while pastor Dr. George C. Rafter stood on the gallows "praying earnestly and audibly for the doomed man's soul" as Tom Horn died.

Twelve years later, on August 31, 1915, St. Mark's hosted one of the most sorrowful funerals in the history of Wyoming. Mrs. Frances Warren Pershing—wife of Spanish-American war hero Brigadier General John J. Pershing—and three of their four children perished tragically in a mysterious August 27 fire in their military home at the Presidio in San Francisco, California. Only young Warren, age six, survived. Frances Pershing had attended St. Mark's as a child with her parents, Senator and Mrs. Francis Warren of Cheyenne.

The stoic general and his young son watched the solemn parade of the horse-drawn black hearse as it wound slowly through the streets of Cheyenne. Heart-broken townspeople, many friends and acquaintances of the Warrens, lined the pathway to Lakeview Cemetery, where more than 1000 floral bouquets lay at the grave site.

Cheyenne became the state capital when Wyoming attained territorial status in 1890. Eleven of Wyoming's governors had been active members of St. Mark's congregation, including possibly the most famous Wyoming head of state of all, Democratic governor William B. Ross.

On October 2, 1924, Governor Ross died

of complications due to an operation for acute appendicitis. Wyoming held a special election to find a replacement for the remaining two years of Governor Ross' term.

The governor's widow, Nellie Taylor Ross, had been content in her role as wife and mother, and had been an active member of St. Mark's Church, dutifully bringing up her two sons in the influence of the Episcopal stone church. Through the encouragement of her friends, as well as political supporters of the late governor, she entered as a candidate in the 1924 special election for governor, spending nary a minute on the campaign trail.

Nellie Taylor Ross won the special gubernatorial election against Republican candidate Eugene J. Sullivan by more than 8000 votes. As such, Nellie Taylor Ross became the United States' first female governor on January 5, 1925, entering office 20 days before Miriam "Ma" Fergusen of Texas.

Although the Cheyenne *State Tribune-Leader* observed that "chivalry and sympathy were the factors of chief consideration" (Larson, p. 457) in her victory, Ross proved to be an able administrator and effective orator. While governor, Mrs. Ross attended services at St. Mark's regularly, occasionally entertaining the Ladies' Guild at the Governor's Mansion. After her term of office, Ross served as Director of the United States Mint from 1933 to 1953.

President Franklin Roosevelt, who faithfully attended St. John's Episcopal Church at Lafayette Square when in Washington, made a historic appearance at the church during a westward campaign sojourn. On October 11, 1936, which happened to be Eleanor Roosevelt's 52nd birthday, the first lady and the president attended services at St. Mark's. Church historian Shirley Flynn described the scene:

> The President and his family were devoted Episcopalians and enthusiastic travelers and usually attended church services wherever they were on Sunday mornings.... That day President Roosevelt and his wife Eleanor, accompanied by Secret Service guards, entered St. Mark's and quietly worshipped with the congregation. A ramp was arranged at the door to enable the handicapped Chief Executive to enter in his wheelchair. The day happened to be Eleanor Roosevelt's 52nd birthday, and she wore a black suit and a new sable scarf, the birthday gift from her husband. (Flynn, p. 35)

St. Mark's pastor, Dr. Charles A. Bennett, had to fight the temptation to draw great attention to the presidential visit. He had promised the Roosevelts he would treat the day's service as any other, and he kept his promise. St. Mark's was one of several stops the Roosevelts made in Wyoming, none of any particular executive significance. Nevertheless, parishioners remember fondly the day the popular Democratic chief executive graced the stone church interior.

Despite the historical significance surrounding Cheyenne's stone Episcopal church, much of the notoriety afforded the sanctuary is due to a mysterious chamber in the shadow of the great stone bell tower. There are those who say this chamber marks St. Mark's importance in metaphysical as well as physical history.

The room sits at the apex of an 85-foot circular spiral staircase winding upwards from the basement. Adjacent to and below the stone belfry, the chamber is described as elegant and charming, featuring Gothic windows, hardwood maple floors, lovely stucco plastered walls, even a chandelier. But the room has no occupant, and apparently no official purpose or use. Some say the "mysterious" chamber is merely a room connected to the original belfry which was never completed. There is, however, another explanation for the odd compartment which has been offered through the years.

In 1886, after nearly 20 years, the blossoming parish finally outgrew the original A-frame church, designed to hold no more than 200 people. Pastor Dr. George C. Rafter and his community set out to design a new church, patterned after the 11th century Stokes Poges Church in London, where Thomas Gray reportedly penned his "Elegy Written in a Country Churchyard." In Wyoming's meager population, however, skilled stone masons proved a scarce commodity.

Fortunately, according to the story, two Swedes, who had recently immigrated to America, crossed the community's path. Neither could read, write, or speak English, but both possessed experience and skills in masonry, carpentry, and general construction. The parish immediately recruited the pair to build the new Old English–style St. Mark's Church.

For weeks the Swedish masons labored over the new sanctuary. They constructed the ground floor; then they began erecting the circular wall designed to encompass the great stone tower. One of the masons would operate the rope-pulley device, which would raise the great quarried stones up to the second mason, standing on top of the structure. The second mason would then guide the stone into place, fastening it with mortar. Eventually, the hardworking masons completed the circular wall, and had raised the tower to nearly 40 feet in height.

One day, parishioners noticed only one of the stone masons working on the job. The rope-pulley operator struggled on his own to complete what he could of the project. Growing noticeably agitated, the lone mason hastily fashioned a wooden roof for the tower. Then, without warning, he mysteriously disappeared as well.

Years later, an elderly gentleman in a Denver, Colorado, residential care home reportedly revealed the fate of the Swedish stone masons. He said he met the second stone mason, who told him his story on his deathbed. The first mason had been accidentally killed when he fell off the stone tower. Fearing he would be accused of the death and face deportation to Sweden, the second mason, who according to the story may have harbored a dubious past in Sweden, anxiously wedged his partner's body inside a section of the circular wall, then covered the space with cement. After a few nervous days, the second mason fled the country, settling in South America, where he reportedly lived the remaining of his guilt-ridden days.

Meanwhile, the distinguished, elderly Dr. Rafter moved into the rooms built by the stone masons, adjacent to the circular wall and belfry. Almost immediately, Rafter reportedly began to noticing strange phenomena emanating from the new church. He could hear the peculiar sound of a hammer pounding from inside the circular wall, as if construction of the wall continued. He could also detect the sounds of muffled voices, like men carrying on an everyday conversation, emanating from inside the wall.

Rafter had the structure searched several times, scouring for would-be squatters settling in the tower. The searches uncovered no one, but the noises continued. Dr. Rafter finally retired in 1904.

The second church was completed in 1888, but construction of the tower remained delayed until 1925. Under the direction of the Reverend Charles Bennett, the parish hired a local construction company to transform the steeple into a stone bell tower. The working crew soon determined they were not alone on the site. Men described the tapping of invisible hammers, the mumbling of disembodied voices, the sounds of footsteps, and the appearance of shadows without bodies. Once the bells were hung in the tower, they would ring by themselves, frightening the crew to the point of resignation. There was no doubt in the minds of the crew: St. Mark's Church was haunted.

The crew, a superstitious but determined lot, devised a plan to appease the specter, which they hoped would allow them to finish their job. They persuaded the good Dr. Bennett, against his better judgment, to allow them to construct a special chamber for the ghost. They hoped the phantom chamber would be found elegant, comfortable and spiritually appealing.

The plan apparently worked. The crew completed its work, and on October 16, 1927, the parish dedicated the newly installed 11 Carillon bell chime inside the freshly completed bell tower.

Despite numerous published articles and stories concerning this stone mason specter, church historian Flynn says her extensive research reveals no factual evidence indicating Swedish stone masons ever worked on St. Mark's Church. There has been conflicting testimony over the years of ghostly phenomena and midnight hauntings: mysterious shadows, floating blue lights, a jellylike substance oozing from baseboards; bells in the tower ringing by themselves, isolated sounds of footsteps.

Flynn insists the ghost of St. Mark's bell tower is mere legend, concocted to scare fanciful children at Halloween. However, the room next to the tower remains empty, serving no apparent use.

Certainly by themselves, the long list of historical events involving St. Mark's Episcopal Church to the Cheyenne community marks the church a true Wyoming pioneer. But if the spectral tale is true, St. Mark's is also a trailblazer in the spiritual realm: the only church in America containing an apartment built and furnished for the comfort and convenience of a ghost.

Sources

Bragg, Bill. *Wyoming's Wealth: A History of Wyoming.* 1876.
Flynn, Shirley E. *Our Heritage: 100 Years at St. Mark's: 1868–1968.* 1968, St. Mark's Centennial Committee, Cheyenne, WY.
Knox, Kirk. "There's a Ghostly Chance." *Wyoming State Tribune.* November 2, 1979, Cheyenne, WY.
Larson, T.A. *History of Wyoming.* University of Nebraska Press.
Munn, Debra. "The Ghost of St. Mark's Bell Tower." *Ghosts on the Range.* 1989, Pruett Publishing Company.

St. Philomena's Church

Affiliation: Roman Catholic
Location: Kalawao, Kalaupapa Peninsula, Island of Molokai, Hawaii
1872

It is a chronic microbacterial infection affecting the skin and peripheral nerves, as well as the eyes, the testicles, and bone. The bacterium burrows into peripheral nerves, destroying them, with a disintegration of tissue. The afflicted lose fingers, toes, noses, ear lobes, and other extremities. Its cause is still somewhat unknown, but it is thought to enter through the respiratory tract, and slowly affect the entirety of the body.

First identified as *Mycrobacterium leprae* by Armauer G. Hansen of Norway in 1873, in modern vernacular the affliction is known by its gentler name, Hansen's Disease. But for most of history, the malady has been known as leprosy.

Since biblical times, the afflicted have been called lepers, vilified and shunned in every community. Lepers have been ostracized as unclean, cursed, and evil. Leprosy was once thought to be a form of venereal disease, adding condemnation to the suffering of the afflicted. The societal treatment isolated them, imprisoned them in the desperate crevasses and pits of society, to let them die without pity or consolation.

Known as *Ma'i Pake* by the Hawaiians, it began appearing in the Islands in the 1840s.

Some theorize it was brought by Chinese laborers imported to Hawaii to work the European and American sugar plantations, but no one really knows how it arrived. For some reason, *Ma'i Pake* seemed to affect natives more than *haoles* or outsiders — another addition to the scourge of foreign diseases that wiped out an estimated 80 percent of the native Hawaiian population.

With no available vaccination or treatment, officials followed the traditional hysterical response, evoked since biblical times: isolation and oppression of the lepers. Those identified as lepers were rounded up and separated from their families. Health officials employed bounty hunters earning five dollars a person to identify, locate, and apprehend lepers trying to hide themselves from officials. Marked children would be pulled from their homes, or abducted from their schools. In all, more than 8000 individuals suffered forcible removal from their homes and loved ones, and banishment to the isolated island that would become known as "the Leper Colony." Most of them died there.

The island of Molokai is located approximately 30 miles southeast of the Island of Oahu, north of Lanai, and northwest of Maui.

The northern Makanalau peninsula features the tallest sea cliffs in the world, which cuts the peninsula off from the rest of Molokai. On the western edge of Makanalau peninsula rests Kalawao, perfectly isolated between the 1600-foot sea cliffs, and the raging Pacific Ocean. It is on this windblown, wave-buffeted rock that the Hawaiian Board of Health, known by the Hawaiian natives as "Board of Death," founded the Leper Colony.

The schooner *Warrick* stranded the first group of lepers on Makanalau peninsula near Kalaupapa in 1866. The ship virtually dumped 124 human beings on the island, to fend for themselves with no shelter and few supplies. They lived in caves, or crude huts of sticks and leaves which they could scratch together for themselves.

On subsequent trips, as the colony grew in size, ships would not even approach the shore, for fear of spread of the dreaded disease aboard ship. Instead, the lepers would be forced overboard into the sea, to swim for their lives, or drown.

Remarkably, some actually survived the horrible journey to Molokai. In 1873, a 33-year-old Roman Catholic priest named Damien de Veuster, arrived at Kalaupapa. Born on January 3, 1840, Joseph de Veuster lived near Louvain, Belgium. Joseph grew up strong and athletic, and gained his carpentry skills as a teenager while working for his father. De Veuster joined the Sacred Heart Community as a deacon in 1859, taking the name of the French saint and doctor, Damien. Ordained in 1864 in Honolulu, he worked on the Island of Hawaii for eight years. When Bishop Louis Maigret asked for a volunteer to work at the Leper Colony at Kalaupapa, Damien came forth.

Fr. Damien immediately led the colonists away from the wind-tormented area at which they'd been stranded. The colony moved inland to a more hospitable location, the tiny village of Kalawao. Under the direction of Damien the carpenter, the lepers built houses, a hospital, and other facilities for their use at Kalawao.

Damien reportedly could be driven and dictatorial as well as compassionate and nurturing. He apparently thought of himself as the benevolent "Father-General" of the colony. Some scholars even question whether he kept a mistress to attend him at Kalawao. Regardless of any human failing, however, Fr. Damien's is the story of an unusually courageous man embarking upon an extraordinary and perilous vocation.

St. Philomena's Church in Kalawao had been initially built by Sacred Heart brothers in 1872, but the maintenance, repair, and enlargement of the church became a lifelong task for Fr. Damien. Named for the 19th century saint and martyr called the "wonder worker," St. Philomena's quickly filled with colonists for the Belgian priest's Sunday mass. The congregation decorated the interior of St. Philomena's in a bright spectrum of color, in the fashion preferred by the Hawaiians. Sunday services became so popular many of the faithful had to view the proceedings from outside at the windows. Damien had holes carved out of the church floor among the pews, so his suffering congregation could cough and expectorate without leaving the sanctuary, and missing any of his sermons. So crowded became the sanctuary that Fr. Damien sometimes felt overcome by the stench of rotting flesh among the congregation.

Eventually, the church required enlargement, and over the years Damien could be found tinkering and working with his church. The last carpentry task of his life became the repair of St. Philomena's roof in 1889, the year of his death.

Sunday services at the little church often seemed to bring the rare moment of joy and belonging to the sorrowful little settlement at Kalawao. Of Sunday mass at St. Philomena's Church, one chronicler wrote, "Whoever saw a Sunday service at St. Philomena's was impressed ... by the fervor of prayers, the beauty of the voices of the Hawaiians singing, and the total seriousness with which the communicants brought their doomed bodies to the sacramental table.... On such days, with the sun shining outside, a gentle trade wind blowing, and the surf adding its soothing bass notes as counterpoint to the Mozart mass being sung by the church choir, it was possible to think of Kalawao as a community." (Daws, *Holy Man*, p. 113)

St. Philomena's Church, Kalawao, Hawaii. (Courtesy Hawaii State Archives.)

In sharp contrast to the custom of the day, Fr. Damien seemed to possess no fear of contracting the disease. He would willingly lay his hands upon the lepers, treat their wounds, and change their fetid bandages. He eventually took to smoking a pipe, so the smell of tobacco would hide the stench of putrid tissue surrounding him every day.

The priest reportedly encouraged the development of a close knit and dignified community at Kalawao. As a result, despite their affliction, the colonists could build as rewarding and enjoyable a life as possible for the times.

In 1881, the colony at Kalawau received a special visitor, Princess Liliuokalani of Hawaii, ten years before she would be made queen. This was Liliuokalani's first visit among the lepers, and she felt deeply moved by all that she saw there: the suffering of the afflicted, the dedication of Fr. Damien, and the continued loyalty of her subjects, even on this most forsaken of islands. Reports described how, as Liliuokalani's barge pulled away from the shores at Kalaupapa, she found a corner of the vessel for her own, and there wept uncontrollably for her suffering people.

Later that year, Damien received a letter from the young Princess:

> I desire to express to you my admiration of the heroic and distinguished service you are rendering to the most unhappy of my subjects, and to pay, in some measure, a public tribute to the devotion, patience, and unbounded charity with which you give yourself to the corporal and spiritual relief of these unfortunate people.... [Farrow, pp. 154–155]

Damien received from Her Highness a decoration of the Royal Order of Kalakaua, in honor of his work on Molokai.

Damien eventually contracted the disease himself, and came to be known as "Damien the Leper." He became as shunned as his parishioners, even by many of his fellow priests, who refused to celebrate mass or share communion with him. But he was not entirely without support; Brother Joseph Dutton and Sister Marianne Kopp eventually joined Damien in his work. Fr. Damien died on April 15, 1889, at the age of 49, of the disease with which he had lived most of his life. He was buried at the cemetery at St. Philomena's Church.

Along the Roman Catholic Church's three steps toward sainthood, Fr. Damien has been both venerated and beatified. Supporters and followers continue to campaign for the third and final step — the entry of Damien's name into the canon (official list) of recognized saints.

Although leprosy is thought of as a disease of the distant past, it still affects a considerable number of people. In 1995, the World Health Organization (WHO) estimated there were 1.8 million known cases of Hansen's Disease worldwide, 6500 in the United States alone. The WHO also estimates 561,000 new cases per year worldwide, with 200–250 in the United States. Fortunately, the shame and the stigma once associated with disease have finally begun to give way in the face of scientific fact and reason.

Study of the disease at modern, research-intensive facilities such as the Gillis W. Long Hansen's Disease Center in Carville, Louisiana, has produced continually developing true knowledge of *Mycrobacterium leprae* which has, fortunately, replaced many of the myths and horror stories. What is now known is that leprosy is curable and controllable. Despite its loathsome reputation, and the quarantine the afflicted have historically faced, it appears that

leprosy is one of the least communicable of diseases, transmitting only among the most susceptible families. This is perhaps why the disease affected Hawaiians more than the *haoles*, since the family lines of the Hawaiians were much less defined and much more intermingled than the Europeans and Americans.

Today, most Hansen's Disease patients never require hospitalization, let alone sequestering. Reconstructive surgery and specialized footwear can compensate for most deterioration of tissue that occurs. Treatment of the disease with antibacterial drugs such as dapsone, rifampin, and clofazimine is very effective. In short, most new patients of Hansen's Disease suffer little disability, provided that the disease is diagnosed early and the recommended treatment procedure is followed.

Kalaupapa, Molokai, is now a National Historic Park, so designated in 1980. Several dozen lepers still live there, although they are now free to leave whenever they choose. But they remain on Molokai, with the graves of the thousands of people who died in isolation, beside St. Philomena's Church, the monument to Damien the Leper. Those who remain on Molokai are living reminders of the terrors that result from social policies developed out of fear rather than reason.

Sources

Beevers, John. *A Man for Now: The Life of Damien de Veuster, Friend of Lepers.* 1973, Doubleday and Co., Inc., Garden City, New York.

Daws, Gavan. *Holy Man: Father Damien of Molokai.* 1973, Harper & Row, Publishers, New York.

Daws, Gavan. *Shoal of Time.* 1968, The MacMillan Company, New York.

Farrow, John. *Damien the Leper.* 1954, Image Books, New York.

Flinn, John. "Hawaii's Cruel Island of Isolation." *San Francisco Examiner*, September 8, 1996.

Health Resources and Services Administration. *National Hansen's Disease Program.* Bureau of Primary Health Care, November 15, 1996.

ZION CHURCH

Affiliation: German Lutheran
Location: Hamilton County, Nebraska
1873

In 1920, with the recent influx of immigrants from Central Europe, xenophobic Americans felt particularly sensitive about sharing their beloved soil with "aliens" and "strangers." With the close of World War I, many Americans remained particularly fearful and resentful toward German Americans regardless of whether they had been native-born, or for how many years or decades they had lived on American soil. Several states passed laws reflecting this anti–German sentiment, and incidents of harassment and even physical assault against German-Americans, in the name of testing their patriotism, had been reported in several states. A conference of governors in 1918 had focused on nationwide efforts to "stamp out disloyalty" among recent immigrants, implicit permission to harass under the guise of "making them real Americans." English-only laws, similar to those passed in the late 1880s and 1890s, had become popular throughout many of the states.

In the state of Nebraska the Siman Language Bill overwhelmingly passed through the state legislature in 1919. Banning all foreign language teaching in elementary schools, it took specific aim at the German language, as Nebraska featured a large German-American community. The tide of resentment seemed to be rising against all immigrants, but particularly those of Rhineland ancestry.

A reversal of trends began at a little elementary school in a small Lutheran church in a rural Nebraska county. Zion Lutheran Church had been founded in 1873 by German Lutherans, with Reverend G.F. Burger installed as the first pastor in 1875. The original church was dedicated in 1883. It became the day school, after the second church was built, for the parish until 1928. The members dedicated the current church in 1897. A graceful white building, its tall, slender steeple used to tower over the landscape of the surrounding village of Hampton.

The Lutheran Church, of course, had been based on the writings of Martin Luther (1483–1546), a German Monk who challenged many of the precepts and practices of the Roman Catholic Church in the 16th century. Luther translated the then Latin Bible into German, making it possible for individuals to read and interpret the Scriptures without clerical interpretation. Individual access to scriptural knowledge became a basic tenet of the Protestant Reformation.

On May 25, 1920, school teacher Robert T. Meyer asked young Raymond Parpart, a fourth grader at Zion Lutheran parochial school, to read a passage from *die Himmelsleither*, or *Jacob's Ladder*. As Parpart read from the book in his German language, Hamilton County attorney Frank E. Edgerton burst into the 60-student classroom, confronted the boy and the teacher, and confiscated *die Himmelsleiter.* Teacher Robert T. Meyer was cited and convicted by the all-male district court of violating the Siman Law, and was fined $25. Outraged by this intrusion, the Missouri Synod of Lutherans refused to pay this or any other fine.

Before the Zion School incident, a coalition of Nebraska Catholics and Lutherans had challenged the "language law" before the Nebraska Supreme Court. At that time, the court had actually ruled the teaching of a religion in a foreign language as permissible, as long as it did not interfere with the instruction of state-required subjects. Zion School, and other schools, extended the lunch hour to 1:30 P.M., to allow time for students of foreign languages to learn their lessons in their native tongues.

But when the case of *Robert T. Meyer vs. State of Nebraska* reached the Nebraska Supreme Court in 1921, the final loophole in the language law closed: the court banned German teaching at any hour, anytime. The court ignored the religious freedom argument, declaring learning German would "naturally inculcate ideas and interests foreign to the interests of the country." Xenophobia had triumphed. The dissenting justice of the Nebraska Supreme Court reportedly attacked Siman Law as "the result of crowd psychology." (Ulmer, P.6)

By 1921, the *Meyer vs. Nebraska* case had attracted national attention. Twenty-one states had initiated legislation regulating the use of foreign language in schools, with two other states absolutely forbidding foreign language in the schools altogether. Oregon went a step further, requiring all children to attend public school rather than parochial school; a step later declared unconstitutional.

When *Meyer vs. Nebraska* finally reached the United States Supreme Court in 1923, the First Amendment had yet to be applied to states and, therefore, the United States Supreme Court could not use it in its argument. By the early twentieth century, there still existed a tremendous gap between laws the states could pass, and how the federal judiciary branch could, or would, act to regulate those laws. Therefore, states were routinely passing laws which, by today's standards, would be considered major infringements on personal and civil rights.

The 1923 ruling on *Meyer vs. Nebraska* became the initial wave that, eventually, would turn the tide. Justice James McReynolds ruled the 14th Amendment denied states the ability to deprive any person "liberty without due process of law." This meant Lutheran parents (or any other parents, for that matter) had the right to direct the education of children, without interference from the state. In other words, Nebraska could not ban teaching of German.

At the same time, McReynolds indicated that within the meaning of the word "Liberty" could be included many other "long-recognized" rights listed nowhere else in the Constitution. These included the right of the individual "to contract, to engage in ... common occupations, to acquire useful knowledge, to marry, to establish a home and bring up children, to worship God according to the dictates of his own conscience, and generally to enjoy privileges, essential to the orderly pursuit of happiness by free men...." On the surface, the 1923 ruling reversed the Nebraska

Supreme Court and allowed German to be used not only in the school, but in all aspects of German-American life—a major victory for the Missouri Synod. The full, long-reaching impact of the case, however, would not be realized for 40 more years.

Between 1965 and 1985, the Warren and Burger Supreme Courts cited *Meyer vs. Nebraska* in 66 separate cases. These cases involved a plethora of civil and personal rights, from the right to wear arm bands to the right to use contraceptives to the right for extended families to live together in a single family unit. In the most stunning decision of all, the citation emerged again during the landmark *Roe vs. Wade* case, which substantively legalized abortion in the United States. Essentially, in writing the 1973 decision in the 7 to 2 ruling by the court, Justice Harry Blackman equated a woman's right to abortion to her right to privacy. He said the Fourteenth Amendment guaranteed neither right could be deprived without substantive due process. Indeed, the theme of all these rulings was "substantive due process," and how the government could not deny civil and personal rights without it.

Ironically, after the 1923 Supreme Court decision, the use of German fairly quickly declined in the Lutheran Church anyway, in the natural process of assimilation which comes with any community finding its place within a larger, foreign community. Despite the paranoia and ballyhoo professed by "real Americans," the immigrants managed to find themselves a productive and substantial role in American society.

The nationwide backlash against immigrants, particularly of Latin American descent, in the United States in the 1990s seemed to many to be a new low point in American domestic policy. Efforts to curb immigration by limiting noncitizen access to public assistance and public health care—such as the Welfare Reform Act of 1996—have been criticized as short-sighted, draconian, fascist, as well as a serious threat to public health. Yet this practice of scapegoating persons of a certain ancestry for the myriad of societal troubles has been a regularly recurring theme in the history of the "land of the free." At one time or another, every ethnic community which has found a home in the United States has had to face systematic harassment and intimidation on both a local and national front. Yet, despite all the persecution, these intrepid immigrants have always found their productive ways into society. It seems they always have. Likely, they always will. Truly, this is what America is all about.

Sources

Bishop, Peter and Michael Darton. *The Encyclopedia of World Faiths: An Illustrated Survey of the World's Liv-*

ing Religions. 1987, MacDonald and Co., Ltd., London and Sydney, pp. 112–116.

Hall, Kermit L. *The Oxford Companion to the Supreme Court of the United States.* 1992, Oxford University Press, New York.

Parrinder, Geoffrey. *Religions of the Modern World, from Primitive Beliefs to Modern Faiths.* 1971, The Hamlyn Publishing Group, New York.

Smith, Hustin. *The Illustrated World's Religions.* 1994, Harper Collins Books, San Francisco.

Ulmer, Richard D., Jr. "From Hampton to the High Court: How Meyer vs. Nebraska made the Law Books." *Sunday World-Herald Magazine of the Midlands.* June 15, 1986.

ST. FIDELIS CHURCH

Affiliation: Volga German Catholic
Location: Victoria, 4 miles east of Hays, Ellis County, Kansas
1876

William Jennings Bryan is remembered as one of the most colorful, controversial, and zealous figures at the turn of the 20th century. An avid advocate of the silver standard, an early supporter of prohibition, and a staunch opponent of United States imperialism, Bryan embodied a fascinating mixture of conservative Christian ideals and progressive political measures. He ran unsuccessfully for the office of United States president three times, but supported the victorious campaign of Woodrow Wilson in 1912. In turn, Wilson named him secretary of state. In 1925, Bryan served as chief prosecutor in the famous Scopes Monkey Trial, in which he successfully defended the teaching of creationism over evolution in public schools.

In 1912, while campaigning for Wilson in the Midwest, Bryan, who hailed from the Midwest himself, passed through the north central area of Kansas. A local politician named D. M. Dreilings of Hays, Kansas, prevailed upon the former presidential candidate to visit the premier architectural attraction of the region, St. Fidelis Church in nearby Victoria.

Under the vast blue prairie sky and beyond the golden level plains, the majestic twin towers of a massive stone church beckoned the gaze of the famed barrister. The wild north Kansas plains emphasized the grandeur of the great structure, then the largest church west of the Mississippi River. William Jennings Bryan was so moved by the sight he immediately acclaimed it the "Cathedral of the Plains," by which St. Fidelis Church has been known ever since. Bryan endeared himself to the people of northern Kansas more in the instant of that pronouncement, than he ever did through his years of political thought.

This Cathedral of the Plains is indeed an impressive structure. Crucible in shape, it stretches 220 feet from the vestibule to the apse behind the altar, and 110 feet wide at the transept. Each of the huge twin bell towers — which could be seen for miles from any direction around the Ellis County plains, stands 141 feet tall. The roof by itself is 75 feet tall. The huge Romanesque facade displays a beautiful rose window over which a statue of St. Fidelis, the 16th century Capuchin friar, stands watch. The interior which seats 1100 features 18 granite pillars, each weighing between ten and 15 tons, stand the length of the nave. Eight horses and 40 men transported each pillar, originally quarried and cut to size in Vermont, from the nearby railroad station to the church construction site.

Interior of St. Fidelis Church. (Courtesy Ellis County Historical Society.)

Immigrants from England and Scotland originally founded the city of Victoria in the year 1873. However, The Cathedral of the Plains can be attributed to a stalwart group of Volga Germans who established the nearby town of Herzog in 1876. Volga Germans are Russians of German ancestry who settled along the Volga River in Russia in the late 18th century.

In 1762, Czar Peter III of Russia was overthrown and presumably killed by his own wife, who was crowned Empress Catherine II. Catherine the Great immediately set about to enhance the image and prestige of 19th century Russia in the eyes of its European neighbors during the Age of Enlightenment. Part of her plan included the settlement and development of underpopulated areas of Russia, such as the steppe region of southern Russia, where the Volga River washes south toward the Caspian Sea. Catherine at age 15 came from Germany's Anhalt-Zerbst region to marry Peter III. She invited peasant farmers from Germany to settle in the area and develop the agrarian lifestyle.

Nearly 72 percent of the Germans who settled near the city of Saratov in the Volga Region practiced the Lutheran faith. Those Germans of the Roman Catholic minority, however, suffered persecution from their Protestant countrymen as well as the Orthodox native peasants. As with all Russian peasants, the Volga Germans could be pressed into serfdom at the virtual whim of the nobility, who in turn fell under the thumb of the autocracy. With the passage of the Universal Military Service Act in 1871 under Czar Alexander II, many who did not become serfs faced involuntary recruitment into the Czar's army, or into construction parties building the transcontinental railroad.

Finally, in 1875, as tensions mounted among peasants and intellectuals throughout Russia, in the wake of the semi-successful emancipation of serfs under Czar Alexander II, a small group of Catholic Volga Germans decided to break free. Hungry for freedom, they decided to risk the dangers of 19th century travel for the prospect of a brighter future in the United States of America. Sailing down the Volga River , they crossed the southwest Russian peninsula to the Don River, which leads to the Sea of Azov. The Volgans traveled across the Black Sea, which leads to the Aegean Sea. Around the Grecian Peninsula, they sailed through the Mediterranean Sea, and across the mid–Atlantic to America. The entire journey covered more than 5400 miles, and took over two months to complete.

Landing in Baltimore, Maryland in November of 1875, the Volga Germans traveled west to Topeka, Kansas, where they spent the winter. On April 8, 1876, the immigrants settled on the eastern bank of the Victorian River. They erected a wooden cross, several sod-hut dwellings, and named the site Herzog, after the small town in southern Russia from which they fled.

Within months, the Germans constructed their first church, a simple wooden lean-to against the house of one Alois Dreiling. Forty feet long by 26 feet wide, the small shelter managed to accommodate only about half the community for mass. Nevertheless, the new immigrants seemed satisfied with their new settlement, and sent word to their friends and relatives along the Volga River. In August of 1876, 286 more individuals from Herzog, Russia, arrived in Kansas, and the settlement of the new Herzog commenced. A second church completed in 1878 and dedicated to Mother of Sorrows emerged to accommodate the growing community.

By 1878, most of the British settlers of Victoria had grown discouraged with their new settlement, and had returned to the British Isles. The Germans, on the other hand, had been toughened by the oppression and hard work of peasant life in the Russian steppes. They remained determined to create a future in Kansas, where they could celebrate their Catholic faith without the persecution perpetuated at the hands of the Lutheran countrymen. The Germans remained, and gradu-

ally populated the hamlets of Victoria and Herzog in northern Kansas.

To this point, the celebration of mass for the community only occurred when missionary priests from a nearby settlement could visit Herzog. But in 1878, the Bishop of Leavenworth invited members of the Capuchin order of friars to settle and work in Ellis County. The Capuchins are actually a moderate offshoot of the Franciscan order, founded by Francis of Assisi in Italy in 1206. Two centuries after the saint's death in 1226, the Franciscan order split between the so-called Spirituals (who adhered strictly to Francis' rule of poverty), and the Conventuals (who were less stringent about poverty, and even chose to own property such as monasteries). The Capuchins, under the leadership of Matthew of Bascio, chose a third path, one which followed the rules of poverty, but seemed more accepting of those who did not. The Capuchins grew rapidly in the 16th and 17th centuries, known as dedicated missionaries and fervent, forceful preachers.

At the request of Capuchin Superior Father Hyacinth Epp, the Kansas Pacific Railroad Company donated ten acres in Victoria on which to build a new church. A third church arose between 1880 and 1884, under the direction of pastor and architect Father Anthony Schuermann, O.F.M. Cap. This church stood 168 feet long and 46 feet wide, with a seating capacity of 600. Its name changed from Mother of Sorrows to St. Fidelis, in honor of the 16th century Capuchin priest and healer who was killed by Zwinglian peasants in present day Switzerland.

The communities of Herzog and Victoria continued to multiply. By the turn of the 20th century, the original St. Fidelis proved inadequate for the needs of the burgeoning parish, which covered all of Ellis County and parts of Russell County to the east.

The present Cathedral of the Plains was designed by architect John T. Comes. The E.F.A. Clark Construction Company of Topeka laid the foundation in 1908. However, the cathedral's nearly miraculous completion is mostly due to the faith of 250 German Catholic families, who rolled up their sleeves and contributed to the project in whatever manner possible. From the native stone quarry seven

St. Fidelis Church, Victoria, Kansas. (Courtesy Ellis County Historical Society.)

miles to the south, the German parishioners hauled and dressed more than 125,000 cubic feet of rock for the construction of the church. Fathers and sons, working in unison, often hauled 70 or 80 loads of stone. Bedford stone from Indiana arrived for the doorways and for the bases and capitals supporting the huge, granite interior pillars. More than one million pounds of cement secured into the church walls the great stone blocks, many of which weighed more than 100 pounds. Horse-powered lifts and pulleys hoisted each block — each too heavy to be moved by hand — into place. After three years of back-breaking toil, the parishioners completed the Cathedral of the Plains in 1911. In 1913 the towns of Herzog and Victoria converged, forming the present incorporation of Victoria.

When William Jennings Bryan conveyed the title of "Cathedral of the Plains," he referred to more than just the physical structure. For as magnificent as the sanctuary is, it serves as a monument to determination that characterized the Volga German settlers of Victoria, Kansas, who overcame nearly unimaginable hardship through ceaseless and willing toil. Indeed, St. Fidelis is a towering emblem of foreign immigrants of the 19th and 20th centuries, willing to venture to the vast heartland of America for what they imagined to be a precious opportunity for self-determination in the New World.

Sources

Andrews, Peter. *The Rulers of Russia*. 1983, Stonehenge Press, Inc., Chicago.

Clarkson, Jesse D. *A History of Russia*. 1969, Random House, New York.

Farmer, David Hugh. *The Oxford Dictionary of the Saints*. 1978, Clarendon Press, Oxford, England.

Nigg, Walter. *Warriors of God*. 1970, Alfred A. Knopf.

Wallace, Robert. *Rise of Russia*. 1967, Time-Life Books, New York.

ANDREWS CHURCH
(The International Mother's Day Shrine)

Affiliation: Methodist Episcopal
Location: Grafton, 17 miles northeast of Clarksburg, West Virginia
1878

Two individual women named A. M. Jarvis resided in north central West Virginia near the turn of the 20th century. Between the two it would be difficult to discern who was the more determined, the more inspired, the more dynamic. Ann Maria Reeves Jarvis (1832–1905) created the Mother's Friendship Day, in an effort to help heal war-torn West Virginia, the only state to be born from the Civil War. Yet her daughter, Anna Mae Jarvis, lobbied for a special day to honor her mother, and created a tradition that would eventually be observed around the world.

Ann Maria Reeves Jarvis was born September 30, 1832, the oldest daughter of Methodist minister Josiah Washington Reeves and Nancy Mosee Kemper. She grew up in Philippi, West Virginia, with two brothers and three sisters. She married Granville E. Jarvis in 1850. Ann Maria gave birth to 11 children, but only four survived the ravages of dysentery and other childhood diseases. In addition to her motherly duties, Ann Maria taught Sunday school in Grafton. One of her favorite lessons was entitled "Mothers of the Bible." She died on May 9, 1905.

Anna Mae Jarvis was born May 1, 1864. As one of only four surviving children in her family, she seemed acutely aware of the fragility of life, and the sufferings her own mother had to bear as a mother. Until the age of 30, Anna Mae lived at home with her mother in West Virginia, at which time she moved to Philadelphia. Anna Mae never married, never had children; yet, she seemed to deify both her mother and the concept of motherhood, something in which she would never share. She died on November 24, 1948, penniless and blind in West Chester, Pennsylvania.

West Virginia in 1865, like most of the

United States, was left ravaged by the Civil War. But the West Virginian experience of the War between the States proved unlike that of any other state. For, before the first mortar shot was fired at Fort Sumter on April 12, 1861, West Virginia did not exist as a separate state, but merely as the northwest section of Virginia. But because northwest Virginians felt so isolated from the rest of the state, and because relatively few of those residents owned slaves, Virginia seemed very much to be two distinctive states in one. Finally, when Virginia seceded from the Union in 1861, West Virginians made the separation final by seceding in 1862 from Virginia. West Virginia developed its own constitution, and became the 35th state in 1863. West Virginians remained unusually, but understandably, divided in their loyalties and sentiments.

In towns like Grafton in northern West Virginia, veterans from both armies returned to common neighborhoods, even to common streets. As wounds healed and property was repaired, the community would have to rebuild, and common bonds would once again have to be secured. The circumstances provided an opportunity for northern Yankees and southern Rebels to begin anew. Yet, even though the war had ended, hateful emotions lingered in the hearts of the ex-soldiers, and the community remained divided. The men reportedly still wore their uniforms in public, arms at their sides, anticipating eruptions of violence.

In 1865, a courageous and inspired Ann Maria Reeves Jarvis, along with other women from northern West Virginia, organized a Mother's Friendship Day, to repair the division which continued to inflict the region. Ten years earlier these women, hailing from towns such as Grafton, Philippi, Webster, Pruntytown, and Fetterman, had organized Mother's Friendship Clubs. These women had experienced first hand the deaths of their children, and their sorrow solidified their commitment to raise the standard of health care and sanitation practices among the dysentery-riddled communities. During the war, the clubs offered comfort and healing for wounded and ill Union soldiers. At one point, General George M. McClellan even used the Jarvis

home to plan the first battle of the Civil War. But after the war, the women's clubs would take action again, to heal much deeper wounds and more intangible ills.

Former soldiers and their families of north West Virginia, invited by the Mother's Friendship Clubs to the Pruntytown Court House, assembled in the square in May of 1865. The men remained fearful of a violent outbreak among the former combatants. Nevertheless, the women insisted, and so Mother's Friendship Day commenced, barely a month after Robert E. Lee surrendered to Ulysses S. Grant at Appomattox Court House.

As the story goes, Ann Maria Jarvis greeted the gathered throng, many of whom wore their military uniforms, in a confederate gray dress. A childhood friend from Virginia wore a union blue dress. The women led the crowd in the singing of "Dixie," then in the singing of "The Star Spangled Banner," and finally in the words of "Auld Lang Syne." Weapons fell harmlessly to the ground, hands clasped in friendship; enemies embraced, neighbors wept, and as legend has it the healing began in earnest.

Forty years later, on her death bed in 1905, Ann Maria Reeves Jarvis made her final request: "Someone, sometime, will found a memorial mother's day, commemorating her for the service she renders to humanity in every field of life." Anna Mae, grief stricken at her beloved mother's passing, made the request her own personal quest for the next ten years.

After Mrs. Jarvis died, daughter Anna Mae Jarvis convinced ministers at Andrews Methodist Episcopal Church, where Ann Marie had taught Sunday school, to hold a special memorial service on May 12, 1907. The next year, on May 10, 1908, Andrews' Church presented a special Mother's Day program to the public. Anna Mae had ordered 500 white carnations, her mother's favorite flower, distributed among the mothers present for the service. Dr. H. C. Howard read from the Gospel of John:

> Now there stood by the cross of Jesus his mother, and his mother's sister, Mary the wife of Cleophas, and Mary Magdalene. When Jesus therefore saw his mother, and the disciple standing by, whom he loved, he saith unto his mother, Woman, behold thy son! Then saith he to the disciple, Behold thy mother!

International Mother's Day Shrine (former home of Andrews Methodist Episcopal Church), Grafton, West Virginia. (Courtesy Thunder on the Tygart, Inc.)

And from that hour that disciple took her unto his own home. [John 19:25–27]

On the same day several ministers at churches in Philadelphia, where Anna Mae had previously lived, delivered sermons on the sanctity of motherhood.

Andrews Methodist Episcopal Church established Mother's Day — the second Sunday in May — as an annual event. Anna Mae, driven by her mother's vision, began launching a campaign for a nationwide Mother's Day observance. Enlisting the help of Henry J. Heinz, the editor of the *Philadelphia Inquirer*, Anna Mae began lobbying churchmen, merchants, editors, and finally legislators for a Mother's Day. On April 26, 1910, she convinced William E. Glasscock, governor of West Virginia, to create a statewide observance. Within a year, every state in the union recognized Mother's Day, and florists enjoyed a heyday. Finally, in May of 1914, President Woodrow Wilson signed a congressional resolution, proclaimed by Secretary of State William Jennings Bryan, to recognize nationally the second Sun-

day of May as "Mother's Day." Mother's Day is now recognized by more than 40 countries worldwide. But the commercialism which has followed the day, which Anna Mae sought to keep simple and sanctified, embittered her through the remainder of her days.

In 1857 the predecessor to Andrews Episcopal Church was a one-room school building. After 15 years, and despite numerous extensions to the original building, the congregation finally outgrew it, and construction of a new church began in 1872. Bishop Edward Gayer Andrews, for whom the church was named, formally dedicated the sanctuary in 1873. After several structural changes, in the 1960s Andrews Methodist Episcopal Church underwent complete restoration to its 1858 state, with white belfry and brick-red facade, its surrounding grounds landscaped into a lovely garden. It officially became the International Mother's Day Shrine in 1968. The church now stands as a memorial to two remarkable women from West Virginia, and to mothers from around the world.

Sources

Barron, William Wallace. "The Story Behind Mother's Day." *Family Weekly*. May 12, 1963.

Crowe, Olive. Notes from "The Anna Jarvis Birthplace Foundation." 1997.

Krythe, Maymie R. *All About American Holidays*. 1962, Harper & Row, Publishers, New York.

ALEXANDERWOHL MENNONITE CHURCH

Affiliation: Mennonite
Location: Goessel, 35 miles north of Wichita, Kansas
1886

A small group of Flemish emigrants from the Przechovka Mennonite Church in Western Prussia neared the end of their nearly 900-mile journey. They hiked along the bank of the Vistula River in what is now Poland. Their ultimate destination was the village of Molostschna, in southeast Russia, in what is now Ukraine. The men of the group walked leisurely ahead of the rest, speaking quietly of the approaching landscape, and the work involved in establishing the new farmlands. Suddenly the men noticed an elegant carriage rolling toward them; its fineries indicated ownership by a nobleman of some distinction. The vehicle stopped and the occupant leaned his head out the window — he was: Czar Alexander I, Emperor of Russia.

The Emperor stepped out and addressed the group: "Where did you come from, my friends? Where are you headed?"

Peter Wedel, elder of the small church, responded, "We are traveling to Molotschna, to find our new home."

"I am familiar with that area," said Czar Alexander. "I have seen your brethren there. I wish you well on your journey, and for prosperity at your new home." The Czar then re-entered his carriage and rolled away.

Later, as the small party drew closer to their new home, they decided on a new name for their church: Alexanderwohl, for the Emperor Alexander had wished them *wohl* (well).

This, according to legend, is how the Alexanderwohl Mennonite Church received its name.

The story of Alexanderwohl Mennonite Church is the remarkable tale of a congregation transposed from West Prussia to south Russia to central Kansas — a journey of more than 6000 miles — in less than 70 years. Yet, despite contact with three separate countries, a variety of cultures and languages, and innumerable hardships and bigotries, the congregation remained intact. Three generations of Mennonites maintained three centuries of traditions and practices, and brought them on their journey to the New World.

The culture from which the Alexanderwohl church originated developed before the 16th century in the northern Netherlands. The Mennonites evolved out of an early 16th century group of radical religious reformers known as the Anabaptists. The Anabaptists rejected the compulsory, infant baptism practices in the Catholic and Reformed churches. They believed that only adults, who understood and believed the commitment they were making, could be baptized as true Christians. This belief threatened the authoritative and economic basis for the institutionalized churches, for which the Anabaptists faced severe persecution, torture, and execution. In 1534, a mob of angry Anabaptists struck back, capturing the city of Munster, Switzerland, further escalating violence between the Anabaptists and the institutional churches.

Many of the Anabaptists sought to distance and distinguish themselves from the violent group that seized Munster, seeking instead a simpler, nonviolent, Christlike way of life. In

1536 a Dutch Catholic ex-priest named Menno Simons (c. 1496–1561), emerged to lead the non-violent Anabaptists towards a new tradition. Menno's followers (later to be called Mennonites) further separated themselves from the other Anabaptists, as well as society at large. Before long, the Mennonites developed their own distinct, separate, self-sustaining communities, in which the members supported each other in a simple, peaceful, practical, agrarian life, modeled after what they perceived as the simple life of the early Christians.

The Mennonites based their lifestyle squarely on the Bible. But rather then developing complicated doctrine and intricate ritual, they focus on the practical, day-to-day life. The Mennonites believed undertaking the imitation of Jesus to be simply too strenuous for individuals. They stressed the urgent needs of the congregation, ardently relying on each other for guidance and support. While the Mennonite churches included elders and ministers, they were not considered the spiritual superiors of the rest of the congregation.

The Mennonites have traditionally been antimilitaristic, practiced in "loving thy enemy." They are antimaterialistic, rejecting the accumulation of wealth and goods, and advocating a simplicity of living. Like the Quakers of 17th century England, the Mennonites opposed oath-taking. They recognized neither the Roman authority of the Catholic Church, nor the local authority of the Reformed churches. Furthermore, the Mennonites maintained the steadfast commitment to always telling the truth. Such practices, apparently, would be viewed as subversive by the established church.

In 1632, at a meeting of the town of Dordrecht, Holland, Mennonite leaders composed the *Dordrecht Confession*, which would come to be recognized as the guiding document of Mennonite principles. One of the important issues addressed in the *Confession* is the question of avoidance: how much should the Mennonite church shun the outside world, including those christened as infants, but never baptized as understanding, believing adults. The Mennonite church has wrestled with the question of avoidance throughout its history;

it rests at the heart of the schism which, in the 17th century, would tear the church in two.

By the beginning of the 17th century, however, many of the Mennonites had settled near Amsterdam and in northern Germany to escape persecution from the established churches. Further migration brought some of them to the Danzig area of West Prussia, between the Vistula and Nogat Rivers, in what is now northern Poland. At first West Prussia welcomed the Mennonites with promises of religious freedom, plus the opportunity to develop the prosperous farmland which has become the Mennonite trademark.

By 1774, Mennonites owned more than 80,000 acres of farmland in West Prussia. They had built roads, orchards, farms, canals, and windmills. But the welcome that once greeted the Mennonites soon passed. Many of their West Prussian neighbors resented their success. When the political tide of West Prussia turned militaristic, the pacifist Mennonites refused to support and join the military, creating even greater hostility. Religious persecution escalated. The Mennonites submitted to a unique form of spiritual extortion, in which local Lutheran and Catholic churches reportedly forced them to pay a kind of a protection fee. In return, the Lutherans and Catholics agreed to allow the Mennonites to worship in peace.

Increasingly, Mennonites could do business only with other Mennonites; opportunities to own and develop land, and a successful economic base, dwindled. With their financial opportunities limited, the Mennonites had little opportunity to provide the education for their children which was so highly valued. Mennonites began looking for other sites and opportunities to settle and grow.

At the same time, Russia had obtained lands to the south and to the east in wars with Poland and Turkey. In the 1780s, under Catherine the Great (1729–1796) — through the scheme of her minister and consort, Prince Grigori Aleksandrovich Potemkin (1739–1791) — Russia encouraged foreign immigrants to settle in the steppes of southern Russia. In particular, the Russians enticed the Mennonites to move; the Russians knew of the Mennonites' success as agriculturalists, the very kinds of immigrants needed to settle the new unoccupied areas of Russia. The same encouragement which caused the Catholic Germans to settle around the Volga River Valley of Russia, brought the Mennonites to Ukraine.

The Przechovka Mennonite Church, derived from the Old Flemish Mennonite Society of Groningen, Netherlands, had settled near the town of Schwetz on the Vistula River in West Prussia in 1540. A conservative order of Mennonites, the church attracted Mennonites from Danzig, Moravia, and Sweden, as well as converted West Prussian Lutherans. But by 1820, opportunities for the Przechovka church had all but disappeared. Elder Peter Wedel led the Przechovka congregation on a journey 900 miles to the south, to the town of Molotscha near Chortitza, in southern Russia. It is this congregation which, after receiving greetings from Czar Alexander I in the vicinity of Warsaw, took the name Alexanderwohl.

Life for the Alexanderwohl Mennonites in South Russia seemed to begin as promising as it had in West Prussia. The Mennonites set up their own community, including distinctive schools, doctors, lawyers, community administrators, separate and relatively uninfluenced by the Russian culture. In the meantime, the Mennonites contributed the agricultural skills and prosperity for which the Russians had hoped, helping to create the mass production of wheat for which the Ukraine would become famous. Mennonites introduced equipment such as four-wheeled wagons, and techniques such as crop rotation and summer fallow. By 1870, the Mennonites of the Dnieper River Valley included 18 villages, 6000 families, 715,500 acres of land, and a total population of 45,000.

But as in West Prussia, the good times for the Mennonites in South Russia quickly came to an end. Under Czar Alexander II, Russian nationalism had begun to spread, with growing pressure to assimilate foreign cultures into Russian society. The Universal Military Service Act passed in 1871, creating compulsory military service for Russian residents. Although delegates from Alexanderwohl and neighboring communities ventured to St. Petersburg to lobby for military exemption due

to matters of conscience, their efforts failed. Facing the possibility of military service, a clear infringement on their religious beliefs, the Mennonite communities almost immediately began looking, once again, for a new home.

A Mennonite grain merchant named Cornelius Janis had read an article about opportunities existing for immigrants in the state of Kansas, in the United States. The Atchison, Topeka, and Santa Fe Railroad advertised for settlers along their expanding thoroughfare, around whom communities could be built as economic support for the railroad. Knowing the plight of the Mennonites in Russia, and knowing of their skill as farmers, the railroad company hoped to lure them to the New World. The railroad offered great incentives of land discounts, free transportation, and even offers to build free immigrant housing for the newly arrived settlers. The Mennonites sent delegates to Kansas to investigate the offer. With the incentives from the railroad, plus financial support from Mennonite communities already established in America, the wave of emigration began. On July 31, 1874, under the leadership of Elder Jacob Buller, 303 adults and 172 children from the Alexanderwohl Church boarded the sailing vessel *Cimbria* at the Sea of Azor. They arrived in New York on August 27, 1874. In October of 1874, the community settled on about 100,000 acres of land between the Cottonwood and Little Arkansas Rivers, near present-day Goessel. The members eventually moved from the immigrant housing supplied by the railroad, into sod houses constructed on the land, and finally to the wooden farm homes that dotted the central Kansas countryside.

Sunday services for the Alexanderwohl Church first took place in an immigrant house, a long barrack-like structure provided for them by the Atchison, Topeka, and Santa Fe Railroad. The community dedicated the first actual church building in 1886. Architect Johann Wall designed the two-story structure with the simple facade. The building featured benches, chairs, balconies, railings, and stairways, all fashioned out of the lumber from the early immigrant houses. A large kettle stove stood in the center of the sanctuary, to heat the con-

Alexanderwohl Mennonite Church (1886–1928) in Goessel, Kansas. (Courtesy of Mennonite Heritage Museum, Goessel, Kansas.)

gregation on cold, winter Sunday mornings. The church underwent remodeling and enlargement in 1928, under the direction of head architect Dan Unruh. But true to Mennonite philosophy, the church building is but a vessel to house the congregation, which remains the focal point of Mennonite life.

The Mennonites are often confused with another distinctive religious society, the Amish. Actually the Amish followed a man named Jakob Ammann, a Swiss Mennonite who broke from the larger community in the Alsace region of northern France in 1693. Among other criticisms Ammann felt the church lost diligence in its avoidance of outsiders and nonmembers. Ammann preached isolation from all outside groups. He believed only those baptized to a pure Christian life could be saved, and all others would be condemned. The larger Mennonite community, on the other hand, felt that while the immediate congregation of believers should be supported and protected, they preferred to leave questions of who would gain salvation to God.

Thus the extreme isolation that characterize the lifestyles of the Amish are rooted in the schism that formed between the followers of Jakob Ammann, and the larger Mennonite church. In America, the Amish settled primarily between Indiana and New York states, while the Mennonites pushed further west. And while the Mennonites choose to venture out and interact intermittently with the surrounding society, the Amish remain as they have for decades, shunning modern society, its customs and its technology.

Today, the Mennonite Heritage Museum in Goessel, Kansas, features displays of old Mennonite architecture, farming techniques, machinery, education facilities, and social customs. It includes artifacts from Bethesda Hospital, built in 1899, the first Mennonite Hospital in America. Meanwhile, the Alexanderwohl Mennonite Church, whose ancestors brought the congregation and its traditions from Molotschna, Russia, 123 years ago, thrives in Goessel, Kansas, and continues to contribute its agricultural forte to America's Bread Basket.

Sources

Bishop, Peter and Michael Darton. *The Encyclopedia of*

World Faiths: An Illustrated Survey of the World's Living Religions. 1987, MacDonald and Co., Ltd., London and Sydney.

Nolt, Steven M. *A History of the Amish.* 1992, Good Books, Intercourse, Pennsylvania.

Solsten, Eric. *Germany: A Country Study.* 1995, Library of Congress.

Wedel, David C. *The Story of Alexanderwohl.* 1974, Mennonite Press, Inc., North Newton, Kansas.

DEXTER AVENUE CHURCH

Affiliation: Baptist
Location: Montgomery, Alabama
1889

She was born on February 4, 1913, in Tuskegee, Alabama, home of Tuskegee Institute, founded in 1881 by famous post–Civil War reformer Booker T. Washington for the education of African Americans. Her father worked as a bricklayer and a carpenter, her mother was a teacher. Her father left the family when she was five and she and her mother went to live with her grandparents on an 18-acre farm in Pine Level, Alabama.

She started picking cotton at a neighbor's plantation when she was seven, and attended Alabama State Normal School in Montgomery at the age of eight. At age 11, she attended Montgomery Industrial School.

She savored her first taste of activism through her husband, Raymond. Longtime member of National Association for the Advancement of Colored People (NAACP), Raymond fiercely advocated for the Scottsboro Boys, nine African American young men, ages 14 to 19, from Scottsboro, Alabama, who were almost randomly picked out as the perpetrators of a rape committed against two white women in 1931. Through a clear miscarriage of justice, a bigoted judge and 12 white male jurors saw all but the youngest of the boys sentenced to the electric chair. But through the intense work of NAACP and the International Labor Defense, none of the eight ever faced execution.

In December 1943, she joined the NAACP

in Montgomery, Alabama, at that point one of only two women to serve in the Montgomery office. She eventually became secretary, and held that office when the NAACP, through the work of a young lawyer named Thurgood Marshall, brought *Brown vs. Board of Education* to the Supreme Court in 1951. This case turned out to be the first in which the highest court in the land declared segregation in the schools unconstitutional.

To support her work in the NAACP, she labored as a seamstress in a downtown Montgomery department store. She commuted to and from her job every day. In the context of that job she would soon be catapulted to national attention, a heroic figure of courage and determination. She would be followed by a city-wide exercise in civil disobedience which would shake the very foundation of the nation.

Her name is Rosa Parks.

He was born on January 15, 1929, in the Auburn Avenue area of Atlanta, Georgia. His father served as Baptist minister for Ebenezer Baptist Church, and his mother worked as a school teacher. After graduating from Booker T. Washington High School in Atlanta, Georgia, he enrolled in undergraduate school at Morehouse College, also in Atlanta. Following his father, he became a Baptist minister in 1947 at the age of 18, and graduated at age 19.

He attended Crozer Theological Seminary

in Chester, Pennsylvania. There, he studied the life and works of Mahatma Gandhi, and the writings of Henry David Thoreau, immersing himself in the ideals of peaceful resistance and civil disobedience. He earned his doctorate of philosophy at Boston College's School of Theology in 1954. In Boston, he met Coretta Scott, who studied at New England Conservatory of Music. They were married on June 18, 1953.

He received his ecclesiastical call from Dexter Avenue Baptist Church in Montgomery, Alabama, in September 1954. Over the next 13 years, as focal point for a growing, nationwide civil rights movement, he would face insults, ridicule, bomb threats, abuse, and jailings. He would tutor the country in lessons of civil disobedience, and mesmerize the crowds with his fiery, eloquent addresses. In Oslo, Norway in 1964, he would be awarded the Nobel Peace Prize. In Memphis, Tennessee, on April 3, 1968, he would perish from an assassin's bullet.

His name was Dr. Martin Luther King, Jr.

The roots of Dexter Avenue Baptist Church can be traced to the fall of 1877, when members of the Columbus Street Church (now First Baptist Church on Ripley Street) decided to form their own congregation. Before the church structure arose, members would meet in private residences, and then at a community hall located between Lawrence and McDonough streets. This hall once served as a Slave Trader's Pen, where slaves confined to tiny cage-like cells awaited sale by their owners.

The property on which the church building was built had been purchased in 1879 for $270.00. Construction began in 1883, with much of the foundation comprised of discarded bricks used during the original paving of Dexter Avenue. The first worship service at Dexter Avenue Baptist Church took place in its basement in 1885. On Thanksgiving Day, 1889, the congregation worshipped in the sanctuary for the first time. For nearly 70 years the red-brick church and parsonage had stood quietly across Dexter Avenue from the Alabama State Capitol and other civic buildings; a harbinger to changing times, a symbol of African American hope in the midst of the "old white square."

Rosa Parks and Martin Luther King, Jr., met for the first time at Dexter Avenue Baptist Church in August 1955, when King appeared as a guest speaker at an NAACP meeting. Dr. King would soon be chosen new president of Montgomery Improvement Association (MIA), and Mrs. Parks would sit on the executive board. While each would play a very different role in spearheading the bus boycott, probably neither's impact upon the civil rights movement would have been so effective without the other. As they exchanged pleasantries on that summer night, neither could have possibly anticipated how their lives would be dramatically altered in little less than four months.

Montgomery's segregation ordinance callously stipulated the seating arrangements on every public bus: The rows in the front third of the bus were reserved for whites only, while the back third of the bus was to be used by blacks. The middle third could be used by either, but blacks were required to yield their seats to whites.

On December 1, 1955, while riding the Cleveland Avenue bus home after work from Court Square in Montgomery, Rosa Parks refused to give up her seat in the middle section of the bus to white passenger James Blake at the Empire Theatre bus stop. In her autobiography, Parks said, "People always say that I didn't give up my seat because I was tired, but that isn't true. I was not tired physically, or no more tired than I usually was at the end of a working day. I was not old, although some people have an image of me as being old then. I was forty two. No, the only tired I was, was tired of giving in...." (Parks, p. 116)

Eventually two Montgomery police officers escorted her off the bus and to the police station, and eventually to the North Ripley Street jail. This incident was the spark which would eventually ignite and later enlighten the city of Montgomery.

Whether due to luck or fate or stupidity or Providence or simple circumstance, the cause of continued segregation in Alabama could not have picked a more unavailing target than Mrs. Rosa Parks. Although there had been individuals who had tested segregation laws in the past, Rosa Parks stood as the most unassuming instigator. She had never been arrested, no

Dexter Avenue Baptist Church, Montgomery, Alabama. (Photograph by Elizabeth Synco.)

scandals haunted her past. A pillar of the community, she had gained respect for her work in the NAACP and throughout the African American community, a model of integrity, honesty, and hard work. As Parks awaited her trial outside the Montgomery Courthouse on December 5, 1955, one young woman was heard to say "They've done messed with the wrong one now!" (Parks, p. 133)

On Monday, December 5, 1955, the municipal court found Rosa Parks guilty of disobeying Montgomery's segregation ordinance, and fined her $14.00. King and E. D. Nixon — the NAACP attorney who posted Mrs. Parks' bond — marveled at the historic blunder of the Montgomery court. Mrs. Parks' would be the test case the NAACP would need to challenge the segregation ordinance in federal court. Nixon immediately posted an appeal bond. Although Mrs. Parks' case was eventually thrown out because of a technicality, it paved the way for the NAACP's suit against the discrimination filed in district court.

On December 2, 1955, King had called a meeting of 40 to 50 spiritual and civic leaders at Dexter Avenue Baptist Church. The community leaders elected him president of the Montgomery Improvement Association (MIA), established Dexter Avenue Church as its headquarters. and began the organization of the Montgomery bus boycott.

That evening at a packed Holt Avenue Baptist Church (due to its more central proximity to the Montgomery black community), King addressed an electrified community meeting, called to consider the implementation of a city-wide bus boycott.

"We are here this evening," he told them, "to say to those who mistreated us for so long that we are tired — tired of being segregated and humiliated; tired of being kicked about by the brutal feet of oppression." (Oates, p. 70) King recalled the Rosa Parks incident, and reminded the crowd of her quiet courage and dignity. He called for unity and commitment to the boycott from the entire community. He proclaimed the righteousness of the boycott, saying, "If we are wrong, then God Almighty is wrong … if we are wrong, then justice is a lie." (Oates, p. 71)

The crowd's emotion erupted at the power of his words, the buzzing energy built to a fevered pitch. Yet, in the midst of the fervor, King's presence of mind called for the peaceful, civil implementation of the boycott. "If we protest courageously, and yet with dignity and Christian love, when the history books are written in the future, somebody will have to say, 'There lived a race of people, of black people, of people who had the moral courage to stand up for their rights. And thereby they injected a new meaning into the veins of history and civilization."

Friend to King and fellow minister Ralph Abernathy presented the demands of the Montgomery Improvement Association to the meeting: (1) Courteous treatment on buses; (2) first-come, first-serve seating, with whites seating, beginning in the front and moving backwards, while blacks sit in the back moving forwards; and (3) black drivers would be hired for predominantly black routes.

Until the city and the bus company met these demands, Abernathy announced, the blacks of Montgomery would refuse to ride the buses. The crowd deliriously shouted its ratification. The Montgomery Bus Boycott began with diligence.

Over the next twelve months, 85 percent of the black bus riders, 14,500 out of a possible 17,000, observed the boycott. During the boycott, bus ridership citywide fell nearly 60 percent, as sympathetic white passengers joined the protest. Revenues from the bus lines plummeted correspondingly. Instead of riding the bus, black workers (who held a considerable percentage of the blue collar and service jobs in the city) would carpool, hitchhike, bicycle, or simply walk to their work sites. While several churches raised funds to purchase station wagons to shuttle boycotters, white housewives who employed African American maids and housekeepers, and who would drive the black commuters to and from work, numbered among the biggest supporters of the boycott. Blacks endured boos, insults, threats, harassment, and in some cases assaults and beatings. Nevertheless, the boycott continued. On January 30, 1956 (the date of Mahatma Gandhi's assassination), a bomb struck King's parsonage at Dexter Avenue (fortunately, his wife and child were unhurt). In February 1955, authorities rearrested Parks under an obscure law — rediscovered by white lawyers — which prohibited boycotts. Still, the boycott persisted day after day, week after week, month after month. In the meantime, the city of Montgomery refused to give into the MIA's demands, while the NAACP's suit against bus segregation had risen to the United States Supreme Court.

Finally, on December 20, 1956, the decision had been rendered: the Supreme Court ruled Alabama's state and local laws requiring segregation unconstitutional. Said a local bystander, "God Almighty has spoken from Washington, D.C."

Eight years later, the Civil Rights Act was passed under the administration of Lyndon Baines Johnson, making racial discrimination specifically illegal in the United States. Four years later Martin Luther King, Jr., was dead. To this day, Mrs. Rosa Parks continues to write, and speak, and appear, to remind people of the year Montgomery led the "Stride Toward Freedom." The struggle for equality continues, of course, with no illusions regarding written laws or lofty rhetoric.

Dexter Avenue Baptist Church stands as a sentinel across the "old white square," perhaps a portent of more things yet to come.

Sources

Haskins, James. *The Life and Death of Martin Luther King, Jr.* 1977, Lothrop, Lee, and Shepherd Co., New York.
Oates, Stephen B. *Let the Trumpet Sound: The Life of Martin Luther King, Jr.* 1982, A Plume Book, New York.
Parks, Rosa. *Rosa Parks: My Story.* 1992, Dial Books, New York.

BUKKYO SEINEN KAI

Affiliation: Jodo Shinshu Buddhism
Location: San Francisco, California
1898

How the single act of one man spending one night under a tree substantially altered countless lives and histories remains an amazing chronicle. Nevertheless, somewhere near the year 590 B.C., Siddharta Gautama arose from his lotus position under the bo-tree, or bodhi tree in Bodh Goya, India. He had conquered his night of temptation, overcoming his *tanha*—his desire and attachment to life, considered to be the root of all distress. Now possessing within him the knowledge of the Way to *nirvana*, the cessation of desire and suffering, Gautama emerged as the Buddha, the Enlightened One, to begin his *dharma*, his teaching ministry.

Twenty-four centuries later, more than half a billion people have been significantly touched by his teachings, which has presented itself in numerous versions to many nations and countless individuals of varying languages and customs. North America, particularly the United States of America, remained one of the last early realms to be reached by the dharma.

But just prior to the turn of the 20th century, the Enlightened One's teaching officially touched the shores of the eastern Pacific Ocean.

Between 1898 and 1910, more than 70,000 Japanese immigrated to the western United States. The great majority of these immigrants came from the prefectures of Hiroshima and Yamaguchi, on the southeast end of Honshu; and Kumanoto and Fukuoka, on the island of Kyushu. Most of these sojourners practiced a denomination of Amida Buddhism known as Jodo Shinshu, whose mother temple called Hongwanji-Ha, stands in Kyoto, Japan.

Many of the new Japanese arrivals did not hold finding religious sanctuary as a priority. Primarily young males in their 20s and 30s, these immigrants had left their families and arrived in the New World alone. Unlike many emigrants to America, the Japanese did not flee persecution in their homeland. Instead, they had come to America seeking individual prosperity which, they hoped, would allow them to return to Japan in an economic strata considerably advantaged over the one they had left. Many of the immigrants found work on farms. Often, the only refuge for the young adventurers could be found in Protestant missions. The Japanese would tolerate the evangelistic zeal of the Christian missionaries in exchange for shelter in a strange land, and a chance to commune with fellow Japanese citizens.

But for others, shelter alone did not fill the void. Many began to seek places where they could practice the traditions and customs of the theosophy on which they had been raised. Nisaburo Hirano, a 21-year-old *Issei* (first generation Japanese immigrant), came to San Francisco in 1891. Like many of his generation, Hirano appreciated the hospitality of the Christian mission, but would not renounce his Jodo Shinto faith for the baptism the Protestants proposed. Professing the need for centers of Buddhist worship in the New World, Hirano returned to his homeland in 1896, to advocate for a Buddhist mission in America. In return, two Buddhist priests named Erya Honda and Ejun Miyamonto embarked on a goodwill reconnaissance trip, arriving in San Francisco in July of 1898.

With the help of local Buddhist immigrants, Honda and Miyamonto formed the first Jodo Shinshu Organization in United States. Known as *Bukkyo Seinen Kai,* the Young Men's Buddhist Association (YMBA) met at the Sutter Street home of Dr. Katsugoro Haidu on July 14, 1898. The association later met at a site called the Pythian Castle Auditorium at 909 Market Street. On July 30, 1898, at the same auditorium, the YMBA adopted its first constitution, and elected its first board of directors. By September 14, 1899, the YMBA rented a building on Mason Street, where weekly Buddhist sutra studies and religious discussions took place. Here the operations of North American Buddhist Mission (NABM), the predecessor for the Buddhist Church of America, began. On November 24, 1899, the First Buddhist Ceremony held in English took place at the YMBA Center in San Francisco.

The YMBA moved about to several other sites, including Stevenson Street, Buchanan Street, Gough Street, and Polk Street. Finally, the name was changed in 1905 to the Buddhist Church of San Francisco and settled on the site of 1881 Pine Street. The new site became the first official church, and headquarters for the North American Buddhist Mission. The new minister, Reverend Koyu Uchida, became bishop and *kantokai* (director) of the NABM.

In 1935, the new NABM bishop Kenju Masayama accepted an extraordinary gift from the Emperor of Siam: A portion of the Holy Relics, reputed to hold the remains of the Shakaman Buddha. In order to properly house the first set of Holy Relics to come to the western world, the Buddhist Church of San Francisco and the North American Buddhist Mission joined forces to build a new Buddhist Church, across Pine Street from the NABM headquarters. The new church would be known as the "Hongwanji Temple of North America." Three stories high, the structure included the Hondo, or worship sanctuary, the NABM offices, and a gymnasium. A stupa, called *Buschari Hoto*, the "Tower of the Holy Relic," crowned the massive columned facade of the new church, where the sacred ornaments would be housed. The new church, completed in February of 1938, stands at 1880 Pine Street.

The Jodo Shinshu sect is one of hundreds of practical interpretations of the *Dharma* (teachings) of Siddharta Gautama, the Buddha. The cornerstone of the Buddhist philosophy is the Four Noble Truths:

Dukkha: The Truth of Suffering

Buddhists believe life itself is Dukkha, suffering. Some have compared life with the wheel not running true on its axis: humans suffer because they do not achieve balance.

Samudhaya: Truth of Origin of Suffering

According to Buddha, all suffering comes from *Tanha,* craving, attachment to life, desire.

Nirodha: Truth of the Cessation of Suffering

Buddha taught the only way to end the suffering is to stop the *Tanha.*

Bukkyo Seinen Kai, San Francisco, California. (Photograph by Penni Thorpe.)

Magga: The Way to Cessation of Suffering

The Cessation of Craving is found by navigating the Noble Eightfold Paths:

Sila
(Kindness of Heart, Moral Integrity)
  Path One: Right Speech
  Path Two: Right Action
  Path Three: Right Livelihood

Samadhi
(Inner Stillness)
  Path Four: Right Effort
  Path Five: Right Mindfulness
  Path Six: Right Meditation

Prahna
(Liberating Wisdom)
  Path Seven: Right Understanding
  Path Eight: Right Aspiration

Jodo Shinshu is a derivative of *Amida* Buddhism, which was founded by Genshin (942–1017). Amida refers to "Birth in Pure Land," which means the "Rightly Established State," the state of Nirvana, toward which all Buddhists strive. Jodo Shinshu emphasizes the aspect of faith of *Shinjin*. Not faith in the Christian sense, since Buddhists proclaim no allegiance to specific gods, Shinjin places trust in the dharma of Buddha. Jodo Shinshu says that trust in practices of Buddhism can bring contentment. An often repeated statement among the followers of Jodo Shinshu is "I put my faith in *Buddha*, in *Dharma* (teachings), in *Sangha* (brotherhood)."

Essentially, the heart of Buddhism is the invitation to an island of sanity in a world of delusion and suffering; *Nirvana* in the midst of *Samsara*. Indeed, the Jodo Shinshu faithful of San Francisco longed to hear the dharma and sutras of Buddha in their native tongues, as the New World indeed proved filled with delusion, suffering, and fear.

A wave of hostile paranoia began building among west coast Americans in the early twentieth century, a wave which would ultimately crash upon three generations of Japanese in America, and Japanese Americans.

The fear of the Japanese grew as Japan rose to world prominence during the Russo-Japanese War. Americans read about the invasion of Korea in 1910, the capture of Tsingtai in 1914, and the intrusion into Siberia in 1918. Suddenly confronted with a little known and seemingly mysterious culture and people, the Americans reacted in the tried and true way: mistrust, bigotry, and hysteria.

The first wave of anti–Japanese hysteria rolled in 1913 and 1920, as Californians passed the "Alien Land Laws." These laws impeded naturalization, terminating Japanese immigrant control of California farm land. The laws' purpose was to discourage the immigration of the Japanese, which by then comprised 2.1 percent of California population.

The second wave fell in 1924, with the passage of the national Oriental Exclusion Act (OEA). The OEA followed the lead of the Alien Land Laws, supporting racial prejudice and exclusion on a national level. The same anti-immigrant fervor which forbade bible teaching in German in Nebraska, discouraged the dharma studies in Japanese in California.

These nefarious attempts to impede the Japanese immigrant population served merely to amalgamate the Buddhist Church and Japanese community. As in the Greek community in Wisconsin, or the Swedish community in Delaware, the place of worship became the centerpiece for the new and growing locale. The Japanese unified around the NABM, which provided comfort and support to their members against the injustices they faced. By 1929, despite the campaigns to halt immigration, 59 Buddhist churches had opened on the Pacific Coast of the United States.

As with all religions, Buddhism had to find a way of accommodating and assimilating into the American way of life. Even Protestantism had to become more Protestant. Coming from a hierarchical, patriarchal tradition, American Buddhism had to adapt to ideas of democracy, feminism, and integration. Presentation of the dharma and the sutras required translation into English, as the Japanese-born Issei gave way to the Americanized *Nisei* (second generation), and eventually the *Sansei* (third generation).

But just as Buddhism seemed to find its foothold on the American continent, the third wave of hysteria crashed onto the lives of the American Japanese. On February 19, 1942, President Franklin D. Roosevelt issued Executive Order 9066, in response to the Japanese navy's attack on Pearl Harbor, Hawaii, on December 7, 1941. Between March 24, 1942, and June 6, 1942, the order gave the secretary of war and the military commanders the authority to: "prescribe military areas ... from which any or all persons may be excluded, and with respect to which, the right of any person to enter, remain in or leave shall be subject to whatever restriction the Secretary of War or the appropriate Military Commander may impose in his discretion." (Kashima, p. 51)

In one of modern history's most blatant examples of massive racial injustice, the Executive Order authorized the involuntary removal and subsequent internment of all persons of Japanese ancestry in the western third of Washington, all of Oregon, and the western half of California. The United States government stripped more than 110,000 individuals of their homes and possessions, relocating men, women, and children to internment camps in Arizona, Colorado, Utah, and other centrally located states. The paranoia and prejudice of the time suggested all Japanese would constitute a threat to the security of the nation by living on the West Coast, where they supposedly could somehow aid a Japanese invasion. Of all Japanese interned, 55.5 percent were Buddhists, and 48.7 percent were American born.

Internment forcibly brought priests of the Jodo Shinshu denomination into interaction with clerics of other Buddhist sects. The blending of traditions brought the usual suspicion and conflict, but also fostered a medium of compromise and understanding. The priests would often offer the camp residents ecumenical services, featuring rites and sutras from the various heritages. The priests began to realize the importance of the evolution of a specifically American Buddhist Church; that is, a church which acknowledged the commonalities shared by American Buddhists, and minimized the differences between sects which had originally developed in Japan — a place many no longer called home. These develop-

ments led to the establishment of the Young Buddhist Association, the Buddhist Brotherhood Association, and finally in July of 1944, the Buddhist Churches of America (BCA).

After three or more years in the internment camps, many of the Japanese Americans formed close bonds with one another, the camps becoming mini communities. But just as suddenly as the camps were activated, they were closed, forcing the internees to again relocate, many now without an economic base. The Buddhist churches followed the internees to Chicago, Cleveland, Detroit, and Minneapolis, as well as back to the West Coast. The churches provided inspiration, fellowship, and support as the Japanese American community returned from its captivity, and reemerged as an important component of American cultural and economic viability.

Today, the national headquarters for the Buddhist Churches of America is located on Octavia Street in San Francisco, the same city in which the BCA's predecessor, Bukkyo Seinen Kai, began just about one century ago. In fact, in July of 1998, the Buddhist Churches of America will celebrate its 100th anniversary. What started out as a young men's mission in a downtown building now encompasses more than six dozen churches throughout the United States and Canada. The BCA continues to infuse American ideals (often not practiced, as in the case of Japanese internment) of democracy, feminism, and integration into the ancient theosophy, which emerged from the shade of the bodhi tree nearly 2500 years ago.

Sources
Bishop, Peter and Michael Darton. *The Encyclopedia of World Faiths: An Illustrated Survey of the World's Living Religions*. 1987, MacDonald and Co., Ltd., London and Sydney, pp. 215–233.
Buddhist Church of America Archives. *75th Anniversary Edition*. 1974, San Francisco.
Davis, Kenneth C. *Don't Know Much About History*. 1990, Avon Books, New York, pp. 299–300.
Kashima, Tetsuden. *Buddhism in America*. 1977, Greenwood Press, Westport, Connecticut, p. 1–65.
Morreale, Don. *Buddhist America*. 1988, John Muir Publication, Santa Fe, New Mexico.

TEMPLE OF ISLAM, #1

Affiliation: Nation of Islam
Location: Detroit, Michigan
1930

The peddler seemed to appear out of nowhere. No one knew exactly where he called home. Some theorized he came from Arabia, others guessed Jamaica. He alternatively used the first names of Wallie Farrad, W.D. Fard, Wallace Fard Muhammad, and Farrad Muhammad. He was reportedly born in 1877 in Mecca, or perhaps Turkey or New Zealand or Syria. He first represented himself as a peddler; later, he would refer to himself as "the Prophet" or simply "God."

In 1930 he began to visit the black neighborhoods of Detroit. He brought with him his wares, silks and trinkets from places in the world he called his customers' "homeland," Africa and Asia. He could be charismatic, articulate, and riveting in his personality. He would humbly enter the people's homes, and display his wares for their perusal. After a while, the customers would find themselves inviting him to stay for dinner. He would sit, and partake in whatever his poor host had to offer. He would eat their food, and bless them for their hospitality. Then he would tell them of other food he eats, food which would better benefit their minds and bodies.

Eventually the talk would come to the Bible, a copy of which might be resting on the coffee table, or on a shelf in the front room. He seemed to be able to explain the teachings of the Bible as if he had written them himself; he could explain the lessons in words that made them immediately comprehensible.

On subsequent visits he would talk further about the Holy Scriptures, but begin to question their content, and their pertinence to his customers. He would begin to introduce the readings of the Qur'an, readings, he explains, which had more meaning for those of African ancestry. Eventually he would denounce the Bible, calling it the text of a white man's religion which systematically diminished and excluded blacks.

Ward made these home visits throughout 1930. At each visit, neighbors and friends of the family would gather from around the neighborhood. The peddler, who had now become known as "The Prophet," would exhort the teachings and wisdom of the Qur'an. He fervently urged his followers to shed their white man's religion, and follow the wisdom of Mohammed, the Messenger of Allah, the One and True. The followers would easily be swept by the emotion and energy of his exaltations, and find themselves denouncing their religion of birth, and contemplating the compelling ideas which the peddler presented.

So great numbered the followers of Fard Muhammad, aka W. D. Fard, that he soon found the houses in the neighborhood no longer sufficient. Fard hired a public meeting hall, possibly in the Paradise Valley area of Detroit, which opened in 1930. The site would eventually carry the name "Temple of Islam, #1." Fard purported to bring freedom, justice, equality to black men in the wilderness of North America. He named his congregation "The Lost/Found Nation of Islam in the Wilderness of North America." It later became known as the Nation of Islam (NOI), the foundations for what the media called the Black Muslim movement in America.

Within three years Fard drew more than 8000 followers. He founded an elementary and secondary school called the University of Islam, and the Muslim Girls Training Class, which trained young women in their proper role as Muslim women. He also founded the Fruit of Islam, the quasi-military arm of the Nation.

Among his early followers was an unemployed auto worker named Paul Robert Poole, born in 1897, and migrating as a boy with his family from his native Georgia to Detroit. Poole quickly became one of Fard's most avid followers, and was eventually renamed Elijah Muhammad, meaning "Messenger of Allah." Fard encouraged followers to relinquish their slave names, in favor of reverential Islamic names. Elijah Muhammad became Fard's chief lieutenant, destined to eventually lead the Nation of Islam to national prominence.

As the organization grew, the Prophet gradually pulled back. In 1934, he mysteriously disappeared. The last official record of Fard is reportedly September 26, 1933, during an arrest by the Chicago police on a charge of "disorderly conduct." Rumors of his fate abounded: some say he had been spotted hastily boarding an ocean liner for some unknown European destination; others said he met with foul play at the hands of Detroit police with whom he had many encounters, or even dissident members. Some even questioned the proximity of Elijah Muhammad's rise, and W. D. Fard's disappearance. In any case, by 1934, Elijah Muhammad became the leader of the Nation of Islam.

Disappointed with the lethargy of the Detroit temple without the Prophet's leadership, Elijah Muhammad left Detroit and established the headquarters for Black Muslims at what was called Temple #2, in Chicago. Muhammad took over the mantle of "Prophet" and "Messenger of Allah," and, fueled by the mystery of the Prophet's disappearance, raised W. D. Fard's status to the embodiment of Allah.

The Black Muslim movement grew substantially under Muhammad, particularly with the conversion of a 22-year-old imprisoned outlaw from Omaha, Nebraska, named Malcolm Little, who would soon renounce his "slave name" and call himself Malcolm X. Between 1947 and 1960, the Nation of Islam gained scores of temples and schools, apartments, grocery stores, restaurants, and farms, mostly due to the integrity and charisma of Malcolm X. Malcolm X became a national figure and, through his charismatic presence and riveting oratory, greatly boosted the visibility of the Nation of Islam. Had Elijah Muhammad not censured Malcolm X for statements he allegedly made in 1963 concerning the assassination of John F. Kennedy, and had Malcolm X not broken away from the Nation due to allegations concerning Muhammad's paternity obligations to six teenage female followers, it is difficult to predict how far Malcolm X would have led the Nation of Islam.

The popularity of the Nation of Islam developed largely due to the positive and powerful vision it brought to African Americans. The Nation of Islam encouraged blacks to develop a sense of dignity, equality, even superiority to whites. Members participated vigorously in the rigors of the religion. The nation required them to attend frequent meetings each month, pray five times a day, and offer one-third of their money to the movement. Vices such as gambling, smoking, drinking, and overeating faced severe discouragement. As a result of this discipline, members often enjoyed a relatively high standard of living, with cash to give to the movement.

The movement preached distrust of whites, instilling the belief that if whites truly wanted blacks to have rights, they would have had them long ago. Although members often refrained from voting, the threat of a powerful voting bloc lingered powerfully, particularly in the 1960s. More than anything, the movement encouraged members to believe, indeed, black is beautiful and divine, and African Americans did not need white Americans in order to achieve full potential and prosperity.

The Nation of Islam attracted a young, predominantly male membership. The Nation reportedly believed in the equality of gender, but also believed in the preciseness of gender roles: males served to be providers and protectors, and females filled the roles of mother and homemaker. Only in these roles, the Muhammad preached, could each sex reach its full value and self-esteem. The Nation also attracted predominantly lower class, almost wholly African Americans (although, interestingly, particularly in the movement's early days, the Nation looked upon nonwhites who experienced much of the same prejudice and reduced opportunities as equal to blacks).

Perhaps the greatest attraction for members to the Nation remained its offer of group solidarity. The Nation framed Christianity as "the white man's religion," preaching that a religion that had brought them so much pain could scarcely bring any benefits. Black Muslims would openly avoid whites, and refuse to accept prejudice toward blacks.

One of the greatest benefits to the African American community is the NOI's presentation of the historical accomplishments of blacks, information rarely highlighted in the Caucasian-dominated media. C. Eric Lincoln in *The Black Muslims in America* illustrates:

> Blacks in Asia and Africa were enjoying advanced civilizations when the whites were eating their meat raw in the caves of Europe. Yet the whites, through their control of the information media (including the black preachers) have succeeded in making the so-called Negroes accept themselves as inferior.
>
> Blacks sat on the thrones of Egypt and Ethiopia, fought beside the Romans in conquering the savages of Britain; discovered America long before Columbus sailed. Blacks ruled Spain and Southern Europe, reigned as popes in the Eternal city of Rome, and built great civilizations on the west coast of Africa. They produced many Moslem scholars of whom the white Christians profess to be ignorant, though the white civilization has stolen much knowledge from them. [Lincoln, pp. 113–114]

Recent scholarship seems to verify these claims. Ivan Van Sertimi, in his book *They Came Before Columbus*, presents compelling evidence of West African sailing vessels capable of utilizing prevailing Atlantic currents and winds to not only navigate to Central and South America, but to do so centuries before Christopher Columbus. And Martin Bernal, in *Black Athena*, demonstrates how various ancient Africans' culture significantly influenced Egyptian and Greek thought and science — the very roots of modern Western Civilization. Yet, much of written western history, penned mostly by white European males, seems to have conveniently forgotten the contributions of Africans to that history.

The Nation of Islam differs from orthodox Islam in many ways, including the deification of W.D. Fard, the belief in bodily resurrection, and the practice of separatism between the races.

The Moslem theology is based on the Five Pillars of Islam, and the Five Pillars of Observance:

The Five Pillars
Belief in One God
Belief in Angels

Belief in Many Prophets, One Message
Belief in the Day of Judgment
Belief in the Qudar

The Five Pillars of Observance
Shahada — The Creed
Salat — Prayer
Zakat — Charity
Siyam — Fasting
Hajj — Pilgrimage to Mecca

The Nation of Islam movement has changed drastically in form and leadership since the initial days of Detroit's Temple of Islam. The membership, estimated at 500,000, essentially split after the 1975 death of Elijah Muhammad. Warith Deen Muhammad, Elijah's son, took over leadership of the Nation of Islam after his father died in 1975. W. D. Muhammad tried to guide the Nation closer to orthodox Islam, which caused the organization to splinter.

Today, there are several offshoots of the Nation of Islam, the largest under the direction of former calypso singer Louis Farrakhan. Farrakhan, calls himself "the National Representative for the Honorable Elijah Muhammed." Farrakhan has revived the name and some of the notoriety of the Nation of Islam. He has been revered for his organization of the Million Man March, and reviled for his derogatory statements concerning Caucasians and Jews.

In whatever form, the Nation of Islam's profound effect on African Americans is unmistakable and enduring. The conversion of charismatic and influential individuals such as Muhammad Ali during Elijah Muhammad's tenure helped raise awareness of the Nation's presence in the consciousness of America.

The Nation of Islam continues to challenge the African American community to elevate its own perceptions and expectations, and open the access to divinity to itself. Its forceful urgings for African Americans to attain the power, integrity and prosperity destined for them has been a potent force in the changing status of the community.

Sources
Cuba, Prince -A-. "Black Gods of the Inner City." *Gnosis: A Journal of Western Inner Traditions*. Fall 1992.

Jones, Linda. "Nations Apart." Michigan: *The Magazine of the Detroit News.* July 17, 1988.

Lincoln, C. Eric *The Black Muslims in America.* 1994, Africa World Press, Inc., Trenton, NJ.

Sertimi, Ivan Van. *They Came Before Columbus.* 1976, Random House, New York.

Wormser, Richard. *American Islam: Growing Up Muslim in America.* 1994, Walker Publishing Company, New York.

BAHA'I HOUSE OF WORSHIP

Affiliation: Bahai
Location: Wilmette, Illinois
1953

The National Baha'i House of Worship in Wilmette, Illinois, is one of the most innovative and visually dazzling structures in North America. One of the world's seven Baha'i Houses of Worship, the Wilmette House is a nine-sided, bell shaped, domed sanctuary, 138 feet high at the apex of the dome, 90 feet in diameter. Designed by architect Louis Bourgeois, the House of Worship required a special mixture of concrete, quartz, and white cement to adequately envelope and adhere to the intricate steel structure. Seating up to 1200 people, the balance and eclectic fusion of architectural styles reflects the ecumenism, unity, and global view of the Baha'i faith, which could be regarded as the prototype 20th century religion.

Followers of the Baha'i faith strongly assert the Baha'i faith is a bonafide, independent world religion, and not a derivative of Islam or any other creed. The name *Baha'i* comes from the Arabic *baha*, which means splendor or glory. Currently, the faithful point out, there are five million members of the Baha'i faith, spanning more than 200 countries and territories around the world. Among the fastest growing creeds on earth, the Baha'i world membership swells at a rate of 3.63 percent per year, more — according to the National Baha'i Center in Illinois — than Christianity, Islam, Judaism, Hinduism, or Buddhism. The followers emerge from a wide variety of backgrounds in race, nationality, economic strata,

and religious upbringing. Apparently, many of the Baha'i faithful are finding fulfillment of their childhood religious indoctrination in the ideologies and practices of this new theology precisely, they say, as the founder of Baha'i had anticipated.

The prophet-founder of the Baha'i faith was Mirza Husayn-Ali, born in 1817 in Persia (Iran), the eldest son of a wealthy landowner and nobleman. Husayn-Ali became an early follower of Mirza Ali-Muhammed, known also as *the Bab* (the Gate), who founded the sect known as Bab'ism, a radical offshoot of Shi'a Islam, which emphasized messianism even more than the Shi'a. Bab'ism swept through Persia, gathering enough early followers to cause mainstream Persian Islam to regard it as heresy. The Bab not only presented a new religious strain, but announced the coming of a greater prophet of God, which further distressed and threatened the orthodox Islamic establishment.

Following widespread persecution which caused the death of more than 20,000 Babis, the Bab faced imprisonment by Islamic Persian authorities in 1847 and execution in 1850. In the Islamic effort to squelch the continuing spread of Babism, many of its followers faced capture and confinement as well. The authorities apprehended Mirza Husayn-Ali in 1852 and imprisoned him in Tehran's infamous prison, "the Black Pit." There, among the stench, filth, and disease of this Persian night-

Baha'i House of Worship, Wilmette, Illinois. (Courtesy Baha'i National Center.)

mare, Mirza Husayn-Ali experienced his revelation: he became God's messenger as prophesied by the Bab.

Husayn-Ali's imprisonment in the Black Pit ended with exile to Baghdad in 1853. He continued in his efforts to revive the Babism following, his radical teachings continuing to alarm the Persian orthodoxy. The authorities further banished Husayn-Ali, sending him to Constantinople (Istanbul) in the Ottoman Empire in April of 1863. By this time, Husayn-Ali publicly proclaimed himself "Baha'u'llah" (Arabic for "the Glory of God"), claiming he was the prophet of God whose coming the Bab had foretold.

In December of 1863, Baha'u'llah was moved again to Adrianople (modern Edirne, Turkey), in Ottoman Syria, then once more to the prison-city of Akka (Acre) in what is now Palestine. Baha'u'llah resided in Akka for the next 29 years, until his death in 1892. Within the prison-city walls, Baha'u'llah lived, wrote his epistles, gathered disciples, and developed the tenets which would become the basis of the religion to be known as the Baha'i faith.

The fundamental premise of the Baha'i faith seems to be unity: There is one God, one Humanity, one World, one Religion. Baha'u'llah presented himself as the latest in a series of historically significant individuals he called Manifestations of God. These manifestations were sent by God to reveal to humankind aspects of the nature of God, and God's intentions for Humanity. Included among these Manifestations are Abraham, Moses, Zoroaster, Krishna, Buddha, Christ, Muhammed, and the Bab. History, according to Baha'u'llah's teachings, has essentially been one extended theological classroom, and each manifestation has been a teacher presenting another lesson on God's relationship to Humanity.

The Baha'is see the development of humankind in history as analogous to the development of a single human in a lifetime. With each stage of development, another revelation has been presented by a Manifestation to humanity, in a context understandable at its particular developmental stage. The Baha'i's consider 20th century humanity to be in its adolescence: it possesses the intellectual and technological capabilities to observe and comprehend the world as a whole, and to respond to it accordingly; it now needs a Divine lesson which will match its current potential. That Divine lesson, according to Baha'u'llah and his followers, is the Baha'i Faith.

Six principles of the Baha'i Faith, as presented by the National Baha'i House of Worship, reflect this vision of One World, One Humanity, One Religion:

- Fostering of good character and the development of spiritual qualities, such as honesty, trustworthiness, compassion, and justice. Prayer, meditation, and work done in the spirit of service to humanity are expressions of the worship of God.

- Eradication of Prejudices of race, creed, class, nationality, and sex. Racism retards the unfoldment of the boundless potentialities of its victims, corrupts its perpetrators, and blights human progress. Recognition of the oneness of mankind, implemented by appropriate legal measures, must be universally upheld if this problem is to be overcome.

- Achievement of a balance between spiritual and practical requirements of life on earth. There are spiritual principles and values by which solutions can be found for every social problem. The essential merit of a spiritual principle is that it not only presents a perspective which harmonizes with that which is immanent in human nature, it also induces an attitude, a dynamic, a will, an aspiration, which facilitate the discovery and implementation of a practical measure.

- Development of the unique talents and abilities of each individual. Through the pursuit of knowledge, the acquisition of skills for the practice of a trade or profession and participation in community life, both the individual and society as a whole are enriched.

- Equality of women and men. The denial of such equality perpetuates an in-

justice against one half of the world's population and promotes in men harmful attitudes and habits that are carried on from family to the work place, to political life, and ultimately to international relations. (Contradictorily, despite the Baha'i Faith's advocacy of sexual equality, the membership of the Universal House of Justice — the primary administrative body for the international church — is limited to men only. According to the Baha'i International Community, "Baha'u'llah himself outlines this stipulation...Baha'u'llah gave no clarification of this feature of Baha'i administration...All that can be said at this time is that it is a matter of faith...." [The Baha'is, p. 44]

- Universal Education. Ignorance is indisputably the principal reason for the decline and fall of peoples and the perpetuation of prejudice. No nation can achieve success unless education is accorded all its citizens.

Spiritual practices of the Baha'i faith include fasting, meditation, and good works. The faithful participate in the Nineteen Day Feasts, held 17 times per year (every 19 days). The Feast promotes the gathering of local Baha'i faithful for spiritual devotion, administrative consultation, and fellowship. Baha'i scriptural study is based on the more than 100 literary works of Baha'u'llah, including the *Kitab-i-Aqdas* (The Most Holy Book) and the *Kitab-i-Iqan* (The Book of Certitude). It also included the hundreds of letters Baha'u'llah wrote from Akka to popes, kings, emperors, and governments worldwide, as well as prayers penned by him. Baha'i scripture also includes interpretations on the writings of Baha'u'llah provided by subsequent leaders of the faithful.

Baha'u'llah died in 1892. He is entombed at his shrine at Akka which stands today. His son Abbas Effendi (1844–1921) known as "Abdu'l-Baha" (Servant of Baha) took over leadership of the Baha'i Faith. Effendi's successor was his eldest grandson, the Oxford educated Shoghi Effendi Rabbani (1897–1957), whose name means "Guardian of the Cause of God."

Their efforts spurred the growth of the Baha'i faith from perhaps 50,000 adherents in 1892, to more than five million. Under their direction, the Baha'i Faith has reached from its middle-east cradle well into Europe, Asia, and North America.

The first exposure of the Baha'i Faith in the United States occurred in 1893, at the World Parliament of Religions at the Columbian Exposition in Chicago. In 1894, a Chicago insurance manager named Thornton Chase reportedly became the first American Baha'i convert. Later that year, four other Americans joined the Baha'i faith. The Baha'is offered their First National Convention in 1909, hosting 39 delegates from 36 different American cities. In the 1920s, the U.S. Baha'i communities, in conjunction with the National Association for the Advancement of Colored People (NAACP), facilitated a series of racial amity conferences, further raising American consciousness to the existence of the Baha'i faith.

By 1930, 18 books of Baha'i scriptures had become available in the English language. By 1944, at least one Baha'i administrative body resided in every state in the union. Today, there are approximately 110,000 American Baha'i in more than 7000 U.S. localities.

Planning for the fabulous National Baha'i House of Worship began with a handful of Chicago faithful in 1903. The blueprints of Louis Bourgeois were selected among the proposals of several other architects. Bourgeois labored diligently over the design for 14 years, until actual construction began in 1917.

Of particular significance is the nine-sided layout of not only the Wilmette House, but the other six Houses of Worship worldwide:

The number nine has significance in the Baha'i Revelation. Nine years after the announcement of the Bab in Shiraz, Baha'u'llah received the intimation of His mission in the dungeon of Tehran. Nine, as the highest single-digit number, symbolizes completeness. Since the Baha'i Faith claims to be the fulfillment of the expectations of all prior religions, this symbol, as used for example in the nine-sided Baha'i temple, reflects that sense of fulfillment and completeness. [*The Baha'is*, p. 52]

Architectural sculptor John Earley completed various sections of the House of Worship at his Washington D.C. plant. He shipped each completed section by train to Wilmette, Illinois, to be adhered to the steel superstructure. The unique design and elaborate ornamentation created difficult problems in not only architecture, but engineering and construction. But finally, after more than thirty-three years of work, the National House of Worship was dedicated in 1953. Each American Baha'i is encouraged, but not required, to make a pilgrimage to Wilmette at least once in a lifetime.

The National Register of Historic Places included the Wilmette Baha'i House of Worship on May 23, 1978.

Sources

Bishop, Peter and Michael Darton. *The Encyclopedia of World Faiths: An Illustrated Survey of the World's Living Religions.* 1987, MacDonald and Co., Ltd., London and Sydney, pp. 173–176.

The Baha'i Faith: An Independent World Religion. 1996, Baha'i National Center, Wilmette, Illinois.

The Baha'is: A Profile of the Baha'i Faith and Its Worldwide Community. Office of Public Information, Baha'i International Community, New York.

ANNUNCIATION CHURCH

Affiliation: Greek Orthodox
Location: Wauwatosa, Wisconsin
1961

Annunciation Greek Orthodox Church in the Milwaukee suburb of Wauwatosa, Wisconsin, represents a paradoxical crossroads of ideas and concepts. It is a modern architec-

Annunciation Greek Orthodox Church, Wauwatosa, Wisconsin. (Courtesy Annunciation Greek Orthodox Church of the Milwaukee Hellenic Community.)

tural creation housing an ancient mode of Christian worship. Built by the iconoclastic American architect Frank Lloyd Wright, it facilitates a religion steeped in rituals, symbols, mysteries, and, indeed, icons. Annunciation church is globular, circular, and horizontal in design and structure. The Greek Orthodox religion is derived from an authoritative, hierarchical, and vertical tradition. Annunciation is one of the country's most exquisite and innovative places of worship, for one of the world's most venerable, beautiful, and perplexing sacred traditions.

The Annunciation congregation formed in early 20th century Milwaukee, when nearly three quarters of the population consisted of immigrants. Already the most German city in America, Milwaukee also harbored a melting pot of newly arrived Poles, Irish, British, Dutch, Norwegians, Bohemians, Jews, Italians, and Greeks.

Among the half million Greek immigrants who settled in the United States between 1905 and 1914, the Milwaukee Greek community numbered around 1100 in 1910, actually one of the city's smallest immigrant enclaves. These Greeks had journeyed from Peloponesus, Arcadia, and Messina in the southeast corner of the Greek peninsula, settling along Wells Street between 3rd and 6th. The Greeks toiled in tanneries, opened coffee houses serving homeland blends and pastries, and worked in restaurants, candy shops, and shoe-shine businesses. Many frugally saved money, hoping one day to return home to Greece. But as years passed, they found themselves gradually assimilating into an American way of life. Between 1912 and 1914, more than 300 of Milwaukee's Greeks actually left America, only to fight in the Balkan war between Turkey and Greece. Meanwhile, the Greek community in Milwaukee began to center around the congregation called *Evangelismotis Theotokou*, meaning "Annunciation of the Mother of God."

One of the first ten Greek orthodox churches in America, Annunciation Greek Orthodox Church originated in 1906, Father Parthenios Kolonis serving as first pastor. This first church, designed by architect Carl Barkhammer and built on the corner of Broadway and Knapp in 1914, stood as an imposing vertical brick edifice.

The Greek Orthodox Church became self-governing in 1850, one of a family of churches which profess to adhere to the original Christian faith, and who practice the Christian worship rituals as they existed before the division of the Christian world between the Roman and Orthodox churches. One of the meanings of "Orthodoxy" is "right belief"; the Orthodox faithful believe their traditions and practices are descended directly from the Apostles and early followers of Jesus.

Between the fourth and eighth centuries, ecumenical councils decided Christian church policy and doctrine. Comprised of the Patriarchs of Antioch, Alexandria, Jerusalem, and Constantinople, as well as the Bishop of Rome, the council met seven times, developing the Nicene Creed, and other essential church standards. As the center of the Roman Empire, Byzantium's Constantinople (present day Istanbul, Turkey) flourished, while Rome and the west plunged into the dark ages.

But in A.D. 800, as the west emerged from the darkness, Charlemagne arose as the crowned king of the new Holy Roman Empire. The bishop of Rome, the Pope, gradually assumed his perceived position as head of the Christian church. When the Pope tried to assert his authority over the eastern churches, the Byzantines refused to accept his authority and the claim of Infallibility. Over the centuries the gulf between east and west widened until, in 1054, the Pope excommunicated the Patriarch of Constantinople, formalizing the schism between Rome and Constantinople, the western Roman Catholic church and the Eastern Orthodox churches. Finally in 1204, Crusaders from the west sacked Constantinople. In an all too often replayed historical scenario, Christians slew Christians as Crusaders looted the glorious Hagia Sophia, Byzantine's most important church. In 1453, Byzantine rule ended in Constantinople with the invasion of the Turks.

Each Orthodox church — whether Greek or Russian or Serbian or Georgian — incorporates church doctrine and tradition into the culture and language of the particular faithful. The Greek community of Milwaukee in the 1920s remained a very conservative and traditional enclave. The church served as the center of the community, and parents sent their children to the Greek School, to learn and perpetuate Greek language and culture. The Greek families in America functioned as strict, patriarchal units. Godparents held revered and responsible positions in the families. Courtships, as such, did not exist, as parents arranged marriages. Easter held more importance than Christmas, and Baptism elicited a greater celebration than birth. As in the strict Orthodox tradition, the church had no pews inside. This forced the congregation to stand with the men separate from the women through the course of the divine liturgy, which could last for up to three hours.

But as the second generation emerged, and the Greeks in America became Greek-Americans, many of the staid traditions for the church began to dissipate. Between, 1920 and 1936 as Greece itself engaged in a tug of war between the Republicans of Venizelos, and Royalists of King Constantine, Greek-Americans struggled between carrying on the traditions of the old country, and developing a unique and relevant way of life in the new land.

Many of the departures from the old ways began at the church. Under Father Benjamin Kolias, the congregation installed pews at Annunciation Church, considered by traditionalists a radical, "Catholic," and therefore unacceptable practice. Men and women could now sit together, family beside family. The youth choir became coeducational, while an organ accompanied the music at the liturgy for the first time.

Gradually, the Greek-American community in Milwaukee grew more affluent, a substantial portion of the second generation having grown up as professionals and businesspeople. With the passing of World War II, the culturally divergent Milwaukee became more accepting of its various factions. Many of the previously separate cultures, including the

Greek-Americans, began to move away from the dirty, cramped inner city to the outskirts of Milwaukee.

Many of the Greeks moved to the northwest suburb of Wauwatosa. The old church on Broadway and Knapp could no longer serve the needs of the expanding community. Facing financial difficulties, the crumbling brick edifice could not tolerate the structural expansion required to accommodate the growing parish community. The downtown location became inconvenient to the expanding community.

Finally, in 1952, under Father Emmanuel Vergis, a building committee established by Annunciation parish decided the time had come to build a new church, one which represented the second and third generations of Annunciation parish. A legal agreement between a building committee and the church materialized, along with a fundraising plan and a site selection campaign. The committee also began to consider the architect to design the new Annunciation Church.

In 1955, the building committee decided to interview fellow Wisconsinite Frank Lloyd Wright for the commission. Most of the committee had assumed it would be impossible to recruit the legendary Wright. Some even balked at the suggestion of Wright, whose reputation for spending over budget and working past deadlines far preceded him. The committee agreed it would be worth the effort, as his name alone would greatly enhance the project.

To the committee's surprise, the 89-year-old Wright accepted the opportunity. It seems the new Annunciation provided an opportunity to develop an innovative idea, and a personal monument in his home state. Plus, he apparently, needed the money. On December 1, 1955, the committee officially selected Frank Lloyd Wright as architect for Annunciation's new place of worship. A momentous relationship had been formed, which would place Wauwatosa and Greek Orthodoxy prominently on the American map.

Frank Lloyd Wright had attained distinction as one of the world's great architects, a status he would maintain and build upon throughout his life. Among his most memorable creations are Tokyo's Imperial Hotel, the Guggenheim Museum in New York, the Johnson Wax Complex in Racine, Wisconsin, and the Civic Center in Marin County, California. His religious creations included Unity Unitarian Temple in Oak Park, Illinois (1905), the Unitarian Meeting House in Madison, Wisconsin (1947), and the Beth Shalom Synagogue in Philadelphia (1954)

Born in Richland Center, Wisconsin, in 1867, Frank Lloyd Wright was the son of a Unitarian minister. He spent his youth in Madison, Wisconsin, and attended the University of Wisconsin. Although his work centered in Chicago for some time, he returned to his home state in 1911, when he established the 600-acre fabled estate of Taliesin (meaning "Shining Brow" in Welsh) at Spring Green, 40 miles northwest of Madison. In 1932 he established the Taliesan Fellowship of artisans and apprentices, who gathered to learn from and work with the master. He established Taliesan West in Scottsdale, Arizona, in 1938.

Apart from architecture, Wright's life often proved contentious, difficult, and lonesome. He endured two stormy marriages, as well as an extra-marital affair with a client's wife, a tragic episode involving adultery, jealousy, murder, and intrigue. Legal entanglements and financial embarrassments beset his career. His life seemed one of endless controversy. He has been described as a "contrarian with king-sized ego," a fierce critic of social mores and other architects, which added fuel to his smoldering life and profession.

His fiery life seemed to cool to manageability when he met Olgivanna Lazovich of Montenegro in 1924. He married her in 1928, and she seemed to bring a sense of order and harmony to his stormy existence. Lazovich had been raised a Serbian Orthodox, and some believe the Annunciation project became a loving tribute to her calming influence on his life.

Within the context of his work, Wright proved to be, indeed, "the Master of Taliesin." Architecture seemed to provide the solace, confidence, passion, and even spirituality he often otherwise sought. He preached architecture eloquently and endlessly. He professed it to be the most complete fusion of art and culture; indeed, in Wright's mind, architecture brought form to cultural ideas. An organic quality permeated his work; he infused characteristics of the natural world into his creations, which reflected his own distinct personality, diversity and individuality, harmony and synchronicity. He believed a successful building to be a seamless whole, not a summation of parts. Such a structure seemed almost a living, breathing entity which, like his own Taliesin, would grow and change with time and passing episodes of life.

Wright had visited Constantinople (which became Istanbul in 1930), and studied the fabulous Hagia Sophia, which means "Church of the Holy Wisdom," but is often called "St. Sophia." Built for Emperor Justinian in the 6th century, it had been Byzantium's dominant landmark, establishing the dome as the chief characteristic of Orthodox church architecture. Wright attained a commanding grasp of Byzantine architecture, and he understood the traditionally required architectural aspects to be incorporated into the new Annunciation Church.

The Orthodox churches fit a cruciform plan, usually patterned as a cross upon a square. The sanctuary always faced the east, and the Byzantine dome spread over the church center. The aisles would have to be wide enough for processions, with room for distribution and display of votive candles. The most astonishing feature would be the icon screen, with a wide central door, which separates the altar and the priests from the congregation. The icons, featuring images of Christ, the Mother of God, angels and saints, seem mysterious, confusing, and often overwhelming to outside observers. The stories and symbolism of the saints and angels interweave to form a rich tapestry of experience, a history of fellow believers to be observed, studied, and emulated. These icons play an essential role in the drama of the liturgy, known as the "holy work for the holy people":

The icons which fill the church serve as a point of meeting between heaven and earth. As each local congregation prays Sunday by Sunday, surrounded by figures of Christ, the angels, and the saints, these visible images remind the faithful unceasingly of the invisible presence

of the whole company of heaven at the Liturgy.... The multitudinous icons express visibly the sense of "heaven on earth." [Gurda]

Practical specifications for the Annunciation community included a church seating capacity of 700, as well as a school accommodating 300, a social hall for 500, and 50-person choir loft. After inspections at several sites, the building commission determined that the location of the new Annunciation Church would be 20 acres at the corner of 92nd and Congress in Wauwatosa.

In August of 1956, Wright suddenly and fluidly drafted the plan for the new Annunciation Greek Orthodox Church, whose theme would be that of the cross inside the circle. In a great departure from the traditional, vertical design, the body of the church formed a graceful bowl resting upon a concrete cradle in the shape of a Greek Cross. Its main floor would be another equilateral cross, the altar on one arm, the choir balcony on the other. Eight hundred seats would cover the circular main floor. No annoying post would obstruct the view; no worshipper would be seated more than 50 feet from the altar. In another radical departure for Orthodoxy, the icon screen with images created by artist Eugene Massellink would be porous, allowing the faithful to view the priests and the altar. The gathered faithful, instead of facing forward toward the lifeless screen, would watch the fervent and contented faces of their fellow believers, enhancing the feelings of community and fellowship.

Persian blue tile would cover the dome roof. Copper would trim the spherical, buff-colored concrete. Sunlight would beam from a series of globular windows, encircling the ridge of the dome like a string of pearls. This ring of light would project the illusion of a heavy dome floating on a fragile cushion of glass. The dome would actually rise and fall upon thousands of ball bearings, allowing it to expand in the heat of summer, contract in the chill of winter. An underground complex, including gardens, a banquet hall and classrooms, would stretch behind the church body.

Wright at once cherished his creation, which he referred to as "Little St. Sophia" or "My Little Jewel." In a published statement concerning his creation, Wright described the new Annunciation as a beautiful melding of the ancient and the contemporary:

> According to the inexorable laws of Change, the spirit of Byzantium lives afresh in the simple design reflecting the beauty of the old life but in accord with those changes that have taken place in our Twentieth Century wherever they are fundamental. Therefore this edifice is, in itself, a complete work of modern Art and Science belonging to today but dedicated to ancient traditions — contributing to tradition instead of living it. [Gurda]

Annunciation Greek Orthodox Church turned out to be one of Wright's last major buildings. The Master of Taliesin died on April 9, 1959, five weeks before the ground breaking ceremony for the new Greek church. His creative fervor refused to break until after he died. Two years and 1.5 million dollars later, on July 2, 1961, Olgivanna Wright attended the dedication on behalf of her late, beloved husband.

The radical departure of Wright's little jewel from traditional church architecture caused a swelling of controversy within and without the Annunciation community. In retrospect the new Annunciation Greek Orthodox Church has been called a bright new beacon for Orthodoxy in the New World, and a national treasure. Recognized as a national landmark in 1974, it has been the subject of countless Wright retrospectives, surveys of American architecture, books, magazines, and even calendars. By 1966, more than 125,00 visitors had come to Annunciation Church, opening for many Americans the doors of understanding into the often mysterious and misunderstood chamber of the Orthodox Church, Greek or otherwise.

In the words of Father Emmanuel Vergis, the pastor overseeing the new church's construction: "The Annunciation Church edifice has done more to promote an understanding of the Greek Orthodox Faith in our community and nationally than any other single force." (Gurda)

Sources

Bishop, Peter and Michael Darton. *The Encyclopedia of World Faiths: An Illustrated Survey of the World's Living Religions.* 1987, MacDonald and Co., Ltd., London and Sydney.

Gurda, John. *New World Odyssey: Annunciation Greek Orthodox Church and Frank Lloyd Wright.* 1986, The Milwaukee Hellenic Community, Wawautosa, WS.

Jones, Cranston. *Architecture Today and Tomorrow.* 1961, McGraw-Hill Book Company, New York.

CHAPEL OF PEACE, INTERNATIONAL PEACE GARDEN

Affiliation: None
Location: Dunseith, North Dakota, United States; Boissevain, Manitoba, Canada
1970

The United States and Canada have been cordial neighbors for so long it is easy to forget a time when such was not the case. In the second decade of the 19th century, however, a period of history unfolded when Canadians and Americans not only fired upon and killed each other, but plotted to invade and conquer the opposing country. Traditional history texts seem to do little in print highlighting this War of 1812 sub-plot. But those who created the International Peace Garden dearly cherish the harmony that has prevailed ever since.

United States proponents of war against Britain in 1812 cited aggressive British activities on the Atlantic Ocean as the primary cause. Between 3000 and 7000 American sailors had been impressed into service aboard British fleets against the French, and more than 400 American ships bound for Napoleonic ports had been seized by the British navy. Although this activity had little to do with Canada, American War Hawks quickly jumped on the anti–British bandwagon. Although New England and the mid–Atlantic regions offered little support for war, the western and southern states sought security against future aggression by the British Empire. The British had developed an unstable but dangerous alliance with Native Americans around the Great Lakes, and helped incite the natives to harass and hinder increasing encroachment of American settlers to the north and the west. Through the fantasized Conquest of Canada, Americans on the western edge hoped to eliminate the dual British/Indian threat in North America, while expanding the North American frontier on which to settle. Victory on land seemed far easier than victory at sea, since the British navy dwarfed any two other navies in the world. To most military "experts" at the time, the overland conquest of Canada by the larger, better-supplied Americans seemed, as Thomas Jefferson suggested, "a mere matter of marching." (Berton, p. 15)

At the dawn of the 18th century, the term "Canadians" referred primarily to French speaking residents living in and near Michigan territory. Other residents of Canada consisted of displaced English natives, and new Americans drawn from the East Coast to the northern frontier at the promise of cheap land. In all, 300,000 individuals occupied the vast British possession, compared to the eight million persons who lived in the United States.

Most Canadian residents apparently felt rather indifferent toward the war. Although they lived in British territory, and took loyalty oaths as a requirement for their settlement, they rarely thought of themselves as British subjects. As farmers and settlers seeking peace on their own pioneer homes, they wished simply to grow their own food and raise their own families. To many of them, the subtle boundary between American and British land seemed irrelevant. Many felt that Upper Canada, the

territory north and west of Michigan, might have naturally become U.S. territory on its own. The war changed any possibility of that. Many Americans, particularly in New England, harbored no passion for the war either. During the Battle of Plattsburg Bay in 1814, for example, Vermont meat producers actually sold beef to the British navy while the sailors waited for battle on the eastern shores of Lake Champlain.

One of the chief characteristics of the conflict between Canada and the United States seemed to be ineptness. Both sides featured poorly manned, poorly commanded, poorly trained, and poorly supplied troops. Both armies fought deep in the wilderness, out of touch and communication with their own leadership. Typical of the pre–Industrial Age war, illness accounted for more casualities than all battles combined. Far from adequate medical care, diseases such as influenza, malaria, typhoid, and dysentery devastated armies on either side.

While no clear victor can be claimed between Canada and the U.S., the Canadian troops certainly succeeded in stemming what the U.S. War Hawks — particularly from the frontier states, such as Henry Clay from Kentucky — promised would be an easy American victory. The Canadians had better commanders; Lieutenant General Sir George Prevost and the brilliant, charismatic General Isaac Brock clearly outshone the aging, diminishing American command. Canadians fought on familiar territory, an historically proven military advantage.

Perhaps the single greatest asset to Canada, however, proved to be its alliance with the developing Indian confederacy under the legendary Shawnee, Tecumseh. Alienated by Indian policies developed under Jefferson, the natives desperately wished to prevent further invasion of Americans on their land. Tecumseh planned to set the boundary of Indian land at the Ohio River and dreamed of building a confederation of northern Native American tribes. Warriors from the Ottawa, Potowatami, Kickapoo, Sauk, Wynadot, Delaware, Mohawk, and Shawnee tribes all joined forces with the British and Canadians. Clearly without Native American numbers, skills, and bravery, Upper Canada would have fallen to the Americans in a matter of months.

Canadians and Americans exchanged increasingly hostile fire between 1812 and 1814. The following synopsize some of the more important battles:

Fort Detroit, Michigan Territory, July 1812

General William Hull represents the dire straits to which the American command in the Canadian campaign had fallen. Aging and alcoholic, soft and gluttonous, red-faced, war weary and shell shocked, Hull harbors a mortal fear of Indians, and begins to exhibit signs of paranoia and depression. Nevertheless in July of 1812, before the War of 1812 had officially begun, Hull (who had never before planned a military maneuver) acts upon the commonly shared delusion that the British threat in North America could be eliminated simply by invading Canada and taking control of the northern neighbor.

Hull marches his ragtag army more than 200 miles in 35 days through the wilderness between Urbana, Ohio, and the Michigan Territory Peninsula above Lake Erie. Many soldiers contract malaria in the wet, swampy terrain, and those who do not die of disease succumb to exhaustion. Hull's British counterpart, General Isaac Brock, Governor of Upper Canada, actually receives word of the war's commencement before Hull, and has time to prepare for the American's maneuvers. Brock's ally, the great Indian leader Tecumseh, actually directs his unnoticed braves to shadow Hull's troops all the way up through Michigan territory.

On July 5, 1812, General Hull and his more than 2000 troops reach Fort Malden, known as Amherstburg, south along the Detroit River. His often mutinous troops resist his commands, and Hull hesitates to advance on the fort even though the Americans badly outnumber the British and Canadians. Soon Brock is able to draw reinforcements to the Fort, and the British hold the outpost.

Hull takes the poorly defended Fort Detroit. But Brock allows a fake document indicating an Indian strength of more than 5000, when in fact it numbered less than 1300, to fall

into the bungling American commander's hands. The report fuels Hull's mounting terror of a native attack. On the morning of August 16, Brock begins to bombard the fort with cannon fire, as the trembling Hull lapses into a near catatonic state. Hull surrenders the fort by noon the same day, later claiming his actions saved the lives of more than 800 civilians. Hull's ill-conceived surrender leads to a court martial for cowardice, followed by an execution order stayed by President James Madison. Reports of the dismal defeat at Fort Detroit shock and dismay Americans back home. The easy capture of Canada dreamed by the War Hawks never comes.

Queenston Heights, along Niagara River, October 1812

Queenston Heights is a ridge south of the village of Queenston, on the west bank of Niagara River. This river flows north/south on a strip of land between Lake Erie to the south, and Lake Ontario to the north. The American Fort Niagara stands on the east bank, while Canada's Fort George is perched on the west side. American commanders feature Captain John Wool and Lt. Colonel Winfield Scott, the future conqueror of Mexico. General Isaac Brock leads the British Canadians.

On October 13, 1812, General Brock commands the battery holding Queenston Heights, when Wool's forces pour over the hill, scattering Brock and troops across the village to a house at the north end. Brock regroups his troops, leading a charge back up heights. To the horror of his men, Brock is killed by enemy gunfire to the chest. In their shock, the troops try to recapture the hill again, but are beaten back once more.

Wool and his band hold the ridge overnight, until Lieutenant General Robert Sheaffe leads a detachment of 1000 troops from Ft. George. Mohawk Indians shadow Sheaffe's 1000, harrying the enemy every step of the way. Avoiding the steep hill which made Brock vulnerable, Sheaffe attacks Wool's troops from the southwest, breaking through Wool's line on Queenston Heights, pushing Wool's forces over the cliff.

General Scott's detachment started with nearly 1000, but more than two-thirds have deserted at the sight of the oncoming Canadians and, especially, the Indians. Scott is forced to surrender, as Sheaffe takes control of Queenston Heights. More than 900 of Scott's soldiers are captured, the vast majority while in the midst of desertion. The British suffer only 14 dead and 77 wounded. One casualty, General Isaac Brock, would be impossible to replace. Brock's funeral is called "the greatest and most solemn" (Berton, p. 252) in history of Upper Canada, while Isaac Brock is lauded as Canada's first hero.

Frenchtown, Michigan Territory, January 1813

Along the River Raisin in the far eastern edge of Michigan Territory, General James Winchester leads 1000 American troops toward Frenchtown. After five months in the wilderness following a succession of defeats, the Americans hunger for victory. Winchester seeks the vain glory of "liberating" 33 fairly apathetic French colonists from the "control" of British and Indians.

At first, the Americans — largely consisting of troops from the Kentucky Militia — drive Indians and British from the small, picketed settlement. The Americans settle into Frenchtown hospitality, gratefully indulging in their first hot food, warm beds, and cozy shelters in weeks. Their comfort seems to foster an air of complacency, which eventually seals their demise.

On January 19, 1813, Lieutenant Colonel Henry Proctor leads 1200 British and Canadian troops, at least half of which were Indians, on an attack from the north against the American-occupied Frenchtown. General Winchester apparently received advanced warning of the raid, but for whatever reason, perhaps due to the intoxication of his comfortable surroundings, he chooses to ignore it. Proctor's troops drive the Americans from the settlement and across the icy River Raisin.

More than 400 Americans are massacred on the spot, their bodies littering the frosty roads and trails surrounding Frenchtown. Hundreds more are captured by the Indians, never to be heard from again. Most are likely butchered, many may be eaten, and the remainder are likely assimilated into tribes to make up for warriors lost in battle.

The massacre at Frenchtown nearly assures that any victory for Americans in Canada is forever lost.

Lake Erie — September 1813

Admiral Oliver Hazard Perry's *Lawrence* squares off against Captain Robert Barclay's *Detroit* for three hours and 15 minutes. Victory means control of Lake Erie and the supply line to Upper Canada. The *Detroit's* long range guns torment the *Lawrence,* which comes perilously close to capsizing. Fortunately for Perry, *Lawrence's* sister ship *Niagara,* under Lieutenant James Elliot, comes to the rescue.

In a rarely used mid-battle naval maneuver, Perry transfers command from the *Lawrence* to the *Niagara.* As Perry and four officers climb into a row boat for the sister vessel, Perry admonishes his lieutenant with the late Admiral Lawrence's now famous line "Don't give up the ship!" With cannons roaring, Perry heads the *Niagara* directly for the bow of the *Detroit,* at the heart of the British fleet. The lagging American formation follows the *Niagara's* daring lead. By 3:00 P.M., the *Detroit's* mast has fallen, other British ships are in flames. The British fleet is captured, the first time so thorough a defeat had befallen Her Majesty's navy. Americans suffer 27 dead and 96 wounded, while British casualties include 41 dead and 94 wounded. Americans gain control of Lake Erie, which virtually ensures against Canadian encroachment into U.S. territory.

Moraviantown, Thames River, Upper Canada, September 1813

With Canadian supplies cut off due to Admiral Perry's victory on Lake Erie, Lieutenant-General Henry Proctor and the warrior chief Tecumseh make a last ditch stand at Moraviantown, on the Thames River, in present day southwest Canada. Facing 9500 American troops under General William Henry Harrison, Proctor and Tecumseh steady the 600 to 800 British Troops, and the 500 to 1000 Indians against Harrison's forces. For Tecumseh and Harrison, the battle is reminiscent of their first meeting, at the Battle of Tippecanoe Creek, Indiana, two years earlier. In Tecumseh's mind, Tippecanoe fortified the need for an Indian Federation, the dream he would pursue through the remainder of his life. Harrison, meanwhile, would build a career on this otherwise rather obscure skirmish, a career which eventually would lead to the White House.

The battle on the Thames River lasts an hour. Harrison's troops break through the Canadian line within minutes. While Proctor and his soldiers break ranks and retreat, Tecumseh urges his braves on, fighting fiercely in the underbrush. The Shawnee hero senses the finality of the battle, which kindles a final effort to defend his beloved native lands. Tecumseh dies in the battle, but his body is never found. His followers gather the body, resting it in a secret burial site, to prevent desecration by the Americans.

The surprisingly light casualties include seven Americans dead, 22 wounded. For the British, deaths numbered 18, and injuries 25, but more than 600 British troops are captured. Proctor is suspended by his superiors of rank and pay, while Harrison returns home a hero.

With Tecumseh's death, the dream of the Indian confederation dies, as there is no one else who can unite the native American tribes against their fate.

Plattsburg Bay, Lake Champlain, September 1814

In a final effort to bring the offensive to the Americans, Lower Canada Governor Lt. General George Prevost launches the invasion of New York State, one month after the British army invades Washington, D.C. The target is Plattsburg, New York, on the western shore of Lake Champlain, twenty-two miles from the present Canadian border. Prevost plans to send 15,000 British and Canadian troops against 3400 American troops, which are supported by an additional 3200 soldiers from the Vermont and New York state militias.

All Prevost needs to implement his campaign is for the British fleet on Lake Champlain, commanded by Captain George Downie, to neutralize the American fleet, and take control of northern Lake Champlain.

The British seem to have the advantage,

with more ships and longer range artillery. But Captain Thomas Macdonough manages to lure Downie and the British ships into Plattsburg Bay, where the Americans' short-range but faster firing cannons take the edge. After two hours of gun fire, Captain Downie is killed, and the British fleet surrenders. American dead number 22, while 58 are wounded. British casualties number more than 600. With Macdonough's victory on the Lake, Prevost is forced to withdraw his troops for Montreal. The invasion of New York is canceled, the last such attempt in the history of the two nations.

After 18 months of fighting costing both sides thousands of lives, no clear victor could be claimed from the conflict between Canada and the United States. Certainly, however, Canada managed to stave off a numerically superior foe, as the United States goal of the conquest of Canada came to naught. The only certainty established by the battles was that Canada would never be assimilated into the United States. The Treaty of Ghent, in December of 1814, clearly established the international boundary between the two countries. The good news is no volley of war fire has ever crossed the boundary since.

On July 14, 1932, recognizing the 118 years since war pitted Canadians against Americans, 50,000 people gathered on the Manitoba/ North Dakota border to dedicate a grand and fitting memorial to the two nations' amiable relations. Three years earlier, Dr. Henry Moore of Islington, Ontario, presented the idea of the International Peace Garden to the Professional Grounds Management Society, which agreed to supervise the project. Forged of the efforts of individuals, numerous charitable organizations, and governments from both sides of the border, the International Peace Garden lies on 2300 acres among the birch and aspen forests of the Turtle Mountains. The state of North Dakota donated 888 acres of agricultural land, while the Province of Manitoba gave 1451 acres of wilderness. Straddling the longest unfortified border in the world, the International Peace Garden lies exactly midway between the Atlantic and Pacific Oceans, on the globe's longest north/south road, connecting Highway 10 in Manitoba to

Chapel of Peace in the International Peace Garden, which straddles the United States–Canada border in North Dakota and Manitoba. (Courtesy International Peace Garden.)

Highway 3 in North Dakota.

The Chapel of Peace, also known as the All Faiths Peace Chapel, is the only structure in the International Peace Garden situated directly on the boundary line between Canada and the United States. Built at the west end of the Garden, this nondenominational sanctuary was built at a cost of $120,000, and dedicated in July of 1970. A simplistic, modernistic design, the chapel seats 200 under the warm glow of amber-hued windows imported from France. A circular fountain pool flows amid four pairs of columns at the center of the sanctuary. The flat limestone walls feature the engraved words of such world-renowned peacemakers as Gandhi, Lincoln, Pasteur, Einstein, Frankl, Kilbourn, and many others.

The Chapel is sponsored by the General Grand Chapter Order of the Eastern Star, a nondenominational fraternal organization, whose purpose is to "provide an organization where women and men with high moral and social character can contribute much time, energy, and wisdom to our Order with Charity, Truth, and Loving-kindness for the good of all mankind throughout the world." Formed by Mason poet laureate Dr. Rob Morris in 1850, the Order of the Eastern Star claims to be the largest fraternal organization in the world to which both women and men can belong.

Miraculously beautiful, the Peace Garden features more than 140,000 annuals, wandering deer, flourishing waterfowl, floral designs, native rock pathways, reflective pools inviting exploration and contemplation for all visitors. In the western Canadian section stands the Peace Tower, 120 feet (36.6 meters) high. The tower's four columns are said to represent the immigrants who journeyed from the four corners of the world, to create two very similar but distinct nations, with a common base of democracy. At the southern United States end is the Lodge, the oldest building in the Garden. Completed shortly after the dedication of the park, the Lodge is the garden's first international effort, with stones gathered from North Dakota, and logs harvested in Manitoba. To the right of the Lodge rests a tablet depicting the Ten Commandments, dedicated by actor Charlton Heston in 1956. The Peace Garden is also home of the International Music Camp, which invites young musicians from around the world for intensive training in music and the arts.

Finally, a cairn stands at the entrance and exit gate, whose message serves as a reminder of the bloody yet distant past on which the Canadian-American link is built. It is a past the two countries seem determined not to repeat:

> We two nations dedicate this garden,
> and pledge that as long as man shall live
> we will not take up arms against one another.

Sources

Berton, Pierre. *The Invasion of Canada, Volume One: 1812–1813.* 1980, Little, Brown, and Company, Boston.

Davis, Kenneth C. *Don't Know Much About History.* 1990, Avon Books, New York.

Greenblatt, Miriam. *America at War: The War of 1812.* 1994, Facts on File, New York.

INDEX